Luminos is the Open Access monograph publishing program from UC Press. Luminos provides a framework for preserving and reinvigorating monograph publishing for the future and increases the reach and visibility of important scholarly work. Titles published in the UC Press Luminos model are published with the same high standards for selection, peer review, production, and marketing as those in our traditional program. www.luminosoa.org

A
*Philip E. Lilienthal*
BOOK

The Philip E. Lilienthal imprint
honors special books
in commemoration of a man whose work
at University of California Press from 1954 to 1979
was marked by dedication to young authors
and to high standards in the field of Asian Studies.
Friends, family, authors, and foundations have together
endowed the Lilienthal Fund, which enables UC Press
to publish under this imprint selected books
in a way that reflects the taste and judgment
of a great and beloved editor.

# Placing Empire

University of California Press, one of the most distinguished university presses in the United States, enriches lives around the world by advancing scholarship in the humanities, social sciences, and natural sciences. Its activities are supported by the UC Press Foundation and by philanthropic contributions from individuals and institutions. For more information, visit www.ucpress.edu.

University of California Press
Oakland, California

© 2017 by Kate McDonald

Suggested citation: McDonald, Kate. *Placing Empire: Travel and the Social Imagination in Imperial Japan*. Oakland: University of California Press, 2017. doi: https://doi.org/10.1525/luminos.34

This work is licensed under a Creative Commons CC BY-NC-ND license. To view a copy of the license, visit http://creativecommons.org/licenses.

This project was supported in part by funding from the University of California Presidential Faculty Research Fellowships in the Humanities, MR-15-328710.

Library of Congress Cataloging-in-Publication Data

Names: McDonald, Kate, 1981- author.
Title: Placing empire : travel and the social imagination in imperial Japan / Kate McDonald.
Description: Oakland, California : University of California Press, [2017] | Includes bibliographical references and index. |
Identifiers: LCCN 2017009063 (print) | LCCN 2017012735 (ebook) | ISBN 9780520967236 (ebook) | ISBN 9780520293915 (pbk. : alk. paper)
Subjects: LCSH: Tourism--Japan--20th century. | Tourism--Political aspects--Japan--20th century. | Japan--Colonies--Description and travel--20th century. | Korea--Description and travel--20th century. | Manchuria (China)--Description and travel--20th century. | Taiwan--Description and travel--20th century.
Classification: LCC G155.J27 (ebook) | LCC G155.J27 M44 2017 (print) | DDC 306.4/819089956051--dc23
LC record available at https://lccn.loc.gov/2017009063

26  25  24  23  22  21  20  19  18  17
10  9  8  7  6  5  4  3  2  1

*For Max*

*For, whatever else it may be, nationalism always involves a struggle for land, or an assertion about rights to land; and the nation, almost by definition, requires a territorial base in which to take root and fulfill the needs of its members.*
—ANTHONY D. SMITH

*It's not just* like *Japan. It is Japan.*
—ARAKAWA SEIJIRŌ, UPON DISEMBARKING AT THE PORT OF PUSAN, KOREA (1918)

CONTENTS

*List of Illustrations*    *xi*
*Preface and Acknowledgments*    *xiii*

Introduction    *1*

PART I. THE GEOGRAPHY OF CIVILIZATION

1. Seeing Like the Nation    25
2. The New Territories    50

PART II. THE GEOGRAPHY OF CULTURAL PLURALISM

3. Boundary Narratives    83
4. Local Color    103
5. Speaking Japanese    135

Conclusion    160

*Appendix: Place Names*    *177*
*Notes*    *181*
*Selected Bibliography*    *221*
*Index*    *245*

LIST OF ILLUSTRATIONS

MAPS

1. Map of Northeast Asia   20
2. "Abbreviated Transportation Map of Korea-Manchuria-China," 1931   21
3. "Abbreviated Transportation Map of Taiwan," 1931   22

FIGURES

1. Map of "Great Japan"   12
2. The remains of a cannon at 203-Meter Hill   37
3. Travelers consult a map as they climb 203-Meter Hill   39
4. The loading of soybeans at Dairen wharf   65
5. Kitashirakawa's uniform on display at Tainan Shrine   67
6. "The Wretched Ruin of the West Tower"   69
7. The Government General Museum and "Secret Garden" at Ch'andŏk. Palace   71
8. "Hakui no Chōsen e yuku" (Going to the Korea of white robes)   104
9. "'Utsukushii shima' Taiwan o nozoku" (Peering into Taiwan, the "beautiful island")   123
10. "Pose of Powerful Coolies."   126
11. "Tsugitaka sanchō o mezashite" (Heading for the summit of Mt. Tsugitaka)   131
12. School for indigenous children at Kappanzan   158

13. "Nihon han'i no shukushō to yon dai shima no mensekizu" (The reduction of the area of Japan and area map of the four main islands)   *167*
14. "Nihon no ichi" (The place of Japan)   *168*

## TABLES

1. A suggested itinerary for Korea–Manchuria travel   *59*
2. A suggested itinerary for Taiwan travel   *60*
3. Place names   *177*

## PREFACE AND ACKNOWLEDGMENTS

This project started with a simple question. What did Japanese travelers see when they went to colonial Korea, Manchuria, and Taiwan? Put differently, what did it mean to "see" Korea, Manchuria, or Taiwan as a Japanese traveler under empire—what did it mean to see territories that were once decidedly foreign and then, suddenly, were not? Japanese travelers in the early 1900s remembered clearly the transformation of these lands into Japanese colonies. But the issue is not one of Japanese history alone. Early American travelers to Hawai'i traveled with memories of the independent Hawaiian kingdom and its overthrow by American colonists in 1893. And though travelers from Great Britain and France operated within empires of longer standing, they too found themselves struggling to negotiate how the many pasts of colonized lands could reasonably be transformed into evidence of the progressive history of their imperial nations.

Because of the global context in which we might ask this question, its answer bears directly on long-held assumptions about the uniqueness of Japanese imperialism. In the first major English-language study of the Japanese Empire as a whole, Mark R. Peattie set out what would become the standard framework for defining the Japanese Empire within the larger history of modern imperialism. "As the only non-Western imperium of recent times," he wrote, "the Japanese colonial empire stands as an anomaly of modern history." He further elaborated on the peculiar nature of Japanese imperialism: "Because it was assembled at the apogee of the 'new imperialism' by a nation which was assiduously striving to emulate Western organizational models, it is not surprising that it was formally patterned after the tropical empires of modern Europe. Yet the historical and geographic circumstances of the overseas Japanese empire set it apart from its European counterparts and gave it a character and purpose scarcely duplicated elsewhere."[1]

For Peattie, the unique circumstances were three. One, Japan had become an imperial power at precisely the moment when it extracted itself from its own unequal treaties with the United States and other Western powers. Thus, the Japanese government saw clearly the significance of territorial expansion to geopolitical power. Two, the Japanese Empire was late to the scene, in the sense that Japan acquired its first formal colony, Taiwan, in 1895. The lateness of Japan's empire meant that there were few unclaimed territories, especially in Asia, which had been the site of intense colonization by European empires for over a hundred years. And three, the cultural and ethnic makeup of the territories Japan did acquire was markedly different from what the world had seen in European and American empires. "Because it was an Asian empire," Peattie argued, "its most important colonies, Taiwan and Korea, were well-populated lands whose inhabitants were racially akin to their Japanese rulers with whom they shared a common cultural heritage. This sense of cultural affinity profoundly shaped Japanese attitudes toward colonial governance once the empire was established."[2]

The idea that its geographic contiguity and internal cultural cohesion set the Japanese Empire apart from European and, indeed, all other modern empires, has had a long life. In their widely influential introduction to *Tensions of Empire*, Ann Stoler and Frederick Cooper refrained from addressing "the meaning of empire in regard to contiguous territory . . . in which the colonial pattern of reproducing difference might in theory be mitigated by the geographic possibility of absorption more readily than was the case overseas."[3] Though Stoler and Cooper have each more recently revised this earlier position, other broad, comparative studies within the growing field of "new imperialism studies" have similarly excluded territorially contiguous empires while simultaneously slipping between theoretical discussions of "modern imperialism" and "modern Western imperialism."[4]

Yet, as did their imperial counterparts in the United States, Great Britain, and France, hundreds of thousands of Japanese people traveled to the Japanese colonies of Korea, Manchuria, and Taiwan during the first half of the twentieth century to pursue precisely this question of whether their imperial territories were, or would necessarily produce, a coherent political, historical, linguistic, and cultural space. Indeed, it was the apparent need for an answer to this question that motivated their travel in the first place. Querying what it meant for a Japanese traveler to "see" Korea, Manchuria, or Taiwan under Japanese colonial rule thus became a concrete approach for exploring questions of deep relevance not just to the provincial realm of modern Japanese history but also to the history of modern empire: what do representations of place have to do with the production and reproduction of imperial formations in the context of colonialism, capitalism, and nationalism? How does place bear on the postcolonial history of settler colonialism, which, since most colonial empires did not abandon the entirety of their colonial holdings, is not so "post" colonial after all? And what does imperial tourism, a phenomenon of equally global provenance, have to do with all of the above?

The answer that this book proposes is that place was a key tool for sustaining imperialism in a period in which the world's major empires, including the Japanese, largely disavowed territorial conquest as a practice of legitimate states. The shift from empire as a project of territorial acquisition to one of territorial maintenance necessitated the production of new social and spatial imaginaries of the nation that could coexist with the imperial territory of the state. In this endeavor, place, like race and ethnicity, served both as an axis along which colonial difference could be defined and exploited and as a symbol of national identity that could encompass the entirety of the imperial territory without distinction. Tourism emerged in this era as the technology par excellence for producing firsthand experiences and representations of the space of the nation and of the colonies as places within it. These experiences and representations legitimated imperial claims to colonized land while at the same time presenting the colonies as spaces of exception to metropolitan political, economic, and social norms.[5]

While many of the conflicts that motivated the spatial politics of Japanese imperialism had contours that were specific to the Japanese Empire, the underlying need to legitimate the territorial claims of the state in the language of nationalist attachments to the land was rooted in the broader social and historical forces that shaped the global transition from a world of empires to a world of nation-states in the nineteenth and twentieth centuries. From this perspective, the historical significance of the geography of the Japanese Empire is not the uniqueness of its contiguity or the cultural cohesion that this contiguity implied. Rather, it is the variety of ways in which colonial boosters and imperial travelers made the relationships between the empire's places meaningful. From history to language to memory and to movement itself, imperial travelers and colonial boosters saw and experienced colonized lands in ways that legitimated their incorporation into the Japanese Empire and promoted the territorialization of a Japanese national identity on colonized land. In other words, the historical significance of the geography of the Japanese Empire lies not its uniqueness but rather in how it exposes the centrality of spatial politics to the survival of empire in the twentieth century.

I began this project over ten years ago, in a research seminar led by Tak Fujitani. The question I explored then was of the politics of tourist guidebooks. In the intervening years, I have found it necessary to expand and revise my analysis of tourism in the Japanese Empire from one that focused on how tourist guidebooks reflected broader discourses of Japanese imperialism to one that argues that tourism was essential to the maintenance of empire itself. In a nearly decade of research, I discovered a truly astonishing quantity and geographic diversity of materials related to travel and tourism in the Japanese Empire—ranging from travel accounts to anticolonial manifestos to the history of national parks. The most important forces behind the evolution of this project, however, were the generous encouragements, suggestions, and critiques that colleagues, editors, fellow panelists, and interested individuals offered at every stage of the project. I am truly grateful for their time and engagement.

My greatest debts are to my advisors, Tak Fujitani and Stefan Tanaka, who guided me through the difficult task of analyzing nationalism and imperialism historically and who, through their regular and rigorous feedback, constantly pushed me to embrace ambiguity and complexity. Sanae Isozumi at the University of California, San Diego Library introduced me to the Japan Travel Bureau library and its collection of the travel magazine *Tabi*. In Japan, I had the great pleasure of working with Mizuno Naoki and Komagome Takeshi at Kyōto University, two scholars whose attention to the inadequacy of general categorizations such as "inner" and "outer" territory to frame the history of the Japanese Empire deeply influenced my own approach. Patrick Patterson introduced me to the history of tourism as a field and gave generously of his time to teach me how to write effective fellowship proposals and presentations, both of which were essential to the completion of this project. Gary Fields introduced me to critical human geography, which shaped the argument of this book and, more broadly, my very approach to history. Max Rorty has been my first and last reader, strongest supporter, and bluntest critic. Every part of this book has benefited from her attention.

Ten years offers a lot of time for research, writing, and thinking. Yet the time would not have been so valuable if not for the many people and institutions whose invitations made it possible for me to develop and receive feedback on each aspect of the project. In Japan, Mizuno Naoki and the Institute for Research in Humanities at Kyōto University hosted me during 2008–2010 for my initial research. Yanagisawa Asobu's generous offer of a temporary visiting appointment at Keiō University's Faculty of Economics in the summer of 2013 allowed me to complete the research for the manuscript. Daniel Milne and Andrew Elliott's invitation to participate in a workshop and special issue on war and tourism for *Japan Review* provided a crucial framework for the revision of chapter 1. Cho Sŏng-un, Itagaki Hiroshi, Kim Baek-Young, Aleksandra Kobiljski, Sang-Ho Ro, Senjū Hajime, and Suzuki Nobuko offered essential conversations, sources, and funding at key points in the project's development.

In the United States, I am grateful to Chris Hanscom, Todd Henry, Shigehisa Kuriyama, Tamara Loos, Ian Miller, Morgan Pitelka, Nathaniel Smith, Dennis Washburn, and Sam Yamashita for inviting me speak on their campuses. These talks were essential proving grounds for the theoretical and historical framework of the project, and the comments and critiques that I received from faculty members and graduate students on each campus enriched the book immensely. Paul

Barclay has been a generous colleague and interlocutor since the first days of my graduate research; many of the images in this book come from the East Asia Digital Images Collection at Lafayette College Libraries, of which he is the director. An encounter with David Ambaras at the Association for Asian Studies annual meeting sparked an ongoing conversation, which fundamentally altered how I thought about the spatial politics of tourism's mobility and led to the research that became chapter 3. At the University of California, Santa Barbara, Sabine Frühstück, W. Patrick McCray, and Luke Roberts have been extraordinary mentors and collaborators.

I owe a special thank you to those individuals who read and commented on the manuscript. In addition to David Ambaras, my modern Japan colleagues Andre Haag, Helen J. S. Lee, and Ryan Moran, as well as my UCSB colleagues Peter Alagona, Sherene Seikaly, and Gabriela Soto Laveaga, each read and commented on the manuscript in its entirety. Mary V. Rorty read the entire penultimate draft and offered many constructive criticisms. Three anonymous readers pushed me to go further in analyzing not just the *what* of imperial tourism but the *why* as well. These gifts of time and attention are the foundation of the scholarly enterprise, yet they are the ones that are the least rewarded. The insightful comments and critiques that each reader offered helped me to refine the foundation and argument of each chapter as well as the manuscript as a whole.

The research and writing for this project would not have been possible without generous financial assistance from the Fulbright IIE Graduate Research Program, the University of California Pacific Rim Foundation, the Joseph K. Naiman Fellowship in Japanese Studies, the Northeast Asia Council of the Association for Asian Studies, the University of California President's Faculty Research Fellowship in the Humanities, the Graduate Division of UC San Diego, and the Academic Senate at UC Santa Barbara. The UCSB Open Access Fund made it possible to publish this book in an open-access format. An earlier version of chapter 5 appeared as "Speaking Japanese: Language and the Expectation of Empire," in *The Affect of Difference: Representations of Race in the Japanese Empire*, edited by Christopher P. Hanscom and Dennis Washburn, 159–79 (Honolulu: University of Hawai'i Press, 2016). I thank the University of Hawai'i Press for permission to print a revised and expanded version of the chapter here. Ellen Broidy at Academic Editorial clarified many of the manuscript's key points and streamlined each chapter. Eun-Joo Ahn, Seokwon Choi, Brett Collins, ChunHui Chuang, Julie Johnson, and Ema Parker provided essential research assistance. The constant good cheer, good sense, and rapid responses of Bart Wright at Lohnes+Wright Cartography made the production of the maps a pleasure. Jennifer Eastman carefully copyedited each page of the manuscript and adjusted her schedule to fit my own, for which I am profoundly grateful. At UC Press, Reed Malcolm and Zuha Khan kept the project on time and on point. Thank you.

# Introduction

This book is about the spatial politics of Japanese imperialism, that is, how the Japanese Empire possessed colonized lands by domesticating, disavowing, and disappearing other claims to that same land. It illuminates how territorializing a Japanese national identity on colonized land shaped the modern Japanese nation and brings into focus how ideas of place sustained the legitimacy of colonialism in a period when the world's major empires, including the Japanese, largely disavowed territorial conquest. This book explores the spatial politics of empire through a study of imperial tourism, which was one of the few institutions of the era to operate on a truly empire-wide scale and one that was uniquely concerned with producing firsthand experiences of colonized land.

Japan was a great imperial power during the first half of the twentieth century. This much is well known. But it is perhaps less well known that between 1868, when the new Meiji government formally colonized the island of Hokkaidō, and 1952, when the Japanese government formally renounced sovereignty over Taiwan, Korea, the Kuriles, the southern portion of the island of Karafuto (Russian [hereafter, R.] Sakhalin), and the League of Nations Mandate Territory in Micronesia (Japanese [J.] Nan'yō), the Japanese government possessed no single mechanism for differentiating, legally or politically, between colonized and Japanese territory. Even after the acquisition of Taiwan in 1895, generally used to mark the beginning of Japan's formal empire, there was never a coherent practice of referring to colonized lands as "colonies" *(shokuminchi)*. Instead, they were the "new territories"; they were "regions"; they were "territories governed by governors general." Anything but colonies. In fact, the spatial order of the empire was so liminal that when the administration of Korea and Taiwan was placed under the aegis of a new

Ministry of Colonial Affairs in 1929, Japanese residents of Korea complained so vociferously that Prime Minister Tanaka Giichi was forced to assure them that the ministry would "not treat Korea as a colony."[1]

In hindsight, it is obvious that Korea and Taiwan were colonies. The Japanese state acquired these lands by conquest and treaty but opted not to extend the full rights and responsibilities of citizenship to their residents. Moreover, the governors general and the imperial government treated these territories as "agricultural appendages" of Japan, setting policies that encouraged the production of basic commodities such as rice and sugar for the metropolitan market while discouraging local industrialization.[2] Internal border controls and overt discrimination in education limited the physical and social mobility of colonized subjects in ways not applied to most Japanese residents of the empire. Similar policies, varying only in their details, were applied to the remainder of Japan's colonized lands—local governments distributed political and economic rights unevenly in Hokkaidō, Okinawa, the Kuriles, Karafuto, and the League of Nations Mandate Territory in Micronesia. At the same time, colonial governments fostered a cultural hierarchy that marked the Japanese language and official culture as the basis for public life.

To put it bluntly, there was an element of instability about the place of these lands within Japan, about the relationship between colonized land, the territory of the state, and the space of the nation. This book examines this instability from the late nineteenth century until the post–World War II period. Through a study of imperial tourism to Korea, Manchuria, and Taiwan, I delineate how the question of where the colonies were shaped the conceptualization of the Japanese imperial nation and how, in turn, this spatio-social imaginary affected the way colonial difference was conceptualized and enacted. In so doing, I explore the significance of spatial politics to the maintenance of colonial hierarchies in a world in which the nation-state form has been globalized but political emancipation has not.

Japan was an empire, thus it is fair to ask why the history of its spatial politics is relevant to the larger colonial and postcolonial history of nationalism and nation-states. Indeed, despite the flexibility with which Japanese officials defined the territories of Korea, Taiwan, and Manchuria in relation to Japan, they were not so shy about describing Japan as "Great Japan," "the Japanese Empire," or the "Great Japanese Empire." Yet the distinction between nation-state and empire was not at all clear. As Ann Stoler has argued, "distinctly rendered boundaries represent . . . only one end of the spectrum" of empire. Imperial formations operate precisely at the "troubled, ill-defined" boundaries of citizenship, territory, and legal rights.[3] The "externalization of empire," the idea that nation-state and empire comprise two entirely different spaces and histories, is best considered a political narrative that arose after World War II than an accurate representation of the relationship between empires and nation-states.[4]

The early twentieth century was a time of global transition. Between the late nineteenth century and the middle of the twentieth, the emergence of the modern system of international relations, with its commitment to the territorial nation-state as the basis for human social and political organization, and the shift from mercantile to monopoly capitalism produced contradictory spatial formations within which imperialist and anti-imperial nationalists struggled to claim a place in the world. Like other new empires, such as the United States and Germany, the Japanese Empire faced these tensions by creating a regional empire that could be used as a resource base for capitalist expansion. In this context, imperialism mediated between the territorializing impulses of the modern state and the de-territorializing impulses of capitalism.[5] Rather than drawing firm boundaries between empire and nation, Japan and other new empires were what we might consider "imperial nation-states."[6] The result was a hybrid form of empire in which the state territorialized a sphere of influence that exceeded the boundaries of the nation but could nevertheless be made available for capitalist exploitation. On the one hand, the idea that the territory of the state was the patrimony of the nation legitimated the state's sovereignty over colonized land. On the other, the need to maintain colonized lands as territories to be exploited in the name of national strength authorized the creation of uneven forms of citizenship and the treatment of the colonies as spaces of exception to national norms.[7]

Over the course of the early twentieth century, the economic, administrative, and discursive structure of empire and nation in the Japanese imperium shifted in such a way that it is difficult, even now, to draw a firm line between the institutions and discourses of the Japanese nation and those of the empire. As scholars working on the history of modern Japan and the Japanese Empire have no doubt encountered, imperial discourse described the space of empire in terms of its places—Korea, Manchuria, Taiwan; Japan; the inner and outer territories. Yet these places did not generally correspond to distinct territorial or institutional jurisdictions; place names appeared as indices to a geographical structure of empire that was itself a chimera.[8] Such is the case, for example, with the term *naichi*, "inner territory." Scholarship on the Japanese Empire routinely uses *naichi* to signify the imperial metropole in contrast to the colonies, or "outer territories." Yet this description implies a concrete-ness of reference that did not exist in practice. The term *gaichi*, "outer territories," only came into official use in 1929, some thirty-five years after the colonization of Taiwan. The term *naichi* was used in a number of ways that were neither geographically nor conceptually overlapping. *Naichi* first appeared as the territorial opposite of the foreign settlements in Japanese treaty ports in the 1850s—ports that the unequal treaties with Western powers had opened to foreign trade. "Inner territory" simply meant "places that foreigners cannot live." Yet in the 1910s the Government General of Korea used "Japanification" (*naichika*, literally, "becoming like the inner territory") to refer to the industrialization of Korean urban areas, while in the 1930s, travelers used "like the *naichi*" (*naichi no yō*) to describe Japanese-language speech that approximated that of a Japanese native, in contrast to the "textbook speech" of colonized subjects. Throughout the history of the Japanese Empire, "inner territory" was a territory, a relative location on a universal trajectory of development, and an essentialized sensibility.

Recent research shows that imperial legal, educational, and political institutions did not create wholly distinct metropolitan and colonial territories. Prestigious metropolitan secondary schools enrolled elite colonized subjects, who had formative political experiences in Tokyo dormitories. The "colonial" legal system was actually at least two in Korea (one for ethnic Japanese and one for colonized subjects) but perhaps three in Taiwan (with separate treatments for Taiwanese Chinese, Japanese, and indigenous inhabitants). Penal systems in the colonies deployed spatial referents to justify treating "people of the inner territory" (*naichijin*) less harshly than "people of this island" (*hontōjin*)—a reference to Taiwanese Chinese—"savages" (*banjin*), and Koreans (*Senjin*). In the case of Taiwan, we must also consider what Hiroko Matsuda has termed the "everyday politics of distinction," which shaped the self-representation of and encounters between migrant laborers from Okinawa, Japanese settlers from the main islands, and Taiwanese Chinese. Unskilled Okinawan migrants to Taiwan, for example, were categorized as Japanese, but Taiwanese Chinese often referred to them as "Japanese aborigines," and Japanese settlers informally excluded them from the elite institutions of settler society, such as the most prestigious schools.[9]

To build on the words of Barbara Brooks, the Japanese Empire was "profoundly conflicted" not only about the status of non-Japanese subjects but also about the status of colonized and metropolitan land.[10] In fact, the spatial politics of the Japanese Empire parallel much more closely the complicated and contradictory history of defining "Japanese" ethnicity and citizenship than they do the history of the expansion and contraction of the Japanese state's territory. It is often argued that, although some rights and responsibilities were divided based on one's place of residence, the household registration system (*koseki seido*) created a "clear dividing line between 'Japanese proper' and 'colonial subjects.'"[11] For example, white-collar workers whose households were registered within the main islands, Okinawa, or Hokkaidō received a "colonial bonus" when they worked in Taiwan.[12] The location of one's household registry also determined one's eligibility for military service (until 1938, when, in the first years of total war, colonized subjects were allowed to enlist).[13] And yet, ethnicity and gender also profoundly influenced the location of one's household registry. A 1921 law formally recognized the intermarriage of Japanese and Korean subjects, for example, but mandated that the location of the household registry be determined by the ethnicity of the male half of the household. A Japanese woman who married a Korean man was entered into the man's Korean household registration, thus legally transforming her into a Korean woman. Korean women who married Japanese men, however, were entered into the Japanese registration. They became Japanese women. A different set of rules applied to children of mixed unions. A child born to a married Korean man and Japanese woman would be entered into the Korean household registry. But if the parents were unwed, the mother could enter the child in her Japanese registry as an illegitimate child, thus conferring upon her offspring the privileges of Japanese classification.[14]

The blurry lines between the space of the nation and the space of empire were not accidental. Rather, the instability of spatial and social boundaries was an essential component of the operation of early twentieth-century imperialism in the Japanese imperium and elsewhere. The present study examines this aspect of the Japanese Empire's spatial formation, the fixing and refixing of colonized lands within the space of the Japanese nation and the concomitant fixing of the Japanese nation on colonized land. For despite this instability, people did talk about places—indeed, an entire industry, tourism, emerged to produce the experience of place, which, as this book argues, became the spatial foundation for the practices of exclusion and dispossession that sustained imperialism after World War I.

## TOURISM AND THE SPATIAL POLITICS OF EMPIRE

One way to understand the history of tourism is to see it as an attempt to stabilize and standardize understandings of place—to produce, in other words, a hegemonic socio-spatial order anchored in specific understandings of place.[15] As an industry, tourism emerged in concert with the expansion of railways and the industrialization of labor.[16] Yet it also emerged during a time of intense geopolitical turmoil, which saw the shocking destruction of the First World War, the reorganization of empires, and the establishment of an organization (the League of Nations) that would, in theory, allow self-determining nations to protect the peace by agreeing upon practices of global imperialism and capitalism that could be imposed upon other, non-self-determining nations.[17] In other words, tourism—an industry devoted to selling experiences of places—was born at precisely the moment when the determination of boundaries, location, and essence was imbued with concrete and intensely debated political stakes. In this sense, tourism and the places it sold were an argument about the global social and geopolitical order.

There is a rich and diverse literature on the subject of tourism and empire. Much of it focuses on how the tropes of touristic literature facilitated and justified formal and informal conquests of colonized lands and on how colonial settlers deployed tourism to articulate their own place within their imperial nations, however geographically distant from the imperial center they were.[18] I am indebted to this literature, particularly to the works of Christine Skwiot, Vernadette Vicuña-Gonzalez, and Jason Ruiz, whose studies of U.S. tourism to Hawai'i, Cuba, the Philippines, and Mexico have laid bare the ways in which particular representations of these destinations and their peoples were—and are—embedded in much broader and long-running attempts by settlers and national governments to sustain claims to colonized lands.[19] Likewise, the works of Ellen Furlough and Inderpal Grewal expose how imperial tourism served as a vehicle for consolidating ideals of national citizenship while at the same time reinforcing the boundaries between metropolitan and colonial territories and between metropolitan and colonized subjects.[20] Together, these works show that the territorialization of the nation did not occur in the empty space of *terra nullius*—territory that colonial states claimed was not under the sovereignty of any state and was therefore available for colonization—but rather through a mutually constitutive process of displacement and appropriation, of possession by dispossession.[21]

This book contributes the first comprehensive study of tourism in the Japanese Empire to the growing field of tourism and empire studies. Earlier studies have illuminated how imperial tourism functioned as "self-administered citizenship training" and as a "memory industry" that encouraged the production of nationalist sentiment toward and the romanticization of colonized lands.[22] Yet the field as a whole has focused on studies of single colonies, and often only in the 1930s. As a result, the striking similarities between touristic representations of Korea, Manchuria, and Taiwan—and the stark contrasts between earlier and later practices of placing—have been overlooked. To explore the significance of these similarities, this book deploys a unique, transcolonial archive of tourist materials from 1906, when the first tours left for Manchuria and Korea, to the late 1930s, when the outbreak of the Sino-Japanese War and the rise of the total war ideology led to a narrowing of tourist discourses and an increased emphasis on the imperial house. The conclusion carries the analysis forward into the early postwar period, when former imperial officials, the Ministry of Education, and the U.S. Occupation worked to reterritorialize the Japanese nation in Asia after the end of formal empire.

A central argument of this book is that the challenge of anti-imperial nationalism and anticolonial liberalism led to a significant change in how imperial travelers and colonial boosters made sense of the place of colonized lands within Japan. In the early years of imperial tourism, representations of the place of Korea, Manchuria, and Taiwan within Japan were structured by a "geography of civilization."[23] Under this geography, imperial travelers and colonial boosters placed the colonies within Japan using three modes: a historical mode, which used the notion of "transition" to naturalize the transfer of power from indigenous states to Japanese colonial governments and the incorporation of colonized lands into the space of Japanese history; an economic mode, which described the colonies and their commodities as part of a network of production, circulation, and exchange made possible through Japanese intervention; and a nationalist mode, which encouraged travelers to forge affective connections to colonized lands and a sense of themselves as national subjects by using sites in the colonies to reenact a Japanese national past. As travelers used these modes to lay claim to the colonies as Japanese national land, they also used them to explain why colonized subjects could be dispossessed of their lands. Under the geography of civilization, imperial travelers emphasized colonized subjects' lack of historical, nationalist, or economic consciousness to legitimate Japanese colonial rule. The result was a core-periphery geography in which colonized lands were imagined to be quickly becoming—or in the case of the nationalist mode, already part of—the national land. Imperial travelers and colonial boosters treated colonized inhabitants as out of place in their own lands.

But the denial of coevalness that the geography of civilization represented could not be sustained in the face of widespread protests, from colonized subjects and Japanese settlers alike, against the uneven territorial-administrative structure of Japanese imperial rule. Starting in the late 1910s, the geography of civilization began to give way to a geography of cultural pluralism, under which imperial travelers *re-placed* the colonies using an ethnographic mode, which represented the space of the imperial nation as one composed of diverse cultural regions and ethnic peoples. If, under the geography of civilization, the colonization of Korea, Manchuria, and Taiwan was justified by marking colonized subjects as out of place in the national land, under the geography of cultural pluralism, the notion of "from-ness"—of subjects who were essentially and unchangingly *in place* in one specific region and only that region—became a key way that imperial travelers and colonial administrations conceptualized and enacted colonial difference. The geography of cultural pluralism fostered new forms of dispossession, internal bordering, and differentiation between colonized and metropolitan subjects in the name of appreciating the essential differences between the empire's cultural regions and its distinct ethnic populations.

What emerges from the transcolonial approach to the study of imperial tourism is the idea that tourism was not just useful for justifying individual instances of colonialism. Rather, tourism was central to the maintenance of empire itself. Imperial tourism was one manifestation of what I call the "spatial politics of empire," the use of concepts of place to naturalize uneven structures of rule.[24] For historians of tourism, spatial politics offers an answer to the question of why tourism emerged as the solution to the particular crises of so many imperial formations in the late nineteenth and early twentieth centuries. It draws together the insights of myriad national case studies of tourism to expose the critical role that imperial tourism played in the colonial and postcolonial history of the modern world. It shows how tourism made spatial relationships meaningful in ways that suited the overall goal of sustaining colonialism and how these spatializations changed over time and in response to broader shifts in concepts of sovereignty and economic structures.[25]

For historians of modern Japan, the concept of spatial politics illuminates how the dramatic changes that the territory of the Japanese state underwent between the late nineteenth century and the end of the U.S. Occupation were not merely a matter of expanding and contracting borders but rather a cause for serious engagement with the problem that imperial territory posed to conceptualizations of the nation.[26] Previous studies have argued that the parameters of the modern Japanese spatial imaginary were set by the early twentieth century.[27] Yet, as the history of the empire's spatial politics makes evident, the problem of maintaining an imperial territory in a world increasingly dominated by the ideals of the nation-state imposed new demands on the spatial and social imaginary of Japan. From the first years of Japanese imperialism, tourism emerged as one of the primary vehicles for spatial politics as Japanese colonial boosters sought to fix and refix colonized lands in ways amenable to the image of Japan as a territorial nation-state rather than an expansive empire.[28]

## PLACE BETWEEN EMPIRE AND NATION

Spatial politics engages a phenomenon central to the history of imperial tourism: the intense focus on producing and circulating firsthand experiences of colonized lands in relation to, but not subsumed within, the politics of race, culture, and language. As Peter Jackson and Jan Penrose argued decades ago, the construction of national identities and of differences within the nation took place on terms that were sometimes racial and sometimes spatial.[29] Yet while numerous works have shown that capitalism and nationalism require the constant production and reproduction of notions of racial, gender, and class difference in order to create the conditions in which exploitation and identity-formation take place, the study of the problem of spatial difference and spatial politics within the nation-state remains a niche issue—the domain of activist scholars of settler colonialism rather than a problem central to the history of the modern world.[30] This book argues that the management of ideas of place was central to the maintenance of empire precisely because, unlike the other two axes of colonial difference, race and culture, its politics directly addressed the problem of colonized land to the territorial nation. Place did not operate in a vacuum. It drew on, buttressed, and challenged prevailing notions of racial and cultural difference. At the same time, to ignore place and the problem of land that it reveals contributes to the erasure of the ongoing nature of colonialism in the postcolonial world.

Place is central to how societies understand themselves and how individuals understand their position within a society. As geographer Tim Cresswell writes, "Looking at the world as a set of places in some way separate from each other is both an act of defining what exists (ontology) and a particular way of seeing and knowing the world (epistemology and metaphysics). . . . In other words, place is not simply something to be observed, researched, and written about but is itself part of the way we see, research, and write."[31] Human geographers, who have been at the forefront of attempts to grasp the humanistic significance of place, treat place both as a social construction and as a phenomenon that makes possible "the very possibility of the social."[32] It is more than a set of ideographically distinct regions. Rather, place has multiple elements. It can be a locale, a site where events occur. It can also be a location or status, a place in relative space. And, of course, it can be an essence or sense, as in the atmosphere of a place or the sense that one gets of being in a unique place.[33]

When shared, understandings of place produce a common language for describing the world and our relations within it.[34] But as geographers from the feminist tradition emphasize, it is, in fact, impossible to conceive of or even analyze place outside of the "power-geometry" of how different groups relate to movement and to each other. In other words, an ontological definition of place always occurs within, not prior to, an epistemology of space and a materiality of social relations. "What gives place its specificity," Doreen Massey argues, "is not some long internalized history but the fact that it is constructed out of a particular constellation of relations, articulated together at a particular locus."[35]

*Place* is thus both a noun and a verb. David Harvey once described *place* as a way of "carving out permanences" in space and time, and it is in this sense that I use it here.[36] Place is both an action and a tool—we use it to identify and individuate objects, people, and events as if it were a static or objective category. At the same time, each time we do so, we create or sustain a particular spatial order of our world. Locating, naming, and bounding places are political acts that represent and reproduce social relationships and political orders. Place is also subject to "perpetual perishing." We enact place each time we use it to describe the world "out there." As we do so, we extend its conceptual life a little bit longer. On the other hand, the enactment of a new place can challenge the dominance of an old order. Place is thus an act of world-making that cannot be reduced to geography or territory—place is an articulation of social relations that is always made from a particular perspective.

Of primary importance to this book's argument is the rise of the territorial nation-state as the "global archetype" of sovereignty and political freedom over the course of the late nineteenth and twentieth centuries.[37] One of the distinguishing features of nationalism is that the nation imagines itself to have emerged from, and to be anchored in, a particular territory.[38] It claims a place. In the words of Edward W. Soja, in the modern era of nation-states, social definitions of territory have been replaced by territorialized definitions of society.[39] For this reason, if none other, the nation-state form placed a new emphasis on territory as the "mediator" between state and people, especially in situations of contested sovereignty.[40] Starting in the late nineteenth century and cresting with the establishment of the League of Nations and later the United Nations, the imperial powers—both the Great and the Late—embraced exclusive territorial jurisdictions as the principal boundaries of sovereignty and the nation-state as the principal guarantor of political freedom. Congruent with theories of state sovereignty established in the late nineteenth century, the nation-state form was based on an understanding that the ideal form of sovereignty was the possession of exclusive jurisdiction over a discrete territory.[41] Yet this process took place without empires abandoning the entirety of their colonized lands or granting political emancipation to all colonized subjects. Indeed, from Hawai'i to Puerto Rico to Australia to Hokkaidō, postimperial states sustained colonialism in new forms. Patrick Wolfe famously underscored this ongoing nature of colonialism when he defined *conquest* not as an event in the history of colonial nation-states but rather as its structure.[42]

It is in this context that spatial politics took their modern form. Attachments to territory were powerful not because they were primordial, but because international relations and official nationalisms increasingly "attribute[d] . . . power and meaning to them."[43] Through geography education, museums, cartography, and collective memory, nationalists sought to produce affective attachments to the state's territory by defining it as the place of the nation. The names for these places were localized, although the concept was not—for example, *Heimat* in Germany, *kyōdo* in Japan, and the *swadeshi* movement in India. Indeed, it is no accident that Ernest Renan's famous 1882 speech *Qu'est-ce qu'une nation?* (What is a nation?) took as its object the problem of Alsace and Lorraine, a region with a distinctly Germanic population that had been recently conquered by Germany but nonetheless remained, in Renan's argument, a legitimate part of French state territory and French national identity. Although for Renan the nation was a form of consciousness, a voluntarist state of mind rather than an organic ethnic identity, part of that voluntarism involved rising out of one's local place to lay claim to the entirety of the territory of the state. Even organicist visions, as Anthony D. Smith argues, relied on an element of voluntarism in that "primordial attachments rest on perception, cognition, and belief."[44] The representation of the territory of the state as the space of the nation, what Thongchai Winikachul has called the "geobody of the nation," thus became a central element in the production of the nation itself as it "provide[d] the ground upon which to stake the claim for nation."[45]

Yet it is perhaps more profitable to think of the idea of the nation as a territorialized community—a nation-state that governs a particular place—as an ideal rather than a reality. The formulation takes for granted what has been a constant struggle for much of modern world history.[46] Nation and state are two distinct and "asymmetrical" spatial identities.[47] The modern state is a product of the modern concept of sovereignty. Its spatial identity is one of territorial administration, of defining jurisdictions, governing the human and material resources contained within the territory, and controlling borders with other sovereign states. In contrast, the spatial identity of the nation is discursive; it is an unstable collection of cultural, historical, and environmental relations that tie a particular community to a particular space but do not *limit* it to that space. While some nations are able to link themselves to particular states, this has not always been the case. Between the late nineteenth and mid-twentieth centuries, the asymmetry manifested in a number of ways, including separatist movements and other sub-state nationalisms, contested borderlands and areas of blurred nationalities, and diasporic communities with a transnational scope but a specific territorial homeland.[48] It was also seen in situations of settler colonialism, when the territory of the state expanded far beyond the spatial identity of the nation or, as in the case of Japanese-controlled Manchuria, the space of the nation expanded beyond the territory of the state.

A map published in a 1919 Japanese geography primer illustrates the problem. The islands of Hokkaidō, Honshū, Shikoku, Kyūshū, and Okinawa are the darkest; the legend informs us that they defined the extent of Great Japan *(dai Nihon)* in 1888, twenty years after the Meiji Restoration. Karafuto and Taiwan are slightly lighter, indicating that in 1898, Japan included these territories as well. The Kwantung Leased Territory, the railway line between Dairen (Chinese [C.]: Dalian) and Chōshun (C. Changchun), and Korea are even lighter, marking these territories as part of Japan by 1907 (a slight fib, since Korea was only a Japanese protectorate in 1905 and was not formally annexed until 1910, while Manchuria was never part of the sovereign territory of Japan). The shading ends with Micronesia, which the legend tells us has been part of Japan since 1914. In contrast to the legend, the accompanying text notes that Micronesia "was under the management of the League of Nations" and that Japan merely leased the Kwantung Leased Territory from China.[49]

The map showed Japan as a historical and territorial entity. Produced by Yamazaki Naomasa, one of the most prominent geographers of the era, it displayed visually what other geographers, such as Odauchi Michitoshi, represented textually through descriptions of Japan's "national land" as divided into "new" and "old" territory *(shin* and *kyū kokudo)*. These depictions committed the sleight-of-hand of equating the spatial identity of the state with that of the nation. To put it more precisely, Yamazaki and Odauchi did not differentiate between the two at all. Yet as we have seen, there were real differences in the administration of colonial and metropolitan territory, and in many respects, these administrative and institutional differences grew more pronounced over time. The space of the nation never fully encompassed the territory of the state. It was in the tension between the two that concepts of imperial nationhood took form.

Indeed, only a couple years before Yamazaki published his map and a couple years after Odauchi published his primer, another definition of the relationship between the territory of the state and the place of the nation appeared, one that helps us to square the circle of spatial politics between empire and nation. In 1915,

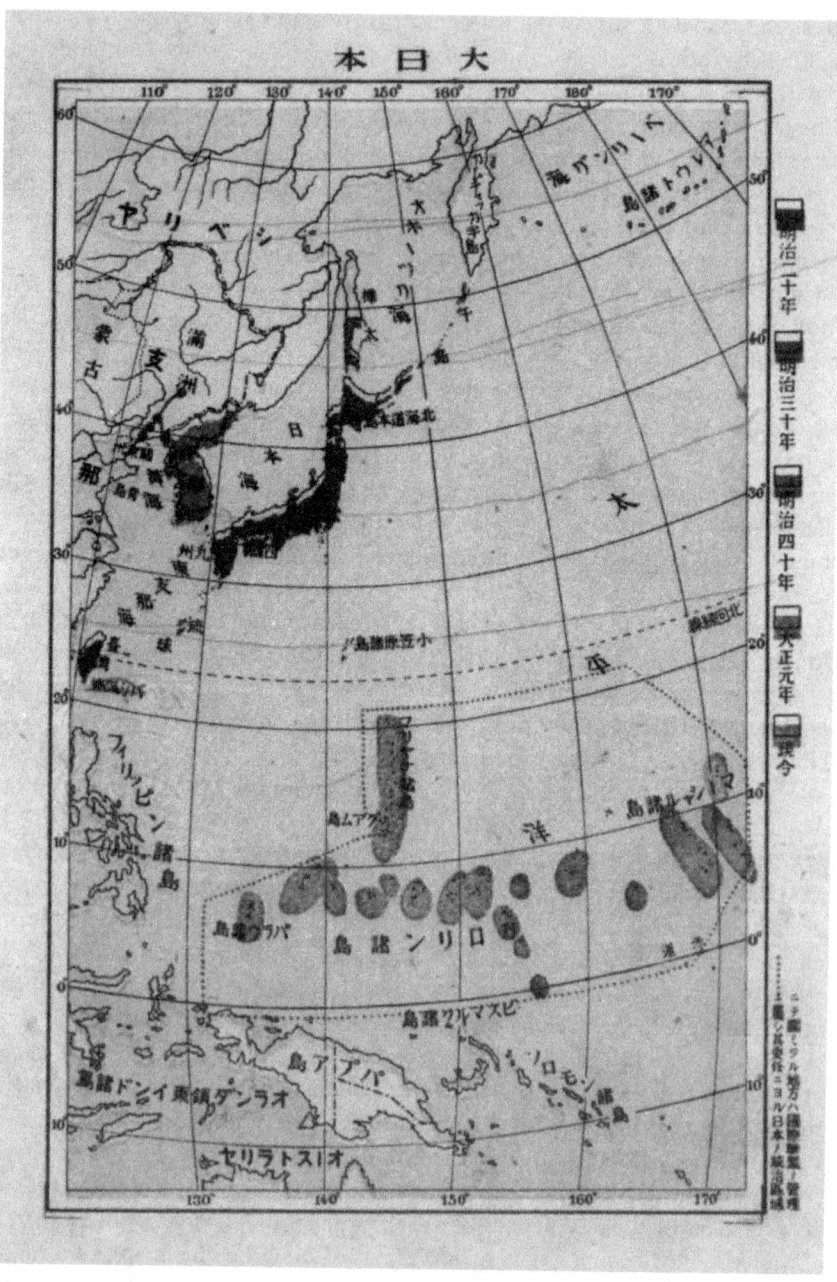

FIGURE 1. Map of "Great Japan."
SOURCE: Yamazaki Naomasa, *Futsū kyōiku Nihon chiri kyōkasho* (Tokyo: Tokyo kaiseikan, 1919). Courtesy of the National Diet Library.

Nitobe Inazō, Japan's most famous scholar of colonial policy, gave a lecture in which he defined *colony* as a "new territory of the state" *(shin ryōdo)*. To justify this definition, Nitobe surveyed the meaning of the word *colony* from the Roman Empire to the British Empire, tracing its meaning in relation to cognate terms such as *territory, plantation, province,* and *dependency*. In its widest meaning, Nitobe concluded, *colony* could refer to an ethnic enclave, as in the case of referring to the treaty port town of Yokohama as a "colony of Westerners." In its narrowest definition, it might refer to just the area in a colonized territory where settlers from the colonizing country reside. Admitting that, "it probably was not precise in the scientific sense," Nitobe offered a middle ground. "All definitions have two components: genus and species," he argued. In this case, "'colony' is of the genus 'territory'; species, 'new.'"[50]

The working definition encapsulated what Nitobe defined as the most important components of a colony: people, land, and "the political relationship with the motherland."[51] But it also illuminated the unstable position of colonies between the territory of the state and the space of the nation. Newness, for example, was subjective. Nitobe defined *new* from the perspective of the colonizing nation. "Through language, customs, institutions, thought, etc., as long as the national people *(kokumin)* think of it as somehow different, the territory is new."[52] Likewise, he chose the word meaning "territory of the state" *(ryōdo)* carefully. Simply referring to a colony as a new territory *(shinchi)* would not do, because a colony is always constituted within a political relationship to the colonizing country—in his words, the "mother country."[53] The term *shin ryōdo,* "new territory of the state," defined colonies as phenomena that were both temporary and permanent at the same time. Indeed, part of Nitobe's purpose in defining *colony* was to offer the field of "colonial policy" and "colonial policy studies" in the service of managing these tensions: "'colonial policies' are the policies that attempt to make permanent the benefits that the mother country accrues vis-à-vis a phenomenon that tends toward the temporary."[54]

Thus, as I use it here, *place* is not in opposition to *territory*. Rather, *place* and *territory* worked in conversation with one another to produce hegemonic spatial imaginaries that fed and were fed by material and political structures of power—the spatial imaginaries that kept the colonies "new" in the eyes of the nation. Imperial discourse used places as signifiers—as the seemingly concrete site of historical events; as territorial homelands for cultures, languages, and ethnicities; as territories in particular spatial and temporal relations to other territories. Placing the colonies and the nation was, in this sense, not distinct from the drawing of borders and the implementation of policy. It was an inherent part of maintaining the uneven forms of citizenship and spaces of exception that defined the colony within the imperial nation-state. Much like Edward Said's imaginative geographies, spatial politics were a way of using representations of place to justify territorial-administrative divisions and the uneven treatment of different populations. They were a way of sustaining particular spatial imaginaries by amplifying and disseminating them to the nation at large through institutions such as education, the print media, and, as the case is here, tourism. As I show, these spatial politics were linked to specific institutions of possession and dispossession—from the use of local color to deny political emancipation to Taiwanese Chinese in colonial Taiwan to the use of theories of native rootedness to legitimate the exploitation of Korean and Chinese labor and to the use of place- and race-based language expectations to limit the social and physical mobility of colonized subjects within imperial society. The geographies of civilization and of cultural pluralism that structured the spatial politics of the Japanese Empire were imaginative, but they were also purposeful.[55]

## OVERVIEW

During the era of Japanese imperialism, tourists visited all corners of the empire, including wartime conquests in China.[56] Of these destinations, I focus on Korea, Manchuria, and Taiwan. This is for three reasons. One, these territories were explicitly outside of the jurisdiction of the 1889 Constitution but within (sometimes ambiguously so) the territory of the Japanese Empire. For this reason, they posed a more troublesome conundrum to travelers attempting to make sense of their relationship to Japan than did Okinawa or Hokkaidō, which had been annexed outright in 1879 and 1868, respectively, and incorporated into the juridical territory of the nation-state as subordinate administrative units. Two, these territories were the site of multiple, well-publicized challenges to imperial rule. Therefore, the place of these lands and their peoples within the territory of the state and the space of the nation were a subject of considerable discussion. There are a plethora of sources, primary and secondary relating to the place of these territories that we can use to explore the relationship between spatial politics and imperial tourism in the Japanese Empire. Three, among all the destinations for imperial travel, Manchuria and Korea—generally referred to as a single destination, *Man-Sen*—were by far the biggest draw. By the 1920s and 1930s, an increasing number of Japanese travelers reached out to Taiwan as well. These territories were the first destinations for imperial tourists and later came to possess the largest and most organized imperial tourist industries. Indeed, as we see in chapter 1, it was the desire to send influential metropolitan Japanese to the new territories of Manchuria and Korea that sparked the formation of an imperial tourism industry in the first place. Later, the domestic arm of the Japan Tourist Bureau, the Japanese government's official tourist organization, largely came into being in order to facilitate travel by metropolitan Japanese to Manchuria, Korea, and Taiwan.

Manchuria is, in this regard, somewhat of a special case. In contrast to the Japan-Taiwan and Japan-Korea relationships, the relationship of Japan to Manchuria is generally described as one of informal imperialism.[57] As a spoil of victory after the Russo-Japanese War, Japan gained possession of the Russian railway concession in Manchuria. This concession was unique among railway concessions in China in that it granted the owner the right of "exclusive and absolute administration" over a 438-mile stretch of railway between Dairen and Chōshun, including a mile of territory on either side of the tracks; this became known as the "Railway Zone." In 1906, these formerly Russian tracks became the trunk line of the South Manchuria Railway Company, a joint-stock company in which the Japanese government held a 51 percent stake.[58] In 1932, the Japanese army stationed in Manchuria attacked Chinese garrisons in Manchuria's major towns, and claimed a far wider territory for a new, putatively independent state, which they called "Manchukuo." From 1932 until 1945, Manchukuo was a puppet state of Japan. In contrast to Korea and Taiwan, which were part of the territory of the Japanese state, Manchuria/Manchukuo was a significant Japanese colony but never formally under Japanese sovereignty.

Yet, despite the many ways in which the political history of the Japan-Manchuria relationship differs from that of the Japan-Taiwan and Japan-Korea relationships, this book finds many similarities in how imperial travelers made sense of these lands as places that were both inside and outside of the social and political boundaries of imperial Japan. While Manchuria presented special challenges to colonial boosters, the practices of placing that they deployed were rarely unique. To the contrary, they were similar in ways that are worth paying attention to. The similarities illuminate how the changes in the geopolitical order that motivated the Japanese government to establish Manchukuo as a puppet state rather than a formal colony also forced colonial boosters and imperial travelers to re-conceptualize the relationship between Taiwan, Korea, and Japan.

We begin our story of imperial tourism and the spatial politics of empire in the city of Port Arthur at the tip of the Liaodong Peninsula, which was located, depending on which nationalist spatial imaginary you employed, either in the Three Eastern Provinces of China or in Manchuria, a place that had always been rather distinct, Japanese imperialists insisted, from China itself. There, a group of Japanese settlers established a society to preserve the battlefield ruins from the Russo-Japanese War. Unlike memorials to the war dead that were established at Yasukuni Shrine in Tokyo and elsewhere in the inner territory, the Society for the Preservation of Manchuria's Battlefield Ruins sought not only to "comfort the spirits of the war dead" but also to "foster unwavering loyalty to the national land."[59] Manchuria was not part of the sovereign territory of the Japanese Empire. It would seem that only a very capacious definition of *national land* would include it.

But it was in the pursuit of affective connections to a national land that exceeded the boundaries of the imperial state that imperial tourism was born, thus it is with this chimeric concept that we begin our investigation of spatial politics between empire and nation. Part 1 explores spatial politics under the geography of civilization. Chapter 1 shows how imperial travel began to reify the abstract concept of a national land by fostering emotional ties between imperial travelers and a small number of sites in Korea and Manchuria. The idea of a national land *(kokudo)* was, like the concept of a national people *(kokumin)*, extralegal and inconsistently defined. At the same time, it was, also like the concept of a national people, an extraordinarily powerful discursive object upon which people acted and which acted upon them. In a reversal of the extant practice of "colonial tours of the metropole," which sought to induce submission to and desire for the metropole among colonized subjects by bringing elite members of these societies to see Tokyo and other urban areas, imperial travel arose to make meaning of the national land by creating a body of subjects who had firsthand experience of it and whose social position authorized them to disseminate their experiences as authentic knowledge.

If affective ties to a national land were the first way in which colonial boosters sought to place the Japanese nation on colonized land, they did little to address what imperial travelers found to be the obvious differences between life in the urban metropole and the colonies. Chapter 2 traces how the Governments General of Taiwan and Korea, as well as the South Manchuria Railway Company, quickly adopted imperial tourism and its central tools, tourist guidebooks and standardized itineraries, to teach imperial travelers to see Korea, Manchuria, and Taiwan as places within the space of the Japanese nation. Rather than simply denying the coevalness of colonized territory, tourist guidebooks used three modes—the historical, economic, and nationalist modes—to place colonized lands within the bounds of a past, present, and future that was both "civilized" and "Japanese," and at the same time, to mark colonized subjects as "out of place" in these same lands. In this, colonial boosters enrolled imperial travelers in the project of constructing a spatial imaginary of the nation that might one day overcome the core-periphery geography of civilization to encompass the entirety of the territory of the state.

Part 2 explores how the crisis of empire that Japan faced after World War I produced a shift from a geography of civilization to a geography of cultural pluralism. In the post–World War I era, the binaries of colony and metropole, colonizer and colonized, Japanese and non-Japanese, were re-constituted as relations between ethnic nations and cultural regions. In a time of growing anti-imperial activism, encounters between travelers and colonized subjects, and between traveling colonized subjects and the state, became sites through which travelers reified a spatial imaginary of Japan as a nation of diverse cultural regions and yet marked the Japanese ethnic nation as the nation's political and cultural core.

Chapter 3 argues that the spatial politics of empire were centrally concerned with movement—as an ideal (free circulation) and as a practice (tourism). In the years after World War I, imperial tourism expanded from an elite practice to what one official called the "democratization and socialization" of travel—what we might think of as mass imperial tourism. At the same time, this era saw the establishment of new boundaries within the state that limited the movement of colonized subjects, especially that of laborers and those engaged in leftist activism. Coming on the heels of unprecedented labor activism and social unrest and concomitant with a political push to universalize male suffrage, the effort to expand imperial tourism in the early 1920s was inseparable from the effort to create a concept of imperial citizenship that could encompass the entirety of the territory of the state while still retaining a hierarchy of colonial difference. Through an analysis of tourism's border-crossing narratives, the chapter shows how the 1920s saw the rise of a new way of spatializing the relationship between metropolitan and colonized subjects. "Citizens" were those travelers with free mobility who were at home anywhere in the empire. "Subjects," on the other hand, were those who the state treated as essentially "from" certain regions and who were out of place when they attempted to travel elsewhere.

The spatial politics of "from-ness" structured new ways of defining colonial difference. These politics were based on an understanding of the colonies as distinct and unchanging cultural regions, with particular natural characteristics that shaped the cultural and ethnic characteristics of the populations that inhabited them. Chapter 4 investigates the rise of a touristic discourse based on this notion of a cultural region: that of "local color." Appearing in response to several high-profile uprisings in Korea, China, and Taiwan against Japanese colonialism, local color discourse co-opted the rhetoric of cultural and linguistic difference upon which anti-imperial groups based their claims for self-rule and independence. Instead, colonial boosters used local color to offer a vision of the nation and empire as a complementary space of diverse cultural regions, defined by history, cultures of labor, and landscape. At the same time, these mechanisms served as the foundation for new practices of dispossession and exclusion, including a spatialized division of labor and the further dispossession of Taiwan's indigenous peoples in the name of preserving the "national land."

Chapter 5 returns to the affective space of the Japanese nation by examining how the geography of cultural pluralism encouraged travelers to experience the empire as a decentered, yet still hierarchical, multiethnic polity. The chapter traces how language became a vehicle for spatial politics as local color discourse shaped travelers' expectations of colonized places and their inhabitants. Rather than reinforce a sense of shared nationality, imperial travelers used Japanese-language encounters with colonized subjects to articulate the impossibility of colonized subjects ever overcoming their place of origin to become authentic members of the nation.

Today, Korea, Manchuria, and Taiwan are no longer part of the territory of the Japanese state. Yet spatial politics did not disappear with the end of formal empire in 1945. The conclusion explores the transformation of the imperial spatial imaginary into an object of memory in the immediate postwar period. In the postwar era, the imperial tourism industry struggled to make sense of its former self. The U.S. Occupation required the production of a spatial imaginary of Japan in which the space of the nation was symmetrical with the territory of the state. Japanese people struggled to re-articulate memories that had been forged under a previous geography, while the next generation of travelers created a new geography of spatial and social relations that addressed Japan's imperial past and uncertain future in Cold War East Asia. In this context, the geography of cultural pluralism continued to structure the representation of Hokkaidō and Okinawa—places that were kept "new," in other words, in the relationship between the nation, colonized land, and the motherland that Nitobe Inazō first defined as *colonialism*.

## A NOTE ON PLACE NAMES

Writing the history of imperial tourism and its spatial politics requires careful attention to the rendering of place names in roman script. Place names have a "semantic depth"; they index networks of relations and shared histories.[60] In the Japanese Empire, place names were an essential part of the larger project of producing and reproducing a social imaginary of the nation that incorporated colonized land into the space of the Japanese nation. Japanese-language tourist guidebooks labeled each place or station with its name in Chinese characters *(kanji)* and its reading in the Japanese syllabary *(hiragana)*. Travelers encountered the cities of Korea, Manchuria, and Taiwan in the language of Japanese imperialism, that is, in Japanese: Pusan, Keijō, Heijō, Antō, Hōten, Chōshun, Dairen, Ryojun, Taihoku, Kagi, and Arisan. The colonial governments Japanified place names—the characters for the name of the Korean capital were read in the Japanese fashion, Keijō, rather than the Korean one, Kyŏngsŏng; similarly, official tourist literature described the reading of the characters for the capital of Taiwan as the Japanese "Taihoku" rather than the Chinese "Taipei"—to demonstrate that these places were now part of the space of the Japanese nation. In Manchuria, Japanified place names were often represented in parallel with Russian and Chinese names as part of a broader move to treat political transitions and imperial expansion as a natural part of the history of nations, as well as, in the specific context of Manchuria, to emphasize the local Japanese government's commitment to the principles of the Open Door policy. The South Manchuria Railway Company's guidebooks, for example, represented "Dairen" through its Chinese characters, bordered by a Japanese pronunciation, a Chinese pronunciation, and a Russian pronunciation. A similar practice of foregrounding the historical geography of place names appeared in the Government General of Taiwan's guidebooks, which invariably recited the history of names for the island of Taiwan. In Taiwan, the chronology of place names served as a convenient tool for illustrating why Japanese colonialism was the most humanitarian of all previous colonialisms—the Spanish and the Dutch, who had called the island "Ilha Formosa," had been concerned primarily with extracting from the island only what was useful for them; in contrast, the Japanese, who called the island "Taiwan," aimed to better the entire island. As we see in the conclusion, deconstructing the shared history of place names was an essential component of constructing a post-imperial social imaginary of Japan that treated the empire as a problem of the past and constituted the present, authentic Japanese social body as an "island nation."

The use of place names as mnemonic sites for imperial narratives of Japanese national history was an important component of the nationalist mode of territorial incorporation, the subject, along with the historical and economic modes, of chapter 2. But the phenomenon is perhaps equally well illustrated by marginalized and colonized groups' use of place names to challenge imperial spatial imaginaries with their own, anti-imperial nationalist renderings of place and spatial order. Just prior to Japan's colonization of Korea, for example, Korea's King Kojong named Korea "The Great Han Empire" *(Tae Han Cheguk)* to signal the independence of Korea. The previous name for Korea, Chosŏn, had been chosen by the Ming emperor in 1394. "Han," in contrast, was "a term traceable to ancient kingdoms on the southern half of the peninsula, an area, most significantly, that had never been invaded by China."[61] When, in one of its first acts, the Japanese colonial government renamed the Great Han Empire "Chōsen," it likewise conjured up a new political relationship, though in this case between Japan and Korea. The Government General stripped Korea of its nationalist name and bestowed upon it the Japanese reading of the name of its last tributary dynasty. In the current era, some Ainu activists seek to territorialize an Ainu identity by referring to the northern island of Japan's archipelago as Ainu Mosir, or "land of the humans," rather than the colonial state's name of Hokkaidō. The territorialization of sovereignty and identity that this conceptualization of Ainu Mosir enacts owes more to a nationalist concept of community than an indigenous one.[62] All the same it evidences the ongoing nature of imperial spatial politics in the post-colonial era.

This book uses the Japanese readings of place names within the Japanese Empire. I found this decision difficult. In the end, however, I decided that the use of the present-day names would have been an anachronistic ascription of a permanent identity to places that were (and are) in flux. It would also have inadvertently effaced a colonizing practice that was an important part of Japanese efforts to naturalize Taiwan, Korea, and Manchuria as places within Japan. Instead, I wish to highlight the significance of renaming to the spatial politics of imperialism, which was part of the broader effort to culturally assimilate colonial populations, such as teaching the Japanese language in schools and converting Korean surnames to Japanese-style names. Whenever possible, I include the current Chinese (pinyin) or Korean (McCune-Reischauer) reading of the name the first time that I mention a place or site. Readers may also consult the appendix for an index of all Japanese place names that appear in the book with their current names in both the roman alphabet and their local script (i.e., Korean *hangul* or Chinese characters).

MAP 1. Map of Northeast Asia. The formal and informal territory of the Japanese Empire encompassed the islands of Japan (including Hokkaidō and the Ryūkyū Islands), Taiwan, Korea, parts of Manchuria, and the southern portion of Sakhalin. Map design: Lohnes+Wright.

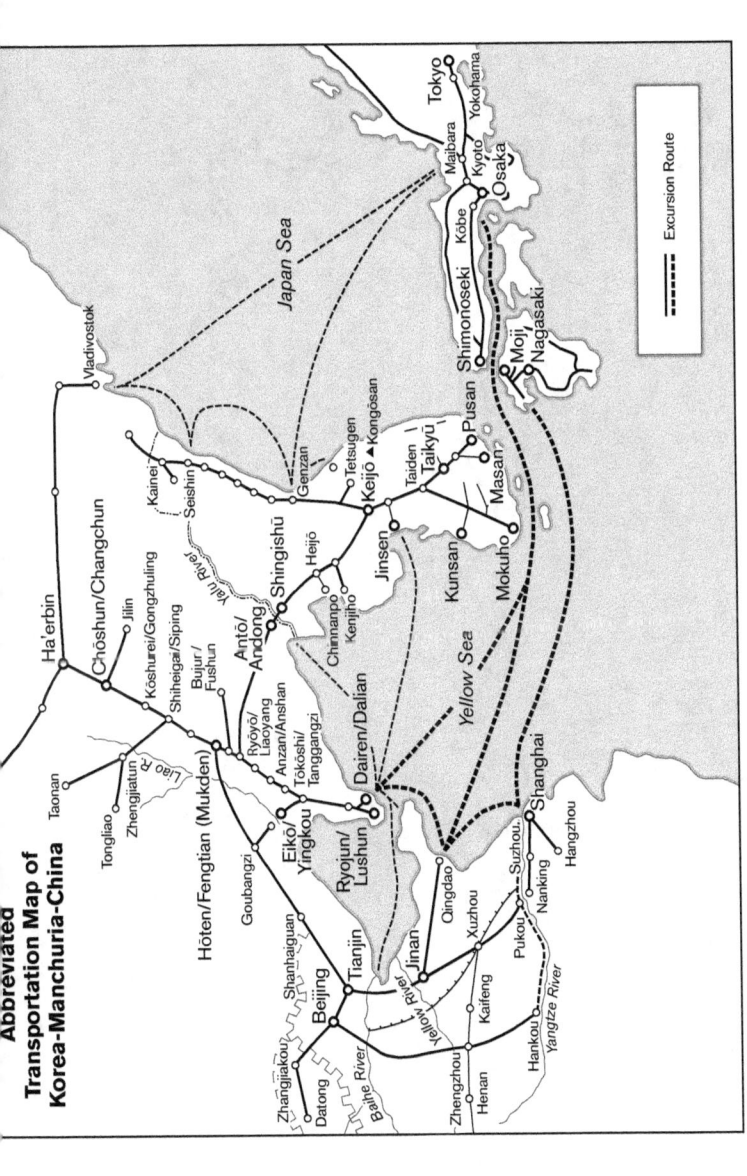

MAP 2. "Abbreviated Transportation Map of Korea-Manchuria-China," 1931. The map shows how the Government General of Korea and the South Manchuria Railway Company suggested that Japanese travelers read the names of station stops along the Korea-Manchuria-China tourist route. Names of stations have been rendered in Japanese for stations in Korea, in Chinese and Japanese for stations along the South Manchuria Railway Line, and in Chinese for other stations within Manchuria and China. The map is redrawn and simplified from Japan Tourist Bureau, ed., *Ryotei to hiyō gaisan Shōwa 6-nen ban* (Tokyo: Hakubunkan, 1931). Japanese pronunciations of place names are from Minami Manshū tetsudō kabushiki kaisha, *Minami Manshū tetsudō ryokō annai* (Dairen: Minami Manshū tetsudō kabushiki kaisha, 1929) and Chōsen sōtokufu tetsudōkyoku, ed., *Chōsen ryokō annai ki* (Keijō: Chōsen sōtokufu tetsudokyoku, 1934). Map design: Lohnes+Wright.

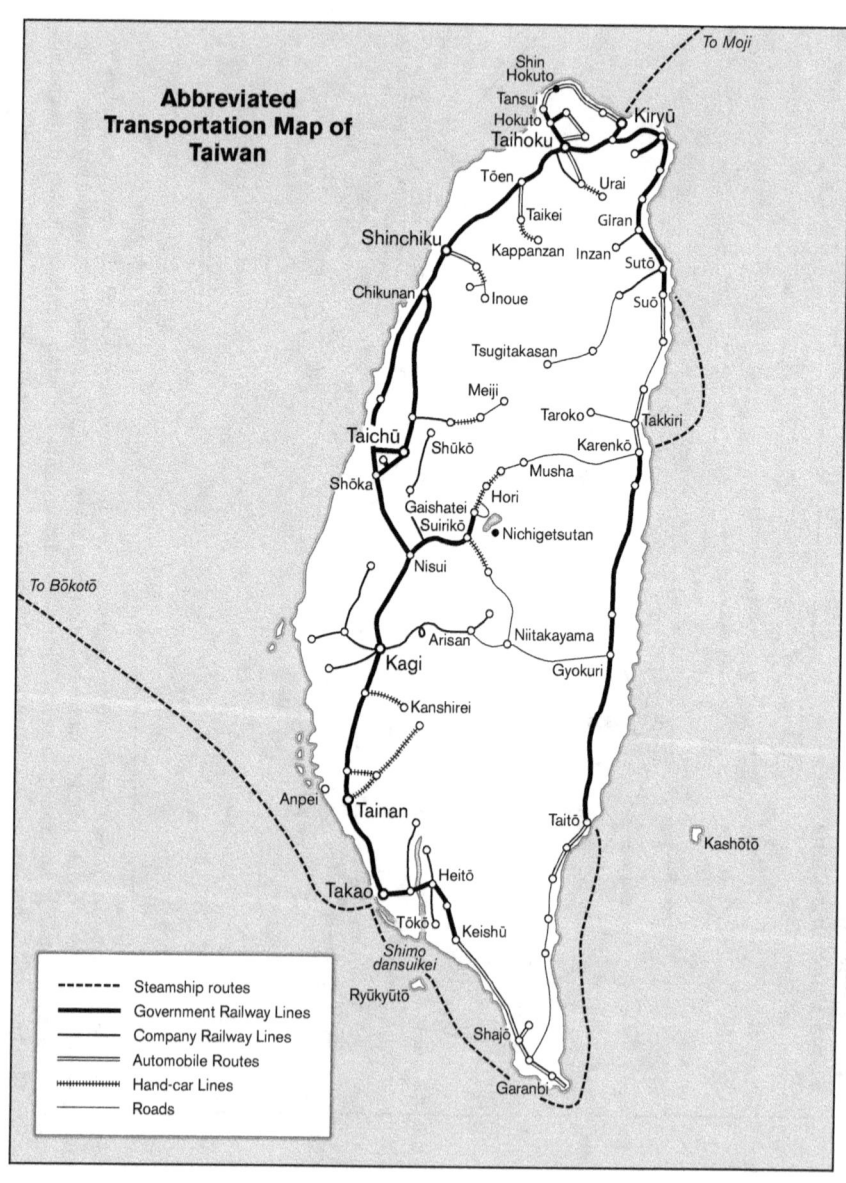

MAP 3. "Abbreviated Transportation Map of Taiwan," 1931. The map shows how the Government General of Taiwan suggested that travelers read the names of station stops in Taiwan. Names of stations have been rendered in Japanese pronunciation. Map is redrawn and simplified from Japan Tourist Bureau, ed., *Ryotei to hiyō gaisan Shōwa 6-nen ban* (Tokyo: Hakubunkan, 1931). Japanese pronunciations of place names are from Taiwan sōtokufu, *Taiwan tetsudō ryokō annai* (Taihoku: Taiwan sōtokufu, 1927) and Sawada Hisao, *Nihon chimei daijiten*, vol. 2 (Tokyo: Nihon shobō, 1937). Map design: Lohnes+Wright.

PART ONE

# The Geography of Civilization

1

# Seeing Like the Nation

In 1936, Nakanishi Inosuke articulated his frustration with what were called "observational travelers" and their not very observant travelogues: "The experts who write the authoritative accounts know geography, human feelings, and customs well of course. But they are writing nothing more than guidebooks. They do not have 'eyes.' Because of this, they do not have a worldview. And because of this, they are not painting a picture of today."[1]

Nakanishi was a prolific proletarian writer. He had worked in Korea in the 1910s as a journalist. Upon his return to Japan in 1919, Nakanishi turned to writing novels. His books never won awards, but they remain some of the most interesting Japanese-language works to wrestle with the dislocation and dispossession that attended Japanese colonialism and imperialism. His 1936 *Shina Manshū Chōsen* (China Manchuria Korea) and 1937 *Taiwan kenbunki* (A record of things seen and heard in Taiwan) are two of only a handful of travel accounts published during the imperial period that were overtly critical of imperialism.[2]

For Nakanishi, to have "eyes" meant to be able to see the structural effects of colonial rule, to see objects and peoples not as representatives of static "places" but as manifestations of social relations. In an essay entitled, "Okoreru Korea" (Angry Korea), Nakanishi described in poignant detail what he meant: "Describing a group of Koreans as a wave of white robes has become a dream of the past. They [now] wear the khaki and gray clothes of dirty laborers."[3] The sights that seemed to represent "Korea" only obfuscated the reality of an imperial economy built on low-wage colonial labor. To write without eyes meant not only to write without a worldview but also to perpetuate "outrageous" distortions that fueled imperialism and masked what Nakanishi saw as the true state of a world defined by class exploitation.

Nakanishi was right to critique travelers' accounts of the colonies for their lack of a critical perspective on social relations within the empire. But Nakanishi was not quite right to say that they lacked a worldview. Japanese imperial travelers and colonial boosters had eyes—just not for the unequal social relations that Nakanishi sought to expose. To borrow James C. Scott's phrase "seeing like a state," imperial travelers "saw like the nation."[4] Modern states make terrain legible and manageable through procedures such as cadastral surveys and urban planning. Similarly, imperial travelers and colonial boosters sought to construct a place for the nation by observing colonized lands through the eyes of a *kokumin*, or national subject.

In the first decades of imperial tourism, to see with nationalist eyes meant to unsee the obvious differences between the experience of the individual and the experience of the nation as a whole, and instead, to see in the collective past and future tense. Gotō Shinpei, who was as much a pillar of Japanese colonialism as Nakanishi was a critic of it, described perfectly what this meant in an article on tourism to Taiwan. "If one does not recognize that it was the blood and souls of many pioneers commended to the mud of this land and the frantic toil and management of our predecessors that has at last called forth the sugar of today," he wrote, "one's observation stops at that of the simple naked eye—the eye of the mind stays shut." To see meant to look, to refine one's gaze and filter it through one's imagination: "If we turn our eyes to the future, it is possible to see how Taiwan will gradually abound in splendor—complete proficiency as a land of industrialized agriculture, the complete development and extraction of that which is now hoarded in the land—and if we don't see this future then we are not fulfilling the job of seeing Taiwan."[5]

Imperial travelers filtered their observations of the empire through a nationalist lens. They saw the present in terms of a national future and a national past. They abstracted from their own limited experience an observation about the nature of a place that they imagined would hold true for all national subjects who viewed the same territory—if they chose, unlike Nakanishi, to view it that way. Upon their return, imperial travelers presented their perspectives as the authoritative ones through a combination of their elite social position and the value attached to "firsthand observation" of the colonies.

We start with the question of imperial travelers' eyes because in order to understand why the territorialization of national identity on colonized lands revolved so closely around imperial tourism, we must first understand the relationship between the practice of observation that imperial tourism encouraged and the social position of the travelers who were chosen to undertake it. Like Mary Louise Pratt's eighteenth- and nineteenth-century European travelers, Japanese imperial travelers sought to make imperial expansion "meaningful and desirable, even though the material benefits accrued mainly to the few."[6] If early modern European travelers described Africa, the Americas, and Asia in terms of a "planetary consciousness" and framed their observations as the discovery of natural laws and natural social orders that would be beneficial to all of humankind, early twentieth-century Japanese imperial travelers framed their observations in terms of an intertwined planetary and national consciousness. On the one hand, they sought to describe particular observations in terms of their broader historical meaning, to define the key sites of Japanese imperialism and colonialism as episodes in a larger story of human progress.[7] On the other hand, they also denied how class shaped their experiences and that of others by representing their observations as those of a universal Japanese national subject, a traveling everyman.

The method and results of their observations tell us much about the practices and politics of firsthand observation that would make imperial tourism such an appealing vehicle for spatial politics and imperial travelers such willing participants in the process. We focus here on imperial tourism to Korea and Manchuria because it was in the context of fostering affective connections between national subjects and these "new territories of the state" that imperial tourism first emerged, in the years immediately following the Russo-Japanese War in 1905. Imperial travelers' observed Korea as a place firmly on its way to becoming Japanese. These observations differed markedly, as Helen J. S. Lee has argued, from those published by largely lower-class Japanese settlers, who portrayed Korea as a place "awash with tension, struggle, and competition" between Koreans and Japanese.[8] Imperial travelers' accounts of Manchuria—in particular, their observations of the site of 203-Meter Hill, the site of the Russo-Japanese War's most famous battle—likewise represented Manchuria as a site of national triumph, in contrast to soldiers' far more circumspect recollections of the battle, which questioned the value of the sacrifices that the largely conscript army had been asked to make in the name of territorial acquisition. Indeed, it was precisely in this erasure of conflict and competition from the present and its displacement onto the past that the worldview of imperial travelers emerged.

## A CRISIS OF EMPIRE

The problem was this: Japanese subjects did not seem to care about empire. They did not care enough, anyway. And when they did, they sometimes cared in the wrong way (for example, when "caring about empire" meant suggesting the illegitimacy of territorial conquest). Hindsight, they say, is twenty-twenty. But in this case, the clarity with which history has explained Japanese imperialism—as the logical complement to mass nationalism in an era of geopolitics and as the logical outgrowth of industrialization in the metropole—obscures the extent to which many Japanese imperialists saw imperialism as a project constantly in crisis.[9]

Perhaps *crisis* is too strong a word. Yet if we are to use our "eyes," in Nakanishi's terms, to read the history of imperial tourism and its spatial politics, we must be prepared to suspend our received notions about the symmetry of state and nation. Instead, we must put one foot into the shoes of those colonial boosters who saw imperial tourism as essential to the production and maintenance of emotional bonds between the nation and its imperial territory and the other foot into the shoes of imperial travelers, who went forth to recast colonized territory as "the national land" *(kokudo)*.

Our story starts, at least provisionally, in 1905. In this year, Japan claimed victory in the war against Russia, a war that had been fought primarily in Manchuria and Korea. The Japanese victory came at the cost of some eighty thousand (largely conscripted) Japanese lives. The end of the war was for that reason, if none other, widely celebrated. But the central government and the media had also worked hard to foment mass nationalism during the war, and in this sense the victory was celebrated not only as an end to the killing but also as Japan's triumph on the world stage. Though the promotion of mass nationalism had begun in earnest with the 1894–95 Sino-Japanese War, it was helped immensely a decade later by the large number of conscripted troops fighting in Manchuria and Korea—nearly ten times the number that had fought in the Sino-Japanese War—and by the introduction of new technologies for bringing the battlefield to the home front. Newspapers ran photographs of battlefields and competed for the most up-to-date reports, which they received via telegraph. The live narration of silent newsreels of battles brought audiences in Tokyo and Osaka to a fever pitch of jingoism, while new infrastructure, such as Hibiya Park in Tokyo, encouraged mass sentiment as never before.[10] It was this reservoir of patriotic sentiment upon which the *Tokyo Asahi shinbun* (*Tokyo Asahi Newspaper*) drew when it invited applications for the first travel expedition to Japan's newest territories a year later: "Go! I will go too—to the new paradise that our Japan has opened up after two years of great hardship."[11]

But all was not as celebratory as the advertisement suggested. Jingoistic press statements about the expedition contained elements of performance and coercion. The Treaty of Portsmouth, which settled the conflict, transferred to Japan the Russian leasehold and railway concession in southern Manchuria and placed Korea under the guidance of Japan as a "protectorate." While Korea and southern Manchuria were under Japanese management, however, they were not placed under Japanese sovereignty. Nor was Japan granted an indemnity from Russia to cover the extraordinary costs of the war, a practice that had been a standard component of previous conflicts between Western and Asian states and had, in fact, even been part of the resolution of the previous Sino-Japanese War. At the news of the settlement's paltry terms, some thirty thousand people in Tokyo gathered in Hibiya Park to demand that the emperor reject the treaty. In other words, they rallied in opposition to, rather than in support of, the government.[12] Protestors overturned streetcars and set fire to police boxes. Clashes with police resulted in nearly one thousand casualties.

The technologies and practices that made the Russo-Japanese War such a powerful vehicle for fomenting mass nationalism also made possible powerful and widely disseminated critiques of the war. In some areas within Japan, the construction of memorials to what the government and local elites termed the "honorable war deaths" and "voluntary sacrifices" of Japanese soldiers began even before the war had ended. But so had criticisms of the war. The increased taxes to support the war effort fell heavily on the urban lower classes, especially rickshaw pullers and craftsmen, who joined in demonstrations to protest the cost of the war. People in the villages of those conscripted made pilgrimages to shrines to pray for the safety of their hometown kids—not, as Naoko Shimazu points out, a necessarily jingoistic act.[13] Poets even inaugurated a new theme for the era—"war-weary poetry"—that lamented the human costs of the conflict. Emblematic of this group was Yosano Akiko, whose poem to her conscripted younger brother, "You must not die" (Kimi shinitamaukoto nakare), earned her the opprobrium of the pro-war literary establishment, one of whom called the poem "unforgiveable as a Japanese national *(kokumin).*"[14]

> You now indeed, succeeding a loved father,
> Are master of that house which in Sakai
> For countless years has kept the merchants' code.
> O no, my brother; no, you must not die.
> Let the damn fortress at Port Arthur fall
> Or let it stand, what difference can it make
> To merchant folk who are not called to cramp
> Their lives in patterns cut for samurai?[15]

The wartime debate over the legitimacy of the war coalesced around the question of who the *kokumin*, "national people," were and what their best interests would be.[16] Yosano's critique was one of many. But it spread widely because, in the words of Sho Konishi, it "poetically rendered" a central concern of antiwar activists—that the fight to claim territory in Manchuria was not, as the government would have it, in the interests of the nation but rather in the interests of the few.[17] Were the *kokumin* a horizontal community of compatriots that existed prior to the state? Or, as in Yosano's formulation, was the idea of a *kokumin* merely an ideological tool that reframed the interests of the few as the needs of the many? Fueling the debate was the fact that *kokumin* itself was an extralegal category, a type of political identification that emerged in thought and action rather than in ethnicity or nationality.[18] It was not the same category as that which was used to define legal Japanese citizenship—the category of Japanese, *Nihonjin*, was defined by the 1899 Nationality Act as those born to a Japanese father. Nor was it the category used to describe all of the people within the territory of the state, who were instead defined by the Constitution as the emperor's subjects, *shinmin*. Moreover, the term was not linked to any static geography of inside and outside or new and old territory but instead moved in little relation to, as we shall see in chapters 3 and 4, the hardening of a geographic structure of imperial citizenship. It was likewise unrelated to the franchise. The right to vote was extended to Hokkaidō residents (who met tax qualifications) in 1904, and residents of Okinawa got the right to vote in 1912, while in 1925 the Universal Suffrage Act excluded both Japanese and colonized residents of Korea, Manchuria, and Taiwan from voting for parliamentary representation.[19] Yet, particularly after the 1930s, even colonized subjects were expected to perform *kokumin*-ness through the use of the Japanese language and eventually, for men, through military service in order to demonstrate their suitability for the rights and responsibilities of citizenship.

Instead of a strict legal category, then, *kokumin* was an affective and performative one. Commentators used it to further their own political positions on how Japanese nationals ought to behave and how the government ought to behave toward them. When the term first emerged, it was as a liberal rallying cry during the 1870s Freedom and Popular Rights Movement, in opposition to what these activists saw as the statist centralism of the ruling elite. Other activists used *kokuminshugi*, "national people-ism," to connote a political formation based around the protection of liberal individualism.[20] But the powerful also used *kokumin* to coerce particular behaviors out of the less powerful—to encourage subjects to behave as *kokumin*. In the lead-up to the promulgation of the 1889 Constitution, the state quickly co-opted the term to denote "patriotic citizens," especially those who promoted what Carol Gluck has called the "civil morality" of the state.[21] During the Russo-Japanese War, the government continued to use the *kokumin* ideal to exhort the Japanese people to support the war effort and, more broadly, to encourage loyalty to a government that was, through tax qualifications on voting and the separation of administration from parliamentary representation, largely insulated from the public.

The war also brought to the fore tensions in the modern nation-state ideal itself. As Sho Konishi argues, the antiwar movement forwarded a powerful critique of modern international-relations theory and its vision of a peaceful world founded on a global order of territorial nation-states. As articulated by figures as wide ranging as Theodore Roosevelt, who presided over the settlement of the Russo-Japanese War, and Nitobe Inazō, the founder of colonial policy studies in Japan, conflict was not an inherent component of the Western concept of civilization but rather external to it, the fault of barbarous societies stuck in a "state of nature." In this framework, the expansion of civilization and its spatial framework of territorialized nation-states was a necessary and morally defensible goal of civilized nations. For Yosano and her fellow antiwar activists in the leftist press, however, the idea that the placement of all the world's territory under the sovereignty of individual nation-states would lead to world peace "was not just a jargon of diplomacy to mask the intent of territorial gain."[22] It was a delusional, "utopian" logic that countenanced colonialism and wars of imperialist expansion, such as the Russian and Japanese battle over the control of Manchuria and Korea, in the name of a future of peace and order.[23]

In the context of the scramble for territory and spheres of influence in early twentieth-century East Asia, generating affective ties to these new territories of the state and, through this process, producing "good" national subjects became a serious concern of both the central government and colonial boosters in Manchuria and Korea. Fearing that the Japanese public would quickly lose interest or even turn against Japan's expansion abroad, at war's end, the government embarked on new programs of indoctrination to reclaim the narrative of the Russo-Japanese War as a victory for the nation. The emperor appeared at celebration rallies and issued rescripts proclaiming his support for the peace treaty. The Ministry of Education renewed its commitment to teaching ethics in schools—classes that encouraged students to see their primary responsibility as service to the state.[24] And in July 1906, two ships departed Japan for Manchuria and Korea, territories that had been the site of the most recent battles and were now—with the peace settlement within the internationally recognized sphere of interest of the Japanese state. One was the *Tokyo Asahi Newspaper*'s four-hundred-participant "Manchuria-Korea Travel Ship" (Man-Kan jun'yū sen).[25] The other was a ship carrying nearly six hundred students and teachers sponsored by the Ministry of Education and the army.[26]

## THE BIRTH OF OBSERVATIONAL TRAVEL

The departure of the two travel expeditions for Manchuria and Korea marked not only the "birth of overseas travel," but also the birth of "observational travel" (*shisatsu ryokō*) as a core component of the government's larger project of producing good national subjects.[27] Given its nationalistic overtones, this practice has understandably been called "self-administered citizenship training."[28] But the production of nation-states and national subjects did not take place in a vacuum, with the territorial domain and national consciousness of each individual nation-state expanding outward into a white space of unclaimed territory. It was embedded in the presumptions of the modern inter-state system, within which Japanese leaders imagined Japan as one of many centers around the globe from which civilization would emanate, and in the system's utopian logic, which countenanced territorial expansion as a necessary evil for the larger good. In other words, observational travel was not only a way of teaching national subjects to understand Japanese citizenship in the context of a national land that incorporated conquered territory. It also positioned that territory within a future global order of territorial nation-states. The firsthand observations of travelers took place within this dual order of the geography of civilization. Thus observational travel might more profitably be considered a practice rooted not in the pathology of a particularly Japanese nationalism but as a new stage in the larger—and longer—project of naturalizing the imperialism of civilization around the globe.[29]

Travel itself was not new to Japan. Domestic travel had been a popular leisure activity in Japan since at least the late eighteenth century, when pilgrimage and "medicinal hot springs travel" were the only recognized reasons for a commoner to leave home. Presenting a famous shrine or a hot spring as their official destination, commoners would tour a wide area to and from that spot, visiting local sights along the way.[30] Moreover, the Meiji government had already been sending elite students and officials on sponsored study travel to the United States and Europe for nearly fifty years.[31] In the 1880s, higher schools adopted this practice by sending students out on educational trips to local areas so that they might practice disciplined observation outside of the classroom. And since 1893, an unofficial organization of political and commercial elites, the Welcome Society (Kihinkai), had facilitated the travel of elite foreigners to Japan.[32]

But observational travel to the new territories differed from these previous practices in two senses: one, the purpose of travel was neither leisure nor the experience of particular sites but rather the observation of the national land and its component parts; and two, it was heavily managed by the central and colonial governments and by colonial enterprises to achieve a particular political end—the production and reproduction of Japanese national subjects who had emotional bonds to colonized land. It was not the act of travel, in other words, that produced the good national subject, but rather the act of observing—or, more precisely, the way in which imperial travelers translated their experiences into "observations."[33]

To observe the national land meant to see the landscape within the dual order of the geography of civilization—in terms of the history of the Japanese nation and, at the same time, in terms of a future global order of interlinked and commensurable nation-states. The next chapter addresses the latter half of this equation. Here, we direct ourselves to the first problem—what it meant to see the land in terms of the history of the Japanese nation. It is here that travelers began the work of constructing observations of the national land that collapsed the gap between their personal experiences or relations to historical events and the official history of these events. Kanō Shigoro, the principal of Tokyo Higher Normal School, laid out the rules as he dispatched his students to Manchuria and Korea in 1906: "A great many *kokumin* know only part of the layout of the battlefields and the conditions of warfare from a few newspapers or magazines, and chances to witness the sites of victory are scarce," he wrote. "Because of this, they are not able to form deep impressions of the war."[34] Kanō encouraged his charges to go beyond this. "Those who will become teachers must not stop at simply reading accounts of battles or gaining information about the war from conversations with others," he exhorted. Rather, "they must go themselves to the battle sites, reflect deeply [on them], and use these materials to enlighten today's subjects and guide the next generation."[35]

The idea that firsthand observation of objects or phenomena in isolation produced knowledge is, of course, a (if not *the*) foundational principle of scientific thought. Training in scientific observation was a core component of the educational curriculum in Japan, as elsewhere. But observation was also a "transposition of the real" into received categories of experience and explanation, and it was in this vein that the first imperial tours were envisioned.[36] Such a practice was already at the core of new methods of education in Japanese primary schools, where educators used Swiss pedagogue Johann Heinrich Pestalozzi's "developmental learning" method to improve students' individual faculties through direct experience and sensory-based observation.[37] One of the goals of the Meiji state's educational system was the reorienting of local life around the abstract categories of modern society—developmental time, civility, and the nation. In this context, the boundary between the categories of "knowledge" and "experience" necessarily blurred. Experience came to be determined not by "what is around the individual, but how that environment connects with abstract criteria—knowledge, be it objectified by science or a national common sense."[38]

Geography education was particularly suited to active learning. Meiji-era elementary school teachers often took their students on field trips in order to transform the local landscape into a laboratory of geographic observation. The purpose of these trips, which visited local monuments, historic sites, and topographical landmarks, was to "increase the child's powers of observation" by fostering "the students' capacity to observe what is in front of their eyes."[39] But what students actually learned to observe was the metageographic relationship between their locality, their region, and the nation-state, in which "local materials" such as historic monuments and shrines linked the students' home communities to the nation as a whole.[40] For Meiji-era elementary school students, for example, part of seeing Nagano Prefecture's Mt. Ontake was seeing it as "the second highest mountain in Japan after Mt. Fuji."[41] For older students, the destinations were farther afield, but the process of observation was the same. One 1902 all-Japan guide for school travel built upon the local-regional-national metageography by organizing the sites to be seen by prefecture, starting with the publisher's locality of Osaka and combining to make up all the sites to be seen in Great Japan *(dai Nihon)*.[42]

The "blurring of the difference between knowledge and the sensate in the logic of the nation" is readily apparent in the accounts of the first imperial travelers to Manchuria. Imperial travelers attempted to describe the knowledge that they gained through travel in the terms of a nationalist metageography of exclusive and stacking territorial relations.[43] Relaying his impressions of his journey to Manchuria and Korea, for example, Miyatsu Kenjirō of Kōbe, a member of the 1906 *Tokyo*

*Asahi Newspaper* expedition, chastised his fellow countrymen for their failure to nest Russian Dairen within the space of Russia itself. He had heard from many people who were impressed by the achievements of the Russians in Dairen and who worried about whether Japan had the resources to rebuild the infrastructure that the Russians had first installed, let alone develop Dairen further. But to truly observe the current situation in Manchuria, Miyatsu argued, one had to understand how to organize the land under observation into the larger territorial categories of the modern world. In this sense, those who made one part of Russia stand in for the whole of the country had it precisely backward. This was an "error in observation." Instead, one should see Russian Dairen in the context of Russia as a whole, where, he noted, there were many internal disturbances that were weakening the country. Dairen did not describe Russia; rather, Russia described Dairen. Applying his style of "correct" observation to the now Japanese city in front of him, Miyatsu argued that the spirit of the nation would ultimately determine the fate of Japanese Dairen. "Even if it is a major power, Russia lost the war. . . . If Japan goes forward by uniting agriculture, commerce, and industry with the Yamato spirit, Japan will advance to a promising future," he concluded.[44]

The line between correct and incorrect observations—and the line between where one nation's spirit took over as the agent of history from other nations occupying a given land—was not so easy for every traveler to determine. In the context of imperial nationalism, the nationalist metageography that worked so neatly in the provinces of Japan's main islands existed in uneasy tension with the core-periphery metageography of the expanding empire.[45] Fellow traveler Kitamura Kikujirō of Osaka stumbled over the indeterminate boundaries and political geography in his observation of the region. "Even though I had a bit of knowledge about Manchuria and Korea through reading books and hearing lectures, it wasn't until I actually set foot there that I thought, *Oh, I see*, and understood," he wrote. Acquiescing to the problem of perspective—"ten people will have ten different impressions, depending on their own positions"—he nevertheless felt confident that Manchuria and Korea were now in some sense part of the territory of the Japanese state and perhaps part of the space of the Japanese nation. "Our Japan is a victorious country and an advanced country," he concluded, "and now I feel deeply that as individuals and as a group we have a heavy responsibility toward the national people *(kokumin)* of Manchuria and Korea."[46] The already vague meaning of *kokumin* makes this statement particularly hard to parse. It is not clear if Kitamura intended to indicate that the people of Manchuria and Korea were distinct national peoples. Manchuria remained sovereign Chinese territory, even if parts of its territory were under Japanese administration. If Kitamura was indeed referring to the people of Manchuria and Korea as distinct national peoples, one expected that he would speak of the national people of Korea and China. Moreover, Kitamura envisioned some relationship between Japan or the Japanese *kokumin* and the national peoples of Korea and Manchuria, but he likewise left the precise nature of that relationship undefined. Kitamura's confusion should not be taken as a sign of his own failure of observation but rather of the confused reality of the burgeoning system of territorial nation-states, as opposed to their theoretical ideal. It also reflected the more intentional obfuscation of the national status of Manchurian residents that Japanese imperialists undertook in order to undercut Qing objections to the expansion of Japanese control over the region.[47]

If observing these lands meant first constituting them within a nationalist metageography, placing them within the history of the Japanese nation also required the exertion of the self as an active agent who held affective ties to what Timothy Mitchell has called the "world of representations."[48] In this sense, the idea of national land emerged as a vehicle for bridging the gap between the idea of Manchuria and Korea as new territories of the state—an idea that some, like Kitamura, struggled to populate—and the space of the nation. If observing the new territories meant deploying territorial containers that were themselves subjective and historical frameworks for parsing the world, it also demanded the deployment of the travelers' subjective selves far more directly in terms of its requirement that travelers bear witness to the national land. In this sense, national land was a resource for the nation and its spatial reproduction not only in terms of the use and exchange value of its commodities but also as a site through which travelers could produce a sense of themselves as having an authentic claim to a particular piece of land.

Part of the value of observation for travelers was the ability to claim what Dean MacCannell has termed the "authentic" knowledge of the tourist—the kind of knowledge that comes from the tourist feeling like he or she understands "the truth" of the site in a way that is not available to those who have not seen it firsthand.[49] Indeed, even as travelers claimed a universal perspective, the authenticity of the tourist's knowledge demanded, in some sense, the acknowledgement of a subjective position, of a body that had traveled to see the land firsthand. This was, as Nicholas Entrikin has put it, the "betweenness" of place—the existence of a here and a there was a matter of both objective certainty and subjective perspective.[50] Observation of the national land thus transposed the real in yet another register, by engaging travelers in emotional reenactments of a Japanese national history as if their experience of a particular site could represent the experience of the nation writ large.[51] The emotional component was particularly important in the aftermath of the war, when commentators worried that nationalist sentiment was fading even among the more well-to-do. In another of the unintended consequences of mass nationalism, the postwar generation took the Meiji state's mantras of "rich country, strong army" and "to rise in the world" *(risshin shusse)* and transformed them into calls for individual success and individual wealth over state loyalty. Tokutomi Sohō, editor of the pro-government newspaper *Kokumin shinbun* (Citizens' news), complained that the younger generation had lost "all, or at least a major portion of, the national awareness" that had characterized the previous generation.⁵²

Indeed, unlike other mnemonic sites relating to the extra-archipelagic history of the Japanese nation—sites that included a growing number of memorial and commemorative monuments to the Russo-Japanese War in Japan, visits to the Toyokuni shrines of Toyotomi Hideyoshi (the architect of two late sixteenth-century invasions of Korea), and exhibits at expositions—the first tours of Manchuria and Korea brought travelers to the sites of historical events to anchor the oftentimes fuzzy space of national history in actual (contested) territory. A visit to Genbu Gate in Heijō (K. P'yŏngyang), for example, allowed one student on the 1915 Hiroshima Higher Normal School trip to "look back on that time twenty years before, when our empire first appeared from behind the curtain on the world stage"—a reference to the 1894–95 Sino-Japanese War, which was fought largely in Korea.⁵³ The preservation of sites assisted in this reenactment. "Heijō's old battlefields are things from twenty two years ago," he wrote, "but [markers along] the pathway explain the preserved battle sites so that you are somehow able to put yourself back in that time."⁵⁴ The school's other diarist noted that "the land we walk on now contains innumerable historical marks made by our countrymen (*kokumin*) hundreds of years ago."⁵⁵ Pusan (K. Busan) likewise sparked the second diarist to imagine himself in a relationship with the soldiers in Katō Kiyomasa and Konishi Yukinaga's sixteenth-century armies. Pusan was the site where Hideyoshi's invasion force landed; the student wrote, "[It is a place] where the blood of countless of my countrymen runs."⁵⁶

But it was the battlefield sites of the Russo-Japanese War that received the most emphasis in these early years. This was for two reasons. First, the Treaty of Portsmouth did not settle the conflict between Japan and China over the control of Manchuria; it simply shifted the terms of debate from whether Japan would have a stake in the territory to how much of a stake it could claim. Second, as we explore in the next chapter, the growing number of Japanese residents of the Kwantung Leased Territory, generally white-collar workers attached to the South Manchuria Railway Company and its growing kingdom of industries, felt their place within the nation to be unsteadily acknowledged by their metropolitan counterparts. For both issues, however, the response was the same—to bring imperial travelers to the battlefields of the Russo-Japanese War so that they might develop affective ties to the contested territory. Standing under a hole in the roof of the Memorial Exhibition Hall at Port Arthur (J. Ryojun; C. Lushun) and hearing the story of how it got there, for example, prompted students to contemplate the sacrifice of Russian and Japanese soldiers. One Hiroshima Higher Normal School student noted that the hall had been the Russian general headquarters during the war. But, "our army" (*waga gun*) launched a shell that went right through the roof, which "made the meaning of the memorial all the more deep."⁵⁷

FIGURE 2. The remains of a cannon at 203-Meter Hill. Postcard, c. 1910s. The ruins of battle were left on the hill like props on a stage. Digital image courtesy of East Asia Image Collection, Lafayette College Libraries, Easton, PA. Image ip0162.

At 203-Meter Hill, the government of the Kwantung Leased Territory provided tour guides, often former soldiers, to narrate the events of the battle. The battle of 203-Meter Hill had been the bloodiest of the entire war. For months, wave after wave of Japanese soldiers climbed up a barren hill toward dug-in Russian machine-gun positions at the top. Thousands were killed. The eventual capture of the hill led directly to the artillery bombing of Russian ships in the harbor of Port Arthur, which could be sighted from the top of the hill, and thus the battle was quickly commemorated as the highpoint of the war and of the patriotic sacrifice of the soldiers who fought in it. Tour guides' narratives were laden with emotional content, and in later years, guides would compete to be known for the particular way in which they retold the story of the final battle.[58] But the landscape itself also played a role, as tour guides linked the narration of the battle with the experience of walking up the hill.

Student travelers described how they vicariously experienced what the soldiers had felt. The report from one student in the Tokyo Higher Normal School's English Club illustrates how the students made use of the emotional narrative and the physical terrain to imagine themselves in the shoes of the soldiers. The students gathered at the top of the hill, listening to an officer recount the story of the battle.

> According to the officer, the last assault began at five in the morning, as planned. Taking advantage of the fast gathering darkness, our soldiers pressed on [toward] the rampart, but the sword-like hills, the irresistible machine-guns, the scattered bodies of the killed and the wounded were serious impediments to their progress. Now marching, now stopping, they came always closer to the rampart. Just then, strains of our national anthem arose from the left wing of our army. All cleared and encouraged, they overthrew the enemy, who now appeared to give way somewhat, and sprang over the rampart in high spirit. A hand-to-hand fight ensued, and at daybreak our regimental flags of the Rising Sun arose high above the heap of the enemy's dead.[59]

The student quickly transposed the guide's narration into his own observation, neatly using his own firsthand experience of the hill to claim an authoritative memory of the event. "Well, our schoolmates," he wrote, "I can imagine how the brave soldiers this time forgot the strain and exertion of the furious attack in the joy of victory and in shouting the deafening 'Banzai!'" Indeed, for this student, reenacting the event on the site itself animated the land with the emotional force of patriotism. "Greatly moved by the officer's lectures and standing still on the traces of this memorable fortress," he concluded, "I was quite oblivious of all else and absorbed in deep meditation."[60]

Standing at the memorial that was later erected atop 203-Meter Hill, Hiroshima's second diarist also had a visceral experience of the terrible battle. He transcribed the words of the group's guide as he described how the Japanese battalion attacking the hill went from eighty soldiers to only tens in the first day. Yet that night, they made earthen defenses, and by the next day, after climbing over the bodies of those who had died before, they planted the Japanese flag on top of the hill. The diarist then jumped in to narrate the story relative to his own perspective: "They stood atop that hill. That place is right next to today's memorial tower and viewing platform."[61] Indeed, the hill itself did much of the work for the tour guides in emphasizing the patriotic sacrifice of the soldiers. As one student from Keijō Public Middle School later wrote, "If it is this hard to climb the hill on this nice road, it must have been a nightmare to climb it during battle."[62]

The reenactment of a Japanese national history in situ encouraged particular forgettings and unseeings that were essential to the maintenance of the fiction of a *kokumin* defined by a shared historical experience. Battlefields were preserved, as the Society for the Preservation of Manchuria's Battlefield Ruins (Manshū senseki hozon kyōkai) explained in 1914, to "make public our everlasting loyalty to the national land" *(kokudo)* and to remind the world of the "national strength" of Japan.[63] And to a certain extent, the transformation of Port Arthur into a "town of historic battlefields" *(senseki no machi)* evidenced the concern of Japanese officials and residents in the Kwantung Leased Territory and the Railway Zone over the tenuousness of Japan's claim to the territory. But if the ambiguity of Japan's

FIGURE 3. Travelers consult a map as they climb 203-Meter Hill. Postcard, c. 1915. The stamp reads, "203-Meter Hill, sightseeing souvenir" *(kengaku kinen)*. Digital image courtesy of East Asia Image Collection, Lafayette College Libraries, Easton, PA. Image ip1201.

informal colonial rule in Manchuria fostered an emphasis on the national land in this context, it also exposed the underlying territorial anxiety of Japan's imperial nationalism. Indeed, as the remainder of the book suggests, the certainty with which the international community recognized Japan's formal colonization of Taiwan in 1895 and Korea in 1910 did little to lessen colonial boosters' sense of the need to constantly reanimate and reenact the nation's claims to these colonized lands. Nor did it dampen the amount of forgetting and re-remembering that such "observations" required.

Though Yosano Akiko would make no such claim herself when she traveled to Manchuria and Mongolia in the late 1920s, the Yosano of 1905 might have suggested that imperial travelers visiting the sites of Hideyoshi's campaigns in Korea consider what the stakes were of transposing a history of samurai—the class of military-aristocrats who governed the archipelago's feudal domains prior to the establishment of the centralized Meiji state—into a history of the *kokumin*.[64] Official Japanese imperial nationalism argued that for centuries the Japanese state and its people had been trying, unsuccessfully, to reunite Korea with the Japanese imperial house and thus liberate Korea from its oppressive tributary relationship with China. Textbooks cast Hideyoshi's sixteenth-century campaigns as one moment in a history that stretched back sixteen hundred years to the invasion of the peninsula by Empress Jingū and the establishment of Mimana, a (mythical) small fief in the southern peninsula, and all the way forward to the colonization, or "annexation" *(heigō)*, of Korea by Japan in 1910.[65] Such a narrative organized the past in terms of the present. It cast the kind of tributary relations that structured foreign relations in East Asia prior to the advent of the Westphalian system as a necessary prehistory to the emergence of the nation-state, the harbinger of civilization and modern international relations, and thus trapped Korea behind Japan's supposedly more advanced temporal location.[66] In reenacting this history, however, the transposition of a samurai invasion into national history also encouraged imperial travelers to understand the past of the archipelago not as a fundamentally different social order but rather as one in which Japanese-ness—in the sense of a national community—was always latent within the islands' people. Reenactment thus fostered in travelers the sense of themselves as products of and participants in the history of the nation rather than—as some who opposed the Meiji state in previous decades had argued—as products of a far more recent ideological campaign to reshape social life on the archipelago into the categories of an international order premised on competition and cooperation between nation-states.

Even within the category of "nation" and "national experience," imperial travelers' observations were fictionalized re-enactments of a national history rather than representations of shared experiences. In the European context, the "myth of the war experience" refashioned the memory of World War I into a "sacred experience, which provided the nation with a new depth of religious feeling and put at its disposal ever-present saints and martyrs, places of worship and a heritage to emulate."[67] In the case of 203-Meter Hill, what the student travelers needed to forget in order to remember was the fact that, as elite students, they were not and largely would not have been asked to fight. Conscription, as Kikuchi Kunisaku has written, was a "poor man's lottery."[68] As the next generation of leaders, the government offered elite students special terms of military service, which Kikuchi calls "government-authorized draft evasion," that included six-week service for normal school students and pay-your-own-way volunteer one-year service for other elite school graduates with access to significant financial resources (in contrast to the three-year terms of other conscripts).[69] But in writing about their visit to Port Arthur, these students—even those on the 1906 Tokyo Higher Normal School trip, for whom the war was a recent memory—conveniently elided the uneven demands the state made of its subjects during the war. Instead, they argued that their firsthand encounter with the battlefield gave them the authority to observe the meaning and history of the landscape in a way that those who had only read it about it could not.

The students' reenactments of the battle of 203-Meter Hill as an intentional and meaningful sacrifice contradicted an ever-growing body of literature in the metropole about the futility of war. Much of the objection to war among the intelligentsia had been animated by the writings of Leo Tolstoy, who emerged during the war as a "symbol of antihierarchical cooperatist anarchist internationalism and moral resistance to the war and Japanese imperial expansion," as Sho Konishi puts it.[70] Critics writing for the *Heimin shinbun* (People's newspaper) amplified his reframing of the war as a conflict not between Russian and Japanese soldiers, but between oppressed peoples and their oppressing states.[71] Following the war, critiques of the management of the war and, in particular, the wanton disregard for the lives of the conscripted, began to appear. One reason for the high number of casualties was not the violence of modern warfare but the inadequacy of supply chains, which left Japanese soldiers dead from beriberi (a vitamin B deficiency that would again be a problem in the Asia-Pacific War) and infection. Tayama Katai, a realist novelist known for his works *Futon* (Futon) and *Inaka kyōshi* (The country teacher), highlighted the meaninglessness of such deaths—and, by extension, the gap between nationalist fervor and individual experience—in his short story "Ippei sotsu" (One soldier).[72] The story recounted the fictional tale of an injured soldier, who tried for days to get back to his battalion at the battlefront, only to die of beriberi before he could get there. That Tayama had been a journalist embedded with the army during the war lent the tale the air of realism. One former junior officer confronted the notion that the soldiers' deaths were purposeful sacrifices for the nation more bluntly: "Death in war is not about dying because one wants to die. One gets killed without really knowing what's going on. What's more, there is no guarantee of being killed. I personally don't believe that one can die that easily."[73] Yet imperial travelers readily clung to the "myth of the patriotic soldier," reenacting their courageous fights and honorable deaths on hills left purposefully devoid of such complicating factors.[74]

## THE COLONIAL ORIGINS OF IMPERIAL TRAVEL

What I have sought to establish is a case for treating imperial tourism and its observational methodology as a particular kind of fiction, one that sought not only to place the Japanese nation on colonized lands but also to construct a vision of the Japanese nation as a coherent social body that could possess—with homogenous affect—a particular land. What I will suggest in closing is that the particularities of imperial tourism's fiction point to a genealogy that traces the practice's origins not to Europe's Grand Tour or to Tokugawa-era hot springs travel but rather to the practice of bringing elite colonized subjects on tours of the metropole. This genealogy reverses the standard narrative of tourism in which imperial railways expand outward, metropolitan subjects follow to gawk at the backwardness of colonized subjects, and then, many years later, colonized subjects who have adopted the bourgeois mentality and practices of the empire follow the same path back to the metropole to subvert the "tourist gaze." Instead, it suggests that both practices were part of the larger effort to produce and reproduce a hegemonic social imaginary in which identity was territorial and difference spatial. While this discourse existed in conversation with other tropes of colonial difference that circulated around race, ethnicity, and culture, it also existed as its own separate concern—one that could not be wholly addressed by recourse to racialized concepts of difference in the context of the burgeoning territorial nation-state system. The spatial politics of this social imaginary elided what Doreen Massey calls "geographies of solidarity" and what Nakanishi simply called "eyes" in favor of a territorial-national lens.

Subsequent chapters bear out this story for our largely metropolitan body of imperial travelers and the colonial boosters who sought to transform the new territories of the state into (new) national land. But it is worth pausing here to note that in the context of the Japanese Empire, the idea of using tourism to produce affective ties to particular territories—in this case, desire—began in 1897, in Taiwan. Indeed, the word for "tourism," *kankō*, was first applied not to imperial elites but rather to a group of thirteen indigenous leaders from Taiwan who were brought to Tokyo and other areas within Japan in 1897. As Jordan Sand points out, the characters that the government used to represent tourism "suggested both a civilizing function and the idea of duty to a sovereign."[75] The 1897 trip was followed in 1911 by a second trip (and then seven more before 1929).[76] Over time, these "tours of the inner territory" *(naichi kankō)* were expanded to include other groups of colonized elites, including Koreans and Micronesians.

These tours of the metropole brought influential colonized subjects to Tokyo and other sites in the hope that a firsthand encounter with inner Japan would "shock and awe" these groups into submission.[77] The Government General of Taiwan's early tours for Taiwan's indigenous peoples heavily emphasized the military might of Japan, but also the abundance, knowledge, and peacefulness of Japanese society.[78] The itineraries suggested, not particularly subtly, that if indigenous peoples would put down their arms, they too would gain the benefits of Japanese modernity. In 1912, one group visited military garrisons in almost each town they stopped at, as well as a cannon factory, a bullet factory, and an armory in Tokyo.[79] But they were also taken to sites emphasizing the lineage of the emperor, the beneficence of the imperial government, and the knowledge of the world and its flora and fauna that Japanese society possessed: the Meiji Memorial Colonization Exhibition in Tokyo, Asakusa Park, the zoos in Kyōto and Ueno, the aquarium at Sakai near Osaka; the Momoyama tombs near Kyōto; and the gardens at Kyōto's Myōshinji Temple.[80]

The Government General of Korea instituted a similar practice of tours of the metropole for Korean elites in 1909, just before the colonization of the peninsula. In the first decade of Japanese colonial rule, the Government General of Korea, the Japanese-owned Oriental Development Company, and the major pro-Japanese newspapers sent over a dozen "inner territory observation tours" (*naichi shisatsu dan*) to Japan.[81] In line with the Government General of Korea's formulation of its mission in Korea, the Korean tours emphasized governance, industrialization, and agricultural science over the displays of military power that formed the core of itineraries for indigenous travelers. The Government General of Korea sought more than submission to Japanese rule. They aimed for a complete reformation (*kairyō*) of Korean society. For this reason, the Oriental Development Company also took Korean travelers to sites that exemplified local government and the cooperative nature of Japanese capitalism at the village level. They visited village governments, trade associations, and cooperative societies far off the beaten path, such as the Kako-gun Ishimori Village Buying, Selling, and Manufacturing Cooperative Credit Society in Hyōgo Prefecture.[82]

From this perspective, the observational travel of the new territories that began in 1906 offered a sort of photographic negative of the many Japans of colonial tourism. If for colonized travelers, tours of the metropole presented a vision of the inner territory that suited the needs of each particular colonial formation, for imperial travelers, one of the goals of observational travel was to subsume the many different subject positions that existed within the Japanese Empire to a singular relationship of a national subject to a national land. These were the dual "eyes" of imperial travelers—on the one hand, the eyes of an elite tasked with educating the masses and, on the other, the eyes of a generic national subject whose experiences of the colonies could believably stand in for the experience of any of his or her compatriots. Indeed, Kanō, the principal of Tokyo Higher Normal School, embedded this idea of a social imaginary in his description of the work of enlightenment that student travelers and future teachers would do. He did not use the word associated with the eighteenth-century European Enlightenment (*kaika*) but rather the word for *enlightening* as a pedagogical act (*keihatsu*), a word that was closer to *illuminating* or *edifying*, the enlightenment children experience through education.[83] Kanō argued that travel to Manchuria was "witnessing" or firsthand observation, but really it was meant to be a kind of training in a particular orientation to colonized territory as national land that leaders in education and the army hoped would be transmitted to the population at large. For this reason, the *Tokyo Asahi Newspaper* argued that teachers should also be sent. Sending elementary school teachers would give these influential figures the "knowledge necessary to grant present and future children the qualifications for being new subjects (*shinkokumin*) of a newly powerful country (*shinkōkoku*)."[84] An arrangement of partial central government support was soon announced for teachers. The travelers themselves would cover the remaining costs, though in many cases, prefectural governments provided considerable support.[85]

It was precisely this act of transposition and dissemination that the framers of imperial travel hoped to achieve. The elite status of early travelers presented a rather different group than what we might expect from a history of tourism, which has long been considered to be a form of mass leisure, in contrast to the more individualized and elite travel cultures that came before.[86] But while domestic travel had been a popular leisure activity in Japan—and would continue to be so throughout the twentieth century—travel to the colonies was prohibitively expensive. The initial student tour of Manchuria in 1906 cost thirty yen—roughly what one higher normal school student could expect to spend in a year. This was despite the fact that the Japanese Imperial Army provided complimentary transportation to Dairen on army ships.[87] Even seventeen years later, in 1923, the Japan Tourist Bureau estimated the cost for a two-week trip through Korea and Manchuria at 140 yen for a third-class ticket and a whopping 287 yen for first class.[88] Given that tuition for one year at the prestigious Keiō University ran 120 yen and one year at Waseda University cost 110 yen, even a third-class trip would have been a considerable luxury.[89] Travel to Taiwan was even further out of reach. The Osaka Mercantile Shipping Company published new sixteen-day itineraries for travel to Taiwan in 1924, which listed the price of first-class travel at 374 yen, second class at 261 yen, and third class, an option that had not been available the previous year, at 170 yen.[90]

The central government, colonial administrations, and colonial enterprises endeavored to lower the cost to individuals. Student discounts provided by the South Manchuria Railway Company and the Osaka Mercantile Shipping Company, whose steamers replaced complimentary army travel, brought the student itinerary down to eighty yen. Itō Takeo, who later published a memoir of his time as a member of the South Manchuria Railway's Research Bureau, described a seventy-five-yen trip through Korea, Manchuria, and China he took in 1917 as "cheap," but this determination reflected either his position as a student at the prestigious Tokyo Number One Higher School or his understanding that the price was cheap relative to the cost of such an endeavor outside the context of student group travel.[91] By the 1920s, when government support waned, colonial enterprises, such as Mitsui Heavy Industries and Bank of Chōsen, also sponsored scholarships for higher commercial school students.[92] While the expense of each trip slowly lowered as transportation companies developed further discounts for travelers, a tour of the empire never became cheap enough to be affordable to the masses. In 1930 the majority of Japanese households (some 65 percent) reported an income of between 200 and 800 yen a year, with some 17 percent earning less than 200 yen per year. While a wide range, these figures suggest that sending a single traveler on an 80- to 110-yen journey would, at best, have cost the average family more than one month's income. It was more likely, however, was that such a trip was far beyond the financial capacity of most.[93]

But the elite status of imperial travelers allowed them to amplify their observations of the new territories upon their return, and for this reason, they were the target audience in imperial tourism's early years. In contrast to Japanese settlers, who crowded belowdecks to travel to Korea and Manchuria and often had bring enough food to sustain themselves and their families for the trip, early imperial travelers went forth with as much pomp and circumstance as government ministries and local newspapers could muster.[94] When Tochigi Prefecture's *Shimotsuke Newspaper* sponsored a group of industrialists on an observational trip to Manchuria and Korea in 1909, for example, the Japanese Bureau of Railways spared no expense in taking advantage of the publicity that the newspaper sponsorship offered. For their trip from Tokyo's Shinbashi Station to Shimonoseki, where they would board the ferry to Pusan, the Bureau of Railways attached a special second-class car that seated seventy-one people, so the group could stay together. On the outside of the car, the bureau painted "Tochigi Prefecture Industrialists' Manchuria-Korea Tourist Group Sponsored by *Shimotsuke Newspaper*" (Shimotsuke shinbun shusai Tochigi ken jitsugyōka Man-Kan kankōdan) on both sides.[95] For the journey between Hōten (C. Fengtian; English [E.] Mukden) and Chōshun, the South Manchuria Railway Company provided a special first-class car, which the members of the group found so luxurious they all instantly declared their intention of becoming shareholders in the joint-stock company.[96] Upon their arrival, they were guided and feted by local chambers of commerce and prefectural associations, such as the Pusan Tochigi Prefectural Association, whose members met the arrival of their ferry waving large banners that read, "Welcome Shimotsuke Tourist Group."[97]

For students, their elite social position likewise granted them the ability to disseminate their observations through the privileged venues they had access to. There was a vibrant market for their new knowledge. Student travelers spoke to their peers as well as to alumni and others interested in hearing what these travelers had learned about the empire. The Tokyo Number One Higher School Travel Club organized, for example, exhibitions that displayed photographs and memories of the trip, as well as a lecture series where students could present their findings.[98] Other schools also offered public presentations and published reports in alumni magazines. By far the most common evidence we have of the self-consciousness of these students about the social value of their travels, however, are the extensive travelogues that many groups published upon their return. Often running hundreds of pages, these reports detailed the journey from beginning to end so that they might serve as a blueprint for future travelers. They also included essays on the current state of various industries and institutions, such as elementary education and banking, "not only so that the students' observations *(kenbun)* might be disseminated, but also because the results of their investigations and research deserve attention."[99]

Like the industrialists, who one impoverished Japanese settler complained spent their time "running around in all directions looking for business opportunities," the students saw imperial travel as a chance for personal gain.[100] In this way, imperial tourism united the nationalist "to rise in the world" *(risshin shusse)* ideal of Tokutomi Sohō with the younger generation's more individualistic version of the slogan of which he was so critical. As members of the growing "new middle class," elite student travelers treated their firsthand knowledge of colonized lands as, in the words of one Hiroshima Higher Normal School traveler, "our capital for the future."[101] Like the trans-Atlantic "sociological grand tours" of American progressives in the early twentieth century, for rising members of Japan's new middle class, firsthand experience from the front lines of empire was particularly coveted as a mark of distinction and knowledge.[102] Some students would use their firsthand knowledge directly as teachers of the next generation. Others would serve as bureaucrats in the metropolitan and colonial administrations, faculty in Japan's universities, and white-collar labor in a growing industrial and financial sector that now extended into Taiwan, Manchuria, and Korea. Indeed, while records of the individuals who traveled to the continent during this period are scarce, the roster of the 1912 Tokyo Number One Higher School trip to Manchuria and Korea reads like a who's who of the next thirty years of Japanese intellectual, cultural, and political history. Yasui Seiichirō went on to head the Tokyo Social Welfare Department before serving as private secretary to Governor General of Korea Ugaki Kazushige and then, in 1940, governor of the prefecture of Niigata. Wada Sei became a professor of Oriental history, authored numerous works on the history of Manchuria, Mongolia, China, and East Asia, and managed the Oriental Library (Tōyō bunko), prewar Japan's most prestigious library and research center for the study of Asia. Capping them all was Yanaihara Tadao, who took over the chair of colonial studies (Shokuminchi seisaku gaku) at Tokyo Imperial University from his mentor, Nitobe Inazō, and went on to become one of the most vociferous and well-known critics of Japanese colonial policy in the 1920s and 1930s.[103]

Student travelers relished the position of responsibility that Kanō had placed upon his students, casting themselves as privileged guardians of the nation's future. Sightseeing in the Russian-controlled city of Harbin (C. Ha'erbin) in northern Manchuria on July 30, 1912, students from Tokyo Number One Higher School received a call from the consulate with the news that the Meiji emperor had died. "I thought of the future and cried," one diarist wrote. "As the generation of the future, our group of twenty-four had no choice but to cry."[104] Another student, this time from the 1915 Hiroshima Higher Normal School trip, felt his future responsibility settle over him as the group gathered on the pier in Pusan: "As we boarded the Shiragi-maru in preparation for leaving the continent, the position of our empire came to mind. Our responsibility as educators pierced our chests anew."[105] Local officials reinforced the message. Another student recalled a particularly memorable meeting in Port Arthur with Shirani Takeshi, the civil governor of the Kwantung Leased Territory. "How is it?" he asked, after the students visited the memorial to Japan's war dead atop 203-Meter Hill. "Have you come to understand the value of Japan?"[106]

Both colonized and metropolitan travelers found ways to critique the representations of spatial difference and territorialized identity that they encountered. Colonial and metropolitan police censored the official reports of the trips of the colonized subjects, in some cases even revising the original comments into more positive statements.[107] But critical comments trickled through. Indigenous travelers mocked the Japanese government's insistence on its own peacefulness, wondering why such a peaceful country would spend such time and resources stockpiling weapons. Others found the stark core-periphery logic of the civilized metropole and savage frontier unconvincing, commenting that Japanese people (naichijin) "live like ants."[108] Moreover, submission to Japanese rule was no given. Mona Rudao, the alleged leader of the 1930 Musha uprising in Taiwan, was a participant in one tour. Likewise, some Korean students reported discovering the extent of colonial discrimination through tours of the metropole, when they saw the difference between the science laboratory facilities at metropolitan schools and those at their own colonial schools.[109]

In the case of Japanese travelers, overt critiques were likewise rare. But one in particular was prescient. Reversing observational travel's practice of collapsing the experience of one into the shared affect of many, one diarist for Hiroshima Higher Normal School commented on the potential for individuals in Dairen to create problems for the many. "Once you've familiarized yourself with this place," he wrote, "you can't help but agree that, like one wave becoming ten thousand waves, an action by the people on the South Manchuria Railway Company route will come to the metropole and become a problem for the whole country."[110]

## CONCLUSION

In the years after the Russo-Japanese War, the Japanese government, colonial governments, and colonial institutions set about creating a nation that had affective ties to Manchuria and Korea. Imperial travelers were, for the most part, willing participants in this process, performing their *kokumin*-ness through their emotional involvement with the national land. Indeed, despite the wide range of critiques that circulated during and after the war, the basic premise of a territorialized national identity would largely go unchallenged by imperial travelers in their writings on empire. Instead, the debate turned to whether and how these colonized lands ought to be placed within Japan. But critiques of imperial travelers' nationalist eyes, such as Nakanishi's, would continue to play a significant role in shaping the spatial politics of empire—if only, as we shall see in later chapters, to outline the boundary beyond which the issue could not be debated.

The point to be gleaned from the emergence of observational travel to the new territories at this time is that the state's concern with producing subjects with affective ties to colonized land was as much a project of naturalizing the territorial nation-state as it was legitimating the scope of Japan's empire. As we shall see in later chapters, the images of Korea, Manchuria, and, later, Taiwan, as places within the Japanese nation and the image of Japan as a nation in place on these lands were shaped by crises more concrete than a conceptual kerfuffle over territoriality and community in a system of territorial nation-states. At the same time, we should not ignore the centrality of the land to the ideological project of observational travel and imperial tourism. Imperial tourism was one component of a spatial politics that sought to construct a social imaginary of the nation that was inseparable from its spatial imaginary. In the broad sense, the spatial politics that emerged in the early twentieth century drew on symbolic-cultural elements of nationalism, such as commemorative practices, geography education, and landscape ideology, as well as its political and technological practices, such as establishing international boundaries and cadastral surveys, to make the land under Japanese administration manageable as territory of the state and meaningful as the space of the nation. In the more narrow sense, the Ministry of Education and other actors conceived of observational travel's contribution to that spatial politics as mediating and, in some sense, fostering ties between state and nation through the observation of the land itself.

This suggests that the story of the social imaginary of modern Japan—what Marilyn Ivy calls the "national-cultural imaginary" of Japan—must necessarily be "re-routed" through Manchuria, Korea, and Taiwan.[111] In the first place, the ideological force of observational travel begins to illuminate how the boundaries between practices of "nationalization" and "imperialization" were intertwined, with colonial travelers brought to the metropole to develop a sense of themselves as part of the space of the Japanese Empire and metropolitan travelers sent to the colonies to develop a sense of themselves as a part of a nation that included colonized lands. Of course, the stakes of "becoming Japanese" differed starkly for each group. But for neither group was the spatial imaginary of the nation a natural phenomenon. Rather, it had to be taught and, the colonial boosters hoped, internalized in order for imperial nationalism to be reproduced. Indeed, it is for that reason that this book begins with the intertwined relationship of national people *(kokumin)* and national land *(kokudo)* that travel produced, rather than with the expansion and integration of the imperial transportation network, a more standard starting point for histories of tourism.

In the second place, specific understandings of Japan and its place in the world emerged from imperial travelers' and colonial boosters' attempts to place these colonized lands within the space of the nation but without, as Nakanishi argued, its tangled web of social and historical relations. In this chapter, we explored the production of a shared history through the reenactment of a national past in Korea and Manchuria. These wars of conquest remain central elements of popular and official national history. They also remain powerful tourist sites, with travelers returning to Port Arthur and to the remains of Hideyoshi's invasion of the Korean peninsula even today. Such "nostalgia tourism," as Mariko Tamanoi has argued, not only "represents the nation's yearning for the landscapes, lifestyles, and spectacles of the lost empire" but also sustains the basic erasures of imperial observational travel by "assisting the Japanese people to forget the power of their own state, which once dominated ordinary Chinese people in a place where they now entertain themselves."[112] Indeed, as Scott Laderman has argued in the case of U.S. tourism to Vietnam, nostalgia tourism reproduces nationalist history's "taking" of places by reducing them to waypoints in a narrative of national rise and decline while at the same time erasing other perspectives on the meaning of these sites and of the power relations that shape what constitutes meaningful history for different audiences.[113] Nostalgia tourism has not erased the history of empire, in other words, but rather has sustained the concept of a national land that exists as a place distinct from the other past-places that share the same land.[114]

A history of imperial tourism that stretches not from 1905 to 1945 but from 1897 to the present raises questions for our idealized imaginary of the nation-state as a territorialized community. What the prevalence of so many different tools, discursive and material, for territorializing a Japanese nation on colonized land suggests is that the territorialized nation is largely a myth. This is not to say that nations did not or do not imagine themselves to be rooted in a particular territory. It was, of course, precisely this pursuit of territorialization that motivated imperial tourism and other modes of addressing the gap between state and nation. But to define nations as themselves territorialized implies an achievement; instead, we ought to be analyzing a process. Shifting our terminology from *territorialized* to *territorializing* calls attention to the continuous work required to sustain the spatial imaginary of nationalism and to how this work is never complete but rather must persist in order to respond to the changing conditions of empire and nation.

2

# The New Territories

The irony of imperial nationalism was that it was through movement that the "sedentarist metaphysics" of the territorial nation-state took hold.[1] The steamship and the railway carriage produced practices of seeing and self-knowing that encouraged imperial travelers and colonial boosters to observe colonized peoples as outside of the Japanese nation in space and behind the Japanese nation in time. But it was not enough to deny the coevalness of colonized peoples—imperial travelers and colonial boosters also had to affirm the place of the nation on colonized land.[2] In this, their methods of locating colonized lands illuminate an aspect of the spatial politics of empire that studies of the representation of colonial difference in the context of Western empires and previous studies of travel in the Japanese Empire have overlooked. Colonial boosters and imperial travelers did mark colonized *peoples* as not-yet-civilized, as primitive, and as backward. Yet this, in and of itself, was not justification enough for colonialism in an era in which the project of empire was transitioning from one of territorial acquisition to one of territorial maintenance. Colonial boosters and imperial travelers also had to locate colonized *land* within the nation in space and in synchronicity with the nation in time.

In the decades following the Russo-Japanese War, colonial boosters turned to tourism to create a social imaginary of the nation that incorporated Korea, Manchuria, and Taiwan as places within the space of the nation. These colonial boosters were a loose confederation of colonial officials, industrialists in the colonies and metropole, and, increasingly, public-private booster organizations, such as the Japan Tourist Bureau, the Taiwan Association, the Korea-Manchuria Information Bureau, and the Manchuria-Mongolia Culture Association, who worked to shape the public image of these places for both Japanese and foreign audiences. The individuals in these organizations would not likely have recognized themselves as members of a larger group called "colonial boosters." Nor did they always agree—settlers, for example, were oftentimes critical of decisions by the governors general that limited the privileges of settlers vis-à-vis colonized subjects or their ability to capitalize on colonial resources to the fullest.³ But they did share a desire to make permanent Japan's colonial holdings and to get their compatriots to see these places (if not their peoples) as necessary components of the nation. In that, they shared much with the boosters who inaugurated imperial tourism to other colonial sites, such as New Zealand, the American West, and the Caribbean.⁴

In the face of growing anxiety over the future of Japanese colonial rule in Korea, Manchuria, and Taiwan, the colonial governments and the South Manchuria Railway Company intervened directly to shape how imperial travelers understood the place of the new territories within Japan. One strategy they adopted was mounting industrial exhibitions in colonial capitals to draw metropolitan travelers to the colonies, and sending elaborate pavilions to be displayed at exhibitions in the metropole.⁵ But metropolitan attendance at colonial exhibitions was generally low, and the complications of shipping flora, fauna, and historic artifacts limited what could be sent abroad for display. Rather than rely solely on short-term, big-ticket exhibitions, the colonial governments and the South Manchuria Railway Company turned to tourism and its central technologies, the itinerary and the tourist guidebook, to transform select portions of Taiwan, Korea, and Manchuria into permanent exhibitions. By carefully curating what travelers saw and how they made sense of these sights, the colonial governments and the South Manchuria Railway Company sought to teach imperial travelers to see Korea and Taiwan as places within the space of the Japanese nation, and Manchuria as a place that was, if not within the space of the Japanese nation, then at least outside of the space of the Chinese nation.

Colonial boosters encouraged imperial travelers to place colonized lands within Japan through two acts of transposition. One was the transposition of the landscape into a position within the space of civilization, in which relations within networks of circulation and exchange and a progressive historical time of development determined the essence and location of a place.⁶ The another was into the space of the nation, in which the location and essence of a place was primarily determined by its relation to an imagined end point of History, that is, of the nation's coming into being in its present-day territory. If, in earlier eras, it had been enough to declare conquered lands *terra nullius*, by the mid-nineteenth century, empires began to locate their conquered lands within what we might think of as the "mosaic" or "jigsaw puzzle" metageography of the international system of nation-states.⁷ The nineteenth century was, after all, an era that saw the particularization of civilizing missions in terms of national futures, such as Manifest Destiny in the United States or "Japanification" in Japan, as well as the incorporation of the

United States and Japan into the European system of states with its idealization of the territorial nation-state.[8] Intellectuals in Japan and the United States understood that the history of civilization was also a history of national becoming.[9]

Rather than simply denying the coevalness of colonized territory, colonial boosters used three modes—the historical, economic, and nationalist modes—to place Korea, Manchuria, and Taiwan within the bounds of a past, present, and future that was both "civilized" and "Japanese," and at the same time, to mark colonized subjects as "out of place" in these same lands. In this, colonial boosters enrolled imperial travelers in the project of constructing a spatial imaginary of the nation that might one day overcome the core-periphery geography of civilization to encompass the entirety of the territory of the state. Thus the boosters' project was, in fact, threefold. One, they sought to teach travelers to see the colonial landscape as already part of a global space of civilization, rather than as places that remained forever behind the inner territory in developmental time. Two, they sought to teach travelers to see the colonies in such a way that it would be possible, in the present and in the future, for metropolitan Japanese people to see the progressive force of Japanese history as being located in the "new territories" as much as it was in the "inner territory." And three, in the service of the first two goals, they applied the same discursive mechanisms that they used to place the Japanese nation on colonized land to *dis-locate* or *dis-place* colonized subjects from the colonized territory that they inhabited.

## THE WORLD OF JAPAN: AS SEEN FROM THE CORNER—OR PERHAPS THE CENTER

By the time the Government General of Korea published its first tourist guidebook in 1915, the territory of the Japanese state had taken the form that it would hold until the establishment of a puppet state in Manchuria in 1932. After an initial period of colonization, which claimed Hokkaidō and Okinawa, the Japanese state acquired Taiwan in 1895. The settlement of the Russo-Japanese War netted the empire the southern portion of the island of Karafuto, the Railway Zone in southern Manchuria, and the Kwantung Leased Territory at the tip of the Liaodong Peninsula in 1905. In 1910, the Japanese state annexed Korea, making the peninsula a formal part of Japanese territory. Then, in 1914, the state claimed the German colony of Micronesia, a conquest that the League of Nations would later ratify by declaring Micronesia to be a Class "C" Mandate Territory under the guardianship of Japan.

Representations from the imperial center described the relationship between the territory of the state and the space of the nation as one of a progressive outward expansion, in which the space of the nation expanded along with the territory of the state. The 1919 textbook map we examined in the introduction is one example. But the representation of Japan as an expanding national-historical space stood in stark contrast to the actual structure of imperial rule, in which Korea and Taiwan were excluded from the jurisdiction of the Constitution.[10] Likewise, this representation ignored the very real differences between the government of the main islands, Japan's formal colonies, and its informal possessions in the Kwantung Leased Territory and the Railway Zone in Manchuria.

Colonial discourse defined Korea, Manchuria, and Taiwan as uncivilized places, for it was this lack of civility that justified the treatment of the colonies as spaces of exception to national norms. Cadastral surveys, for example, were one mechanism by which the colonial governments incorporated colonized lands into the territory of the state while still marking them as outside of the space of the nation. Undertaken by the Government General of Taiwan from 1898 to 1903 and the Government General of Korea from 1910 to 1918, these surveys became a means by which the Governments General translated the discourse of colonial incivility into actual practices of dispossession. In Taiwan, the Government General delineated the mountainous interior region of the island as a special administrative zone because of its "savagery," and declared all the land within that zone to be public land. In the Government General's argument, indigenous peoples who resided in the area did not have a concept of private property and therefore could not have owned the land prior to the establishment of the Japanese colonial government. The Government General's own research later contradicted this assessment. Nevertheless, it became the basis for the large-scale transfer of legal ownership of land to the Japanese colonial government.[11] In Korea, it was not the cadastral survey itself that led to the dispossession of Korean landowners but rather its subsequent effects. In its determination to make Korea an agricultural appendage of Japan, the Government General encouraged individual landowners to shift their production to rice, which would be sold to consumers in the industrializing metropole, and sweetened the deal by subsidizing improvements necessary to increase production. When the price of rice collapsed in the 1920s, however, so did the welfare of a majority of Korean farmers. In the aftermath, the Japanese-owned Oriental Development Company became the largest landowner in Korea.[12]

The colonial legal system likewise translated the discourse of colonial incivility into institutional exceptionalism. The Governments General operated under two laws, known as Law 63 in Taiwan and Law 30 in Korea, which granted the governors general the authority to issue ordinances that had the power of law—to bypass, in other words, the Imperial Diet and any local legislative bodies and to rule by decree instead. In the inner territory, such power was reserved for the emperor. Enabled by Laws 63 and 30, the governors general enacted penal rules for the colonies, such as the use of flogging to punish colonized subjects, which were specifically disallowed by the inner territory's Civil Code. These practices were necessary, the colonial governments argued, because colonized subjects lacked a level of development that would enable them to respond to more "civilized" punishments.[13]

Manchuria was a slightly different case. Yet even here the discourse of incivility enabled special practices that marked Manchuria as a place both within and without the space of civilization. For example, Japanese residents enjoyed the privilege of extraterritoriality in Manchuria. The practice originated in the so-called unequal treaties that Western powers signed with China and Japan, and later Japan with China, in the late nineteenth century. These treaties granted foreigners the right of extraterritoriality in China because, the argument went, local courts were uncivilized, and foreigners ought not to be subjected to their barbaric justice. In Manchuria, Japanese residents had the right to be tried in Japanese consular courts staffed by Japanese magistrates, who would determine their fate under the rules of Japanese, rather than Chinese, law. Moreover, extraterritoriality justified the creation of a Japanese consular police force, whose duty it was to protect the property rights of Japanese residents.[14] From this stemmed the establishment of a Japanese court system whose rulings superseded those of the Chinese magistrates (at least the Japanese court argued as such) and would come to form the foundation of a large-scale transfer of Chinese land to Japanese ownership in the 1920s.[15]

In each case, the Governments General and the South Manchuria Railway Company legitimated practices of dispossession through the legal and administrative constitution of Korea and Taiwan as somehow apart from the space of the nation, and Japanese Manchuria as apart from both China and the space of civilization. At the same time, the representation of these places and their peoples as somehow outside of the Japanese nation in space and behind the Japanese nation in time imparted to many Japanese residents of Korea, Manchuria, and Taiwan a sense of precarity. In the case of Manchuria, settlers worried that Japanese politicians and officials cared little about the future of the Railway Zone and the Kwantung Leased Territory. They were not wrong to worry—indeed, commentators in the metropole questioned the "worth of the whole enterprise."[16] Despite early imperial travelers' insistence that Manchuria constituted an essential component of the national land, others argued that the permanent colonization of Manchuria was a dangerous and unnecessary endeavor. In the years immediately after the establishment of the South Manchuria Railway Company in 1906, powerful voices advocated pulling back, while others, such as Gotō Shinpei, demanded pushing forward toward direct colonization. Itō Hirobumi, a towering figure in Japanese politics, succinctly summed up the problem. "Japan's rights in Manchuria are nothing more than the leased territory . . . and the railway," Itō stated. "Today, officials and even businessmen speak readily of 'managing Manchuria.' But Manchuria is in no way part of Japan. It is no more and no less than one part of China's territory. We have no right to speak of exercising sovereignty in a territory that doesn't belong to us."[17] Japanese expansionists continued to pursue territorial gains opportunistically throughout the 1910s and 1920s—most famously through the presentation of the "Twenty-One Demands" to the Chinese government in 1915, one of which resulted in the extension of Japan's leasehold in Manchuria to ninety-nine years. Yet others worried that the international embrace of the territorial nation-state as the foundation of world peace, combined with the rise of the Chinese nationalist movement, meant that further territorial expansion in Manchuria would be perceived as aggression against an extant state rather than expansion into the fictive white space of *terra nullius*.[18] As it had been during the Russo-Japanese War, the question of whether Japanese expansion into Manchuria was in the best interests of the nation remained an active question.

Japanese settlers and colonial administrators in Korea likewise felt the tension of their not-quite-in / not-quite-out status. Japanese colonial discourse emphasized the long, shared history of Japan and Korea and argued that a Japanese "annexation" *(heigō* or *gappei)* of Korea would be a reunion between two civilizations with shared ancestry yet disparate histories. Yet travelers' representations of Korea in the early twentieth century gave short shrift to the common ancestry thesis and instead described the peninsula as a strange and dirty backwater. Okita Kinjō's description of Korea in his 1905 *Rimen no Kankoku* (Korea behind the mask) is illustrative in this regard. Okita acquiesced to the geography of civilization's insistence on defining regions in terms of what they produced for exchange. But he described Korea's products as ones of questionable value to civilization's market: according to Okita, the "seven major products" of Korea were "shit, tobacco, lice, courtesans, tigers, pigs and flies."[19] Such a discourse certainly buttressed Japanese claims for the legitimacy of the Government General's civilizing mission.[20] Yet it also fostered the insecurity of Japanese settlers, who, by the early 1910s, were fighting to overcome the strictures that the idea of Korean backwardness placed on their own economic activities in the peninsula.[21] Some commentators feared that life in Korea was Koreanizing, or "*yobo*-izing" Japanese settlers (*yobo* was a derogatory term that Japanese settlers applied to Koreans) instead of Japanifying Koreans.[22]

Further intensifying the spatial and territorial anxieties of Japanese setters in Korea were metropolitan attitudes toward the project of colonialism itself. In the lead-up to the opening of the 1915 Korean Products Competitive Exhibition in Keijō, the press and the Government General of Korea expressed concern that residents of the metropole were disengaged from the task of assimilating Korea—a practice that aimed to Japanify Koreans through language training and other external changes, such as customs and social organization.[23] As one editorial in the *Tokyo Asahi Newspaper* put it, the major goals of colonial development depended on the ability of the Government General to invest the Japanese nation in the future of Korea. It was not enough for Japanese to stand by and watch colonization happen, the editorial argued. The project required participation.[24] None was more conscious of this than the governor general himself, who could project no near-term future in which the colonial administration would not be operating at a deficit.[25]

In the case of Taiwan, the discourse of colonial savagery and weak metropolitan commitment likewise flustered Japanese settlers and the colonial government. In the 1895–96 military campaign to wrest control of Taiwan from Chinese guerrillas and indigenous peoples who opposed Japanese rule, the metropolitan media introduced Japanese readers to the "customs" of indigenous life—hunting, gathering, and headhunting—while likewise portraying Taiwanese Chinese as lawless bandits, whose ragged uniforms and lack of valor contrasted with the spotless white uniforms and bravery of the Japanese soldiers.[26] By the turn of the century, however, the equation of Taiwan with savagery struck colonial boosters in both Taiwan and the inner territory as both old news and the key cause of the lack of metropolitan investment—both financial and emotional—in the future of the island. In the face of the steep expense of establishing a colonial government, there had been calls to sell back the island to China at any price.[27] In response, boosters proposed ways of increasing metropolitan appreciation for Taiwan. In 1899, for example, Nakahashi Tokugorō, the president of the Osaka Mercantile Shipping Company, which enjoyed a government monopoly on regular services from the metropole to the island, suggested renaming the island Nan'yōdō (South Seas province), because people associated the name Taiwan with the savagery and death of Japan's past encounters with the island. "Therefore," he argued, "it's necessary to change it to a splendid and beautiful name that bears no relation to anything that came before."[28] Likewise, members of the Taiwan Association (Taiwan kyōkai), a booster organization headquartered in Tokyo, attempted to elevate the civilizational status of Taiwanese Chinese in the metropolitan imagination by referring to them in a way that did not condemn the island as a whole to an image of savagery and lawlessness. The Taiwan Association argued that referring to Taiwanese Chinese as "Taiwan natives" *(Taiwan dojin)* conjured up comparisons to "Hokkaidō natives" *(Hokkaidō dojin)*, in other words, the Ainu, and therefore, of an entire island that was "savage" in character. Instead, the boosters suggested "people of Taiwan" *(Taiwanjin)* or "islanders" *(hontōjin)*, two terms that lacked any overt reference to a linear trajectory of civilization development or pejorative characterization of the island's essential nature.[29]

Tied in with these concerns was, for the largely Japanese population of boosters around the empire, the problem of how to refer to Japanese people themselves. As the Taiwan Association pointed out, though official and popular discourse oftentimes referred to Japanese people as "inner territory people" *(naichijin)*, this moniker only made sense if one thought of Japanese identity from the perspective of a colonial periphery looking back on a metropolitan core. It naturalized a hierarchical division between inner territory and new territory that settlers hoped to eventually overcome, at least in terms of their own place within Japan. Instead, Taiwan boosters suggested "people of Japanese culture" *(wajin)*, in contrast to "people of Chinese culture" *(kanjin)*—a division that incorporated all Japanese people, regardless of place of residence, into the same category and upset the spatialization of the inner territory as the center of the empire.[30] In Manchuria, the leaders of Japanese civil society in Dairen likewise referred to themselves as "imperial national people" *(teikoku kokumin)* or "Japanese subjects" *(Nihon shinmin)*, two terms that expanded the space of authentic Japanese nationality to include Manchuria. In Korea, settlers slipped between referring to themselves as "inner territory people" *(naichijin)* and as "Japanese people" *(Nihonjin)*, a term that defined Japanese-ness in terms of parentage rather than location.[31]

## PLACING THE NEW TERRITORIES

In the years between the first tours of Manchuria and Korea in 1906 and the creation of an imperial tourism industry in 1918, the number of metropolitan residents traveling to observe the new territories grew steadily.[32] It was in this context of colonial anxiety and a growing market for imperial travel that the colonial governments and the South Manchuria Railway Company embraced tourism as a tool for *re-placing* the new territories in the metropolitan imagination. In 1908, the Government General of Taiwan published the first Japanese-language tourist guidebook to Taiwan, the unimaginatively titled *Tetsudō ryokō annai* (Guide to railway travel). The South Manchuria Railway Company followed in 1909 with its first Japanese-language guidebook, *Minami Manshū tetsudō annai* (Guide to railways in southern Manchuria). The Government General of Korea entered the field in 1915 with its own official guidebook, the *Chōsen tetsudō ryokō annai* (Guide to railway travel in Korea).

A few years later, the colonial Governments General and South Manchuria Railway Company were aided in their efforts to facilitate imperial travel by the Japan Tourist Bureau and the Korea-Manchuria Information Bureau. Eager to promote the growing trend of imperial travel further, in 1918 the empire's major transportation institutions joined with the Japan Tourist Bureau (JTB) to begin services for domestic travelers. The new services built on those that the Bureau of Railways, railway and steamship companies, and hotels had begun offering to foreign travelers through the JTB in 1912. At that time, the JTB opened offices not only in Yokohama and Kōbe, two major ports of entry for travelers coming across the Pacific Ocean, but also in Hōten, Dairen, Keijō, Pusan, and Taihoku, where the JTB offered tourist information and guide services. With the turn to the domestic market (which, in this case, also meant the imperial market), the JTB updated its physical footprint as well. In 1925, the organization added offices in locations that catered to the circuits and pathways of Japan's growing middle class—Osaka, Kyōto, and Tokyo's Nihonbashi Mitsukoshi department store. Other tourist organizations began services as well, such as the South Manchuria Railway Company's new Korea-Manchuria Information Bureau, which in 1923 set up offices in Tokyo's Marunouchi Building, Osaka's Sakai-suji Street, and in front of the station at Shimonoseki, the gateway to Korea.[33]

Concomitant with its turn to the domestic market, the Japan Tourist Bureau published its first compendium of tourist itineraries in 1920. The South Manchuria Railway Company's Korea-Manchuria Information Bureau followed soon after with its own set of itineraries in 1923.[34] These itineraries guided travelers through their observations of colonized lands with little emphasis on encounters with colonized cultures or peoples. Instead, the itineraries directed travelers to sites that signified the success of the Governments General and the South Manchuria Railway Company at placing colonized lands within the space of civilization and the space of the nation: sites of production and circulation, sites that defined the past of each colonized land as a linear history of transition to Japanese rule, and sites that located colonized lands within the affective space of the national land and a collectively experienced national past.

Together, tourist guidebooks and itineraries did not present a "Japanese" view of the colonies in contrast to a colonized one. They presented a boosters' view of the nation, one directed at metropolitan Japanese who did not have the level of attachment to the new territories that colonial boosters' desired. In fact, the guidebooks differed markedly from another "Japanese" representation of the colonies. In 1913, the Japanese Bureau of Railway's published its first English-language guide to the empire, *An Official Guide to Eastern Asia*. Modeled after the Baedeker guides in Germany, the *Official Guide* sought, in the words of its primary sponsor, Gotō Shinpei, to "advertise Japanese culture and the Japanese spirit to the entire world." For Gotō, this meant moving from an understanding of Japan in the universal terms of civilization to one more particular to the Japanese nation. "In other words," he wrote, "to contribute to making rapid progress in moving from 'Japan in the World' to the 'World of Japan.'"[35] To introduce foreign travelers to the world of Japan, the *Official Guide* included pages and pages on Japanese, Manchurian, and Korean geography, history, and customs (Taiwan and Okinawa were contained in volume 2, *Southwestern Japan*). The guidebook represented East Asia from the perspective of the Japanese Empire, which was cast as the point of translation, both in terms of transport geography and knowledge, between East and West.[36]

The guidebooks published by the Governments General and the South Manchuria Railway Company for Japanese travelers likewise sought to translate the landscape into terms readily understandable by metropolitan travelers. But they were far more circumspect about the necessity of knowing anything about colonized subjects. "This book," the Government General of Korea wrote in the opening pages of the 1915 *Chōsen tetsudō ryokō annai*, "notes almost all of the famous places, historical ruins, and scenic sights along the lines of the Korean

TABLE 1  A suggested itinerary for Korea–Manchuria travel. This two-week itinerary was the shortest itinerary for Korea–Manchuria travel. Longer itineraries took travelers farther afield in Manchuria, to the Russian-controlled cities of Harbin and Kirin in the north and to the port of Eikō on the Liao River.

| Day | Location | Sights to Be Seen |
|---|---|---|
| 1 | Tokyo | [none] |
| 2 | Kobe | [none] |
| 3 | At Sea | [none] |
| 4 | At Sea | [none] |
| 5 | Dairen | Wharf, soybean oil factory, city |
| 6 | Dairen–Port Arthur–Dairen | Hakugyokuzan Memorial Tower, museum, memorial exhibit hall, various battlefields, old and new cities |
| 7 | Dairen | West Park, Electric Amusement Park, South Manchuria Railway (SMR) Central Laboratory, SMR Sakakō (locomotive) factory, SMR Ceramics Laboratory, Hoshigaura |
| 8 | Hōten–Bujun–Hōten | Open-air mine, Mondo tile factory, various mines, other factories |
| 9 | Hōten | Inner castle [Chinese city], palace, Northern Tomb, new city, West Tower, Golden Temple, Hōten Park, Shōkawanuma Pond, Southern Manchuria Medical School |
| 10 | Heijō | Daidō Gate, Renkōtei Pavilion, Botandai Pavilion, Otsumitsudai Pavilion, Genbu Gate, Fuhekirō Pavilion, Yōmeiji Temple |
| 11 | Keijō | Nanzan Park [Keijō Shrine], Government General building, Museum, Keifuku Palace, Pagoda Park, Commercial Products Exhibit Hall, Arts Manufactory |
| 12 | Keijō–Pusan | [none] |
| 13 | Shimonoseki–Tokyo | [none] |
| 14 | Tokyo | [none] |

SOURCE: Japan Tourist Bureau, ed., *Ryotei to hiyō gaisan Taishō 12-nen* (Tokyo: Japan Tourist Bureau, 1923), 256–58.

Railways." With its comprehensive guide to Korea's sights to be seen, the guidebook was "truly the best companion for those who wish to travel Korea."[37] It was possible, in this formulation, to know Korea without learning a thing about contemporary Koreans, as the guidebook contained nothing related to Korean customs or culture in present use.

In fact, the first editions of official Japanese-language tourist guidebooks contained few textual descriptions of colonized subjects or colonial cultures. They did occasionally include a picture of colonized subjects, but only as part of a photo

TABLE 2  A suggested itinerary for Taiwan travel.

| Day | Location | Sights to Be Seen |
|---|---|---|
| 1 | Tokyo | [none] |
| 2 | Kōbe | [none] |
| 3 | Moji | [none] |
| 4 | At sea | [none] |
| 5 | At sea | [none] |
| 6 | Kiryū–Taihoku–Maruyama | Museum, Taihoku Park, Government General, Botanical Garden, market; Taiwan Shrine, Kenzawa Temple, Maruyama Park |
| 7 | Taihoku–Taichū | Taichū Shrine, Taichū Park, market, Teikoku Sugar Taichū factory |
| 8 | Taichū–Nichigetsutan | Sun-Moon Lake, Savage Tribe |
| 9 | Nichigetsutan | [none] |
| 10 | Kagi–Arisan | Mt. Ari Shrine, Sacred Tree |
| 11 | Mt. Ari–Kagi | [none] |
| 12 | Kagi–Hokkō–Tainan | Timber factory, Kagi Shrine, Kagi Park, Hokkō Shrine, Oriental Sugar Hokkō Factory |
| 13 | Tainan–Takao | Kaizan Shrine, Confucian Temple, Prince Kitashirakawa memorial sites, market, Fort Provincia, salt fields, Anpin Port, Tainan Park, Kaigen Temple |
| 14 | Takao–Heitō–Takao | Heitō Park, Taiwan Sugar Heitō factory, Takao Port, Lighthouse, Mt Hōtai |
| 15 | Hokutō | Hokutō hot spring, Fudō Falls |
| 16 | Hokutō–Taihoku–Kiryū | Port under construction, Sharyō Island, Courbet's Beach, Senton Cave |
| 17 | At Sea | [none] |
| 18 | At Sea | [none] |
| 19 | At Sea | [none] |
| 20 | Kōbe | [none] |
| 21 | Tokyo | [none] |

SOURCE: Japan Tourist Bureau, ed., *Ryotei to hiyō gaisan Taishō 12-nen* (Tokyo: Japan Tourist Bureau, 1923), 287–95.

meant to capture something else—generally a site of production or circulation. The one exception to this rule was the Government General of Taiwan, which featured images of "native customs" from at least 1916 on, as well as a recommendation to visit the "tamed" indigenous village of Kappanzan (C. Jiaobanshan). On the broad scale, however, colonial boosters did not encourage what we have come to know as "ethnic tourism," in which "the native is not simply 'there' to serve the needs of the tourist; he is himself 'on show,' a living spectacle to be scrutinized, photographed, tape recorded, and interacted with in some particular ways."[38]

The omission of any discussion of colonized cultures or peoples is particularly curious in the context of the widely publicized and debated assimilation policy *(dōka)* in both Korea and Taiwan, which was predicated on long-running scholarly and popular discourses about the backwardness and savagery of Koreans, Taiwanese indigenous peoples, and Chinese people in both Taiwan and China—the same discourses that legitimated the political and legal distinctions between the inner territory and the new territories. Yet the Bureau of Railways argued that Japanese-language tourist guidebooks did not need to include information on colonized subjects. In the preface to its 1919 translation of the Korea, Manchuria, and China volumes of the *Official Guide*, the Bureau of Railways explained that, "For readers from the United States and Europe, it was particularly necessary to provide explanations of such things as the conditions of countries *(kokujō)* and customs. But the general Japanese traveler does not necessarily require [such explanations], and, as such, we have omitted them."[39] In the end, colonial boosters presumed the imperial traveling public to be entirely too familiar with the customs and character of Koreans, Chinese, Taiwanese Chinese, and Taiwan's indigenous peoples, and thought that they might prefer to learn about the land and its contents instead.

Colonial boosters used tourist guidebooks and itineraries to convince Japanese travelers of the success of Japanese colonialism and the legitimacy of Japan's claims to colonized land. Central to this argument was the idea that the place of colonized *land* could be distinguished from the place of colonized *people*. In other words, that it was possible to describe parts of Korea, Manchuria, and Taiwan as "like the inner territory" at the same time that one described the colonized peoples who occupied that land as "out of place in this world." To make this argument, tourist guidebooks and itineraries used three modes to define the place of colonized lands: the economic mode, with its emphasis on sites of production and circulation; the historical mode, which narrated the past of colonized lands as linear histories of transition from primitive existence to unified states and then to incorporation into Japan; and the nationalist mode, which located colonized lands within the affective space of the national land and a collectively experienced national past. Each of these modes instructed travelers to understand the place of the land as a matter of location within global networks of exchange, developmental time, and the history of the colonizing nation. Not part of these representations of colonized land were concepts of place as essence or of place as a specific cultural region. Rather, tourist guidebooks and itineraries treated the place of colonized lands as malleable. Moreover, the modes overlapped in contradictory ways, which kept the place of colonized lands liminal—always both within and without the space of the nation.

## PORTS, PRODUCTS, AND THE CIRCULATING MISSION

In teaching Japanese travelers to see the territories of Taiwan and Korea as part of Japan, and Manchuria as not a part of China, the colonial governments and the South Manchuria Railway Company directed travelers' attention to the infrastructure of circulation and production. They portrayed Japanese imperialism as a "circulating mission" as well as a "civilizing" one. By the mid 1910s, new ports, railway lines, and steamship services had integrated the metropole and the new territories into a smoothly operating transportation network. Sites of circulation, such as bridges, wharves, and vehicles themselves, and sites of production, such as coal mines and sugar factories, featured heavily in the colonial governments' and South Manchuria Railway Company's representations of their own achievements in transforming the new territories into part of a new Japan.[40] Blurring the boundaries between metropole and colony, these guidebooks argued that not only had the new territories been fully integrated into metropolitan circuits of production and exchange but also, through the intervention of Japanese colonialism, they were now significant places in their own right within the global market.

Tourist guidebooks and itineraries gave ports special consideration as gateways: sites where colonial boosters could contrast the smooth movement of goods and people between territories with the imagined isolation of the pre-colonial landscape. Pusan, for example, was a testament to the progress of the Government General of Korea's Japanification project. The 1923 *Chōsen tetsudō ryokō benran* (Quick guide to railway travel in Korea) painted a picture of the port in words, explaining how development under the Government General of Korea had transformed Pusan into a mirror of Japan: "Like a mirror, you see the crowd of steamships and sailboats, and the scene of the town with buildings lined up from the shore to the mountainside, and wonder if you are again looking at Shimonoseki or Moji [the two neighboring ports from which the connecting ferry departed]."[41] The 1921 *Chōsen tetsudō ryokō annai* put it more succinctly: "Pusan has been so Japanified, it doesn't even smell like Korea anymore."[42]

In fact, few cities in Japan boasted the size and facilities of the port of Pusan. Rural areas, particularly in the northeast, lagged far behind major cities in any part of the empire in terms of electrification and urban modernization. Tōhoku, for example, in the northeast of the main island of Honshū, received startlingly little of the infrastructure development dollars that benefited the nation's more urban areas. In 1930, for example, there were fifty-seven electric light bulbs for every one hundred people nationally; there were only thirty-four per hundred people in Tōhoku. As the decade progressed, the disparity worsened. By 1935, Tokyo boasted more than one light bulb per person while Tōhoku actually lost light bulbs.[43] In other words, the process that the Government General wished travelers to see as "Japanification" had little to do with an actually existing Japan. Rather, colonial boosters used geographic signifiers to place Korea within an imaginary Japan that they defined as a space of industrialization and circulation.

Although the term "Japanification" was rarely used outside of Korea, official guidebooks and itineraries for Taiwan and Manchuria followed a similar strategy for placing these territories firmly within an economic space of empire defined not by inside and outside or advanced and backward, but by production and circulation. Sites of connection, such as ports and bridges, showed travelers a map of Japan shaped by transport rather than geographic barriers. And though there was little commentary on the destination of colonial products, the heavy emphasis on production demonstrated how colonial territory was flourishing under Japanese management.

As the port of arrival and departure for the Osaka Mercantile Shipping Company's regular service to the Japanese port of Moji, the port of Kiryū (C. Jilong; E. Keelung) was a routine stop for imperial travelers arriving at and departing Taiwan. Eager to highlight the Government General of Taiwan's efforts to bring Taiwan into the world of industrial movement, JTB itineraries explicitly labeled the "renovations to the port of Kiryū" as a sight to be seen.[44] With railways that ran right to the docks, the 1921 *Taiwan tetsudō ryokō annai* (Guide to railway travel in Taiwan) reported the new port of Kiryū was "very convenient for connections between land and sea travel." Making clear the role of the colonies in the construction of a new Japan (and thus going beyond what the Japanification of Pusan implied), the guidebook helped travelers to see the port in comparison: such a convenient land-sea connection was "perhaps something rarely seen in our country."[45] A new Japan was being born—in colonial territory.

Although Manchuria was an informal rather than formal Japanese colony, the South Manchuria Railway Company's Passenger Bureau pursued a strategy similar to that of the Governments General of Taiwan and Korea. Guidebooks for southern Manchuria began with Dairen, which the South Manchuria Railway Company ensured would be the most active port in Manchuria through its policy of "Dairen centrism" *(Dairen chūshinshugi)*.[46] Dairen was the key port for the transshipment of Manchurian goods and the headquarters of the South Manchuria Railway Company. As the 1909 *Minami Manshū tetsudō annai* (Guide to railways in southern Manchuria) described it, however, the wharf at Dairen was emblematic of the whole of Japanese-controlled Manchuria itself; it was "a grand construction project" whose "vast scale" made it a "rare sight in the Orient."[47] For some travelers, the wharf marked Dairen as a place that was no longer in Asia or China, but rather served as a gateway between the West and the East. As one of the Hiroshima Higher Normal School diarists described it, Dairen was the "Marseilles of the Orient," a reference to Marseilles' role as the gateway between France and North Africa.[48] The wharf was so central to the railway company's promotion of southern Manchuria that the first image included in the 1909 guidebook was a pullout panoramic photo of the wharf—showing clearly the railway that connected the piers to the wharf and three steamships tied alongside. In later editions, the South Manchuria Railway Company used a line drawing of a steamer tied up to the pier at Dairen as the guidebook's inside cover (see the cover of this book).

While ports showed the efforts of the South Manchuria Railway Company and the Governments General to bring the new territories into the pathways of modern circulation, sights inside the colonies showed travelers the resources that Japanese industries were turning into valuable commodities. Early guidebooks and itineraries placed commodities front and center. Itineraries for Taiwan reflected the colonial government's vision of Taiwan as an agricultural appendage of Japan. The JTB's 1923 itinerary for Taiwan, which required three weeks, sent travelers on a journey through Taiwan's raw materials and industrial production sites. At each stop, the itinerary suggested seeing sights of industrial and agricultural modernization. In Taichū (C. Taichung), travelers were to see Imperial Sugar's Taichū factory. In Hokkō (C. Beigang), the sight to see was Oriental Sugar's Hokkō Factory. In Heitō (C: Pingtung), Taiwan Sugar's Heitō factory. Other forms of industrial production dotted the remainder of the itinerary, from the Eirinjo Timber Factory in Kagi to the salt flats at Takao (see table 2). The Government General of Taiwan's 1916 *Taiwan tetsudō ryokō annai* underlined the significance of these sights with data that described the volume of production at each factory and gave a description of the "major products" of the area that surrounded each station stop. All told, administration, sugar factories, and industrial agriculture constituted nearly sixty percent of all the sights noted by the 1916 guidebook.[49]

To further promote these sights, the Government General of Taiwan's guidebooks highlighted the high levels of productivity of sugar and timber factories. The description provided by the Government General was concise, defining as quickly as possible the power of the new productive infrastructure. In Kagi, the main sight to be seen was the Kagi Timber Factory, which operated the "latest machinery to process timber from Mount Ari."[50] Photos included alongside showed a large, Spartan factory poised on open flatland next to a railway line. Imperial Sugar's factory at Taichū was "capitalized at five million yen and could run at 1,050 horsepower." In 1916, the guidebook reported that the factory had produced fifteen thousand tons of sugar in the most recent season.[51] Subsequent editions did little to elaborate on the merits of each sugar factory, except to note a staggering increase in sugar production. Taiwan Sugar's Heitō factory, which consolidated sugar from

FIGURE 4. The loading of soybeans at Dairen wharf. The picture accompanied the South Manchuria Railway Company's 1909 description of Dairen wharf. It shows the three tracks of the dock railway, a ship that runs almost the length of the wharf itself, and dozens of Chinese laborers carrying and stacking hundreds of bags of soybeans. The sight to be seen was the transport of goods, not the people.
SOURCE: Minami Manshū tetsudō kabushiki kaisha, ed., *Minami Manshū tetsudō annai* (Dairen: Minami Manshū tetsudō kabushiki kaisha, 1909).

all of Taiwan Sugar's local factories, produced forty-five million tons of sugar in 1926.[52] Dai Nihon Sugar's Hokkō factory, nearby, produced over thirty million tons the same year.[53]

If sugar and timber evidenced Taiwan's place in a global market as well as a Japanese economy, soybeans and coal defined Manchuria in similar terms. Beginning with the first South Manchuria Railway Company guide in 1909 and continuing through each subsequent edition, the soybean dominated the representation of Manchuria's unique place within the world. The 1919 edition included photos of stacks of soybean cakes ("the collection and distribution of soybean cake") and a vast warehouse full of bags of soybeans.[54] In addition to seeing the soybeans ready for export at the wharf, travelers were also encouraged to visit one or more of the nearby soybean oil factories, sixteen of which were noted on the guidebook's map of Dairen. The Tokyo Number One Higher School made its first stop at the soybean warehouse in Dairen in 1912. The size of the warehouse impressed the student diarist enough that he quoted how many beans per square foot it could hold.[55]

Second to soybeans in South Manchuria Railway Company guidebooks was coal. The production of coal centered on Bujun (C. Fushun), the central colliery of Manchuria and one of the South Manchuria Railway Company's major industrial enterprises in Manchuria.[56] Here, the rhetoric of Japan's leadership in the production and circulation of commodities continued. The sights to be seen in Bujun were sooty, loud, and industrial. The South Manchuria Railway Company included Bujun in all its itineraries, and its guidebooks included images of the smoking Mondo Tile Factory, coal elevators above the underground mines, and a "sand-gathering machine" on the banks of a nearby river. The 1919 guidebook devoted a number of pages to describing the investment the South Manchuria Railway Company had made in increasing the efficiency and productivity of the mines, contrasting this with the "makeshift" methods employed under the Russian China Eastern Railway. The guidebook also detailed the South Manchuria Railway Company's past interventions and outlined plans for the further economization of mining operations. The mines had once produced only three to four hundred tons a day, but by 1919 the mines were producing seven thousand tons a day. "Bujun," the guidebook concluded, "is on the verge of becoming a great industrial area."[57]

## JAPANIFICATION

In contrast to the economic mode, which described Korea, Taiwan, and Manchuria as places within a space that was defined sometimes as "like Japan," sometimes as "civilization," and sometimes as "like the West," guidebooks used the national and historical modes to place colonized lands within the space of the Japanese nation. From the first days of imperial travel, battlefields were sites where travelers were encouraged to experience colonized lands as national land through emotional narratives of patriotic sacrifice. This was true even in Manchuria, which was not part of the sovereign territory of Japan (see chapter 1). Early tourist guidebooks and itineraries expanded the nationalist mode to include Shintō shrines, which helped travelers to situate the new territories within a form of spirituality that Japanese ideologues portrayed as uniquely associated with the Japanese state. Colonial shrines often housed gods associated with empire. For example, the Taiwan Shrine in Taihoku (C. Taipei) housed the "three gods of exploitation" *(kaitaku sanjin)*, who had first been deified in the establishment of a shrine in Hokkaidō, and the spirit of Prince Kitashirakawa as a "protector deity" of the nation.[58] Prince Kitashirakawa had been a celebrity of the campaign to subdue Taiwan after the transfer of sovereignty in 1895. The popular illustrated magazine *Fūzoku gahō* (Customs illustrated), for example, exulted in his daring exploits against the guerrilla resistance in its pages. After his death, the cause of his celebrity shifted from military prowess to martyrdom. In a practice similar to that of the reenactment of Russo-Japanese War battles in Port Arthur, the Government General of Taiwan's guidebooks

FIGURE 5. Kitashirakawa's uniform on display at Tainan Shrine. The uniform was one of several items related to Kitashirakawa that Government-General tourist guidebooks suggested imperial travelers see on their tours of Taiwan. Like this uniform, each item on the "trail of Prince Kitashirakawa" was described as one that Kitashirakawa "really" (*jissai ni*) used prior to his death in Taiwan in 1896.
SOURCE: Tainan jinja shamusho, ed., *Tainan jinjashi* (Taihoku: Tainan jinja shamusho, 1928).

encouraged travelers to follow the "trail of Prince Kitashirakawa" to see places that he "actually" slept, traveled, and died on Taiwan, especially Tainan Shrine.[59]

Just as shrines and battlefield sites encouraged travelers to use the verisimilitude of their locations to reenact a national past and reflect on a national spirit, guidebooks and itineraries likewise used historical sights to encourage travelers to observe the process of historical transition from non-modernity to modernity and from non-Japanese to Japanese rule. They adopted strategies that made the past of each place comprehensible in terms of a linear narrative of unification and incorporation into Japan. Beginning with the first tourist guidebooks and continuing to the end of the empire, the colonial governments and the South Manchuria Railway

Company gave Korea, Manchuria and Taiwan a historical character by assigning each an ancient and a modern capital.

More so than guidebooks for Taiwan and Manchuria, guidebooks for Korea emphasized historical sights. To a certain extent, this emphasis reflected the differences between the policies of the Government General of Taiwan and the South Manchuria Railway Company, the former of which worked to transform Taiwan into a source of agricultural products to feed the growing industrial workforce in the metropole, and the latter of which, in lieu of sovereignty, focused on anchoring Japan's claim to Manchuria in its "management" of the region's human and material resources for the benefit of the global market. But the emphasis on historical sights in Korea also reflected the colonial discourses circulating at the time. While Taiwanese Chinese people in Taiwan and Chinese people in Manchuria might have been members of an East Asian cultural sphere that Japanese ideologues defined as "same script, same race" (*dōbun dōshu*), Japanese colonial discourse depicted Koreans as people who also shared a common ancestry with the Japanese. For colonial discourse on Korea, the challenge was to explain how the outcomes of two nations, which were in theory composed of the same people, were so different—one an empire, one a colony. In contrast, Manchuria and Taiwan were described as vast, untapped territories that had been colonized only recently by the Chinese. The emphasis in these cases was on differentiating Japanese colonialism from the Chinese and European colonialism that had come before. Thus, in Taiwan, the ancient capital of Tainan (C. Tainan) and the modern capital of Taihoku served as the two poles of recorded insular history. In tourist materials, the two capitals told the story of the shift from a Dutch and Chinese imperialism that sought to benefit only itself to a Japanese imperialism that benefited "the whole island."[60] In Manchuria, the two halves of the city of Hōten—one "Chinese" and old, the other simply "new"—served as the ancient and the modern capitals of Manchuria, describing the city's arc from capital of the Manchus to a dusty, forgotten city—when the Manchu rulers became the Qing emperors in Peking—and then to the forefront of the modernization of East Asia with the Japanese construction of the new city.[61]

Placing the territories in developmental time naturalized imperialism by normalizing transition. In the case of Korea, the guidebooks identified five historic capitals of Korea—Puyo (K. Buyŏ), Keishū (K. Kyŏngju), Keijō, Kaijō (K. Kaesŏng), and Heijō. The Government General's guidebooks used the multiple capitals to underscore the argument that Koreans had failed to develop successfully as a people because they suffered from too many transitions. This failure was constituted, always, in contrast to the successful development that Japan had experienced due to its supposedly unbroken imperial line.

Overlaid on the narrative of multiple transitions was the story of how Korea became part of the Japanese state. The Government General of Korea's guidebooks

FIGURE 6. "The Wretched Ruin of the West Tower." Postcard, c. 1910s. The South Manchuria Railway Company used historical sights, such as the West Tower, to tell a story of Manchuria's historical abandonment by the Manchus. Together with the former Manchu palace inside Hōten's city walls, colonial boosters' used the West Tower to describe the early glory of the Manchu rulers and the subsequent decline of their infrastructure after they left Hōten for Peking, where they ruled as the emperors of the Qing dynasty (1644–1912). Historical narratives such as these served to justify colonial boosters' claim that Manchuria was not an authentic part of China. Digital image courtesy of the East Asia Image Collection, Lafayette College Libraries, Easton, PA. Image ip0084.

paired Heijō and Keijō as "ancient" and "modern" capitals to reify a narrative of development and transition that culminated in the "annexation" of Korea and the reunion of the Korean and Japanese peoples. The guidebooks presented Keijō, the first major stop after arriving at Pusan, as a grand vista of peninsular history, from the early history of the Paekche kingdom to the transfer of power to the Government General in 1910. Layered among the city's many sights were ruins and remains of three dynasties, as well as the new infrastructure that made the city the "capital of the peninsula," a reference that sought to remove the city from the connotations of feudalism that came with the name "Chōsen."[62] But despite the thousands of years of peninsular political history in the city, the significance of all of it was exceeded by the Chosŏn dynasty (1392–1910)—the last dynasty prior to the annexation by Japan. Of nineteen sights listed by the 1921 *Chōsen tetsudō ryokō annai*, only one traced its significance solely to the Paekche.[63] Rather, the guidebook's suggestions centered on sights related to Chosŏn dynasty and colonial rule: the Ch'andŏkkung and Kyŏngbokkung palaces, government buildings, Independence Gate, tombs of the Chosŏn dynasty's ruling Yi family, and sites of enthronement and conflict.

The tourist guidebooks rarely described Chosŏn dynasty sights as impressive in their own right; they valued them for the story they told of the transition to Japanese colonial rule. For example, although in 1921 the Government General headquarters was still located in the former headquarters of the Resident General, an ornate Victorian building in the Japanese settlers' quarters, the 1921 guidebook stressed that Kyŏngbokkung, the palace of the Chosŏn dynasty, was going to be the new headquarters of the Government General of Korea. This practice of layering the new Japanese government over the previous Chosŏn dynasty included Japanifying the palace's name: "Keifukukyū: Although the new Government General office is now under construction here, this place is the first palace where the founder of the Chosŏn dynasty undertook the great work of rule."[64]

Other Chosŏn dynasty sites, such as the Ch'andŏkkung Palace, were similarly made to speak to the transition from Chosŏn to Japanese rule. In its description of Ch'andŏkkung, a residence for the Yi family, the 1921 guidebook described the layout of the palace and then quickly moved to the botanical gardens, zoo, and museum, which were located on the palace grounds. These areas, the guidebook pointed out, used to be part of the secret gardens of the Ch'andŏk Palace, "but are now opened to the public" *(kōkai sareteiru)*.[65] As Noriko Aso argues, the creation of public spaces connected with the imperial families was a key component of official narratives of modernization in both Korea and Japan.[66] Such notions were popular in urban planning, from the transformation of Tokyo into a modern capital in the late nineteenth century, to the Great Han Empire's push to the reform the space of Hwangsŏng, the city that would become Keijō under Japanese rule, "to create a symbolic national center from and through which to integrate the previously stratified groups of Koreans into national subjects of King Kojong."[67]

In the colonial context, tourist guidebooks used the conversion of private space into public space to construct a narrative of historical transition to a modern society that was Japanese in terms of its language and state but was universal in its embrace of the free circulation of people, goods, and ideas. In this formulation, what distinguished Japan, and the modern nation-state more generally, from the politics that had come before was that modern government was a public good. Indeed, in the historical overview that preceded the description of what to see in Keijō, the guidebook portrayed the transition from the Chosŏn dynasty to the Government General not so much as one of political turnover but of the next stage in the development of government on the peninsula: "From [the establishment of the first Chosŏn palace in Keijō] over five hundred years ago, the palace and the city have been rebuilt countless times after fires and disturbances. Yet its

FIGURE 7. The Government General Museum (above left) and "Secret Garden" (below right) at Ch'andŏk Palace. The caption explains that although the gardens were actually the residence of the Yi royal family, a part of the gardens had been opened to the public. The vertical placement of the images of the garden and the museum provides a visual narrative of the transition from private to public resources that the Government General argued characterized Japanese colonial rule in Korea.
SOURCE: Minami Manshū tetsudō kabushiki kaisha Keijō kanrikyoku, *Chōsen no fūkō* ([Keijō]: Minami Manshū tetsudō kabushiki kaisha Keijō kanrikyoku, 1922). Courtesy of the National Diet Library.

prosperity as the capital of the peninsula has never changed. In particular, the last ten or so years have shown surprisingly rapid progress *(chōsoku no shinpo)* and expansion."[68] Without even mentioning the Government General, Keijō was made to demonstrate the long history of unified rule over the peninsula and, most importantly, the grand achievements that had come in the past ten years with the transition to colonial rule.

The path of the express railway arranged travelers' encounters with Korea such that Heijō, the "ancient capital" *(koto)*, immediately followed Keijō, the "capital of the peninsula." As the former capital of multiple dynasties but present capital of none, the role Heijō played in the progress of peninsular history was more ambiguous than that of Keijō, which had the presence of the Government General and the last unified peninsular dynasty to demonstrate the orderly transition of rule. In Heijō, the Government General used the city's history to undercut Korean nationalists' claim that Koreans were an independent ethnic nation. The sights of Heijō emphasized the ambiguity of the origins of the Korean nation and linked the ancient history of "the country of Chōsen" (*Chōsenkoku*) to tributary relations with China. For all the talk of Heijō's turbulent ancient history, however, the sights the guidebook recommended ultimately told an overarching story similar to that of Keijō: the transition to Japanese rule, in this case not from independent Korean dynasties but from Chinese to Japanese influence. In this, it was a distinctly state-oriented narrative of origin and transition rather than an ethnicity-oriented narrative, in contrast to those put forth by Korean nationalists such as Sin Ch'ae-ho.[69]

As an "ancient capital," the guidebooks made Heijō embody the heterogeneous origins of Korea as a unified political territory and celebrate the transition from Chinese to Japanese rule as a result of Japan's victory in the 1894–95 Sino-Japanese War. As the 1921 entry on Heijō began, "Ages ago, the people of the country enthroned the god Tan'gun, who had been born under a spindletree on Mount Paektu, and made a capital at Heijō. Thus, from a mysterious legend begins the history of this place." The first recorded history cited by the guide dated from the time of the Zhou dynasty (1046–256 BCE), "when it is said that a branch of the Kishi family moved to Chōsen and made Heijō their capital." The founding of the first historic Korean capital by a *Chinese* nobleman was confirmed, the guidebook continued, by the true history of the Song dynasty (960–1279 CE): "Ryōyō Province, from olden times [known as] 'the country of Chōsen,' is a place that was ruled by Kishi. Today's Chōsen probably took the old name."[70] The historical overview continued to emphasize the turbulence of Heijō's history as capital: Heijō ceased to be the capital of Kishi (K. Kija) Chōsen when the descendants died during the time of the Han empire (206 BCE–220 CE); the Han established the Lelang Commandery (108 BCE–313 CE), but were eventually thrown out by the Koguryŏ (37 BCE–668 CE); following the fall of the Koguryŏ, Heijō became a western capital for the Koryŏ (918–1392 CE), under many names. To emphasize further the changing fortunes of Heijō, the overview concluded with a literary read on the city's main river, the Daidō (K. Taedong): "[And the blue Daidō river] looks as if it holds the secrets of antiquity and is sneering at the glory and decline of the human world."[71]

Subsequently, Heijō was the site of encounters of Japanese and Chinese armies during Hideyoshi's sixteenth century invasions of Korea and the 1894–95 Sino-Japanese War. Indeed, the majority of the city's sights told the story of Konishi Yukinaga's defeat by the Ming army in the Bunroku campaign (1592), and the Japanese army's rout of the Qing army in 1895. Renkōtei (K. Ryŏngwangjŏng), a pavilion dating from the Koguryŏ era, was the site "where Konishi Yukinaga fell into the trap of the sinister scheme of Ming Ambassador Shen Weijing" during the

Bunroku Campaign, which "was the basis for his crushing defeat at Heijō."[72] The "sinister scheme" referred to the secret drugging of the commander of the Japanese army defending Heijō by a Korean courtesan. The sleepy commander was then beheaded by the leader of the Ming army, and Japanese forces were forced to retreat. Similarly, Otsumitsudai (K. Eulmildae), a pavilion also dating to the Koguryŏ era, was where "the enemy made . . . their stronghold and hung their uniforms on the tree branches to make dummy troops and menace Yukinaga" during the Bunroku campaign. Botandai (K. Morandae), a neighboring pavilion, was where Konishi Yukinaga "put his main headquarters and sucked up the pain of a defensive battle" when "he found himself surrounded by the Ming army."[73]

Neighboring these sights that staged the loss to Ming China were the sights that told the story of Japan's eventual victory over Qing China. The Futsū Gate (K. Pot'onmun), a nine-hundred-year-old gate that dated to the Koryŏ period, was where the Ming army entered the castle walls of Heijō to begin the battle with Konishi Yukinaga's forces. Three hundred years later, it was the site from which one battalion of Japanese forces attacked the Qing army during the Sino-Japanese War. The Shichisei Gate (K. Ch'ilsŏnmun) marked the northern entrance to the castle and had been the site of pitched battles in both the Bunroku campaign and the Sino-Japanese War. During the Sino-Japanese War, Qing troops took the high ground and "rained down" an attack on the Japanese army. Otsumitsudai and Botandai, which were famous as sites of defeat during the Bunroku campaign, served double-duty as sights of glorious victory during the Sino-Japanese War. At Otsumitsudai, "the Qing General made this his headquarters, where he was made to worry about the two [incoming Japanese] army branches from Gensan." Previously well known as the site of Yukinaga's "painful" defensive battle against the Ming, Botandai became the site of a "famous struggle" during the Sino-Japanese War and the source of a "new memory for the world."[74]

## IN PLACE / OUT OF PLACE

In their efforts to rehabilitate Korea, Manchuria, and Taiwan in the metropolitan imagination, colonial boosters used similar strategies to place colonized lands within the space of civilization and the space of the nation. The histories told were explicitly not the histories of the colonies' ethnic nations. The South Manchuria Railway Company guidebooks, for instance, had no interest in Han Chinese residents, other than to represent them as cogs in the machine of soybean and coal production and circulation. Similarly, the state-centric story of Korean origins disconnected Korea from Koreans and therefore from the progressive history of the peninsula. Despite some small-scale discussion of the "native customs" and "tamed villages" of Taiwan's indigenous peoples, Taiwan's history was restricted to the narrative of transition from the ancient capital of Tainan to Taihoku, limiting the story to the western, plains areas of the island and erasing indigenous people from the island's history, which was now told as a progression of Dutch, Spanish, Chinese, and then Japanese colonial rule.

The economic, historical, and nationalist modes displaced and dislocated colonized subjects from the spatial and social imaginary of the nation by disconnecting their pasts and futures from that of the land. But this is not to say that colonized subjects were tangential to the project of placing colonized lands within the nation and the nation on colonized lands. Their labor was essential to the operation of civilization's modern transportation infrastructure. From the Chinese conductors of South Manchuria Railway Company streetcars in Dairen to Korean and Chinese construction workers, miners, and farmers, and those who moved goods from the railhead to the city, the networks of exchange simply could not have functioned without their labor.[75] Moreover, the figure of the colonized subject played a significant role in defining travelers' experiences of the colonies as places that were becoming part of the space of the nation. Like colonial boosters, imperial travelers used the historical, economic, and nationalist modes to define their own sense of belonging, or "in-placeness," in Korea, Manchuria, and Taiwan, while using these same modes to mark colonized subjects as out of place.

For imperial travelers, these modes structured their imagination of a normative landscape of the nation, which was reified through the contrast between the ideals that the modes professed and the colonized subjects they saw.[76] Arakawa Seijirō, who traveled to Manchuria and Korea as part of a 1918 tour of businessmen from Utsunomiya, used a scene at the Manchurian port of Eikō (C. Yingkou) to illustrate the incongruity of Chinese people in spaces of circulation, embodied in this case by the railroads. He compared the Chinese Government Railways station with the South Manchuria Railway Company's Eikō Station. The South Manchuria Railway Company's station had been bustling. But the Chinese station was different: "There didn't seem to be even one person in charge at the station. . . . Two or three people came in noisily, but even so there didn't seem to be any passengers." There was only one soldier "lumbering" around with his gun.[77] In Keijō, Koreans appeared out of place in the modernizing peninsula. As one imperial traveler wrote in a 1915 report: "When I look at Koreans walking through the Japanified town, it seems like somehow they are a race *(jinshu)* that has come from another country."[78] The poet Kawahigashi Hekigotō described the out-of-placeness of Koreans more bluntly. It was not that "Korea falls, but at least there are mountains and rivers," he wrote. Rather, referring to the common colonial practice of denigrating Korean men for their clothing, Kawahigashi thought the process was more akin to "the country dies, and there remain outstanding clothes and hats."[79]

If, in the historical mode, out-of-placeness was determined by a failure to transition, in the economic mode, it was a failure to organize one's life or society around the principles of circulation, exchange, investment, or the production of value. Nagasawa Sokichi, a speaker of the House of Representatives who toured eastern Taiwan in 1916, explained that indigenous people misunderstood the purpose of money. Describing a situation closer to slavery than wage labor, Nagasawa noted that "recently, because of labor shortages, sugar companies and the like don't even bother with offering to employ the savages *(banjin)*, since if they request [indigenous labor] from the police, the savages will do whatever the police say. They come from each village like forced labor." But he explained that sugar companies used compulsory labor not to exploit indigenous people but because indigenous people were unable to grasp the value of the money. "If you try to pay them with paper money, they won't take it," Nagasawa wrote, because "they fear that it will rot." The solution was to try to pay them in silver coins, but even this did not work: "They use them to do things like dig holes, decorate their necks, or to decorate their swords by driving them in [to the handle]. They do this because they don't understand that [money] is used as a medium of exchange."[80]

The student diarist for the Hiroshima Higher Normal School dwelled similarly on how the failure to understand concepts such as "investment" could lead to rapid changes of fate. In Hōten, he remarked, "nobody can avoid thinking of the last days of the Qing."[81] When the students visited the Northern Tomb in Hōten, however, they placed the blame for its fragile state not on the vicissitudes of history but on the failure of the Chinese nation as a whole to embrace investment. "If it's not actually about to crumble, the Chinese won't fix it," the diarist explained.[82] Hayasaka Yoshio, another resident of Tochigi Prefecture's Utsunomiya City, who published an account of his travel through Korea, Manchuria, China, and Taiwan in 1922, used an encounter with Korean rickshaw pullers in Keijō to likewise condemn the Korean people. Hayasaka recounted how he asked two different rickshaw pullers for a ride to the Higher Common School, only succeeding after walking a considerable distance and trying for a third time. "What does the above story tell us? If I were to put it in one word, I would say that it shows the laziness *(taidasei)* of the Korean people," he wrote. What Hayasaka called "laziness" was not an unwillingness to work; it was an unwillingness to plan ahead. "Their level of living is extremely low, and if they earn enough to live for one day they sleep or drink or eat or gamble. Tomorrow's matters are tomorrow's, and next year's matters can be dealt with next year."[83]

Yoshino Sakuzō, Japan's most famous prewar liberal, summed up how colonized subjects' failure to join the modern world of investment and exchange necessitated Japanese stewardship over their lands. In his 1916 report on Manchuria and Korea, he spelled out how important it was to recognize the gap between how Japanese settlers and officials understood the purpose of labor and how the "natives" *(dojin)* did. The Koreans he spoke to on his trip objected to the massive road construction projects being undertaken by the Government General, because the labor they were compelled to contribute was both unfair and bothersome. Yoshino did not agree with their claims. Nonetheless, he argued that it was important to take them into account when formulating colonial policy. "An ignorant people most certainly cannot endure losses today in the name of a long future of profit," he explained. While he agreed that it was "logical," when faced with these sorts of complaints, "to argue that the thoughts of the natives are mistaken," he advocated that colonial officials work with local Korean leaders to find a language that both sides would understand. "You can't govern the natives on logic," he concluded.[84]

Like most of the concepts and categories that structured colonial boosters' and imperial travelers' efforts to place colonized lands within the nation, the notion that colonized subjects were out of place in modern, industrial society, particularly in terms of attitudes toward circulation and labor, was not only a Japanese notion. In the entry on railways in his *Things Japanese*, for example, the early Japanologist Basil Hall Chamberlain wrote, "A railway journey in this country is apt to be anything but a joy."

> Owing to some cause not yet explained, the Japanese who, when abiding in their own native ways, are the very pink of neatness, become slipshod, not to say dirty, when introduced to certain conditions of European life. . . . In fact, the whole thing is queer and unpleasant, unless of course the traveler be a philosopher to whom every novel experience supplies welcome material for meditation. Such a philosopher will perhaps enquire the reason of the stripe of white paint across the windows of the third-class cars on certain lines. It is a precautionary measure adopted for the safety of country bumpkins; for it has happened that some of these, lacking in personal experience of glass, have mistaken it for air and gashed themselves horribly in the attempt to shove their heads through what, in their innocence, they supposed to be a non-resisting medium.[85]

Chamberlain's comments, like those of Japanese imperial travelers, were on par with how British travelers described railway transportation in Egypt and India. Nineteenth-century European imperialists argued that modern civilization and tradition occupied two different worlds: one, a world in which people used tools to dominate nature; the other, a world in which people lived according to nature's whims. The difference was psychological as much as material. There, British travelers treated the railway tracks as part of the space and time of the modern and the surrounding land as a completely separate territory in both space and time.[86] On the same page that he noted that the arrival of "a dense crowd of natives" to an Indian train station provided "much that is amusing to a curious observer," G. O. Trevyelan observed that civilization and nature were like oil and water, never to share the same location. "Stroll one hundred yards from the [railway] embankment," he wrote, "and all symptoms of civilization have vanished."[87]

The point is that imperial travelers did not simply deny the coevalness of colonized subjects. They used their out-of-placeness as the measure against which they calculated the Japanification of the land. The "Japan" of Japanification was ambiguously territorialized—marked by generic industrial infrastructure and the sensibility of the observer as much as it was by cultural symbols such as Japanese place names or state-centered mnemonic sites. In this, colonial boosters enrolled imperial travelers in the project of constructing a spatial imaginary that contained the possibility of a floating "center" rather than one that would always be located in the inner territory. This practice constituted the problem of colonial difference as the out-of-placeness of colonized peoples and justified the incorporation of colonized lands in to the present space of nation.

Over time, the outbreak of anti-imperial nationalist movements and boosters' own frustrations with the uneven structure of colonial rule would force imperial travelers and colonial boosters to find ways to place colonized peoples within the space of the nation if they were to maintain the place of the nation on colonized lands. Yet in this early era, imperial travelers marked colonized subjects as out of place in both the space of civilization and the space of the nation, and they used that representation of out-of-placeness to define the modernity of Japan, the new territories, and imperial travelers themselves. Tayama Katai summed up this attitude best in a report on his travels through Manchuria and Korea in 1924 (sponsored by the South Manchuria Railway Company). He juxtaposed the new, modern, and Japanified Korea against what he saw as the out-of-placeness of Koreans. Koreans watched as time passed by—Korea the place moved forward while Korea the people stood still. Because of this, they were a "dying nation" (bōkoku suru).[88] Surveying the scene around him, Tayama commented to his companion, "For the people of Korea, Japan being in charge must be a very difficult thing, don't you think?" "Yeah," Mr. M responded, "that must be true. After all, it seems like there are a lot of people thinking about the past." Tayama described the people of Korea as the "ordinary people of Korea" (Chōsen no jinmin), a term that connoted a people who had not yet recognized their own subjectivity, in contrast to "national people" (kokumin), who embraced their national identity, or even imperial subjects (shinmin), who understood themselves to be a people in relation to the emperor. This designation likewise suggested a temporal difference between the development of Koreans and of the Japanese national people. "But surely they will gradually realize that they are mistaken, right? A good thing is a good thing, no matter what you say," Mr. M continued. Tayama sighed and shook his head. "Customs have strong roots," he explained. He looked out the window of the train. There, among the villages scattered about the low hills, "a Korean wearing dirty white clothes lazily stopped his plow and watched the train passing by."[89]

## CONCLUSION

The many modes through which colonial boosters demonstrated the successful incorporation of colonized land into the space of the nation and the space of civilization—and their concomitant displacement of colonized subjects from the temporality of their own lands—illuminates how spatial politics emerged through the malleability of place. In this transitional moment between a world of empires and a world of territorial nation-states, it was not enough to simply disappear colonized subjects under a blanket of civilization or to deny their coevalness. Rather, colonial boosters recognized the significance of placing the Japanese nation on colonized land as well. Doing so required the deployment of multiple strategies, which, taken together, kept colonized lands "new" but also made a clear case for their legitimate place within the space of the nation.

The Governments General and the South Manchuria Railway Company deployed similar strategies for representing colonized territory as already integrated into or in the process of becoming part of a Japanese national space. These modes spatialized the relationship between metropolitan and colonial territory—as a synchronic economic relationship of circulation and exchange; as an allochronic relationship of progressive transition to the metropolitan present; and as an affective relationship of national people to the places of national history. The fact that these spatializations overlapped in contradictory ways—Korea and Taiwan were, for example, both becoming Japan and already part of Japanese history and the nationalist land of patriotic sentiment—did not dampen their potential as ways that imperial travelers cum national subjects could understand their own place in a Japan that included the empire. Rather, these overlapping modes offered a shifting sand of relationships that kept the place of colonized territory perpetually in question and thus served as a productive site for imperial travelers' continual reaffirmation of the legitimacy and desirability of colonial rule.

In parsing the place of the colonies through these modes, travelers and colonial boosters operated within a geography of civilization. On the one hand, they saw the space of the nation in terms of an expanding sphere of civilization centered on the inner territory. On the other hand, the territoriality of the geography of civilization was ambiguous. It defined the space of Japan as a liminal location between the universal space of civilization in colonial modernity and the particular civilization of the Japanese nation-state. Likewise, the economic mode and its representation of Japan's circulating mission in Korea, Manchuria, and Taiwan emphasized the liberatory nature of new circulatory technologies, but largely in the frame of a universal discourse of civilization. It was through history, which we discussed in this chapter and will return to in chapter 4, and language, which we will discuss in chapter 5, that colonial boosters and imperial travelers made the case that colonized lands were being incorporated into a specifically Japanese national space. This case rested on the notion that the culmination of the historical process of national expansion and integration would result in the disappearance of visible manifestations of cultural difference in Taiwan and Korea. In the South Manchuria Railway Zone, the case was less clear, though ultimately these representations too emphasized the idea that China, the Chinese people, and the ruins of Manchu history in Manchuria were residues of a dead past. In contrast, the neatly and generically "modern" architecture of Japanese-controlled cities signified the future that was to come.[90]

In their insistence on the significance of the changes in the land that the colonial governments had wrought, colonial boosters adopted the modernist notion that the assimilation or modernization of the people would follow that of the land. In the inner territory, the late nineteenth and early twentieth century would see numerous attempts to resolve the so-called social problem of industrial capitalism—persistent poverty and, with the rise of the concept of public health, the recognition that the dangers of industrialism's dark side could not be contained within its dark places—with the redesign of the urban habitat. City officials, architects, and transportation companies attempted to produce modern subjects by transforming the urban landscape into a consciously organized space that materialized an imagination of the city as a microcosm of industrial social life: open spaces, pathways that emphasized the flow and circulation of commodities over congregation, and distinct divisions of space into places of work, leisure, and residence.[91]

From one perspective, then, the production of the colonies as places both within and apart was a "spatial resolution" *(kūkanteki ketsugi)* to political economic contradictions born of global capitalism.[92] Capital accumulation and resource extraction could proceed with fewer hurdles than in the metropole. The well-being of colonized subjects was not of significant concern to the colonial governments in these early years. The Governments General were quite content to let colonized subjects die through flourishing sales of opium (a government monopoly in the Kwantung Leased Territory and Taiwan), exceedingly harsh and poorly remunerated wage labor, forms of punishment declared too barbaric for the metropole, and squalid living conditions for the lower classes that were made worse through inept government management of services such as sanitation.[93]

From another perspective, however, the overlap between colonial boosters' conceptualization of the relationship between people and land and that of urban planners in the metropole suggests that—despite the territorial-administrative differences between Korea, Taiwan, the Kwantung Leased Territory, the South Manchuria Railway Zone, and the inner territory—the spatial imaginary of the nation was for all self-consciously national subjects an act of voluntarism. In other words, the production of the colonies as problem places also required national subjects to adopt a particular spatial imaginary of the nation against which the colonies could be marked as different, "new," or "not yet" Japanese. It was a sense of self defined by a sense of place. It was an act of choosing to connect oneself to a place whose location was defined by global and national networks of circulation and nationalist metageographies and whose essence was likewise defined in the commensurable spatial and temporal terms of nations in a global world. It was this act of voluntarism that the colonial policy of assimilation sought to elicit from Taiwanese Chinese and Koreans. And it was likewise an act of voluntarism that colonial boosters and urban planners sought to elicit from metropolitan travelers.

If, in rhetoric, the ability to participate fully in the nation was a matter of voluntarily constituting one's sense of self within a new spatio-social imaginary, in practice, it was a far more complex matter. In the post–World War I era, the demand that citizens and subjects rise out of their local place would collide with a new regime of internal and external borders that disproportionately affected the mobility of colonized subjects. It was in this context of democratization and bordering that the primary axis of spatial politics would shift from a geography of civilization to a geography of cultural pluralism and the mobility of the tourist would become a central ideological mechanism through which colonial boosters produced an imperial spatial and social imaginary for a second generation of imperial subjects.

PART TWO

# The Geography of Cultural Pluralism

# 3

# Boundary Narratives

A young Korean man waited patiently on the deck of the Kōrai-maru. Three policemen stood between the third-class crowd, many of whom had emerged on deck two hours before, after a long and unpleasant night below, and the upper-class passengers, who paraded off the ship and into the waiting room of the neighboring train station. Finally, the third-class passengers were allowed to leave. The young man walked down the gangplank, searching for the detectives he suspected would be waiting for him. He tried to blend in with the Japanese passengers. He tried to not hold his breath. To no avail. Calling out "Yobo!"—a derogatory name for Koreans—the Pusan port police pulled him aside. The young man, a student at a prestigious private university in Tokyo, recognized that he could not be as brusque as he had been with the customs police in Kōbe. He silently handed over his luggage and sat down to await permission to continue on his way.[1]

The previous chapters laid out a case for treating imperial travel as both a methodology for analyzing the spatial politics of empire and a manifestation of that phenomenon. In chapter 1 we explored how the ideological work of observational travel revolved around the use of historical reenactment to produce a homogenizing and hegemonic "national" memory of and affect toward the "national land." In chapter 2, we looked at how colonial boosters used tourist guidebooks to represent colonized land as part of the space and time of the nation while *dis-placing* colonized subjects from that same land. In both cases, imperial tourism produced particular fictions that made possible travelers' internalization of a sense of self and nation that incorporated colonized lands as places within the nation and that produced affective ties to the nation as a place that contained colonized land.

The story of the Korean student on the Kōrai-maru illustrates the way in which the representation of the empire as a space of circulation—a circulating mission—elided the increasingly restrictive and unevenly applied terms under which that circulation was allowed. In 1918, the Japan Tourist Bureau, whose mission had previously been restricted to the enticement and facilitation of European and American travel to Japan, began to offer services to Japanese travelers. In subsequent years, the Japan Tourist Bureau was joined by a number of organizations, such as the South Manchuria Railway Company's Korea-Manchuria Information Bureau, which likewise sought to facilitate the travel of metropolitan residents to the so-called new territories. An imperial tourism industry was born.

In terms of its central methodology—the observation of colonized lands through the particular categories of colonial modernity—the kind of travel practices that the imperial tourism industry promoted were not significantly different from those of the observational travel that came before. Yet in another sense, tourism differed sharply. Whereas the founders of observational travel had understood its ideological work to be intimately connected to the elite status of the travelers, the mission of Japan's domestic tourism industry was to promote the travel of the masses. Financial considerations meant that this ideal was never achieved, but the shift in rhetoric and orientation was profoundly significant in shaping the meaning of imperial tourism in the context of an empire in which the distinction between being a "subject" and being a "citizen" was increasingly drawn in motion.

National belonging in imperial nations was a complex process that involved the negotiation of legal and subjective notions of nationality, subjecthood, and citizenship.[2] As Tessa Morris-Suzuki writes, the post–World War I years saw "the tendency for most colonial empires to develop an increasingly sharp distinction between the formal status of nationality (shared by all or most inhabitants of the empire) and substantive citizenship (rights to participate in the political process, which were unequally distributed between colonizers and colonized)."[3] In the Japanese Empire, one of the key ways in which this growing divide was experienced was through mobility. This is perhaps best illustrated by the Japanese state's work to deny Korean independence activists access to the Paris Peace Conference, where they were expected to press their case for Korean independence. In December 1918, Syngman Rhee, future president of the Republic of Korea, and Chŏng Han-gyŏng (Henry Chung), applied to the U.S. State Department for passports in order to travel to Paris. The State Department recognized that, under international law, the men were subjects of the Japanese state. The State Department then forwarded their application to the Japanese consulate, where it was promptly denied.[4] Rhee and Chŏng were simultaneously recognized as Japanese nationals and denied the rights of Japanese citizenship. Indeed, activists in other contexts also articulated the difference between imperial subjecthood and citizenship on precisely this axis. Addressing his writing to the population of newly enfranchised voters in the metropole following the passage of universal male suffrage in 1925, Taiwanese Chinese activist Cai Peihuo complained that Taiwanese Chinese—and only Taiwanese Chinese—were not allowed to travel directly from Taiwan to China but instead had to route their travel through the inner territory.[5]

The ideological work of tourism emerged in conversation with its denial of the differential mobility of colonized subjects. In this way, mobility came to serve as one of the axes along which travelers experienced the difference between subjecthood and citizenship as well as an axis along which the boundaries of citizenship were enforced. In its promotion of tourism as the work of all national people, the imperial tourism industry defined free mobility within the empire as one of the core or shared values of the nation.[6] Yet the frustrations of immobility became a common theme through which colonized subjects articulated their own experiences of disenfranchisement and racialization. It was in motion that they encountered this new understanding of colonial difference. In contrast, it was in motion that imperial travelers came to see themselves as "at home" anywhere in the empire.

## FROM A GEOGRAPHY OF CIVILIZATION TO A GEOGRAPHY OF CULTURAL PLURALISM

Practices and experiences of movement defined the contours of national identity in the context of an empire rapidly shifting from a project of territorial acquisition to one of territorial maintenance. Indeed, movement is particularly important to our story, because it is here—in motion—that we begin to see the transition from a geography of civilization, which conceptualized colonial difference primarily in terms of the expansion of the space of the nation over time and the concomitant erasure or "assimilation" of colonial cultures, to a geography of cultural pluralism, which envisioned Japan as a variegated nation of diverse cultural regions. If, under the geography of civilization, the social imagination of the imperial nation was one that equated the Japanese nation with Japanese culture and Japanese history, the dominant social imaginary of the geography of cultural pluralism was of Japan as a multinational state and the Japanese people as a multiethnic nation.[7]

Around the world, cultural pluralism was a response to competing, often oppositional positions as migrants and colonized subjects challenged nativist discourses of assimilation. For this reason, Mae Ngai refers to it as an "immigrant intervention" in the case of the United States.[8] But cultural pluralism was also an imperial intervention to stave off self-determination's threat to the legitimacy of an imperial imaginary grounded in assimilationist models of civilization and national culture. The post–World War I era saw a turn to regionalism and cultural pluralism around the globe as empires struggled to address the intertwined crises of economic depression, labor activism, and anti-imperial and anticolonial activism.[9] In interwar

France, as in Japan, the nation was increasingly understood as a matter of "unity in diversity," which, in the words of Gary Wilder, both "reflected the confidence of an organized empire at the height of its power" and "revealed the anxiety of a colonial project . . . facing an imminent crisis of colonial authority."[10] In the Soviet Union, planners debated how to articulate the relationship between Russia and its multinational peripheries, shifting between what Francine Hirsch has termed the "ethnographic" and "economic" principles of administrative-territorial division. The former argued that internal territorial divisions should follow ethnographic boundaries—in essence, arguing for a multinational state. The latter, by contrast, suggested organizing the empire in terms of economic expediency and a dismissal of national rights, such as self-determination.[11] Uniting the two was the common vision of a state defined by regional diversity rather than homogenizing national expansion.

Within the framework of the multinational state and the culturally pluralistic nation, one of the key terms for both imperialists and anticolonial activists was *mobility*.[12] Under the terms of the post–World War I geography of cultural pluralism, national belonging increasingly revolved around intersubjective claims to "in-placeness" in the empire and its opposite, the official and unofficial denials of the mobility of colonized subjects. Imperial tourist literature and imperial travelers expressed these claims through representations of the national subject as a traveling citizen and themselves as deracinated national people *(kokumin)*. In contrast, colonized subjects, particularly those who circulated within the elite institutions of imperial society, pointed to the state's denial of their own right to circulate freely within the empire as a defining feature of their status as colonized subjects. It exposed the lie at the heart of the assimilationist ideal—speak Japanese, orient your life around circulation and exchange, think of yourself as Japanese, and you will become Japanese. Instead, the contrast between the free mobility of ethnic Japanese subjects and the restricted mobility of colonized subjects showed an empire that was quickly moving from treating colonial difference as a matter of time and development to treating colonial difference as a matter of race and place.

## A CRISIS OF EMPIRE

The end of World War I brought political and economic challenges to empires around the world. In the British Empire, deflation lowered the value of the raw materials the empire extracted from its colonies, while, in the aftermath of the destruction caused by the war, the military and financial cost of maintaining colonial rule appeared suddenly steeper and, for some, undesirable or even unsustainable.[13] The economic crisis felt around Europe was matched by an equally powerful challenge to the rhetoric and legitimacy of imperialism's civilizing missions. While Woodrow Wilson did not invent the principle of nationality, his 1918 Fourteen

Points speech suggested a framework—a league of nations—within which such an ideal might be translated into a reality. Anticolonial activists around the globe quickly incorporated the ideal into their movements.[14]

It is important to recognize, however, that the principle of nationality appealed to imperialists as well as to anti-imperial nationalists. As Susan Pedersen writes, the establishment of the League of Nations was not the end of the question of empire but rather the beginning of a new era of its discussion.[15] The early years of the league were dominated by high-stakes discussion about how to reconcile wartime territorial conquests with the ideal of liberal internationalism. The crisis of empire was not so much whether imperialism would continue but of what form it would take. Territorial conquest and direct rule, as in France and Italy? Or the establishment of imperial commonwealths that fostered semi-independent governments whose economic and foreign relations were largely determined by the demands of the imperial metropole, as was advocated by the United States and Britain? The distinction was a bit facetious, as each empire maintained colonial holdings that were territorialized in multiple ways. The League of Nations even added a new category, that of "mandated territory," to the menu of imperial options.

The World War I years and their aftermath were a time of intense social and political turmoil in Japan. Japan emerged from the war much stronger—economically, politically, and territorially. Japan was now a global military power and a creditor nation with a primarily industrial economy. At the same time, Japan's rise to Great Power status did little to quell the discomfort with imperialism that had shaped discourses of Japanese colonialism since the colonization of Taiwan in 1895. If the need to differentiate the Japanese Empire from Western empires had initially kept the Japanese government from formally designating Taiwan, and later Korea, as "colonies" (shokuminchi), the economic and political crises of the post–World War I era brought to the fore the contradiction between the designation of Taiwan, Korea, and Manchuria as unique administrative territories in name and their treatment as colonies of exploitation and settlement in fact. Moreover, institutions such as the colonial education and legal systems, which had been established in the name of assimilation, were increasingly glaring markers of colonial discrimination. Ironically, colonial tours of the metropole, which were supposed to make colonized subjects see themselves as a part of Japan, sometimes led them to recognize the degree to which they were not.[16]

If, in the first years of territorializing a Japanese national identity on colonized land, it had been possible to imagine that assimilation would simply disappear colonized peoples from colonized lands, in the years during and after World War I, anti-imperial and anticolonial activism made such a vision increasingly hard to sustain. In Taiwan, Taiwanese Chinese activists pursued both violent and nonviolent strategies. The Government General suppressed the violent rebellions brutally.[17] Nonviolent movements were allowed more leeway. Inspired by the contradictions between the imperial rhetoric of "all subjects are equal under the emperor's gaze" and the reality of colonial discrimination, Taiwanese Chinese elites began a campaign for full assimilation into the institutions and opportunities of the metropole in the mid-1910s. When the assimilation movement was unsuccessful, they shifted to an even more vociferous campaign for self-rule, which became known as the Movement for a Taiwan Parliament (Taiwan gikai).[18]

In Korea, activists rejected the deferred promises of imperial assimilation and instead launched an anti-imperial independence movement in the name of the Korean nation. The 1919 uprising, known as the March First Movement, took Japanese colonial authorities completely by surprise. On March 1, 1919, a day set aside to commemorate the recent death of the Korean king, Kojong, Korean students and activists submitted a declaration of independence to the Government General. The language of the declaration was the language of self-determination, which tied the Korean nation to the Korean territory: Korea was a nation of "twenty million united people" who had a history of over "forty-three centuries."[19] As they read the declaration out loud in Keijō's Pagoda Park and elsewhere in the city, the crowds grew into massive protests around the peninsula. The Government General responded with a violent suppression campaign that left 150 Koreans dead and five hundred injured in the first six weeks alone.[20]

In China, students challenged Japan's economic dominance and foreign impingements on China's economic and territorial integrity. In 1919, not long after the March First Movement touched off battles in Korea, student leaders demanded an end to the Great Powers' infringement on Chinese sovereignty through such practices as extraterritoriality and concessions. They made Japan a specific target of their activism, demanding that the League of Nations refuse Japan's Twenty-One Demands—through which Japan had converted its twenty-five year leasehold in southern Manchuria into a ninety-nine year lease in 1915—and compel Japan to return the former German concession of Shandong to full Chinese sovereignty, which the Treaty of Versailles had transferred to Japan after Germany's loss in World War I.[21] When the Paris Peace Conference refused to acquiesce to Chinese demands, what had been a single protest on May 4 exploded into a full-fledged nationalist movement whose influence extended long into the twentieth century.[22]

In the face of anticolonial and anti-imperial activism in the colonies, the colonial and imperial governments searched for ways to defuse the political conflicts that the structure of colonial rule created without ending colonialism itself. One approach was the liberalization of rule. In 1918, Hara Takashi took office as the first "party" prime minister, the first prime minister to be chosen by the majority political party in the Diet. Hara had long critiqued the Government General system and its institutionalization of the colonies as territorial-administrative exceptions to the Constitution. As prime minister, Hara advocated a policy of "extending the metropole" (naichi enchō) in order to normalize the position of

Korea and Taiwan within the Japanese political and legal systems. By promoting liberal institutions throughout the empire, Hara argued that the policy of extending the metropole would "[turn] Koreans from the Koreans of old into new Japanese citizens *(kokumin)*, which will bring about their happiness and development."²³

Similarly liberal policies were applied in Korea and Taiwan. In Korea, the Government General pursued a policy of "cultural rule," which replaced the previous policy of military rule. Colonial officials opened the door for Korean participation in and advancement within the colonial system through a vernacular press, schools and universities for Koreans, and the admittance of Koreans to the colonial police force. As Michael Robinson argues, these measures were designed to function as an "escape valve" for anticolonial sentiment amongst the Korean population. It also delimited the boundaries within which Koreans could express a distinct cultural and political identity.²⁴ In Taiwan, the policy of extending the metropole led to the appointment of Den Makoto, the first civilian governor general, in 1919 and the revision of Law 63 by the Diet to allow for the wider application of inner territory laws to Taiwan and a reduction in the number of ordinances issued by the Government General.²⁵

The second approach to the growing political conflict within the empire was a kind of cultural pluralism, known as "harmony" *(yūwa)*. In its ideal form, harmony suggested the peaceful coexistence of the many ethnic groups within the Japanese Empire. First introduced by the Governor General of Korea as *naisen yūwa* (Japan-Korea harmony) in the aftermath of the March First Movement, it quickly became associated with the post–World War I civil morality of the imperial state. Japanese students in the metropole wrote essays on how best to achieve Japan-Korea harmony; Japanese settlers in Keijō established a Dōminkai (Association of same people) to further harmonious interactions between Koreans and the Japanese in the colony; and the colonial governments began promoting intermarriage as a way of achieving, on the level of the family, ethnic harmony and integration. In practice, colonized subjects saw quickly that harmony was a new ideological tool for compelling colonial subservience to imperial rule rather than a commitment to actual multiculturalism. One Korean member of the Dōminkai wrote in 1924, "The Japanese constantly harp on *naisen yūwa* and urge Koreans to promote harmony . . . while flaunting special privileges and a sense of superiority."²⁶ Hamada Tsunenosuke, a former chief of the Bureau of Colonial Affairs who traveled around the empire in 1924, exposed a similar logic of cultural pluralism operating in Taiwan. Noting most shops had closed for the New Year's holiday, Hamada was surprised to find a number of shops still open. They were operated by Taiwanese Chinese, and, while bright and well run, such a failure to observe a national cultural holiday was "yet another example of how inner territory–Taiwan harmony has yet to be achieved."²⁷

## BREAKING BOUNDARIES

The transition from observational travel as a self-consciously elite activity to imperial tourism as a practice for all national subjects took place in the context of increasing challenges to the core-periphery structure of the empire. As anti-imperial and anticolonial movements demanded new ways of drawing boundaries within and without the empire, the imperial tourism industry began suggesting to Japanese travelers that the empire was in fact a border-less space.

Imperial tourism trafficked in boundary narratives, that is, in stories that travelers used to make sense of the social collective to which they belonged and to define the boundaries of that sense of self and collective identity.[28] Unlike the traditional formulation of boundary narrative, however, tourism's narratives did not focus on boundaries as borders between different peoples or customs. Rather, tourism's boundary narratives told the story of how the infrastructure of tourism broke the social and topographical barriers that divided the Japanese nation. In this sense, imperial tourism offered a sense of self, social collective, and space that mapped neatly on to the notion of the nation as a horizontal community of national people who occupied a particular place on the globe.

The vision of the nation as a horizontal community undergirded the liberalization of Japanese government in the 1910s and 1920s. It also reflected the dramatic change in the economic structure of the country over the course of World War I—from primarily agrarian to primarily industrial, which sparked its own new industry of leisure and consumption. This culture of play did its own boundary work as it drew heavily on the notion of the "masses" to transform what had been considered uncultured amusements into commercialized experiences of "the leisure of the masses" *(minshū goraku)*.[29] Even the higher-end palaces of consumption packaged their services in the architecture of boundary breaking. To encourage frequent visits to its Nihonbashi Mitsukoshi department store Information Bureau, for example, the Japan Tourist Bureau and Mitsukoshi revamped building policies to allow patrons to enter the store without taking off or covering their street shoes.[30]

Colonial boosters' tourist guidebooks and itineraries emphasized the boundary-breaking work of infrastructure. The Government General of Korea heralded, for example, the Shimonoseki–Pusan Connecting Ferry, whose departure times were coordinated with the arrival and departure of the Shinbashi (Tokyo)–Shimonoseki Special Express Train and the Pusan–Keijō Express Train. "More than the danger of one thousand mountains and ten thousand valleys," the 1923 *Chōsen tetsudō ryokō benran* stated, "in the distant past, the hundred-*ri* [240-mile] sea route had a danger disproportionate to its distance. Between Shimonoseki and Pusan, there was an insurmountable 121-*kairi* [nautical mile] border." "But," the guidebook continued, "now it is one pipeline between the same national land—the progress of science has overcome the power of the natural world and the path hardly takes eight hours."[31] The text emphasized the parallel history of the removal of the topographic and geopolitical boundaries between Japan and Korea and the incorporation of Korea into the space of the Japanese nation. For "border," the guidebook used the word *kokkyō*, which signified a border between states. For "land of the same country," the word was *kokudo*, "national land." The connecting ferry had consolidated Korea and Japan into the same national land.

Colonial boosters likewise made the Yalu River Rail Bridge speak to the destruction of the border between Korea and Manchuria: "In addition to increasing the economic relationship of the two countries *(ryōkoku)* year by year, the transportation between the two cities of Shingishū [K. Sinŭiju] and Antō [C. Andong] has become remarkably convenient because of the footpath built into the bridge. The border has been mostly broken down and the two cities have become one."[32] The editors of the magazine *Chōsen oyobi Manshū* (Korea and Manchuria) looked forward to building a "new Japan" now that the bridge had "completely obliterated" the biggest waterway that "isolated" Korea from Manchuria.[33] In Taiwan, the completion of a railway line that ran the entire north-south distance of the island in 1908 led the new governor of Tainan, Tsuda Sōichi, to declare that the so-called Main Line railway had "assimilated" *(dōka)* Taiwan into the metropole.[34] Twenty-four years later, Tanaka Keiji, a prominent geographer and the leader of a group of geography and history teachers on an observational tour of Taiwan, used similar language to praise the Osaka Mercantile Shipping Company's new 10,000-ton class ships. Though they would operate on the Japan–Taiwan line, the ships were powerful enough to make the trip between Europe and the United States. From his perspective, "it is clear that the contribution of these ships to bringing the inner territory and Taiwan closer together is not small."[35]

The discourse of technological and infrastructural boundary breaking was mirrored by the discourse of tourism itself, which advocated for a new travel culture that broke down the barriers between elites and the masses. As Miriam Silverberg argues, the mass culture that dominated the era "presumed and produced" individuals as "consumer subjects" who engaged in subjective formation through the consumption of mass media. This act of consumption contributed to the production of subjects because media content was shaped, in more and less subtle ways, by state ideology.[36] Tourism likewise presumed and produced the individual as a citizen-traveler, who enacted his or her participation in and belonging to the nation through the practice (that is, the consumption) of travel.

Colonial boosters emphatically rejected earlier representations of imperial travel as the purview of elites. Instead, they insisted that imperial travel was the duty of all national subjects. Hayashi Takahisa, principal of Miyakonojō Higher Commercial School, articulated this sentiment in his 1931 preface to the school's report on their journeys to Korea and Manchuria. "The need to know about the colonies is not a problem that is confined to a few special people. Rather, in these days of enlightenment, it must be part of the common sense we have as national people."[37] In this phrasing, "common sense" had two meanings: one, a shared basis for making good judgments; and two, a shared sensibility of what it meant to be a national subject of Japan. Both would be facilitated through travel to the colonies. Yet Hayashi's use of *kaika* for "enlightenment," in contrast to Kanō Shigorō's use of *keihatsu* in 1906, also illustrated the shifting meaning of "national subject." In contrast to Kanō's *keihatsu*, which was associated with education, *kaika* was more closely associated with the concept of (Western) Enlightenment, and the opening of Japanese society to that Enlightenment in the late nineteenth century (known as *bunmei kaika* or "civilization and enlightenment"). In Hayashi's formulation, the "common sense we have as national people" was not a common sense that would be communicated from elite travelers to the masses, but rather a kind of knowledge that every national subject should gain for himself or herself. In this formulation, the community of national subjects was horizontal rather than hierarchical.

Indeed, one of the interventions that the Japan Tourist Bureau and its associated agencies sought to achieve with the opening of services to Japanese travelers was the democratization of travel knowledge and culture. Contributing to the fledgling industry were a host of organizations devoted to disseminating what became known as "travel culture" *(ryokō bunka),* such as the JTB's Japan Traveling Club (Nihon ryokō kurabu) and the Ministry of Railways' Japan Travel Culture Association (Nihon ryokō bunka kyōkai) and its flagship magazine, *Tabi* (Travel).[38] In the first issue of *Tabi* in 1924, Arai Gyōji, the head of the services department at the Ministry of Railways and future head of the Japan Tourist Bureau, defined the travel culture of the era as the idea that all national subjects should and could travel. He referred to the mission of the tourism industry as one of disseminating an elite travel practice to the masses. Making reference to two of the country's most famous literary travelers—Matsuo Bashō, author of the late seventeenth-century haiku collection *Oku no hoso michi* (The narrow road to the deep north), and Saigyō Hōshi, a twelfth-century poet whose poetic journeys to the north inspired Bashō's—Arai contrasted the travel cultures of earlier eras with the current moment, in which the combination of the liberalization, industrialization, and mechanization of Japanese society placed new constraints on travel at the same time that it made possible a new form of mass travel. "In a world in which the struggle for existence is so clamorous as to be blinding," Arai wrote, "traveling like Saigyō or Bashō is not something that most people are allowed. It is a pleasure that only one part of the people can enjoy." It was time, he argued, to use the power of science and civilization to make the pleasure of travel available to a great number of people, rather than the elite few. It was time not only to "democratize" *(minshūka)* travel but also to "socialize" it *(shakaika).*[39]

## TOURIST MOBILITY, COLONIZED MOBILITY

The rise of the imperial tourism industry coincided with practices that placed uneven restrictions on mobility within the empire, and it is here that we must interrogate how tourism contributed to the maintenance of empire and the reproduction of an imperial social imaginary under the new conditions that internationalism, anticolonial activism, and anti-imperial nationalism presented.

Much of the actual work of containing the threat of anti-imperial and leftist activism took place through restrictions on the circulation of people and information within the empire. The Government General of Korea imposed travel restrictions on Koreans in the immediate aftermath of the March First Movement. The restrictions, which included language-proficiency examinations, cash-on-hand requirements, and the requirement that Korean travelers present letters of certification from both their local authorities and the port police in Pusan, were sustained in official and unofficial forms until 1939.[40] The Government General of Taiwan restricted information about the Korean uprising, leading Taiwanese Chinese activist Cai Peihuo to complain: "Since March 1, 1919, you can't even say the word 'Korea' in Taiwanese media."[41] The Government General of Taiwan sustained the Taiwanese Chinese passport system, originally established in 1897 by the Qing provincial government, and imposed further measures, such as police surveillance, to track the activities of Taiwanese Chinese people in southern China.[42] Police crackdowns on the circulation of communists and communist-related materials even led to the establishment of what Annika Culver has termed an "underground railroad" between Korea and Moscow. Wary of being stopped and searched on the railway, Korean communists traveled on foot along the route of the South Manchuria Railway to bring the annual report of the Korean Communist Party to the Comintern in Moscow. Nakano Shigeharu described the route in a short story, called "To Moscow" (Mosukowa sashite), which was published in the *Musan shinbun* (Proletarian times) in 1928. Though the story was critiqued for romanticizing Korean resistance, it illustrated the way in which the representation of the empire as a space of circulation—a circulating mission—elided the increasingly restrictive and unevenly applied terms under which that circulation was allowed.[43]

The routes and itineraries that the tourism industry offered, however, hid these distinctions and instead represented the internal borders of the nation as gateways to be passed through on the way to one's destination. The Japan Tourist Bureau's 1923 itinerary for a two-week trip through Manchuria and Korea, for example, noted that travelers would undergo a customs examination at three places: at Dairen Station, when departing on northbound trains (which, although part of the Railway Zone, were covered under different tariff agreements with the Chinese government); at Antō Station, when crossing into Korea; and on the connecting ferry from Pusan to Shimonoseki.⁴⁴ The latter was to enforce internal tariffs on items such as tobacco, which were cheap in China and Korea but taxed as luxury items in the metropole.

A subsequent edition of the Japan Tourist Bureau's itinerary compendium emphasized that these examinations were necessary and were "not an inconvenient, complicated process."⁴⁵ The accuracy of this statement depended, however, on the experience of the traveler. One of the diarists on the Hiroshima Higher Normal School trip in 1915 grumbled when he could not get his tobacco through customs on the connecting ferry from Pusan. He had carefully counted his cigarette and cigar purchases and had bought less than the maximum amount in Shanghai. Yet when he presented his bag to the customs official on the ferry, the official pulled out the cigars and threw them in the garbage bin. The student was furious. "What are you doing?" he asked, his voice, according to his own report, "full of both utter amazement and anger." The customs official replied, "It is fine to bring up to one hundred cigarettes. It is also fine to bring up to fifty cigars. I am throwing one of them away." The student noted that the official delivered this news "with a cold smile." Feeling defeated, the student went back downstairs to his cabin. "When I came back up to the deck a second time," he wrote in conclusion, he saw the garbage bin, "full to the top with various kinds of tobacco."⁴⁶

Hayasaka Yoshio, who traveled through Korea, Manchuria, and China in 1922, had a rather different experience, one much more in line with the statement about customs examinations in the Japan Tourist Bureau's suggested itinerary. In a section of his travelogue entitled, "Kind Customs" (Yasashii zeikan), Hayasaka described his encounter with customs officials at Antō as he entered Manchuria from Korea. "I worried, because there were five or six boxes of Korean tobacco in my bag," but the customs official waved him through.⁴⁷ He had a similar encounter at Shimonoseki at the beginning of his trip as he waited to board the connecting ferry to Pusan. It was a completely mundane experience: "As the customs official opened my bag, he asked, 'Have any tobacco?' 'No.' 'Do you drink?' 'Sometimes.' And that was that." For Hayasaka, the bigger story was his own seasickness—he was relieved to be through with the examination so that he could lie down.⁴⁸

For both the Hiroshima student and Hayasaka, the examinations were uncomfortable experiences (at the very least). At the same time, neither of them imagined that their experience was shaped in any way by ethnicity. The Hiroshima diarist's status as an student in an elite school afforded him a certain amount of leeway when interacting with officials, and it was this sense of entitlement that allowed him to question the customs official with an angry tone of voice—he even used a grammatical construction that was somewhere in between polite and impertinent (*nani suru desu*). For Hayasaka, the customs experience was simply something to be suffered through along the way to something else.

In contrast, Korean novelist Yŏm Sangsŏp painted a picture of Kōbe–Pusan travel shaped entirely by his status as a Korean. In his short story "On the Eve of the Uprising" (Mansejŏn), which formed the basis for the vignette that opened this chapter, the protagonist, Yi Inhwa, attempts to board a ship bound for Pusan at Kōbe only to be hassled by a plainclothes customs officer on the docks. The officer peppers him with questions: "Your age? School? On what business? Destination?" "Helpless and irritated," the protagonist writes, "I wanted to ask out loud why on earth he needed to know."[49]

Retiring to the third-class bathing area on board the ship, Yi finds himself surrounded by Japanese people, who, after an initial period of attempting to determine whether the poorest-looking member of the group is Korean, strike up a conversation about the laziness and gullibility of Koreans, using the derogatory term *yobo*. Soon a Korean working for the port customs office arrives to order him off the boat with all of his belongings, so that he might be inspected and interrogated by the port police.[50] Throughout this, Yi negotiates constantly with the customs officials, who describe their own constraints—they can only open the bags in his presence, for example—alluding to the way in which the singling out of Korean travelers for special scrutiny was enacted within the confines of professional identity and respect for the rule of law. Ultimately, the officials allow him to re-board the steamer two minutes before it departs. After a journey marked by contention and conflict, Yi arrives in Pusan a day and a half later. As told at the beginning of this chapter, he attempts to disembark without drawing the notice of the port police in Pusan, but the police find him anyway and harass him one more time. In contrast to the Hiroshima student's comfort in expressing anger and disbelief at the arbitrary nature of customs enforcement on his return from Pusan to Shimonoseki, Yŏm's protagonist felt the need to adopt a strategy of conciliation at Pusan, where he felt more vulnerable than he had in the metropole.

The story of Yi Inhwa was fictional. But Yŏm's underlining of the differential mobility of travelers within the empire contained important kernels of truth.[51] On the one hand, Yŏm Sangsŏp was a Korean nationalist and socialist, who spent four months in prison for organizing protests of Korean students and laborers in Osaka in support of the March First Movement. "On the Eve of the Uprising" was a work that presented an anti-imperialist nationalist challenge to Japanese colonial rule. Yŏm also portrayed the colonial government's exploitation of class differences; Yi expresses his rage at the thought of Japanese labor recruiters deceiving Korean laborers about the wages and conditions they could expect if they contracted to work in the metropole. In this sense, the story might be read more as a manifesto than a documentary account of cross-straits travel. On the other hand, Yŏm's turn to mobility in this moment to expose the fundamental contradictions of the colonial assimilation policy and its geography of civilization illuminates how the ability to move freely throughout the empire was seen by at least some colonized subjects, particularly those who moved within the elite institutions of imperial society, as the sine qua non of full membership in the imperial nation. He attended Keiō University in Tokyo, one of the most prestigious private universities in the empire. This pathway was facilitated by his brother, who was a lieutenant in the Japanese imperial army.[52] For Yŏm, then, it was apparent that no matter how well they spoke Japanese or what prestigious institutions they belonged to, colonized subjects would be treated differently by colonial and metropolitan institutions.

Yŏm was not alone in this assessment. Writing under the name Priest Go, a Taiwanese Chinese author protested the discrimination that Taiwanese Chinese students experienced at the borders of the inner territory. Seeking to demonstrate his willing participation in the colonial regime of Japanification, one Taiwanese Chinese student—whose surname was 林, which was "Lin" in Chinese and "Hayashi" in Japanese—identified himself to customs officials at Kōbe as Hayashi. In response, Priest Go reported, the customs official rejected the student's claim to Japanese identity with the retort, "Don't try to fool me. Aren't you really a Rin?" By offering a Japanified pronunciation of the Chinese reading of the student's last name—changing "Hayashi" to "Rin"—the official insisted that the student's authentic identity was Chinese. It was incidents like these, Priest Go argued, that illuminated the contradiction in Japanese imperial society. Why should the student bother to demonstrate Japanification when people like the customs official at Kōbe would never recognize him as Japanese?[53]

At the heart of imperial tourism's ideological function was its representation of the traveling-citizen as a free subject and of space as absolute—the nation and empire as a space that one passed though regardless of body or perspective, space that existed rather than was produced. Although border officials harassed colonized subjects or sometimes even denied them passage, imperial tourist promotions described the routes of travel within the empire in universal terms, erasing the empire's internal and embodied borders. When the Osaka Mercantile Shipping Company inaugurated its new travel magazine, *Umi* (The sea), in 1924, it included a number of articles designed to teach travelers the how-tos of Taiwan travel. Articles such as "To China! To the South Seas!" advertised the company's routes between Taiwan and southern China—precisely the route that was forbidden to Taiwanese Chinese travelers without prior government permission. The article made no mention of how travel requirements differed for different populations. One might object that these were materials directed toward a particular touring audience, one from the inner territory. Yet tourist guidebooks and route advertisements were multipurpose items. The Government General of Taiwan's 1927 *Taiwan tetsudō ryokō annai*, for example, contained information on how to travel with a corpse (tip: it costs 50 percent more to travel with a corpse if you opt for an express train service).[54]

Other how-tos and travelogues for Taiwan emphasized the ease with which travelers could pass through the island's internal border between the plains areas and the Government General's special administrative zone in the central mountainous region, the so-called Savage Territory. For the indigenous peoples residing inside the special administrative zone, the border marked a line they could not cross without police permission. Colonial authorities worked hard to communicate this fact to indigenous leaders. As part of a "savage tour" *(banjin kankō)* of the island, colonial police screened a film that showed an indigenous man being electrocuted by the electrified border fence.[55] The representation of the guard line as a strict and impassable boundary elided the way in which, as Paul D. Barclay has argued, the line also worked as a "contact periphery" between Japanese officials and indigenous residents of the highlands.[56] At the same time, passage through the boundary was at the whim of and in the service of Japanese colonial rule. As Kirsten Ziomek relates in her accounting of the life of Yayutz Bleyh, even indigenous people who participated in the colonial regime found themselves stymied at times by the vagaries of the police. Bleyh—an Atayal woman who had served in the Aboriginal Affairs division of the Government General and as a translator for a group of indigenous leaders touring the metropole—applied to the Government General of Taiwan for permission to travel to the inner territory, where her common-law husband, a Japanese man, lay on his deathbed. The Government General dragged its feet and demanded more documents, delaying her travel by three months. Her husband died shortly after her arrival.[57]

Quite in contrast, Japanese travelers experienced the "savage border" as a line to be crossed. One of the most popular tourist sites in Taiwan was the village of Kappanzan, which was relatively close to the main railway and offered the chance to "survey the state of life of the savages *(banjin)*."[58] Ogi Zenzō described his experience of the border as one of frictionless passage: "Those of us who were going up [to Kappanzan] stopped at the Taikei ward office to request permission to enter the Savage Territory. As we applied, the officer called up to Kappanzan to let the office there know we were coming, and instructed us where our lodging was for the night."[59] The Japan Tourist Bureau's compendium of tourist itineraries described such an experience as the norm. Under the heading, "Observing the Savage Territory," the compendium explained that "the process is very simple—just report orally and permission will be given immediately."[60]

If touristic representations differentiated the nation of traveling-citizens at all, it was by class—first class, second class, and third class. Yet such representations also elided the common practice of ethnic differentiation that structured the railway car and steamship cabin. The third-class cabins located under the stairs on the Shimonoseki-Pusan Connecting Ferry were designated for Korean travelers. Though the ship was technically divided into three classes, Japanese travelers referred to these cabins as "fourth class."[61] As Kō Sonbon points out, even if unofficial policy did not differentiate cabins by ethnicity, income did the same work.[62] First- and second-class cabins were extraordinarily expensive, and as Akimori Tsunetarō noted in his 1935 account of travel in Korea, the Government General's policy of encouraging lower wages for Korean workers and granting "colonial bonuses" to Japanese workers meant that even third-class fares were largely unaffordable to Korean travelers.[63] Such a system was enforced in Taiwan and Manchuria as well, where railway conductors and railway guards expected Taiwanese Chinese and Chinese passengers to ride in second or third class.[64]

Imperial travelers were cognizant of this expectation, even if tourist guidebooks did not make it plain. Indeed, in one incident, it was precisely because they were riding in second or third class that a railway guard mistook a group of Tokyo Number One Higher School students for Chinese exchange students. On board a second- or third-class carriage at Eikō Station, a Japanese soldier boarded to check the cabin. "Are you all Chinese?" he asked. "We're Tokyo Number One Higher School students!" they responded, "in a high-handed manner." The soldier, determined to find out if there were in fact any Chinese people aboard the car, kept up his questioning: "Well, are you foreign students then?" The question suggested that the students were Chinese students studying at Tokyo Number One Higher School on exchange. The students just burst out laughing, for, they said, "What else could we do?"[65] For other imperial travelers, riding the third-class cars represented an off-the-beaten-path experience of imperial travel. Matsuda Kiichi, a middle-school student from Osaka, congratulated himself for riding "with the islanders" in third class as he traveled south from Kagi in 1937. The sleeping cars were full, and, he declared, he had little interest in "ordinary travel" anyway.[66]

It is possible to suggest that all of these travelers were different types of travelers—that a Taiwanese Chinese person would not consult a Government General tourist guidebook or an Osaka Mercantile Shipping Company advertisement to find out how to travel to southern China, nor would a Korean traveler consult the Japan Tourist Bureau's itinerary compendium to look for which cabins they were eligible to reserve on the connecting ferry. But the colonial governments themselves engaged in ideological work to teach colonized subjects to imagine the space of the nation as one of free movement and themselves as national subjects with the right to move freely. In that sense, imperial tourism's boundary narratives were directed at the national people as a whole even if, in practice, they applied only to a subset of national subjects. Elementary school Japanese-language textbooks produced for the Governments General of Taiwan and Korea, for example, included travelogue and letter-from-abroad readings, such as "Letter from Keijō" (Keijō dayori), "From Kiryū to Kobe" (Kiryū kara Kōbe), and "I Rode the Connecting Ferry" (Renrakusen ni notta).[67] The texts represented the territory of the state as a space within which social and topographical borders had been eliminated. "I Rode the Connecting Ferry," for example, described the journey of a Korean student and his father between Pusan and Shimonoseki. Even though the text was published in 1924, one year after the end of the official travel certification system and the beginning of unofficial restrictions on Korean movement to Japan, it did not address the common conflicts that Korean travelers and migrants faced on the connecting ferry. Instead, "I Rode the Connecting Ferry" represented the journey between Korea and the inner territory in the way that imperial travelers experienced it. The story reported none of the restrictions and interrogations that Yŏm's Yi Inhwa endured. Rather, the student's narrative described their arrival at Pusan Wharf at ten o'clock in the evening and how they quickly boarded the Tokuju-maru, one of the three sister ships that formed the third generation of connecting ferries. The story ends with their arrival in Shimonoseki at seven the next morning and their quick transfer to the local inn.[68] Like the first colonial tourist guidebooks, the elementary-school primer situated this moment of Japan-Korea travel within a progressive history of imperial transition and ever-increasing speed. They meet a friend of his father's aboard the ship who says, "When this connection was done on ships such as the Iki-maru and the Tsushima-maru [the first generation of connecting ferries], it took twelve whole hours. Now, though, they got the three ships—the Keifuku-, Shōkei-, and Tokuju-maru—and it only takes eight hours. The trip is convenient."[69]

## THE BOUNDARIES OF BOUNDARY BREAKING

For the fictional Yi Inhwa, as for real colonized travelers, the experience of internal borders within the empire was one of the rejection of shared nationality through the denial of recognition; it was one of reinforcing, or perhaps even constituting, a sense of their own place within the imperial nation. This sense of place was based not on eventual cultural assimilation but of ethnic difference. Nor was it limited to colonized subjects. Rather, when faced with boundary breaking by colonized subjects, imperial travelers reinforced the distinction between the Japanese ethnos as the empire's traveling citizens and colonized subjects as those who still required constraints. To put it bluntly, they put colonized subjects in their place.

When combined with the rhetoric of expanding the metropole and imperial harmony, ethnic discrimination in border crossing and travel fostered both a sense of collective identity among colonized subjects and a sense of the need to maintain institutional policies of ethnic differentiation among imperial travelers. One observational travel group's story illustrates how this process unfolded. The spread of travel culture to Taiwanese Chinese children impressed Tsukahara Zenki, a teacher traveling with the 1932 All-Japan Geography and History Teachers' Association trip to Taiwan. He noted, "Taiwan's islander children also enjoy playing deck billiards [shuffleboard] back and forth."⁷⁰ His fellow travelers Urakami Shūe and Yamaguchi Shunsaku recorded a rather different experience of Taiwanese Chinese travel culture with the Japanese Empire, however. Upon boarding the Yoshino-maru in Kōbe, Urakami's group noticed that the cabin that had been reserved for their party had, in fact, been "occupied" *(senryō)* by Taiwanese students *(Taiwan gakusei)*. The word that Urakami used for "occupied" was the same word associated with a military occupation, though he did not register the irony. More interesting was the students' reaction to the ship's secretary's insistence that they vacate the cabin. "When the ship's secretary tried hard to get them to change rooms, I saw the attitude of the students get very threatening. They all stood up and roared things like, 'We are also Japanese *(Nihonjin)*! We paid the same fare so what are you doing differentiating us?' while they held their canes in their hands and beat the columns and stomped their feet. Their manner was ghastly."⁷¹ Discussing the incident afterward, the travelers searched for explanations. One, based on a discussion with a Japanese official in Taiwan, was that "educating Taiwanese requires extremely careful consideration" because of the rise of anticolonial thinking among Taiwanese Chinese scholars.⁷² For others, however, the reason for the outburst was not that difficult to locate. "It wasn't a mystery at all why they did something like this," Yamaguchi Shunsaku wrote. "Afterward, I heard that islanders are prejudiced against inner territory people."⁷³

## CONCLUSION

In the midst of a crisis of empire and nation, the Japan Tourist Bureau and other imperial transportation enterprises set about representing the empire as a space of free movement and the empire's subjects as traveling citizens within that space. Their representations elided, however, the internal and embodied borders that shaped the travel of colonized subjects within the empire. Despite imperial travelers' own embrace of boundary breaking as the foundation of observational travel, they found ways to turn a blind eye—or, in some cases, exploit—the boundaries that travel within the empire imposed on colonized subjects. Movement, in other words, should not be considered an afterthought in the history of tourism but rather a central site in which its politics, both of practice and representation, emerged.⁷⁴

In telling the history of imperial tourism from the perspective of the kind of spatial experiences it presumed and produced, I have sought to avoid what Saskia Sassen has called the "endogeneity trap" of trying to explain the significance of a phenomenon solely by the studying the phenomenon itself.⁷⁵ Indeed, a central aspect of the ideology of imperial tourism was its representation of the national people as traveling citizens. Writing, then, of a history of tourism that focused solely on the experiences and movements of the empire's most powerful subjects would re-create rather than challenge the spatial politics of empire. Instead, this chapter has shown how the ideological work of tourism emerged in conversation with its erasure of the differential mobility of subjects. In this way, mobility came to serve as one of the axes along which travelers understood their own status as "citizens" as well as an axis along which the boundaries of citizenship were enforced.

Though imperial tourism represented mobility as a project of increasingly convenient point-to-point travel, the uneven experiences of intra-imperial borders illuminate the fact that "contact zones" do not occur solely at a traveler's destination. The differentiation of space into discrete and internally homogenous "familiar" and "alien" places is its own kind of fiction. Yet it was one that would become increasingly central to the work of territorializing a Japanese national identity on colonized land—and to the conceptualization and enactment of colonial difference. Imperial tourism's erasures expose how everyday practices of distinction increasingly marked Korean, indigenous, Taiwanese Chinese, and Chinese bodies as subject to special scrutiny. While in their journeys to battlefields and other sites in the nationalist mode, imperial travelers treated national membership as a performative and affective category, through their own encounters with the growing internal borders of the empire, colonized subjects demonstrated that membership in the nation was a matter of recognition as well.

The differentiation of travelers based on ethnicity and place was the underside of the liberalization policies and "harmony" rhetoric that Japanese officials deployed in the face of growing anti-imperial and anticolonial activism. As harmony activists envisioned it, ethnic difference was a value if it could be contained within the nation. What was required was the recognition of the different strengths that each ethnic group brought to the nation and the embrace by all groups of certain shared values. Those promoting liberalization policies likewise recognized the existence of distinct ethnicities within the nation, arguing that the extension of the legal and political institutions of the metropole would create a homogenous space of the nation within which local ethnic populations could achieve "happiness" as Japanese nationals while retaining their ethnic identities.

As colonized travelers experienced it, however, the rhetoric of the nation as a homogenous space encompassing the entire empire did not live up to the reality. Ethnicity and place were linked—it was not only their identity as Taiwanese Chinese that made Taiwanese Chinese travelers subject to special scrutiny. It was also their attempt to travel from Taiwan to the inner territory—to move from the place that official policy insisted they belonged, to a place where official policy and unofficial practice constituted them as alien. Likewise, it was not just in movement that Korean travelers found themselves relegated to a lower class of service. It was in movement along the empire's rail and steamship lines, which the "circulating mission" discourse of Japanese colonialism constituted as the space of a civilized

Japanese nation in contrast to that of colonized subjects, who were out of place in the space of civilization.

The geography of cultural pluralism was thus both a weapon and a tool. For anticolonial and anti-imperial activists, the idea that Taiwan and Korea were distinct cultural regions with distinct ethnic populations served as the basis for powerful challenges to the structure of Japanese imperial rule. For colonial boosters and imperialists, however, the same concept became a way of envisioning a future Japanese imperial nation that fully integrated the new territories and their peoples at the same time that it used notions of place to reinforce an ethnic and cultural hierarchy within the nation.

# 4

# Local Color

In 1935, an article entitled "Going to the Korea of White Robes" (Hakui no Chōsen o iku) appeared in the popular Japanese magazine *Tabi*. The article's byline credited the account to Kobayashi Chiyoko, and while the article provided no biographical information, it is likely that the author in question was, in fact, the famous singer of the same name. She had recently recorded the first Japanese version of the Korean folk song "Arirang" for the label Nippon Victor. Its lyrics and melody evoked a Korea curated for the Japanese colonial imagination—a land of "simplicity, melancholy, and wit" that was also a "reflective mirror" of Japan's modernity through which Japanese people could connect to the "primeval emotions and lifeways" of an imagined premodern Japan.[1]

The Japan Tourist Bureau sent Kobayashi to the peninsula as its special correspondent. Like her version of "Arirang," Kobayashi's description of Korea represented the colony as both exotic and familiar. "You'll be surprised to find that just by crossing one sea, there are scenery and customs that are so different," she wrote.[2] The Korea of white robes was a leisurely place, a preindustrial paradise. The white-robed men were not just Koreans, they were emblematic of Korea itself—slow and unchanging, a land that was both close to and far away from what a subsequent correspondent referred to as "the rapidly changing inner territory" of the Japanese Empire.[3]

In the late 1920s the geography of civilization gave way to a geography of cultural pluralism. From Taiwan to the inner territory to Manchuria, imperial tourism shifted away from representing the place of the colonies in terms of their progress toward Japanification and industrialization and instead offered the experience of "local color" as its primary product. No longer was the value of the first-hand

FIGURE 8. "Hakui no Chōsen e yuku" (Going to the Korea of white robes). The cover to Kobayashi Chiyoko's special report on travel to Korea linked culture and territory by placing a typical colonial image of a Korean man above a map of the Korean peninsula.
SOURCE: *Tabi* 1935, no. 7. Courtesy of the Japan Travel Bureau Library of Tourism Culture.

experience of the colonies solely the observation of their incorporation into the circulatory pathways of civilization or their place in the national land. Rather, colonial boosters and imperial travelers increasingly portrayed the importance of imperial travel as the sensory experience of regional difference that it offered.

In emphasizing the value of regional difference to the national people, local color representations like Kobayashi's suggested a spatial and social imaginary of Japan that integrated colonized lands and peoples into a Japanese nation that was now understood to be a variegated space of diverse and commensurable cultural regions and a national body composed of multiple ethnic nations. This new spatio-social imaginary posited an elevated status for those citizens who could make use of regional difference, for it was those who circulated throughout the empire who could contribute their experience of Japan's diversity to the wealth, knowledge, and well-being of the nation. The emphasis on circulation changed the meaning of observation as well, which now was not only observing the sight at hand but also appreciating the differences between regions and peoples.[4]

Local color tourism invoked new modes of territorial incorporation and modified the old. Tourist materials no longer erased colonized subjects from the prescriptive lists of sights that defined each territory. Rather, local color introduced an ethnographic mode of territorial incorporation, advertising the observation of colonized subjects as a fundamental component of the experience of regional difference.[5] The historical mode adopted "indigenous peoples" *(genjūminzoku)* as the subject of the regional histories of Taiwan, Korea, and Manchuria, while the nationalist mode emphasized the necessity of preserving diverse regional landscapes for the well-being of the national people. Most significant, however, were the modifications to the economic mode, which now treated commodities as natural resources endemic to particular regions rather than products made marketable through Japanese industrial know-how. Local color likewise represented physical labor as a product of the natural aptitudes of particular peoples rather than as an unfortunate holdover from a previous nonindustrialized era. In this, local color suggested a spatial and social imaginary of the Japanese nation that defined it as an economic body whose relations were constituted through a "mutual exchange of advantages" between ethnic groups and cultural regions.[6]

Local color's treatment of culture as something that one could consume reflected a broader shift to an everyday life defined by commodities and consumption, what has been called the rise of the *kokumin* as "consumer-subject" as well as citizen-subject in the late 1920s.[7] Mass culture even—or, perhaps, especially—commodified sentiment through the production of consumers' desire for "the new," which, in the case of local color tourism, manifested as a desire for "the exotic old."[8] What distinguished local color tourism from other examples of the "erotic grotesque nonsense" culture of the mass consumption era, and what makes it central to the analysis of the spatial politics of Japanese imperialism, however, is that local color was about the consumption of place. Local color represented particular identities as endemic to particular territories in a manner that took both the territories and the identities outside of History.

The exhortation to imperial travelers to consume the nation's local colors necessarily involved them in the broader struggles of imperial and anti-imperial nationalism that shaped the 1920s and 1930s as the empire transitioned from an era of territorial acquisition to one of territorial maintenance. With the notable exceptions of anarchists such as Sin Ch'ae-ho in Korea and proletarian internationalists like Nakanishi Inosuke, who imagined politics to be an unstable conflict between classes and individuals imbricated in multiple subject positions, the conflict over the future of the imperial nation-state could not but invoke territorialized identities as the basis for political legitimacy.[9] Native ethnographers used local color to foment ethnic nationalism in Japan, and Korean anti-imperial nationalists used it to lay claim to an independent Korean nation in Korea. Representatives from Japan's "second cities" used it to challenge the dominance of Tokyo in the determination of Japanese culture at the same time that Taiwanese Chinese activists used it to demand self-rule.[10] The Japan Tourist Bureau used local color to emphasize the need for continued colonial rule in Taiwan, while the Japanese Kwantung Army used it to justify the formal separation of Manchuria from China and the establishment of the putatively independent state of Manchukuo. If the geography of civilization had emphasized the transformational power of History over custom, local color flipped this relationship on its head to argue that Culture and Ethnos were ontological properties of territory that must be protected from History.

The use of local color to fight so many different political battles suggests the further naturalization of the territorialized nation as the global archetype of political community. At the same time, it illuminates how such a concept could also be used to naturalize a multinational state that legitimated past colonialism in the name of future protection and prosperity. Indeed, it was precisely local color's utility to several movements—the imperial national, the anti-imperial nationalist, and the anticolonial liberal—that made local color tourism such an important political tool. In an era when anti-imperial and anticolonial activists took to newspapers, magazines, and even children's literature to challenge the legitimacy of Japanese imperialism and, in some cases, of nationalism and the territorial nation-state, local color suggested a way of seeing the nation not as a project of future homogenization but as a constructed cultural body. Culture, in this context, was understood as both the ontological local culture of the state's diverse regions as well as the voluntarist culture of the nation as a whole. Such a project naturalized the territoriality of the nation as a composite of its territorialized subcultures, which were represented as inseparable from the environment that had forged them. In its claim to protect and curate the empire's diverse regional cultures, local color provided a raison d'être for a liberal, imperial state that superseded the logic of national self-determination.[11] Local color tourism naturalized this new imaginary by emphasizing the sensory experience of difference between places—now understood to be static and fixed—and encouraged travelers to reproduce this imaginary through the act of appreciating the complementary capacities and commodities that each region and ethnic nation had to offer.

This chapter shows how colonial boosters used the idea of local color to articulate a vision of Japan as a nation and empire of diverse yet complementary regions in Korea, Manchuria, and Taiwan. It focuses on two of local color's common terms, *labor* and *landscape*. It was through these interlinked terms that colonial boosters transformed the threat that colonized subjects posed to the legitimacy of the Japanese Empire into an argument for the authenticity of a multiethnic nation of Japanese *kokumin* that nevertheless incorporated colonized lands and peoples on uneven terms. Though histories of the sublime—a sensory experience of beauty or grandeur that inspires awe—suggest that the production of a romantic landscape relied on the erasure of visible labor, central to local color's spatial politics was the territorialization of a hierarchical social imaginary through the figure of the indigenous laborer.[12] Colonial boosters used local color to define the empire's ethnic nations as essentially "from" a particular territory while at the same time representing the imperial nation as the complementary union of an imperial division of labor and natural resources. Such representations constituted the colonies as places within and yet somehow apart from the nation by positing an imperial social imaginary in which relations between ethnic nations were defined as a mutual exchange of advantages between the empire's regions and peoples. They also fostered new forms of dispossession in the name of "appreciating" the differences between the natural aptitudes and diverse histories of each region. The chapter traces the contours of local color in Korea, Taiwan, and Manchuria to illuminate how the representation of land and labor used specific political conflicts over the future of each territory as a resource for reproducing place-images that fueled, rather than undercut, imperial travelers' sense of the "newness" of the colonies.

## THE SECOND GENERATION PROBLEM

Behind colonial boosters' enthusiasm for local color was a hint of exasperation. The second generation of imperial tourists had grown up on the accounts of the first—accounts that described Korea, Manchuria, and Taiwan as places that felt, looked, and smelled different from Japan—and it was this experience of difference that they sought to acquire through travel. Yet the geography of civilization framed these experiences of difference as uniformly negative. While travelers were perfectly willing to recognize the modernization of colonial infrastructure, industry, and governance, they experienced colonial differences as negatives—aspects of colonial life that needed to be ameliorated before the colonies could truly become part of the Japanese nation. It was this negative valuation of difference that Matsukawa Jirō pointed to in his 1925 guidebook, *Shi go nichi no tabi* (Four- and five-day trips). While Western-style buildings and street cars made the city center of Keijō "far more splendid than the city of Kyōto," the city's native differences lingered: "in the places where in between [the street cars and autobuses] white-robed Koreans *(Senjin)* lumber around, carrying tobacco pipes that might as well be three feet long, there is the unmistakable color *(kara)* of Korea," he wrote. "If you take one step from the flourishing [central] district toward the poorer quarters, you are led to a squalid Korean town where the streets are narrow, and low houses made of dirt are jumbled together."[13] It was likewise this negative sense that sparked protest from one alumnus of Miyakonojō Higher Commercial School, who resided in Keijō. Major changes had taken place in the colony in the last ten years, including the construction of a new Government General Building, the widening of roads, and the introduction of asphalt. But, he complained, the country had not yet taken notice. "It is my strong desire," he asserted, "to see this travelogue used throughout the country and to see it introduce the true conditions of Korea-Manchuria widely throughout the realm."[14] Itō Ken, a prolific literary critic, voiced a similar complaint in his 1935 *Taiwan annai* (Guide to Taiwan): "[The Japanese] *(Nihonjin)* lack clear and correct knowledge of this complete picture. If you immediately think of 'savages,' 'venomous snakes,' 'bad illness,' or 'terrible heat' when someone says 'Taiwan,' it must be said that you are very ignorant. If you are Japanese, then it really is an embarrassment not to truly know Taiwan."[15]

Japanese settlers in the colonies found themselves fighting against a metropolitan imaginary that turned the terms of the geography of civilization against them. In the early 1920s, movements against Law 63 and Law 30—the laws that empowered the governors general of Korea and Taiwan to issue ordinances without the involvement of a parliament—gained strength as organizations of Japanese settlers joined with elite colonized subjects to advocate for the full incorporation of the colonies into the metropolitan political and legal systems. Yet in 1925, colonial residents found themselves further excluded from the imperial polity when a universal male suffrage bill was passed that formally denied residents of Korea, Taiwan, and Manchuria the right to vote in national parliamentary elections. Whereas, previously, suffrage had been based on tax qualifications, thus limiting the electorate to some five percent of the population, the 1925 act defined eligibility by age, sex, and place of residence. Only males twenty-five years and older whose official place of residence was in the inner territory could vote. The act thus enfranchised many colonized subjects residing in the metropole but excluded Japanese residents of Korea, Taiwan, and Manchuria. The act also, however, mandated a full year of residency at the voter's current place of residence, a rule that disproportionately disenfranchised the heavily Korean community of migrant laborers in the metropole.[16] The exclusion frustrated many settler and colonized elites, who continued to debate whether the best route toward achieving a political voice would be by demanding complete assimilation (the policy known as *naichi enchō*) or by seeking autonomy from the metropole in the form of local parliaments and self-rule, the strategy taken by the largely Taiwanese Chinese activists who participated in the movement for a Taiwan parliament.[17]

In both Korea and Taiwan, colonial elites chaffed against the continuation of the Government General system, which had been justified, in part, by the argument that colonized peoples were not civilized enough to participate in liberal government.[18] In Korea, the Government General was challenged by a nascent coalition of Japanese and Korean commercial elites, who opposed the government's proposal to maintain Korea as an agricultural appendage of Japan. Seeking a stronger voice in governing the colony, they rejected the notion that the political status of the entire territory should reflect the popular—and, they claimed, often inaccurate—notions of the developmental status of colonized subjects. In Taiwan, the lines of conflict were drawn differently. Taiwanese Chinese elites opposed the continuation of the Government General system, while Japanese settlers largely supported it as an important source of their special privileges on the island.[19] Yet as Itō Ken's complaint shows, even as settlers argued that Taiwanese Chinese people should remain second class citizens, they too argued that the geography of civilization ought to be replaced with a new spatio-social imaginary that treated the territory of Taiwan as fully part of the Japanese nation. In Manchuria, Japanese settlers in Dairen feared both the rise of Chinese nationalist claims to Manchuria and the Japanese government's apparent lack of commitment to Japan's "special interests" in Manchuria. A number of settlers campaigned vigorously for election to parliamentary office in order to protect these special interests and won five seats in the 1928 election. (The suffrage law prevented Japanese residents of Manchuria from voting, but these settlers were able to bypass that restriction on their voices by running for office—the residency requirement for holding office was determined by the location of one's household registry rather than actual place of residence.) As Emer O'Dwyer points out, the significance of the election was to be found not so much in the election of Japanese residents of Manchuria to the Diet, but in the political parties' adoption of the concerns of Japanese settlers in Manchuria and elsewhere as a core component of their own platforms.[20]

If colonial elites found themselves frustrated that the uneven geography of empire was likely to continue for a second generation, metropolitan officials and colonial administrators likewise found themselves confronting the prospect of a second generation of colonized subjects who had little patience for the empire's empty promises. Though they were not threatened by the renewal of Laws 63 and 30 or disenfranchised by the Universal Suffrage Act, government officials were tasked with maintaining the viability of imperialism in an increasingly hostile domestic and international environment. Hamada Tsunenosuke, the former chief of the Bureau of Colonial Affairs, noted this in his 1928 report on travel to Taiwan:

> Among today's young students . . . there are those who have embraced treachery, using big exaggerations like so-called ethnic self-determination *(minzoku jiketsu),* Taiwan self-rule, or Taiwan independence. And there's also a group of inner territory people like members of the Diet who fan [their anger]. These guys think it's a good thing and run around making noise. The hot-blooded youth go along with the crowd. The problem gets bigger. Won't it be the case then that before too long phrases like 'establish a Taiwan parliament,' just like phrases like 'independence for Korea,' [will] penetrate the minds of elementary school children? That's what I worry about.
>
> I'm convinced that probably nothing will happen with the current generation of islanders. But what about the second generation? It seems as if they're heading in the direction of absolutely opposing the Government General's policy of assimilation, and inviting the result of that opposition. This is the thing that I can't stop being afraid of.[21]

Within the borders of the Japanese imperial state, the moral renewal of imperialism revolved around the concept of "harmony" *(yūwa).* Officials hoped that the pursuit of harmony would mitigate anti-imperial activism among colonized subjects by encouraging Japanese citizens to appreciate more actively the virtues of colonized subjects. Harmony associations in Osaka and Yokohama, two cities with large populations of Korean workers, for example, encouraged students to write essays about their feelings toward Koreans and Chinese people and, in particular, to emphasize the contributions that each ethnic group made to the imperial whole. The associations saw composition as a particularly powerful vehicle for achieving the internalization of a multiethnic national identity because, like reports on imperial travel, the essays required students to write in the first person.[22] Reforming the attitudes of the second generation of imperial subjects would also, officials hoped, help with the growing second-generation problem among colonized subjects by decreasing the instances of overt interethnic antagonism.[23]

But the challenges could not all be fixed with adjustments to the public image of empire or to its prescribed method of interethnic relations. Colonized subjects also challenged the empire to live up to its own rhetoric. Writing a few years after Hamada, Taiwanese self-rule activist Cai Peihuo argued that assimilation's promise of eventual inclusion had brought the empire to an inevitable turning point. "Is this what the imperial command of 'all subjects are equal under the emperor's gaze' is supposed to mean?" he asked. He described in detail how the Government General of Taiwan's sugar monopoly artificially lowered the prices that Taiwanese Chinese farmers could get for their crops. "In this era of popular rights, in one corner of a Japanese Empire that absolutely protects the right to private property," he exclaimed, "there is this place called Taiwan, where we do not have the freedom to sell the sugar cane that we ourselves have produced."[24] For Cai, the passage of universal suffrage fundamentally transformed the character of Japanese imperialism. If before it had been possible to see imperialism as the work of a small group of vested interests making decisions on behalf of a largely disenfranchised population in the colonies *and* the inner territory, after 1925, imperialism was now truly a matter of a metropole ruling over colonies. Cai argued that universal suffrage represented a turning point in the history of Japanese imperialism.

> Those of you who were in the position of being without prestige and being ruled are now suddenly in the position of controlling us. . . . While we celebrate your new life, we also eagerly hope that you will not forget the bitter and terrible taste that you experienced in the past as those who were controlled, who were underestimated and put down. . . . So as not to harm the rights that we have as human beings, we are asking of you that we be allowed to follow a different course. Why? If not, . . . Japan, whose imperialism has been dominated by a small number of vested interests, will really become in name and fact an imperialist country.[25]

The second-generation problem called into question one of the fundamental premises of Japanese imperialism—that assimilation would transform colonized peoples into new Japanese subjects and colonized territory into Japanese national land. It seemed possible that the results were not as promised. Not only was ethnic nationalism on the rise, but metropolitan residents were also stuck in their erroneous views of the colonies. As Cai argued, the extension of universal suffrage created a moment of opportunity, but one that was fraught with moral stakes. No longer could empire's contradictions be written off as a matter of time or as a project of elite vested interests—"rulers"—making decisions for the "ruled," the unpropertied and disenfranchised. From his perspective, Japanese citizens of the metropole had to either affirm Japan as a culturally pluralistic nation or accept that they were embarking on a new era of outright imperialism.

Ultimately, those who sought in this moment of democratization an end to empire were sorely disappointed. The Diet voted to renew Laws 63 and 30, the two laws that granted the Governments General of Taiwan and Korea the power to govern through ordinances rather than representative democracy. In 1929, one year after Cai's manifesto, the metropolitan government decided to bring the colonial governments under its formal control by placing the Governments General of Taiwan, Korea, the Kwantung Leased Territory, Karafuto, and Micronesia under a new ministry, the Ministry of Colonial Affairs. The decision to go forward with the Ministry of Colonial Affairs was, in some sense, a victory for imperial democracy, in that it was largely motivated by the desire of the metropolitan political parties to take control of the Governments General, especially that of Korea, by formally incorporating them into a cabinet ministry and, therefore, into the system of political spoils.[26] Yet with the establishment of the Ministry of Colonial Affairs and the official introduction of the term "outer territory" (*gaichi*) for Korea, Taiwan, Micronesia, Karafuto, and the Kwangtung Leased Territory, the metropolitan government imposed a seemingly permanent geographic hierarchy on metropolitan and colonial territory that previous policy had insisted would be temporary.[27] Three years later, in 1932, the imperial government affirmed the establishment of the state of Manchukuo, and the state's officials began constructing a history and ideology that would justify the permanent independence of Manchukuo from China and a relationship of complementary dependence with Japan.

## SEEING WITH CULTURALLY PLURALISTIC EYES

It is in this context of myriad challenges to the spatial order of empire and questions about the future of the Japanese imperial nation that we must interpret the significance of imperial tourism's turn to local color. The establishment of the Ministry of Colonial Affairs in 1929, combined with the exclusion of colonial residents from the franchise in 1925, marked the sedimentation of a territorial-administrative structure that divided metropole from colony. Yet it did so without admitting to Cai's proposition—that Japan really was "becoming . . . an imperialist country." Instead, imperial discourse increasingly emphasized that colonized subjects were also *kokumin* and that Korea and Taiwan were "regions" (*chihō*) of Japan. A similar denial of imperialism shaped the official discourse of the new state of Manchukuo, in which the government prioritized its claim to sovereignty over members of the state's "five races"—Manchurian, Mongolian, Chinese, Japanese, and Korean—with an official history that stated that Manchuria had been colonized by multiple ethnic groups and therefore no one group could claim an authentic link to the territory.[28] In this sense, the politics of local color went far beyond legitimating colonization to the construction of a new "metaethics of national life" that revolved around the triple categorization of difference as ethnic rather than temporal or socioeconomic, of ethnic identities as territorial ones, and of a new ideology of the state that located its legitimacy in its management of relations between ethnic groups and their regional "homelands."[29]

Beginning in 1927, the Japanese Ministry of Railways, the Governments General of Korea and Taiwan, and the South Manchuria Railway Company each revised their guidebooks to include numerous essays on local customs, languages, geography, and history. Previous guidebooks had not included this introductory information, considering it unnecessary. But the second generation placed it front and center. The 1927 *Taiwan tetsudō ryokō annai* included, for example, "Exotic Taiwan and the Manners and Customs of Taiwanese: A Quick Guide to Taiwan."[30] The Government General of Korea and the South Manchuria Railway quickly followed with their own local color guidebooks emphasizing the unique history, geography, and culture of the regions. The turn to regionalism extended even into the inner territory, where the Ministry of Railways produced its own local color guidebook series for Japan, which divided the inner territory into seven distinct cultural regions.[31]

Colonial boosters portrayed the change as a response to metropolitan desires. "Today's tourists don't want to only see famous sights and historic remains," wrote Mōri Motoyoshi, the director of the Keijō Tourism Association, in the magazine *Kokusai kankō* (International tourism). "They also want to have their fill of that land's *local color (rōkaru karā)* and *local attractions (rōkaru atorakushon)*."[32]

Rather than describe metropolitan desires, however, local color guidebooks and magazines took the lead in prescribing new ways of seeing the space of the nation. Consider the Keijō Tourism Association's own description of the local color of Korea: "Since the Japan-Korea annexation of 1910, all of Keijō has been completely changed. Yet although the appearances of modern culture, such as the construction of tall buildings and modern houses, the supplementing of roads, and the [modernization of] clothing, are being furnished, Korea's particular customs will add an exotic spice everywhere that will please the cameraman, starting with the ancient architecture of the Kinsei Palace at Keifukukyū, . . . the white-robed people walking on the street, the clothes-washing of the *omoni* (wives), and the *suljip* (sake shops) along the roadside."[33]

On the one hand, the Keijō Tourism Association used the Japanese readings of the names of local cities and sights to locate Korea within Japan, continuing the practice of Japanifying place names that had begun with the geography of civilization. On the other hand, the tourism association altered the framework for making meaning out of difference by treating it not as an element to be eventually eliminated but as a value to be appreciated. The tourism association represented Korea within Japan by spelling out the Korean words for "wife" and "sake shop" in *katakana*, the Japanese syllabary reserved for foreign words. Next to these words, in parentheses, the association included the Japanese characters. The tourism association also suggested that the appreciation of the value of local color was a universal characteristic of cosmopolitan—that is, modern—people. The "exotic spice" of Korea's customs would "please the cameraman," a figure who is described in terms of affect—his appreciation for cultural difference—but not ethnicity or nation. But since, as we saw in chapter 3, the ability to travel without ethnicity or nation was limited, the association's cameraman signified those who enjoyed the privileges of imperial citizenship, those who experienced travel as the act of passing through borders that defined distinct places rather than those for whom their place traveled with them. Most significant, the tourism association did not suggest that the presence of a visible Korean culture was in any way antithetical to the legitimacy of Japanese rule. The tourism association defined the culture of Korea as a commodity. It was to be consumed and transformed into value for the traveler. It was not a political or historical statement.

Colonial boosters marketed the colonies as a welcome break from the rush of life in the metropole, drawing on a notion of the sublime that was not distinct from industrialization and labor but whose value to the nation was, in fact, constituted within the temporality of industrial life. The product, in this case, was less the site itself than the affective response that the experience of difference produced. In her special report, for example, Kobayashi Chiyoko marveled at how "white-robed Koreans" epitomized not working and that "she could not help but smile." "Slowly, slowly the old white-robed Korean men put on their black hats and walk around, neither sweating nor making noise," she wrote.[34] Hamada Tsunenosuke mobilized wonder and awe in his description of laborers in Dairen's soybean oil factories. Responding to the idea that coolies wore little while they worked because they were uncivilized, Hamada argued that the nakedness was a sign of their specialized knowledge—it was not because it was too hot but because they knew that the oil would spit and get on their clothes. A neutral observer might suggest that having one's skin burnt by oil several times a day would likely motivate a more well-remunerated workforce to purchase protective attire (or, better yet, demand that it be provided by the employer). But in Hamada's retelling, the coolies were "strong" and "patient" workers. "Us inner territory people have a lot we must learn from them," he concluded.[35]

Colonial boosters and imperial travelers transposed their experiences into an imagination of the nation as a space of unique regions whose value emerged from their natural complementarity and the sensory experience of difference they offered. In 1929, the Japan Tourist Bureau advertised travel to Korea and Manchuria with the tagline "Can you see THIS in Japan?" "This" meant, "some thousands of coolies" laboring under the "white sun" at Bujun and the grand historical ruins of Hōten. But "this" also meant the "feeling of a life of freedom" that one got from looking down the Yalu River. These were all things that could "only be seen on the continent." These sensations were unavailable in the inner territory: "One cannot get such a deep emotion from the scenery of an island country."[36] Students on the Miyakonojō Higher Commercial School trip to Manchuria and Korea agreed. One student marveled at the scenery—all "I saw and heard through the railway carriage window was strange."[37] Doi Ichirō, a student from Tokyo Prefectural Number One Commercial School, even went so far as to enumerate the differences between rail travel in the metropole and the continent in his reflections on their 1932 trip to Manchuria and Korea. Invoking the authority of the traveler as first-hand observer, he listed the differences "just as I saw them, just as I felt them, and just as they were":

1. The trains carry more power and go faster because of the wide gauge;
2. The rail beds are rocks rather than sand;
3. The outside of the passenger cars is green rather than brown, as it is in the inner territory. Additionally, first class is yellow, second class is grass

colored, and third is red-brown (just a little bit darker than the red of Japanese third-class cars);
4. There are fewer windows than in the inner territory, and they are smaller. The window glass is double weight because of the harsh continental winter;
5. The third-class seats are fancier than inner territory seats—they are about the level of second-class seats in the inner territory;
6. The Korea-Manchuria trains run lower to the ground;
7. The trains ring their bells in the "American style," that is, with the sound "garan garan!"
8. They sell food on the train (because there are not as many options for buying lunch boxes at the station as there are in the inner territory);
9. On the South Manchuria Railway Company lines there are pistol-carrying guards aboard the trains, and the uniform of the conductors is very high quality;
10. In terms of general impressions, the stations and people of Korea are really calm, not like the inner territory. It is a grand feeling to board a South Manchuria Railway Company train rushing across the vast plains of the continent.[38]

Matsuda Kiichi, a middle-school student who traveled by himself through Taiwan in 1937, could not contain his excitement at the thrill of difference. Looking through the window of a train car heading south, Matsuda exclaimed, "The mountains of Taiwan! The rivers! The houses! Even if there is a bit of the feeling of the southern country, nothing at all resembles the inner territory's suburbs or the nostalgic landscape of my homeland."[39]

These expressions of awe and wonder at the strangeness of the landscape were a far cry from the Government General of Korea's 1921 exclamation that the port of Pusan had "been so Japanified, it doesn't even smell like Korea anymore."[40] As these accounts suggest, by the late 1920s, to see with nationalist eyes meant something more than it had in the first years of imperial travel. In this era of economic and political turbulence, to observe colonized lands meant not only to territorialize a space for the nation but also to treat observation as a practice of appreciating the differences between places within the space of the nation. When the students of Hiroshima Higher Normal School toured Korea and Manchuria in 1915, both diarists commented that the colonial government's policy of Japanification had gone so far as to even change the weather. Thunder was not often heard before the Japanese arrived, wrote the first diarist, "so even the atmosphere is being Japanified." For him, this meant that human power—the power of an industrial society to reengineer social life through changes to the landscape—"had even taken control of nature."[41] When students from Miyakonojō Higher Commercial School traveled to Korea in 1930, however, their diarists read the landscape in an entirely different fashion. Watching the countryside pass by outside the train's window, one student said, "it was as if the 'white-robed peasants' emanated the atmosphere of Korea."⁴² The atmosphere in this case was not the weather, but the sweatiness and "lazy movements" of the farmers in the fields. It was a welcome break, a valuable strangeness. In the words of another student, they enjoyed the "strange scenery" outside the window: women doing the washing, farmers in white robes, children playing strange hand games.⁴³

Some struggled with the mandate to see with culturally pluralistic eyes. Kamata Yoshio discovered as much when he toured Korea and Manchuria with his classmates from Miyakonojō Higher Commercial School in 1926. Reporting on the events of the day's tour of Keijō, Kamata related a discussion that he had with his guide, a member of the Miyazaki Prefecture Residents' Association (Miyazaki kenjinkai). "Koreans do a lot of goofing off and wandering around, huh?" Kamata asked, noting a number of Koreans relaxing in the Botanical Gardens at Ch'andŏk Palace. "Well," the guide responded, "it looks like that, right? But, even in the inner territory, think about Asakusa Park in Tokyo. People with nothing to do are just lying about. Now, when foreigners see that, they think that there isn't a people in the world that plays around as much as Japanese people. In other words, it's the same as what you're thinking about Koreans." Not having achieved the confirmation of his observation that he desired, Kamata tried a different tack. "Well," he said to the guide, "Koreans *are* smelly." Again, the guide offered a broader perspective. "Yeah, they are," he acquiesced, "but that has to do with what they eat. Foreigners think that Japanese smell like daikon radish, and Japanese say that foreigners stink of foreignness *(ketōkusai)*. If you go to China, Chinese people stink. No matter where you go, you smell what you call the stink of that country. So, really it's not right to say that Koreans stink."⁴⁴ Kamata described his conversation with the guide as a moment of almost enlightenment. "I heard this and thought, *Oh! Now I see*. It was a mistake to think of Koreans as a stinky people or a lazy people." But then he reconsidered: "I thought that [it was a mistake]. But then again, I actually could not think [of Koreans] otherwise."⁴⁵

For others, the mandate to see with culturally pluralistic eyes also served to demarcate the boundaries of acceptable behavior and national expectations. In this sense, appreciating cultural differences encouraged imperial travelers to reproduce the norms and expectations of the nation. For example, one Miyakonojō student incorporated a central tenet of Japanese colonial discourse on Manchuria when he described the thrill of riding on the Ajia Super Express, the South Manchuria Railway Company's most famous and technologically advanced high-speed train, as the thrill of traveling through "an unpeopled region at super high speed."⁴⁶ The land was not unpeopled. But Japanese colonial discourse often represented it as such, for this justified the larger discourse of Manchukuo as a blank canvas where the state could build a new "paradise" by combining technological modernity with a commitment, however chimeric, to multiethnic harmony.

In his discussion of "Chinese leisure" (Shinajin no kyōraku), Takahashi Gentarō likewise reproduced a point that imperial travelers had made constantly to legitimate de facto Japanese control over Manchuria under the geography of civilization: that the problem with China was that Chinese people did not understand the need to invest in the future. But now, under the geography of cultural pluralism, the argument was cloaked as appreciating the essential differences between Chinese people and other nations. He started with a comparison that drew on the common description of coolie leisure as "drinking, betting, and buying." "In Japan we also say, 'drink, bet, buy,'" Takahashi's interlocutor, Mr. Kuchino, began. "But for Chinese people, it's not a factor of three but five," he continued. He explained that Chinese people also add mahjong and joking to the three standard amusements. Moreover, Chinese people revel in China's extraordinary cuisine: "They say that the dogs in China are all skinny," Mr. Kuchino reported. "Why?" asked Takahashi. "Because [Chinese people] eat the part that they are supposed to give to the dogs."[47]

In this manner, Takahashi's fictional conversational partner appreciated "Chinese customs," while presupposing the opprobrium or moral judgment of the Japanese reader/traveler. Appreciation became a vehicle for defining the limits of acceptability. Takahashi continued by explaining the differences between the two nations in a way that contrasted the presumed stability of the Japanese and Manchukuoan state's protection of private property with what he portrayed as the lawlessness of Chinese life: "Based on what you describe, Mr. Kuchino, it seems that for Chinese people, the guarantees of life and property are not adequate, and so for that reason, they think that they had better enjoy themselves while they can." "Yes, exactly," Mr. Kuchino concurred.[48]

## THE SPATIAL POLITICS OF "FROMNESS"

The act of appreciating the differences between regional cultures necessarily involved the definition of what the authentic culture of each region was. Local color tourist materials placed great emphasis on indigeneity. The Government General of Taiwan's 1927 *Taiwan tetsudō ryokō annai* described the population of Taiwan as divided into three groups: inner territory people, Han people who migrated from China, and "the so-called savages, who are the native residents of Taiwan."[49] The Government General of Korea's 1929 *Chōsen ryokō annai ki* (Notes for Travel in Korea) emphasized that the history of Korea was a story of both "indigenous peoples in the Korean peninsula" and migrant peoples from Manchuria, Japan, and the Shandong region of China.[50] A later edition distinguished between an "indigenous Korean people" in the southern peninsula and an "indigenous people" in the north, who intermixed with various peoples of Manchuria and China.[51] In contrast, the 1929 *Minami Manshū tetsudō ryokō annai* (Guide to railway travel in Manchuria) steadfastly refused to use the term "indigenous" to describe any of the region's peoples. Instead, it noted that, "until the middle of the Qing period, Manchuria was managed by a race considered to be of the endemic Tungus family."[52]

A variety of terms were used to indicate indigeneity, each of which carried specific connotations. The Government General of Taiwan described the indigenous peoples of Taiwan as *dochaku no jūmin*, literally "the people who live on the land." This term connoted "natives" rather than the self-conscious identification that the term "ethnic nation," or *minzoku*, implied. In Korea, the use of *genjūmin* for "indigenous" co-opted the language of national self-determination by differentiating between an ethnic Korean people (*genjūmin taru kanzoku*) in the south and a migrant and mixed population in the north. The description went on to link the history and security of the southern Korean people with the Japanese state by explaining that it was the southern, "indigenous" ancestors of the Korean people whom the Japanese state had historically supported against the dominance of the Chinese dynasties and with whom the Japanese people shared common ancestors. In the case of Manchuria, the South Manchuria Railway Company used the word "manage," *keiei*, to cast the relationship between the Tungustic people and the land not as one of indigeneity but of supervision—precisely the same word that the railway used to describe its own relationship with Manchuria between 1906 and 1931.[53]

In the aggregate, local color tourism engaged in what we might think of as a politics of "fromness"—marking certain bodies as essentially "from" certain places and using this to justify particular inequalities and restrictions. The politics of fromness "incarcerated" colonized subjects in place on the terms of the post–World War I era.[54] One aspect of this was guidebooks' new emphasis on the idea that certain peoples were indigenous to certain places. Despite the variety of terms and connotations thereof that guidebooks used to define indigeneity, each took pains to address the issue, even if, as in the case of the South Manchuria Railway Company, the intention was to deny the possibility of its existence entirely.

The way that local color tourism defined the authentic culture of each region and the significance of that culture to the imperial whole spoke to specific political conflicts in each territory. In the case of Manchuria, colonial boosters argued that the region's lack of an indigenous people defined its local color and delegitimated Chinese claims to sovereignty over the region. In its description of Manchuria's history as one of an "endemic" (*koyū*) Tungusic people who "managed" (*keiei*) Manchuria, for example, the South Manchuria Railway sidestepped the thorny issue of authenticity by implying that the early Tungusic peoples held an inauthentic, non-sovereign relationship with the Manchurian region that was similar to the railway's own non-sovereign relationship with Manchuria. After 1932, when, as guidebook author Ōtsu Toshiya pointed out, "the era of 'the management of

Manchuria'" came to an end, the 1935 *Minami Manshū tetsudō ryokō annai* offered more specifics on the ancient history of Manchuria but continued to refrain from describing any group as indigenous to the region.⁵⁵ Manchuria's history now began with the Sushen (J. Mishihase or Ashihase) and Yilou peoples, who "gathered in completely uncivilized villages without any regulation" and who, over time, "invaded" the cultural area to the south—that is, China—and were themselves settled by migrant groups from the northern part of China.⁵⁶ In this, the railway's history preserved its emphasis on the inauthenticity of any one people's relation to the territory claimed by the puppet state of Manchukuo.

Indeed, the guidebook described the unique local color of Manchuria as the result of this particular aspect of its history. It emphasized the history of Manchuria as one uniquely marked by conflicts of an ethnic character. For example, "The Yuan, who were a Mongolian race *(Mōko shuzoku)*, were destroyed by the Han race *(kan jinshu)*." But later, the Aisin Gioro family emerged (from the Tungusic Jurchen people) and destroyed the Ming.⁵⁷ According to the guidebook, the landscape of Manchuria reflected this history. "Because Manchuria is a land in which races *(minzoku)* have risen and fallen since ancient times, there are not a few buildings that have been left behind by the various races. The stone castles atop Mount Daikoku (C. Dahei Mountain) and Tokuri Temple (C. Tei-li-ssu), the earthen castles in Kishū (C. Guizhou), and the stone-tiled castles in the flatlands of Kinshū (C. Jinzhou), Ryōyō (C. Liaoyang), and Hōten are examples of this."⁵⁸ And, of course, seeing such sites in their proper historical context was an important aspect of seeing the "true" Manchuria: "Passengers can glimpse [these sites] from the train window or can visit the sites themselves at their leisure."⁵⁹

Guidebooks and local color materials for Taiwan took a different approach. They recognized the island's indigenous peoples as the source of the island's authentic local color. In contrast, guidebooks described the island's Taiwanese Chinese population as representatives of the Chinese ethnic nation *(Shina minozku)* who had "migrated" to Taiwan.

While guidebooks and travel magazines represented Taiwanese Chinese culture as an important component of the experience of Taiwan, it also took care to represent the true nature of the island's land and landscape as indigenous.⁶⁰ For example, Matsuzawa Akira, who authored a guidebook for travel to Taiwan in 1929, described Taiwan's difference from the metropole as primarily environmental rather than developmental.

> The Island of Takasago—Hōrai Island. . . . The many flowering grasses that color the ever-green ground, or the dark red of the hibiscus flower in which we forget that winter comes, or the breeze that softly shakes the coconut palms, the rich fruits that coax out the sense of taste of the travelers who come in all seasons, the dusky forests, the stately figure of that sacred mountain Niitaka, the endless sugarcane fields, the herds of water buffalo, bamboo rafts, or the fascinating life of the savage tribes . . . for travelers, there is not one thing [about Taiwan] that is not exotic.⁶¹

Matsuzawa used indigenous people as the central image in the ethnographic representation of Taiwan. He did not erase Taiwanese Chinese people, or "islanders" *(hontōjin)*, from the picture. Rather, he simply pointed out that they, too, were migrants, in contrast to the indigenous people. "There are approximately 4,000,000 people living in Taiwan," he wrote, "but of this number, 3,700,000 are members of the Chinese ethnic nation *(kanminzoku)* who have migrated [to the island] and 200,000 are inner territory people. The rest are what we call 'savages' *(banjin)*. Savages are the indigenous residents of Taiwan *(Taiwan no dochaku no jūmin)*."[62] Matsuzawa was not alone in this position; other official tourist publications made the same arguments. Writing in favor of a gradual policy of assimilation into the political system of the metropole, Morishige Shūzō argued in *Tabi* that the true nature of Taiwan was defined by its "primitive savages" rather than its Taiwanese Chinese. Using a nationalist keyword from Japanese geography education, Morishige argued that Taiwan was the "native place" *(kyōdo)* of the indigenous people, while the "culture of southern China" had only been "transplanted" to the island.[63]

Those writing from the perspective of the Movement for a Taiwan Parliament argued that it was precisely this transplantation that made Taiwan a unique place. As Cai Peihuo wrote in his manifesto, *Nihon honkokumin ni atau* (To the metropolitan citizens of Japan), "Just like you are not the same as us because of the effects of a thousand years of history and a special landscape, we also have special qualities that differ from you."[64] In contrast, Morishige and later Japan Tourist Bureau publications argued that the government of Taiwan should be determined by the needs of its indigenous population. In Morishige's words, the fact that "our Taiwan . . . jumped directly from the Stone Age to the Iron Age without hitting the Bronze Age" suggested the need for a "developmental" approach to political incorporation.[65] In this formulation, Taiwan was not ready for self-rule because its true nature was that of its indigenous population rather than its Chinese population. While Taiwanese Chinese assimilation activists such as Cai saw at least part of the solution to the "Taiwan problem" as one of differentiating the island's Chinese population from the indigenous population (as they saw this lumping together of the two as one of the sources of Japanese discrimination against Taiwanese Chinese and against Taiwan in general), colonial boosters saw this differentiation as a solution to a different conceptualization of the Taiwan problem—that of Taiwanese Chinese challenges to the structure of empire.[66] To that end, Matsuzawa did not follow Cai in linking the exotic nature of Taiwan to the need for self-rule. Instead, he followed the practice of the Government General, which in the early 1920s heeded calls from local Taiwanese Chinese to engage in "effective propaganda" to correct metropolitan misunderstandings about Taiwan but left off their demands for equal treatment.[67] He simply touted the island's exotic nature and modern infrastructure and erased its recent history.

Like the guidebooks' use of indigeneity to define the authentic character of each region, colonial boosters used indigeneity to define the place—quite literally—of colonized subjects within the territory of the state and the social imaginary of the nation. If, in its historical mode, local color tourism waded into the issue of national self-determination by differentiating regions on the basis of their indigenous occupants, in its economic mode, local color tourism integrated those regions into a labor hierarchy determined by ethnic aptitudes rather than exploitative structures. In the nationalist mode, it likewise drew on the spatial imaginary of local regions to constitute the figure of the colonized subject as one element of an exotic landscape to be appreciated and consumed by the national people.

In local color representations, the colonized subject did not appear as a political figure but rather as a laborer and a defining element of the landscape. Local color literature went to great lengths to insist on the locality of this labor. Colonized subjects were no longer referred to as deterritorialized "savages" or placeless "coolies." Instead, colonial boosters argued that the figure of the laborer symbolized the unique landscape of the place itself. In Korea, for example, Government General publications emphasized the figure of the burden bearer, or *chige-kun*, as a must-see for travelers.[68] Arakawa Seijirō's 1918 report on Korea had included a description of *chige* that marked them as a sign of Korea's general disarray: the reason why *chige* were necessary in Korea was because "the roads are bad, thus horses and carts can't be used. Most of the hauling is done instead on human shoulders by these *chige.*"[69] By 1934, however, the Government General completely altered the significance of the *chige*—making them no longer a sign of lack of development. The 1934 *Chōsen ryokō annai ki* included a special inset on *chige* and insisted that they were an essential element of Korea's local color: "In places such as the crossroads of flourishing cities, the wharves of ports, and the entrances of stations, Koreans in ragged clothes carrying long wooden frames on their backs are wandering around. When they see people returning from shopping or passengers carrying luggage, they gather around from front and behind, right and left. In Korean, these are called *chige-kun*, and they are people whose trade is hauling. It can't be fixed labor, but rather what we might call work without art or place (*ikichi*)."[70] While the guidebook argued that burden-bearing was "place-less" work, it made an attempt to localize the specific figure of the *chige* as an element of Korean culture and history: "When we say *chige-kun*, we hear the *kun* as *kun* [n.b.: *kun* is a Japanese term of respect added to the end of a name and is also the first character in the word for 'monarch' and 'sovereign']. For this reason, we think, 'Wow, *[chige-kun]* are important.' But actually, *chige* is a name for a carrying device and *kun* is the word for 'person' in old Korean."[71]

Each representation of colonial labor as local color emphasized the mutual constitution of labor and landscape. In the case of Taiwan, it was the sight of laboring indigenous people that produced the sense that Taiwan was both exotic and integrated into the Japanese social body. The caption to the cover photo of a 1939 *Tabi* special issue on Taiwan described the labor of Taiwan's indigenous people as part of Taiwan's landscape. "Known to the world according to its name 'Formosa' (beautiful island), this island truly does not contradict that name but is a paradise of evergreens and a land of scenery." The caption concluded by linking indigenous people to the island's major industries as both a labor force and a consumable experience in their own right: "The cities are cleanly bright, and in the countryside, the figures of the Takasago-zoku working tirelessly, along with the rice, sugar, and fruit industries, gives you a deep understanding of Taiwan."[72] In 1935, the Government General prohibited the use of *seiban*, "raw savages," in official documents in favor of "Takasago-zoku," or the "tribal peoples of Taiwan."[73] Takasago-zoku, the name by which the 1939 *Tabi* special issue referred to the Amis people that it featured, naturalized the figure of the indigenous person as part of Taiwan's natural landscape by collapsing the distinction between the Amis people featured (only one of the nine indigenous ethnic groups that the Government General recognized) into a single "tribe." Through this renaming, the Government General also placed Taiwan into the larger history of Japan. "Takasago" was an archaic Japanese name for the island, which came from the name of a Japanese settlement in southern Taiwan that was abandoned in 1628.[74] With its reference to the early Japanese settlements, "Takasago" territorialized indigenous peoples as the local color of all of Taiwan at the same time as it incorporated the island into the historical and linguistic space of Japan.

In case of Manchuria, colonial boosters took a slightly different approach to the practice of localizing labor as landscape. The South Manchuria Railway Company emphasized the "coolie" as one of the most significant elements of Manchukuo's local color, along with other aspects of social life in the region that they categorized as representative of "Chinese" culture, such as the "Little Thieves Market" in Hōten.[75] Indeed, despite a dominant Japanese political discourse that overwhelmingly rejected the idea that Manchuria was in any way an authentically Chinese territory, even imperial travelers saw the passage across the Yalu River from Korea to Manchuria as an act of crossing a cultural border between the "white robes" of Korea and the "black robes"—those worn by Chinese people—in Manchuria.[76]

Colonial boosters went to great lengths to describe these low-wage laborers as essentially Chinese. In his *Shin Manshūkoku kenbutsu* (Sightseeing in new Manchukuo), Takahashi Gentarō used an imaginary dialogue to explain the place of Chinese labor within Manchukuo and within the East Asian labor hierarchy as a whole. Looking at laborers carrying towers of soybean cake, Takahashi's imaginary partner asked, "These laborers are what we call 'coolies,' I suppose?" Takahashi contradicted him: "Yes, but, instead of calling them 'coolies,' if possible, I would like to get into the habit of calling them 'Chinese laborers' *(kakō)*, or what the

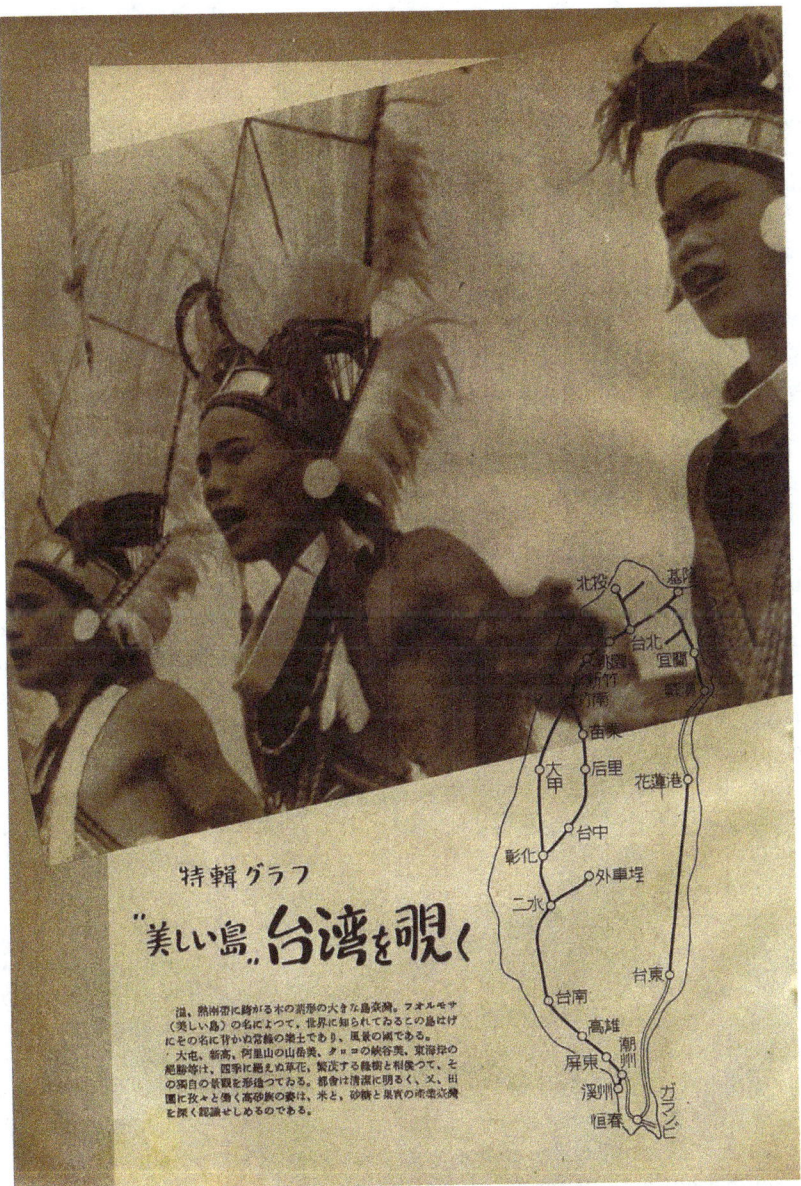

FIGURE 9. "'Utsukushii shima' Taiwan o nozoku" (Peering into Taiwan, the "beautiful island"). The cover of a 1939 *Tabi* special issue placed an image of men of the Amis people over a map of the entire island of Taiwan. The image effectively erased the island's majority Taiwanese Chinese population from the representation of Taiwan's authentic culture. It likewise represented the dancing men as the authentic people of all Taiwan by describing them as "the Takasago people" rather than as Amis people.
SOURCE: *Tabi* 1939, no. 5. Courtesy of the Japan Travel Bureau Library of Tourism Culture.

Chinese themselves call them, 'laboring people.'"[77] A 1936 guide to Manchukuo in *Tabi* magazine even referred to the Dairen housing facility for Chinese laborers, which had been known in tourist itineraries and guidebooks as Coolie Camp *(kūrī shūyōjo)*, by its new name: Camp for Chinese Laborers *(kakō shūyōjo)*.[78]

Yet even though the "Chineseness" of these laborers was an important part of Manchukuo's multiethnic local color, it also served to emphasize the state's argument that Chinese people were essentially foreign to Manchukuo. Indeed, in May 1935, such a perspective became part of Manchukuoan labor law, when new restrictions on foreign labor required Chinese laborers to secure permission before entering Manchukuo, without which they were considered "illegal aliens."[79] Yet even as colonial boosters encouraged an understanding of Chinese laborers as inherently from elsewhere, they also taught travelers to appreciate the natural aptitude of Chinese people for hard labor—and to understand that the low wages they received for this labor were a reflection of Chinese history rather than South Manchuria Railway Company policy. Takahashi argued, for example, that the new terminology of "Chinese laborer" was to call attention to the skill required to perform the work of a laborer in Manchuria, which sometimes involved carrying as many as forty-five layers of soybean cake. "Japanese laborers can't even compare" to the skill and price of Chinese laborers, Takahashi argued.[80] A South Manchuria Railway Company publication elaborated on the origin of the wage differential: "During the past four hundred years, the powerless inhabitants of China Proper were continuously under the yoke of either vacillating regimes or selfish warlords. The privations and sufferings of their forefathers have inured these indomitable laborers to meager life and sustenance. The majority of coolies in Dairen are immigrants from Shantung and other parts of China Proper. Endowed with abilities to endure hardships, these energetic coolies are rapidly paving the foundation for stable and elevated life."[81]

In his own account of travel in Manchuria, Nakanishi Inosuke raged at the idea that the origin of the laborers explained their condition. In fact, it was quite the opposite—the fact that they were free migrants from China was the source of their extreme exploitation, because as supposedly "free labor," the South Manchuria Railway Company had an incentive to get as much work out of them for as little renumeration as possible. He concluded: "Those industrial laborers (coolies) are receiving the world's maximum screwing from XX!!"[82] The censors blocked the name of the "screwer," but from the context it was clear that Nakanishi referred to the South Manchuria Railway Company.

Nakanishi was not wrong. What the railway portrayed as an inherent feature of coolie labor was better understood as a product of its own recruiting and employment system. The South Manchuria Railway and other Japanese enterprises primarily hired laborers through the *laoxiang batou*, "hometown boss" system. The *batou*, "head," recruited laborers from his hometown and then traveled with them and served as their foreman when they arrived in Manchuria. The enterprise paid wages directly to the *batou*, who passed them to his accountant, who passed them to the *batou*'s assistant, who distributed the wages to the workers themselves. As the South Manchuria Railway Company's own research suggested in 1944, this system created three different opportunities for wage skimming and left the workers destitute. The railway was perfectly happy to use this system, however, and even to celebrate the low wages it could pay Chinese labor.[83] The South Manchuria Railway departed from metropolitan practice, in fact, when it opted to continue working through the indirect *laoxiang batou* system rather than imposing "scientific" direct management. This choice contributed to the relative lack of white-collar, middle-management jobs—for either Japanese or Chinese residents—in Manchuria by outsourcing management to migrant Chinese laborers.[84] Explaining the difference between the metropolitan and Manchurian labor systems, however, the railway's tourist materials argued that it was simply following local custom. The coolies worked in a "feudal" *(tōkenteki)*, indirect labor system that reflected the underdevelopment of China itself, and the railway was simply acquiescing to the social organization that they preferred.[85]

In the case of Manchukuo, the "fromness" of Chinese labor buttressed a discourse of the natural complementarity of an exploitative division of imperial labor and the legitimacy of the imperial state. In the case of Taiwan and Korea, a similar rhetoric of complementarity justified the ongoing exploitation of local labor and new forms of dispossession. As did Kobayashi Chiyoko at the opening of this chapter, tourist literature for Korea used the notion of complementarity to represent Korea as a slow place that complemented the fast pace of the metropole—in other words, a framework of comparison set by the temporality of industrial society. In her special report on travel to the "Korea of white robes," Kobayashi Chiyoko described Korea as part of Japan's primordial past. Another account lamented the "half-Japanification" of the colonial capital at Keijō, preferring instead the exotic scenery of the nonindustrialized landscape. Describing her arrival to Korea in the page of *Tabi*, Aoi Ikko depicted a landscape coming into focus, with white-robed Koreans as its defining, localizing feature: "First I saw the mountains far across the blue sea, and as we got closer, I could see that the green trees were growing thick. Then, here and there, in high places and in low places, faint glimpses of the figure of white-robed Koreans came to me." For Aoi, the landscape represented an alternative to the clamorous modern: "Ah, this quietness and beauty—maybe this is a dream land? It is too far from the present."[86]

Quite in contrast to earlier touristic representations, which had dispensed with Koreans entirely, local color representations argued that Koreans were a defining feature of Korea itself. And indeed, imperial travelers expressed such expectations. One student from Kyūshū Imperial University's 1933 trip to Korea and Manchukuo argued that if it were not for the white robes of Koreans, he would not have had the

FIGURE 10. "Pose of Powerful Coolies." Postcard, c. 1935. The postcard shows the ambiguity that defined colonial boosters' representation of the place of coolie labor in Manchukuo. On the one hand, the postcard described coolies as an element of the "the customs of Manchuria." On the other hand, by 1935, tourist materials increasingly emphasized the "Chinese-ness" of Chinese laborers to delegitimize Chinese claims to Manchuria by emphasizing the foreignness of the region's Chinese population. Digital image courtesy of the East Asia Image Collection, Lafayette College Libraries, Easton, PA. Image ip0099.

sense of being in a different place at all: "The many Koreans wearing white robes is strange, but otherwise [Pusan] gives off entirely a feeling of the inner territory." It was, in fact, somewhat of a disappointment to this student. Pusan "did not live up to [his] expectations."[87]

Local color tourism fostered the ongoing reproduction of an increasingly sedimented metropolitan social imaginary that equated Koreans with Korea and vice versa, and which had already marked Koreans for different treatment based on the dual facts of their foreignness to the inner territory and the supposedly undeveloped, "slow" nature of Korea itself. It was the idea that Korea had a lower standard of living that had initially authorized the creation of an artificially cheap market for Korean migrant labor in the metropole. But by the late 1920s, Korean labor had become synonymous with cheap, precarious labor—particularly construction day labor. Governmental officials in the inner territory began to comment on the necessity not of cheap day labor but of Korean labor. Koreans were, in the words of one Kyōto city official, "an absolute necessity." This was especially true "in the areas of unskilled labor in public works construction."[88] Deploying language eerily similar to that of the touristic representation of Korea's local color, Sakai Toshio, an official in the Osaka city labor bureau, described Korean workers as perpetual migrants: "Like nomads roving about in search of greener pastures, Korean workers wander the heavens and the earth in search of labor, appearing in Manchuria or in the wilderness of Siberia. Or, crossing the straits to Japan, they come as a white-robed army, a veritable Asian multitude."[89]

The idea that lower-paying, less-secure employment was appropriate for Korean workers relied on the dual notions of Koreans as always essentially from Korea and of an undeveloped "Korean Korea" that existed apart from the industrialized Korea of Japanese colonial rule. Traveler Akimori Tsunetarō articulated and challenged these notions when he critiqued the Government General's policy of paying Korean and Japanese workers different wages. Though the Government General argued that the prevailing wage for labor in Korea was 60 percent what it was in the metropole because it only took 60 percent of what it took in the metropole to live, Japanese (naichijin) working in Korea were generally given a 60 percent boost. In his 1935 self-published travel report, Akimori pointed out that regardless of one's ethnicity, the cost of riding the trains was the same. The disparate wage policy was akin, in his mind, to gradually refusing to allow Koreans to ride the trains, which, for Akimori, was "not good government."[90] Indeed, as Nakanishi Inosuke complained in his 1936 essay "Angry Korea," the image of "the Korea of white robes" encouraged travelers to view social relations as a matter of relations between places rather than between peoples—and that masked the increasing incorporation of Korean laborers into the most precarious positions in the imperial economy.

## THE NATIONAL LAND

Perhaps the best example of the imbrication of local color tourism with the production of a new ethics of postimperial empire is the establishment of national parks in Taiwan in 1937. The 1930s saw a boom in national parks around the world and, though it has largely gone unremarked, nearly half of these parks were established on colonized or semi-colonized land.[91] The designation of three national parks in Taiwan—Daiton, Tsugitaka Taroko, and Niitaka Arisan—took place soon after the designation of twelve national parks in the metropole between 1934 and 1936. Though colonial officials celebrated Taiwan's national parks as the first in the outer territories, they were not the only parks to be established on colonized land.[92] Two national parks—Akan and Daisetsuzan—were also established in Hokkaidō in 1934, Japan's first colonial acquisition.

National parks displayed and preserved scenery that represented the nation through the diversity of its regions—yet it was a diversity defined on imperial terms. The founders of the first part of the national parks movement, which focused on establishing parks in the inner territory, framed much of the appeal of the parks as their ability to encapsulate a particularly Japanese view of nature—in contrast to a Western one—a view that imperial subjects could be taught to appreciate. The areas selected to become national parks not only were rich in resources for "the study of topography, botany, and zoology" but also "held a deep significance as a training ground for the improvement of the nation's knowledge and cultivation of the nation's spirit," because they were rich with historical sites that would attest to the glorious history of the national land.[93] The twelve parks established in the inner territory included scenic landscapes like Mount Fuji; sites of national history, such as the Tokugawa shrine at Nikkō; historical sites relating to the Southern Court, which ruled during an imperial schism in the fourteenth century (and to which the current imperial house linked its line); and sites of imperial mythology, such as Mount Kirishima, the site of the descent of Amaterasu's grandson, Ninigi-no-mikoto, from heaven to the islands of Japan (known as the *tenson kōrin*).

In Taiwan, the Taiwan National Parks Association chose the mountainous regions of Daiton, Tsugitaka Taroko, and Niitaka Arisan to be national parks—areas with scenery that reflected the particularity of Taiwan within the framework set by the metropole. For some, the choice of mountain scenery to represent the uniqueness of Taiwan was strange. In debates over which areas to select, the Government General overruled the suggestion that at least one park represent the tropical plains of the island, which was not only a major component of tourist advertising and the place where the majority of the island's residents lived but also, the author argued, a kind of scenery that was unique relative to the metropole (though in this the author of the proposal ignored Okinawa, perhaps because he imagined it to be outside of the metropole as well). Countering that proposal, the Government

General of Taiwan's Interior Department argued that any area selected for a national park in Taiwan must include mountains, because mountains had been part of the selection criteria—the theme of "big nature" *(dai fūkei)*—for metropolitan national parks (all twelve national parks contained famous mountains). Taiwan's national parks were intended, the Interior Department argued, to remind visitors and local Japanese residents of Japan.[94]

The landscape and natural monuments that Taiwan's national parks represented were thus set by the frame of the metropolitan national parks. Though all three parks were on the island of Taiwan, national parks literature described their uniqueness in the context of Japan. Niitaka Arisan contained the "tallest mountain in Japan, Mt. Ari," while Tsugitaka Taroko was the biggest park in Japan and included the spectacular mountains of the Tsugitaka (C. Xueshan) mountain range. In contrast, Daiton National Park was the smallest national park in Japan, but that made it quite similar to Mount Unzen National Park in Kyūshū, and, given its proximity to the island's capital, Taihoku, it was in the most advantageous location.[95]

Taiwan's national parks further underscored the idea that the authentic identity of Taiwan was indigenous rather than Taiwanese Chinese and, like the representation of Korea and Manchuria, demonstrated the simultaneous incorporation of Taiwan into the nation and its differentiation through the figure of the laboring "native." The framers of Taiwan's national parks incorporated the labor of indigenous peoples into the foundation of the national parks while, at the same time, representing the park as quintessentially primitive, right down to the "savages" themselves, who could be seen in the park and were part of the unique characteristics of the scenery.[96] In an attempt to raise awareness of Mount Niitaka (C. Yushan) and Mount Ari (C. Alishan) in light of their candidacy for national park status, *Tabi* ran a lengthy article that included maps and itineraries for mountain climbers and emphasized the unique features that Taiwan's mountains had to offer. Following two paragraphs on the distinct flora and fauna of the Mount Ari area, the article pointed out that travelers could also see the Tsuo people, the local population, from the window of the Mount Ari Electric Railway. The scenery, in other words, was not limited to peaks, plants, and animals: "The savages who live in the high mountains, in particular the savage girls of Mount Ari, are extremely beautiful in appearance."[97] The national parks enabled the incorporation of indigenous people into the tourist economy as labor and as scenery.

Indeed, a central component of the movement for national parks in Taiwan was to represent Taiwan and Taiwan's indigenous peoples as "in place" in the Japanese nation but, at the same time, to deny indigenous peoples a claim to any particular territory within the nation. Two of the parks—Niitaka Arisan and Tsugitaka Taroko—were firmly within the so-called Savage Territory, and this fact played a central role in their constitution as part of the national land. In order to facilitate tourism, the Taiwan National Parks Law stipulated that the restrictions on entry to the Savage Territory were to be removed as soon as possible. For those in the Bureau of Savage Management (Ribankyoku), this dictate presented worrisome challenges to their dual mandate to undertake the "guided enlightenment" of indigenous peoples while protecting the safety of what would surely be an increased number of visitors to the special administrative zone.[98] But the Taiwan National Parks Association insisted that it was precisely the primitive nature of these sites that made them such a valuable resource for the national people. Like Taiwan's local color more generally, the Government General of Taiwan represented Taiwan's national parks as pure nature.[99] The Government General declared emphatically that the national park sites had no history—or, more precisely, that they stood outside of history. It was that fact that had preserved their scenery, the Government General argued, leaving for future generations a kind of nature to which Japanese in the metropole and Korea would otherwise have no access, because of the long history of civilizational and commercial development in these areas. Because the Atayal residents of the area "engaged in only primitive cultivation," the mountains were "virgin soil."[100] As Yokō Kōsuke, an employee of the Bureau of Savage Management, wrote, "Precisely because the parks are within the Savage Territory, they are natural areas that have been protected by the savages, who we now call the Takasago tribes. They are sacred lands that the gods *(kami)* have left especially for today's cultured people."[101]

The location of the parks offered a special opportunity. Enumerating the special features shared by all of Taiwan's national parks, the vice chairman of the Taiwan National Parks Association pointed out that in addition to the relatively little damage from industrial development that the areas exhibited and the fact that they showed four distinct seasons (another trope of the Japanese national landscape), they were all on state-owned land *(kōyūchi)* and would be very easy to regulate.[102] The distinction of being state-owned land was significant, because it meant that the Government General would not have to negotiate with the present occupants of the land; it could simply assert its rights to use the land as it saw fit. The primary residents of the special administrative zone were, in addition to Japanese colonial police, indigenous peoples. In 1902, the Government General of Taiwan had declared that indigenous peoples possessed no rights to property within the special administrative zone. Arguing that the indigenous residents of the territory recognized no "unified institution" that could guarantee property, the colonial state determined that they could therefore make no claims to ownership. This rule, in fact, contradicted the Government General's own ethnographic surveys, which demonstrated that indigenous communities had a variety of concepts and practices of ownership. Yet it served as a convenient tool for the Government General as it sought to access camphor and timber in the special administrative zone.[103]

FIGURE 11. "Tsugitaka sanchō o mezashite" (Heading for the summit of Mt. Tsugitaka). Okada Kōyō's image of Tsugitaka Taroko National Park shows the centrality of indigenous labor to the representation of Taiwan's national parks as well as to their actual operation. Image courtesy of Okada Kōyō Photo Art Museum. Digital image courtesy of East Asia Image Collection, Lafayette College Libraries, Easton, PA. Image ip1035.

The Government General's Committee on Taiwan National Parks addressed the question of land rights directly, asking, "Won't savages think that their land has been taken?" The response from the director of the Government General of Taiwan's Interior Department was clear: "The Takasago tribes will be relocated."[104] The Government General of Taiwan was not the only participant in the national parks process to suggest such a practice. In his own report to the Government General on the potential of the Mount Ari area as a national park, Tamura Tsuyoshi, one of the founders of the national parks movement in the inner territory, argued that the Government General ought to move indigenous villages out of the park boundaries and incorporate their residents into the promised tourist economy. "Construct a small village," Tamura advised the Government General's Forestry Management Office, "say, of two or three savage houses, above a waterfall near Suganohira, where savages can farm fruits and vegetables, make souvenirs, or, if necessary, serve as guides for Mount Ari and Mount Niitaka."[105]

The suggestion that indigenous villages be relocated was not new. A few years earlier, the Government General had begun a policy of both forced and voluntary removal of indigenous villages from mountain highlands to the lowlands.[106] Tamura himself had encouraged the deployment of a similar "move and work" policy at Hokkaidō's Akan National Park, where Ainu residents were made to move or participate in the tourist economy—either as scenery themselves or as guides or small-time entrepreneurs.[107] Okada Kōyō, who would become famous in the postwar era for his photographs of Mt. Fuji, captured this constitution of indigenous peoples as both landscape and labor in an image that appeared as part of a 1939 collection of photographs celebrating the opening of Taiwan's national parks.

## FROM COLONIAL FRONTIER TO NATIONAL EXOTIC

Between the mid-1920s and the late 1930s, colonial boosters set about attempting to create a spatial and social imaginary of the Japanese nation that decentered the inner territory and its people. In its place, they proposed a cultural and ethnic hierarchy of "harmony" that marked colonized peoples as "in place" in particular regions of the nation but on terms that maintained colonial hierarchies in the name of natural complementarity. The twin ideas of harmony and local color encouraged a second generation of imperial travelers to see themselves as the pinnacle of an imperial division of labor through the productivity of their leisure practices, which constituted the work of observation as a matter of appreciating the empire's complementary diversity of human and material resources.[108] The normative landscape that local color proposed undercut anti-imperial and anticolonial demands for self-rule and self-determination, while positing a place (albeit a subordinate one) for ethnic nations and their historical territories within the Japanese imperial nation. Under the geography of civilization, Korea, Manchuria, and Taiwan constituted the colonial frontier. Under the geography of cultural pluralism, they came to be coded as the national exotic.

Writing on the politics of multiculturalism in Australia, Elizabeth A. Povinelli argues that multiculturalism represents a "new metaethics of national life." If the study of ethics focuses on what is or is not moral in a given society, metaethics examines morality itself. For Povinelli, multiculturalism became the determinant of morality in postwar Australia—to put it simply, laws and practices that promoted the state and social recognition of multiple cultures, particularly of indigenous culture, were moral; those that denied the place of minority and indigenous culture in Australia were immoral. But, as Povinelli points out, recognition is itself a political act, the drawing of lines that bounded not only a "national common sense" but also the realm of possibility for recognizable "cultural" expression.[109]

There are many significant differences between Povinelli's analysis of the politics of multiculturalism in Australia and this book's analysis of the spatial politics of the Japanese Empire, not least of which are the differences that emerge from an ethics of multiculturalism rooted in what Povinelli defines as the apologetic historical consciousness of postcolonial settler modernity and those rooted in the triumphalist historical consciousness of what here is colonial settler modernity. But in many ways, the comparison is illuminating, because it draws our attention to the ways in which the cultural pluralism of imperial tourism's local color discourse was not merely designed to legitimate the possession of colonized land by perpetuating acts of dispossession. It also produced a national subject who understood these practices to be moral under the post–World War I era's new symbolic regime of authenticity.[110]

Tourism's affective productions contributed to the reproduction of an ethics of harmony in ways that incorporated the recognition of indigenous land and labor but denied political emancipation in favor of protecting an imperial cultural pluralism. If colonial boosters located the work of imperial citizenship in the appreciation of place-based difference, they also anchored the morality of cultural pluralism in the duty and power of the state to manage relations between ethnic groups and cultural regions to create a productive complementarity. The challenge of anti-imperial nationalism and anticolonial liberalism made it no longer possible to argue that the temporal and spatial form of imperialism was a project of making the space of the nation symmetrical with the territory of the state. Instead, local color deployed a notion of indigenous land and labor that territorialized a permanent hierarchy of ethnic peoples. This hierarchy emerged, so the argument went, not from the whims of the imperial state but rather from the state's recognition of ethnicity as natural product of environment. While not discounting history entirely, local color downplayed its transformative potential and instead proposed a notion of culture that was indexed by place and largely outside of history.

The rise of romanticized representations of Korea, Taiwan, and Manchuria was as much about producing an ethical or "good" subject of a culturally pluralistic nation as it was about legitimating the continued colonization of any one territory. As we saw in chapter 1, the production of good subjects through the formation of ties to the national land motivated imperial travel and tourism from its inception, immediately following the Russo-Japanese War. What we see here is that the spatial politics of the 1920s and 1930s adapted this practice of observation to incorporate the demands of the post–World War I era's new symbolic regime of authenticity, which argued that nationalism and imperialism were two opposing forces and located morality firmly on the side of nationalism. In practice, the distinction between empire and nation remained fuzzy. No place was this more true than in the case of Manchuria and Manchukuo, which travelers treated as part of the complementary hierarchy of the Japanese Empire, even if it was still not part of the territory of the Japanese state.

The rise of local color tourism illuminates how tourism facilitated the transition from imperial state to multicultural nation by making the appreciation of local difference part of the work of national subjects, that is, part of the culture of imperial nationalism. The 1930s saw the rise of local color tourism in colonized lands around the globe—from Hawai'i to California to Algeria.[111] In Japanese colonial boosters' representation of Korea, Taiwan, and Manchukuo, local tourism industries represented colonized lands as the ancient past of the colonizing nation and as the home of indigenous cultures to be both consumed and protected. Through local color, cultural pluralism became the basis for what we might think of as "post-imperial imperialism," in which the metaethics of cultural pluralism domesticated challenges to the legitimacy of the imperial state by incorporating the recognition (but not emancipation) of multiple ethnic nations into the historical consciousness and practices of "good" national subjects.

## 5

# Speaking Japanese

The spatial politics of local color provided new tools for representing the social divisions of the imperial nation as both complementary and naturally hierarchical. Colonial boosters, particularly those who resided in the colonies, used the language of cultural complementarity to argue for the inclusion of colonized territory into the space of the Japanese nation. For their part, imperial travelers accepted that the bottom rungs of the labor hierarchy would be filled with colonized subjects, whose "natural" aptitude for such work made the project of empire both rational and justified. At the same time, imperial travelers sought grounds upon which they could be said to share a political community with colonized subjects despite the geographic, historical, and cultural differences that separated them.

As imperial travelers went forth investigating colonized lands—the so-called new territories—and the future of their relationship with Japan, they also probed colonized subjects for their willingness and ability to become imperial subjects. The mechanism of this probe was the Japanese language, the one tool that imperial travelers wielded that could cut through volume after volume, article after article, travelogue after travelogue of "truths" about the Japanification of the new territories: *Do you understand Japanese?* Getting right to the heart of the question, imperial travelers questioned colonized subjects in Japanese and about Japanese, and they recorded these conversations as evidence of either the success of assimilation or the need to continue training and evaluating colonized subjects for membership in the nation.

That they chose language for this task is not surprising, given the pervasiveness of the ideology known as "linguistic nationalism" during the late nineteenth and early twentieth centuries. In the late nineteenth century, Ueda Kazutoshi argued that language was the lifeblood of the nation. The leader of the campaign to standardized spoken Japanese, Ueda famously articulated the link between the Japanese language and the "Japanese spirit" in 1894, when he argued that "the Japanese language is the spiritual blood of the Japanese people."[1] During this time, the Governments General in Taiwan and Korea inaugurated intense Japanese-language education campaigns, intending to transform colonized subjects into Japanese people through linguistic conversion. In the metropole, the Ministry of Education waged a similar campaign against what it called "dialect" *(hōgen)*. Schools around the country worked to transform the highly variegated everyday speech of the nation into a "national language" *(kokugo)*. Despite national language advocates' insistence on the essential unity of the Japanese-language speech community, the new "standard" primers for language education in the metropole, which appeared in 1903, proposed to teach the nation what was, in fact, a highly localized version of Japanese: Tokyo dialect.

In this moment of shifting expectations, no individual's definition of "proper Japanese" was self-evident. Rather, speech itself was undergoing a process of definition and redefinition as powerful institutions, such as the Governments General, the Ministry of Education, associations of language teachers, and public intellectuals, linked speech to nation and therefore to one's place in society. In the hands of imperial travelers, linguistic nationalism became the basis for a shifting landscape of inclusion and exclusion that operated in loose parallel with the vision of the empire as a division of labor and cultural regions. Imperial travelers agreed that certain peoples—like classes of laborers—were naturally suited to certain languages and registers (the degree of formality and kind of vocabulary that one uses depending on the social context), and only some could use language to transcend their place of origin. Yet unlike labor, imperial travelers did not treat language as an example of the logic of mutual benefit. A Taiwanese Chinese street peddler's broken Japanese did not fulfill a particular function that allowed other speech communities to attend to complementary tasks. Rather, in their reactions to the Japanese-language speech of colonized subjects, imperial travelers produced a sense of the imperial nation as a community divided by intractable linguistic variation, which they read as a sign of the continued unfitness of colonized subjects for full inclusion into the nation.

## THE PLACE OF LANGUAGE

The idea that language and nation are coterminous, that nation comes from language and that nations are definable through language, is a form of language ideology rather than a historical truth. It would be hard to find a nation that meets the standards of national-language ideologues. Language is notoriously variable, with even the most codified of tongues open to internal debate over the "correct" way to conjugate a verb, how to gender speech, and which registers are appropriate for different classes of people. For this reason, Michael Silverstein has argued that language is a metalinguistic category—a subjective matter of where boundaries between languages, dialects, creoles, and so on should be—rather than an objective description of what they are.[2] Indeed, despite the self-evidence with which they drew the linkage between language and nation, more often than not, nineteenth- and twentieth-century linguistic nationalists found themselves confronting language as a problem to be solved rather than a reality to be embraced.[3] During this era, as Hiraku Shimoda argues, speech diversity "was not a problem of function . . . rather, it was a problem of political psychology."[4] As national-language activist Ueda Kazutoshi saw it, the problem was not that people could not understand each other, but rather that they would not feel like a unified nation if they did not speak the same language. "Dialectism" threated the unity of the nation, because "even though we are all Japanese, it is like meeting foreigners."[5]

Like the landscapes of labor and scenery that constituted the touristic "local color" of Japan's diverse cultural regions, imperial travelers and colonial boosters used language to place colonized lands and colonized peoples within the Japanese nation. Yet unlike those landscapes, the linguistic encounters that travelers recorded offered the possibility of immediate and transparent relations between themselves and colonized subjects, as well as the potential for provocation. Like visible landscapes, travelers constructed linguistic landscapes in ways that created a sense of place in accordance with their own ideological lenses.[6] Early Japanese imperial travelers used Japanese-language encounters to place colonized subjects under the rubric of the geography of civilization. They imagined that the new territories were both already part of the national (linguistic) land and, at the same time, imagined that the recognizable differences of colonized subjects would soon disappear (if they hadn't already) as they too became Japanese. Readily embracing the equation of language and nation, imperial travelers regularly recorded conversations with local residents as part of their travelogues. In Korea, where travelers encountered Korean students on the city trains, conversations provoked astonishment and optimism about the prospects of assimilation. Arakawa Seijirō, for example, believed that "the most difficult and important task" of colonial policy was "to harmonize the feelings of the natives and assimilate them as citizens."[7] On his 1918 trip, the speech of Korean common school students impressed him enough that he wrote about the encounter. After twenty or so Korean students boarded the train, the captain of Arakawa's group brought one student over to share his opinion of Japan. Though Arakawa did not include the content of the student's answers, he appeared pleased that he had answered "promptly and clearly," presumably in Japanese (since no one in the group spoke Korean).[8] The Hiroshima group expressed similarly positive feelings after an encounter with Korean students from Heijō Higher Common School. The Heijō students "spoke national language just like a person from the inner territory," one student reported.[9] In fact, it appeared that the Korean students spoke it somewhat better than people from the metropole. As the other diarist noted, the Koreans' "textbook Japanese was so good that when I was told, 'Your Japanese is a little different,' I broke into a bit of a cold sweat."[10]

In Manchuria, Japanese language signified not assimilation, but an expansion of Japanese territory.[11] As the Hiroshima students reported, when they arrived in Dairen from Nanking, "after ten days of travel for us who had been in contact with the language and scenery of a foreign country, we were extremely happy and nostalgic to finally discover a city that centered on the Japanese language."[12] Yet even in Manchuria, where Japanese-language education was not couched in terms of assimilation into national subjects, the use of Japanese by Chinese medical school students and service workers signified their integration into a Manchurian society dominated by Japanese institutions and aims. The Tokyo Number One Higher School students were impressed with the South Manchuria Railway Company's hiring of Chinese streetcar conductors, for example. "They really thought this out," one student wrote. The policy of having Chinese conductors in the first car would encourage both Chinese ridership and the spread of Japanese language, since the conductors were required to use Japanese.[13] At a common school *(kōgakudō)*, the students met Chinese students who, after only three years of training, could speak "surprising" Japanese. When the Tokyo students approached the school to ask permission to look around, a Chinese student responded politely in Japanese, inviting them in to speak with his teacher. The fluency of his speech prompted the diarist to note, "When he said that, he was basically Japanese."[14] Later, the Chinese students stood up and sang "Kimi ga yo," the Japanese imperial anthem. "When I heard these spectacular little Chinese citizens *(Shina no chiisai kokumin)* rise up together and sing [Kimi ga yo]," he gushed, "I felt an indescribable feeling that was like breaking out in a cold sweat."[15]

Encounters with Japanese-speaking colonized subjects produced a sense of the uncanny. Travelers' responses were part celebration and part concern over what the linguistic aptitude of colonized subjects meant for their own place within the nation and the empire. Imperial travelers were particularly unnerved by the ability of indigenous people in Taiwan to speak Japanese. Travelers were clear in their expectation that indigenous people would not speak Japanese. Or, if they did, that they would clearly distinguish themselves from metropolitan Japanese (by speaking impolitely, inappropriately, or with an accent). In 1918, the painter Ishikawa Toraji captured these unarticulated expectations in "Taiwan ryokō" (Taiwan travel), his contribution to a volume entitled *Shin Nihon kenbutsu* (Sightseeing new Japan). Ishikawa reported speaking with several people, but the only people whose speech he commented on were the indigenous people he met in the Savage Territory. "I grabbed my sketchbook and walked here and there," he wrote.

"Along the way, every male savage I met gripped his sword and greeted me with 'hello' *(konnichiwa)*." The encounter "was somehow uncanny."[16] The appearance of Japanese-speaking indigenous people and, moreover, *polite* Japanese-speaking indigenous people struck Ishikawa as strange and unsettling.

In many ways, the surprise that Ishikawa, Arakawa, and the Tokyo and Hiroshima students expressed is counterintuitive. From the historian's vantage point, it is not at all surprising that many colonized subjects spoke excellent Japanese. Japanese-language education was the centerpiece of assimilation policy in Taiwan and Korea. In the words of E. Patricia Tsurumi, "Education, it was hoped, would secure the cooperation of the natives and perhaps eventually would even assimilate them. . . . Education was seen as an instrument of fundamental social, political, economic and cultural change; it was to transform a segment of traditional China [Taiwan] into an integral part of modern Japan."[17] Language theorists "firmly believed that the mastery of a language would lead to the construction of the personality associated with that language."[18] As one leading scholar of colonial language pedagogy claimed in 1904, "the knowledge, emotion, and quality of the nation, as well as the people's activities and growth, all reside in the language."[19]

To accomplish this goal of transforming colonized subjects into willing subjects of the Japanese nation, the Governments General in Taiwan and Korea invested an enormous sum into education, particularly the study of Japanese. Language education began in the first year of Japanese rule over Taiwan when Isawa Shūji, the acting chief of the Government General's Bureau of Education, started a program of Japanese classes at Shisangyan, near Taihoku. A year later, there were fourteen "Japanese language institutes" in the new colony.[20] The near isomorphic relationship between "education" and "language education" continued throughout the early colonial period. In 1898, the Government General's new Common School Regulations stipulated that the purpose of such an education was, first, to "give Taiwanese Chinese children a good command of Japanese language" and, second, to "teach them ethics and practical knowledge, in order to cultivate in them the qualities of Japanese national subjecthood *(kokumin taru no seikaku)*."[21]

Like their Taiwanese Chinese counterparts, indigenous people within and without the Savage Territory were encouraged to attend school to learn Japanese. In the plains areas, the Government General opened what were known as "Savage Common Schools" *(banjin kōgakkō)* in 1905.[22] Inside the Savage Territory, the Government General established education centers for indigenous children in 1908 as part of a broader plan to claim the territory for the Japanese camphor industry.[23] These education centers differed from common schools in two important ways. One, they were operated by the Government General Police instead of the Bureau of Education. Two, their curricular offerings were far more basic than even the Savage Common Schools, which already used separate textbooks that emphasized "simple" skills, such as reading in *katakana* (rather than

Chinese characters, the language of literature and government) and learning to read only in colloquial, rather than literary, Japanese *(kōgotai,* not *bungotai).*[24] As late as 1927, students in education centers spent two-thirds of their instructional time on Japanese and "practical studies" *(jikka),* which meant farming *(nōgyō),* handicrafts *(shukō),* or sewing *(saihō).*[25] By 1934, there were over eight thousand indigenous children attending eighty-eight education centers, with at least one in every indigenous district.[26] Though linguistic discrimination and social inequality prevented these children from matriculating into the primary school system in high numbers (a point to which we will return to later in this chapter), many learned to speak Japanese fluently. A 1936 report by the Government General documented that the average rate of "national language diffusion" among indigenous people was around 30 percent, with the highest being the Tsuo people, of whom over 40 percent of males and nearly 22 percent of females spoke Japanese.[27]

When Japan colonized Korea in 1910, the new Government General of Korea imported the common school system from Taiwan with the similar intention of transforming Koreans into Japanese subjects via language education. Though Tsurumi argues that the Korean and Taiwanese systems produced quite different results, for our purposes, the point lies in the similarity of intentions, which stemmed from the basic presumption that, to borrow again from the Government General of Taiwan, "the Japanese spirit rests in the Japanese language." For this reason, from the perspective of assimilation policy, it was imperative that colonized subjects "put all effort into using as much Japanese as possible" and that the colonial governments provide the educational foundation for such a spiritual linguistic transformation.[28] By closing many private academies and coercing and otherwise incentivizing attendance at Government General schools, the colonial government in Korea enrolled nearly eighty-eight thousand pupils in over 450 common schools by 1918.[29]

With this history in mind, one might expect Japanese fluency among colonized subjects to be so banal as to be not worthy of mention. And yet quite the opposite was the case. Ōyama Takeshi, an official in the Bureau of Colonization who traveled to Taiwan in 1924, was taken aback by the ability of indigenous people to speak perfect, polite Japanese. In his travelogue, Ōyama reported arriving at a station in southern Taiwan to find dozens of indigenous people, whom he called *seiban,* "raw savages," standing outside the police building. He noted the otherworldliness of their appearance: colorful long cloths on the women, strange jewelry, and arms that were covered from wrist to shoulder in "savage tattoos." Yet, to his surprise, "everyone understood Japanese." "Isn't your belt tight?" he asked. "No, it's not a problem," a smiling man answered. Ōyama noted their barefootedness. "Aren't your feet hot?" he inquired. "No, they are not hot," another answered. Ōyama thought of the men running through the jungle barefoot and asked, "Well, don't you ever get cut and injured by thorns?" "Not very often," the man replied. "And anyway, if we do get injured, we get better within three days." Ōyama considered this last statement to be a thinly disguised sneer at the weakness of Japanese people *(naichijin)*.[30] The man's fluent Japanese, which Ōyama reproduced in polite forms, illustrated for Ōyama the surprising success of colonial education. And yet the encounter also revealed the potential for language to become a new tool for attacking the legitimacy of colonial rule. Ōyama's interpretation of the man's remarks was perhaps colored by an earlier encounter he had had with Japanese teachers in Korea. There, Korean students had taken to demonstrating their fluency by asking, in perfect Japanese, "When will you let Korea become independent?"[31] The content—that is, questions about independence and jibes at Japanese rule—was troubling. Yet the mode of delivery—polite, fluent Japanese—made it all the more troubling, for had not this been the goal of colonial policy in the first place?

## SPEECH, LANGUAGE, NATION

In evaluating their fellow countrymen's Japanese, imperial travelers adopted the official posture of the Ministry of Education vis-à-vis the Japanese language, namely, that there was a *single* Japanese language that could be spoken either correctly or incorrectly. Prior to the 1890s, only the written form of Japanese, known as literary Japanese, *bungotai*, was taught in schools. Literary Japanese, a mix of Chinese characters and Japanese classical grammar, bore little relation to spoken Japanese, which varied dramatically by region. The differences between spoken Japanese in different parts of the islands were so great that Tokugawa Yoshinobu, the last shōgun, once remarked, "[I had] a terrible time in meeting with someone from Satsuma. No matter what he said, I could not understand him at all. . . . Higo people are almost as hard to make out as Satsuma people."[32]

By the 1880s, a movement to reform written Japanese began to build strength. Seeking to use the new compulsory educational system to standardize literacy across all classes, the campaign sought to reform written Japanese so that it reflected a colloquial rather than literary form. Led by the minister of education, Mori Arinori, the movement published new Japanese-language textbooks for elementary schools that used the colloquial form.[33] The movement became official in 1903, when the Ministry of Education began issuing its own standard textbooks, including a primer written in colloquial Japanese. By this point, however, the movement to reform *written* Japanese had morphed into an even larger project to unify and standardize written *and* spoken Japanese so that, for the first time, writing reflected speech and vice versa. Thus, the 1903 textbook explicitly aimed to disseminate a "standard form of Japanese."[34] Yet, in an archipelago characterized by linguistic diversity rather than unity, what version of Japanese speech would qualify as "standard" Japanese? The ministry adopted the Tokyo dialect as the basis for standard Japanese and the colloquial written form.

Speaking "standard Japanese" did not come naturally to most students in the metropole, many of whom were forced to wear "dialect tags" *(hōgen fuda)* as a punishment for slipping into their native tongue at school.[35] Yet this disconnect between Japanese subjects and their supposedly shared national language did little to trouble Japanese linguistic nationalists, who argued that the strength of the Japanese nation lay in its unified tongue. This was particularly true after the 1894–95 Sino-Japanese War, which—among linguists and nationalists—touched off jingoistic paeans to the unity of the Japanese language across classes and regions.[36] Some argued that the reliance on literary forms in written Chinese made China weak. The poet Inoue Tetsujirō, a member of the influential Association to Unify Speech and Writing (Genbun itchi kai), wrote in the *Yomiuri shinbun* (Yomiuri newspaper) in 1901: "the spoken and written languages are in the most incompatible state in Japan and China. . . . It is impossible, even for intelligent people, to express in written Chinese Western ideas such as logic, economics, and philosophy. . . . The Japanese writing system is far more advanced than that of the Chinese; the innovation of adding *kana* [characters representing syllables] to *kanji* [Chinese characters, which represent ideas] words contributed to the development and progress of the Japanese people. . . . [This was] one of the causes that brought the Japanese victory over the Chinese."[37] Shiratori Naokichi, a founder of the field of "Oriental history" *(tōyōshi)* and prominent member of the Tokyo Imperial University faculty, argued that Japan had emerged as the leading power of Asia because of its linguistic independence. In contrast to Korea, "Japan had gradually liberated itself from the Chinese tradition and valued its own language and writing. . . . Every language shares its destiny, its rise and fall, with its nation. . . . Korea was heavily influenced, politically and culturally, by the Chinese race, and therefore was never able to gain its firm independence."[38]

The linguistic nationalism of the years after the Sino-Japanese War produced a particular language ideology among education officials and colonial planners that linked the creation of an ideal national people to the use of an ideal national language.[39] Paradoxically, this meant that all Japanese people had to learn what was ostensibly already the national language *(kokugo)*. In the colonies, as embodied by educators like Isawa Shūji, the chief of the Bureau of Education in Taiwan, the national language campaign *(kokugo undō)* was stripped of its irony and put forth as a self-evident process of assimilating colonize subjects into an already existing Japanese nation and national language.

Wielded in the context of empire, language was a double-edged sword. Outside of the official and highly controlled domains of education and policy,

Japanese-language speech remained highly variable. Though the Hiroshima students equated the use of Japanese in Dairen as a sign of the cozy Japanese-ness of the foreign port city, they also found a comforting Japanese-ness in nonstandard forms of Japanese. At Tōkōshi (C. Tanggangzi) Hot Springs, the group stayed at the Seirinkan, a Japanese-style inn operated by Japanese settlers and managed, it seemed to the diarist, by their seven-year-old daughter, Atsuko. "Uncle, let's go for a walk!" she said to him. The accent of her speech affected him, "She became even cuter as [her] Kyūshū accent *(namari)* mixed in with the beginning of each word."[40] Staring out into the Manchurian plains at dusk, he found it hard to reconcile the severity of the landscape with the bell-like nature of the seven-year-old. "In truth, I never thought I'd spend such a beautiful night in the wastelands of Manchuria," he sighed.[41] Though Atsuko's Japanese was nonstandard, the Hiroshima student nonetheless found it praiseworthy and comforting.

In their evaluation of Japanese-language speech in the colonies, imperial travelers deployed this common double standard: colonized subjects could demonstrate their ability and willingness to join the Japanese nation only by speaking national language properly; Japanese people, however, could demonstrate their authentic Japanese-ness by speaking it improperly. Students from the 1931 Miyakonojō Higher Commercial School trip fell over laughing when Mr. Yamada, a tour guide who also hailed from Miyazaki Prefecture, broke out in Miyakonojō dialect *(Miyakonojō kotoba)* as he introduced his lecture on the Manchurian silver market: "Since I came to Manchuria ten years ago, the hair on this head [indicating his own] has turned white, because I looked at the reports on the silver exchange in the newspaper every day and suffered until my head hurt. Everyone, please look at this head."[42] It was a little taste of home for the travelers—indeed, it was so local that the only reason I am able to include this translation is because the diarist himself provided a translation, knowing that his audience would not be able to make much sense of the dialect. Yet the Miyakonojō students were not as forgiving of other localized styles of Japanese speech. Encountering a group of Korean elementary school children on the train to Jinsen (K. Inch'ŏn), the boys asked them questions while giving them candy. "Their Japanese was skillful," the diarist reported, but "the majority of them couldn't pronounce the voiced consonants *(dakuon)*, so, for example, *densha* [train] became *tensha*, *gojuppun* [ten minutes] became *goshuppun*." Worse: "Moreover, when they talked among themselves, they spoke in Korean *(Chōsengo).*" While remarkably similar to his experience with Mr. Yamada, from such evidence, the student surmised that the Korean students had the potential to become good imperial subjects but were not there yet. "If they could pronounce the voiced consonants, and if they spoke Japanese even when speaking to their friends, there wouldn't be better Japanese imperial subjects *(Nihon teikoku shinmin)* than these Koreans," he concluded.[43]

144    CHAPTER FIVE

## THE LOCAL COLOR OF LANGUAGE

Imperial travelers' representations of colonial speech show how language became a tool for envisioning the space of empire and nation as an unstable linguistic landscape. Imperial travelers expected people from certain places to speak in certain manners. When they did not, which was quite frequently, the travelers began to propose new landscapes, ones tied to their expectations that Japan was or should be a multiethnic imperial nation composed of essentially different ethnic groups who were indigenous to essentially different cultural regions.

Like the local color of cultural regions, the local color of language was a swirling mix of coercive and anticipatory expectations. In the colonies, language was governed by the coercive expectations of the Governments General and the South Manchuria Railway Company. These were official expectations with official consequences: one would speak national language in official settings, one would wear a Japanese-style school uniform to school, and one would treat colonial officials with respect. Imperial travelers brought their own expectations, however, anticipating certain manifestations of colonial difference, such as colonized subjects' inability to speak Japanese, strange customs, and questionable respect for colonial officials. In imperial travelogues, these rival expectations intersected, with travelers expressing surprise at how the colonies were not different in the way that they had expected, and with them then recalibrating how to define that difference. The local color of language was, in other words, another measure that, like mobility, tracked the shift from a geography of civilization, in which assimilation was the presumed goal and endpoint of colonial history, to a geography of cultural pluralism, in which cultural difference was not only expected but enforced. It was this latter notion of Japan as a nation of diverse cultural regions, each of which had its own authentic indigenous people, that imperial travelers deployed to paint a picture of an imperial nation that was both united and comfortably hierarchical.

For their part, colonial boosters promoted a straightforward version of language as local color. In the guidebooks and pamphlets that began appearing in the mid-1930s, colonial boosters depicted language and territory in an isomorphic relationship. Despite the aggressive national language campaigns that the Government General of Korea had enacted to stamp out the use of Korean in everyday life, for example, the 1934 *Chōsen ryokō annai ki* encouraged travelers to learn a few Korean phrases in order to interact more smoothly with locals. The phrase guide described Korean (using the term *Sengo*) as a local alternative within a territory governed by national language.[44] "While nowadays national language has spread to the degree that there is no place where one cannot communicate through national language, for the person who wants to understand Korea and the people of Korea, it is necessary to understand Korean. Even if you only memorize two or three words, you can create an extremely friendly environment."[45] The guidebook provided translations for "hello," "goodbye," "how much," and other everyday phrases. The suggestion that communication between Japanese people and Koreans in Korean held value for both parties differed markedly from previous guidebooks, which insisted that travelers could and should use Japanese language with no difficulty. For example, a 1926 Korea-Manchuria Information Bureau guidebook claimed that, "as the mother tongue has spread throughout the land, travelers from the inner territory should not worry about being unable to communicate."[46] By 1934, regardless of whether communication in Japanese was possible, the guidebook suggested that one make an attempt to use Korean anyway.

In Manchukuo, the Japan Tourist Bureau's Dairen Branch and the South Manchuria Railway Company promoted the local color of storefront signage as a symbol of the region's distinct linguistic culture. The bureau's 1941 *Manshū kanban ōrai* (Manchurian sign travel) taught travelers how to read the Manchukuoan cityscape. The need for colorful signs, the guidebook explained, stemmed from the region's historical high rate of illiteracy. In such a context, a colorful and distinctive signage had developed as a way to identify different shops and services. The small volume offered travelers a chance to see the region as distinctly Manchurian. "When you walk around picking out the signs, you forget the dirt, noise, and bitter thirteen-degree-below-zero cold," the guidebook stated. "You are made to feel keenly the pleasure of Manchuria."[47] Other guidebooks, such as the South Manchuria Railway Company's 1935 *Minami Manshū tetsudō ryokō annai* also incorporated the signage prominently into their depictions of Manchuria. The inside cover of this edition of the railway's guidebook showed sketches of various signs, which replaced the myriad transportation devices that had adorned the inside cover of the previous edition and the sketch of the steamer at Dairen wharf in the edition prior to that.[48]

In these representations, language evoked a concept of the local defined by the history and practices of a particular speech community, not unlike the concept of authenticity-through-language that the ethnologist Yanagita Kunio proposed for Japanese.[49] Here, guidebooks defined speech communities by place (one spoke Korean in Korea), yet presented the affect of that speech community as accessible to outsiders if they joined it (even temporarily). In the colonial context, it is easy to read this representation of the local color of language as an ethno-racial rather than territorial division. In colonial Taiwan, for example, anthropologist Inō Kanori classified indigenous people into eight distinct "tribes" *(shuzoku)* based on language in the late 1890s.[50] Similarly, in post-1932 Manchukuo, language was one of a slippery cast of schemes for categorizing the state's "five races," which also included history, phenotype, religion, and nationality.[51] Yet local language prescriptions in colonial tourist guidebooks appeared simultaneously with local language prescriptions in guidebooks for travel in the inner territory. Thus, as the Government General of Korea exhorted imperial travelers to speak Korean in Korea, the

Ministry of Railways gently suggested to metropolitan travelers that they try out Tōhoku dialect in Tōhoku, Kyūshū dialect in Kyūshū, Kinai dialect in Kyōto, and a little bit of Ainu in Hokkaidō.[52] In these representations, language and ethnicity were not a one-to-one match—popular representations of Japanese ethnicity in the 1930s did not distinguish between Kyūshū and Kinai—whereas language did define a place, and a place, language.

In prescriptive tourist literature, the local color of language was thus a binary concept—the local language was either this or that. Korean or Japanese. Chinese or Korean. This dialect or that dialect. For imperial travelers, however, the reality of language use was far messier. They struggled to differentiate between people in ways that matched their expectation of both a spatial and ethnic differentiation of power and prestige within the empire.

The use of Japanese in the colonies provoked expressions of surprise and praise by imperial travelers. Visiting the Girls' Higher Common School in Keijō, Hayasaka Yoshio wrote that, "[Koreans'] power of memorization is really quite strong. What's more, in things like their power of language, there are places where Japanese people can't even compare."[53] Nagasawa Sokichi had a similar experience in eastern Taiwan, where, he wrote, "The savage children's pronunciation in the national language practicum was perfect."[54] Yet both travelers heard the Japanese spoken by colonized subjects within a relative rather than binary linguistic landscape. For Nagasawa and Hayasaka, rather than a single language that one either spoke or did not speak, "national language" contained degrees of competence. "Actually," Hayasaka continued, "their speech in Japanese and in English is clear and bright, and made me ashamed of our Tōhoku accent."[55] Nagasawa drew similar comparisons, arguing that the indigenous children's pronunciation was perfect and bore "absolutely no comparison to our Tōhoku people."[56]

In his landmark analysis of the 1920s education system, historian Motoyama Yukihiko argued that scholars should approach Japanese education history as a story of capitalism. Previous historians had been inclined to emphasize the policy divisions between the Ministry of Education's incorporation of state ideology into the curriculum in the formative Meiji period (1868–1912) and the tentative "liberalization" of education in the Taishō years (1912–1926). In contrast, Motoyama suggested that the distinction between "state-centered" and "liberal" education was a false dichotomy. Rather, policies from both eras shared the goal of differentiating the population into elites, white-collar workers, and blue-collar laborers for the purposes of strengthening Japanese capitalism.[57] Language served a central role in promoting a division of labor within Japanese society. Kitamura Kae comes to a similar conclusion in her study of indigenous education in colonial Taiwan. Writing about the new guidelines for colonial education that appeared in 1927, which stated clearly that the purpose was to "develop Japanese citizens" (Nihon kokumin), she argues, "Just as the education center symbolized the maintenance of a separate school system under Special Administration [of the "Savage Territory"], the multilayeredness that was established within the *kokumin* is clear. There were distinct differences in the reality of 'the necessary character of a citizen' that [students] were supposed to master."⁵⁸

When Hayasaka and Nagasawa stated that the Japanese spoken by Koreans and indigenous people was far beyond that of the people of the region of Tōhoku in northeastern Japan, they located Korea and the indigenous areas of Taiwan within a division of language that closely mirrored the empire's geographic division of labor. As a region, Tōhoku provided two basic contributions to the imperial economy: wage labor, in the form of workers who traveled to the urban manufacturing center, and material resources, such as rice and coal.⁵⁹ In a situation that elsewhere has been called "the development of underdevelopment," the region provided essential resources for urban industrialization while its population lived with disproportionately fewer benefits from industrialization.⁶⁰ It was these disparities that led ethnographers such as Yanagita Kunio to the northeast in the 1930s to document what they saw as the last remnants of the authentic everyday life of the Japanese people being eroded by the uneven fits and starts of capitalism. In this light, Nagasawa's and Hayasaka's insistence that indigenous people and Koreans spoke Japanese better than the people of Tōhoku suggested not only that Koreans and indigenous people could be integrated into the imperial economy as labor but also—perhaps more important to travelers seeking to create a national space under the terms of the geography of civilization—that they would not necessarily be consigned to the bottom rungs of the labor hierarchy.

No matter how celebratory, however, imperial travelers' accounts of spoken Japanese exhibited considerable anxiety about the place of Japanese-speaking colonized subjects in an imperial society. For Hayasaka and Nagasawa, this anxiety appeared as a concern about whether these Japanese-speaking students, whose pronunciation was flawless, were actually comprehending *(rikai)* the subjects that they studied. Hayasaka suspected that the Korean students' ability to produce Japanese did not correspond to their ability to understand subjects in Japanese. "What about their comprehension?" he asked. Nagasawa, too, wondered if producing speech signified understanding. Responding to critics who suggested that indigenous people could not understand abstract subjects such as math, Nagasawa wrote, "Besides, their grades in math are also excellent." For Nagasawa, this was all good news: "If you look [at the question of assimilation] from these good points, you can say that, of course, they are a people with the power of understanding *(rikai).*" Indeed, it placed indigenous people in a position above that of Taiwanese Chinese, who, in Nagasawa's words, "have a mother country and can't understand right or wrong." "The savages," he concluded, "have a simple character that should be loved [and] will be very easy to assimilate." Meanwhile, in Korea, Hayasaka found that, though their skill in foreign language speech surpassed that of Japanese, Korean students' comprehension lagged behind: "I found that [their comprehension] is not as we imagine it to be. In general, it seems as if [Korean students] excel at geography, history, and national language, but they are inferior in math and science."[61]

Students in the Hiroshima Higher Normal School group found a different, but still effective, method of turning the foreign-language proficiency of the Korean students they encountered into a way of marking Koreans as perpetually failing to measure up to the Japanese. Questioning their teacher about a sign outside the telegraph office in Heijō Station that stated that the office would not handle messages written in "mixed sentences" (Korean and Japanese), the student wondered why this was necessary. Was it because they used mixed sentences to include deceitful things? The student quoted the teacher's response: "Sure, I suppose that there are those things. But Koreans have an extremely high aptitude for learning foreign languages. After four years of common school, they have basically completed [learning Japanese], and after higher common school, they don't even use Korean and are completely free in their ability to speak Japanese." Drawing on the popular Japanese narrative of Korean history as marred by what Japanese commentators called "toadyism" (*jidai shisō*) (in contrast to Japan's supposed 2,600 years of unbroken imperial rule), the teacher enumerated two reasons for what he portrayed as Koreans' extraordinarily skill with language: one, the sounds in Korean are found in all other languages; two, historically, Koreans have always been speaking languages that were imposed by foreign countries.[62]

The concern with comprehension in the classroom, as well as the use of comprehension as a method of belittling the achievements of impressively bi- or multilingual students, had, as its flipside, the praising of pronunciation and politeness. For imperial travelers, using the "national language" was both a skill and an affect. In the terms of sociolinguistics, imperial travelers made explicit metapragmatic statements about how they expected colonized subjects to speak Japanese, and they also expected colonized subjects to perform with an implicit metapragmatic awareness that signaled acquiescence or consent to a hierarchy of examiner and examined, interrogator and interrogated.[63]

Consider politeness. In his 1922 account, Hayasaka reported the following conversation with two "beautiful Korean women" on the night train from Keijō to Hōten. The women, he discovered, were traveling to Heijō, where they attended the Heijō Girls' Higher Common School.

> By the looks of their clothing, they were, without a doubt, educated women. In that case, I thought, they should also understand Japanese *(Nihongo)*. Driven by curiosity, I asked, "Ladies, where are you headed?" The younger of the two responded with a smiling face, as if she were a little embarrassed, "We are going to Heijō." [Her] pronunciation was clear, and in no way inferior to [that of] a female student from Tokyo.... I asked, "What is your principal's name?" The woman said, "He is called

Mr. So-and-So." (I forgot the name.) I asked, "Are the teachers from the inner territory nice to you?" The women, "Oh yes, everyone is kind and deeply compassionate." I had always thought that colonial education would not work without kindness and compassion, and [her statement] coincided exactly with my opinion.... I said, "Well, it is time for us to go our separate ways. If my schedule allows, I might pay a visit to your school." "Goodbye," she said. It was somehow touching. Do female students in the inner territory have such an easy, gentle affect? Koreans *(Senjin)* are not a people whom we should hate. Through kindness and compassion, we must guide them to the level of civilization.[64]

Hayasaka initiated the encounter using honorific forms of verbs and proper nouns, in this case the honorific *mairu* (to go) in place of *iku* and *kijo*, to refer to the women as "ladies" instead of "students" or "you two." They conducted the remainder of the conversation in polite, upper-class Japanese. This was an explicit test on Hayasaka's part. He was intrigued about their ability to comprehend *(wakaru)* Japanese, thus he spoke to them using a considerably polite and affected form of the language. The politeness of his inquiry to the female Korean students contrasted markedly with the language he used in other encounters, for example, with rickshaw pullers. "Hey, Mr. Rickshawman!" he reported calling out in Keijō, "Take me to the Higher Common School, will ya?" *(Oi, shayasan! Kōtō futsū gakkō made itte kuren ka).*[65] When several rickshaw pullers in a row refused to carry him up the hill to the school, Hayasaka declared the entire Korean population to be lazy and unfit for capitalist society. In this instance, however, he interpreted the women's polite response to his polite inquiry as evidence that they comprehended the rules of Japanese-language speech and, indeed, that they had acquiesced to—if not actively desired—Japanese rule.

## NATIONAL LANGUAGE AND THE ETHNO-LINGUISTIC DIVIDE

As these encounters demonstrate, imperial travelers drew the borders of the linguistic landscape in the terms of the geography of civilization—of an expanding space of the nation that already did incorporate the new territories and would soon incorporate their peoples. At the same time, like colonial boosters' early tourist guidebooks, they found ways to mark colonized subjects as "not-quite" in place in this new linguistic space. To mitigate the threat of colonized subjects' mastery of the national language, Hayasaka posited an imaginary of a future Japanese imperial nation that had divisions along class, ethnicity, and gender lines, lines that contradicted the official goal of national language policy and colonial education, which was to create a horizontal nation of national language speakers who shared a particular affect and "national spirit." Politeness, the implied metapragmatic awareness that imperial travelers expected of colonized subjects, served to draw a boundary between populations that appeared willing to assimilate and those that did not. But this boundary also differentiated between those populations that had to prove their willingness and those from whom no such demonstration was expected. Alongside the question of willingness was the question of ability, which, for Hayasaka and others, delineated populations capable of assimilating from those that, in travelers' determinations, were not.

The same year that Hayasaka traveled the empire to investigate the conditions of the colonies, the Governments General of Korea and Taiwan radically altered the structure of colonial education. Linguistic nationalism had, since Isawa Shūji arrived in Taiwan in 1898 to establish his Japanese language institutes, been the ideology underlying the colonial and metropolitan governments' emphasis on the dissemination of standard Japanese. Yet, in many ways, the maintenance of three different education systems undermined such an ideology by differentiating the nation based on class, gender, and ability in the metropole, and by race or ethnicity (as well as class, gender, and ability) in the colonies. The three educational systems were, first, the multitracked primary school system that culminated in university education, which was for social and academic elites in the metropole and for Japanese residents of the colonies; second, the single-track "common" school system for colonial subjects *(kō gakkō)* and nonelite metropolitan subjects *(jinjō gakkō)* that ended with higher common school and that did not share teachers or facilities with the primary school system; and third, the "educational centers for indigenous children," which were equally standalone and underfunded, and ended after only four years.

In 1922, the Governments General of Korea and Taiwan announced changes that would fully incorporate linguistic nationalism into the structure of colonial education by ending, in theory, the use of race and ethnicity to differentiate student populations. Following the emergence of vociferous assimilation, self-rule, and independence movements across the empire, the colonial administrations opted to liberalize colonial education in the hopes of incorporating dissenting groups into the imperial nation.[66] In 1922, Den Makoto, the governor general of Taiwan, presented the Rescript on Education, which declared that all schools would be open to both Taiwanese Chinese and Japanese children. Rather than require Taiwanese Chinese students to attend common school and Japanese students to attend primary school, the rescript declared common schools to be "institutions for non-Japanese-speaking children" and that primary schools would be for Japanese-speaking children "regardless of race."[67] Primary schools were opened to indigenous children as well, provided that they completed four years of education in an indigenous education center and could demonstrate considerable Japanese-language fluency.

Similarly, Saitō Makoto, the governor general of Korea, presented the Revised Korean Rescript on Education in 1922. In the words of one historian of Korean education, the rescript created a "separate but equal" system for Japanese and Korean education by increasing the number of years of education provided by the common schools.[68] Yet here as well, the definition of "Korean" and "Japanese" bears close attention: as the research of Yeounsuk Lee has shown, the Revised Korean Rescript defined Japanese students *(naichijin)* as "those who always use national language" and Koreans *(Chōsenjin)* as "those who do *not* always use national language," thus opening the door for a liberal interpretation of educational policy by allowing a small number of Korean national language users to matriculate into the Japanese system.[69]

As it was for colonial boosters advocating "harmony" through the promotion of a multiethnic spatial imaginary of Japan, the stakes for colonized subjects attempting to matriculate into the colonial education system were high. As we saw in chapter 1, the Japanese education system was consciously designed to produce labor for industrial production as well as future leaders who would govern the nation-state. The majority of students completed their education after six years of compulsory elementary school. The metropolitan educational system was thus both meritocratic and explicitly elitist, designed as it was to divide the population into managers and workers.[70] In the colonies prior to the integration rescripts, the Governments General discarded meritocracy in favor of ethnic hierarchy, though they continued to espouse liberal rhetoric about the necessity of education for social advancement. In Taiwan, the Government General encouraged Taiwanese Chinese to enter the professional classes as either teachers or doctors. At the Taihoku Medical School or the Teachers' College, elite Taiwanese Chinese students received training from Japanese instructors and licenses to practice on the island. Yet these schools remained the culmination of a distinctly inferior and circumscribed track when compared to that offered to Japanese students, who could rise through the primary, middle, and higher schools in Taiwan and then attend a university or specialty school *(senmon gakkō)* in the metropole.[71] In contrast to the path made available to Taiwanese Chinese students in Taiwan, the path for Japanese students in Taiwan carried significantly increased options for professional specialization and access to university education, which was over the course of the early twentieth century an increasingly important prerequisite for membership in the new middle class and access to elite, metropolitan political, economic, and social networks.

The 1922 integration rescripts "intensified the contradiction between liberal culture and ethnic inequalities" in the education system, particularly in the fields that had been reserved for colonized subjects.[72] In Taiwan, the integration rescripts made the previously Japanese-only primary schools open to Taiwanese Chinese students. Yet, as Ming-Cheng Lo has pointed out, it also made the previously Taiwanese Chinese–only medical school open to Japanese students. In Korea, a robust private education sector dampened somewhat the social effects of the discriminatory public education system. Yet, in Korea too, Japanese students used the edict to enroll in the best of the formerly Korean-only institutions, thus further marginalizing Korean students in the public education system.[73] While the integration edicts ostensibly removed official practices of ethnic discrimination from colonial education, in practice, they introduced far more pernicious methods of unofficial discrimination. For example, Japanese students entering medical college after five years of preparatory education did not have to take an entrance exam. Yet, after initially ruling that Taiwanese Chinese students would also be exempt, the Taihoku Medical School reinstated entrance exams for them.[74] While these exams covered many topics, the language of the integration edicts provided the measure by which any non-Japanese applicant could be excluded, regardless of their technical competence in a given subject: fluency in the Japanese language. For this reason, E. Patricia Tsurumi argues that, after the integration edicts, language became the locus of discrimination within the colonial education system.[75] After the integration edicts, those who used Japanese in everyday life could to go "Japanese" schools. In practice, however, "Taiwanese [Chinese] pupils who participated in this form of coeducation never exceeded one percent of those Taiwanese [Chinese] who received elementary education."[76] Contrary to the stated intention of its promoters, the integration edicts altered (rather than eliminated) the mechanism of ethnic and racial discrimination in education by creating a situation in which linguistic competence needed to be evaluated prior to inclusion. These evaluations were differentially applied: "Japanese language backwardness" was routinely used as a reason to limit the matriculation of Taiwanese Chinese students into primary schools, despite the fact that a secret 1923 study by the Government General of Taiwan showed that Taiwanese Chinese students were performing at or above the level of their Japanese counterparts.[77]

Among imperial travelers, language encounters in the post-integration empire reinforced the new ethno-linguistic hierarchy. Rather than represent Japanese-speaking colonized subjects as evidence of the promise of assimilation or as flawed but capable future imperial subjects, imperial travelers enhanced their attention to the "appropriateness" of colonial speech. Though the 1930s have been described as a time when the "vulgar" racism of the early colonial period was discarded in favor of a more "polite" racism,[78] imperial travelers used expectations based on race, ethnicity, and gender to define the boundaries and hierarchies of the imperial nation more explicitly than before.[79] This was particularly true for travelers to Taiwan, who continued to be surprised and fascinated by Japanese-language encounters with indigenous people, yet also troubled by the potential consequences of such linguistic competence.

To be sure, imperial travelers did not see themselves as doing anything to language or to the linguistic landscape. Rather, they used conversations with colonized subjects as a way of emphasizing their own authority as first-hand witnesses to colonial conditions. In contrast to prescriptive materials, which adopted the voice of the omniscient third-person, imperial travelers represented their travelogues as a series of "I statements" that documented the traveler's lived experiences.

No experience was more immediate—and more unavailable to nontravelers—than actual conversations with colonized subjects *in* the colony itself. In other words, for imperial travelers, reporting speech in the form of direct quotations was one of the most valuable ways of representing the entire narrative as both authoritative and uniquely informative.

In these representations of dialogue, imperial travelers engaged in content policing and promoted theories of ethnic opacity that incorporated essentialized ethnic boundaries into the linguistic landscape of empire. The policing of what colonized subjects should or should not say had as much to do with imperial travelers' expectations of whether colonized subjects could (or should) transcend their place of origin and the cultural characteristics travelers ascribed to it as it did with more explicitly political subject matters, such as the question of independence. Ōyama, as we recall, flinched when he heard Korean students using their national language skills to ask when Korea would become independent. Yet imperial travelers had strong expectations more broadly about the kinds of statements colonized subjects should or should not make. Matsuda Kiichi, a middle-school student from Osaka who traveled to Okinawa and Taiwan in 1937, had two entirely different reactions to the Japanese-language speech of indigenous peoples. At Kenbō Shrine in Taihoku, Matsuda encountered an indigenous man paying his respects to the dead. Quoting the man directly, he wrote, "The savage prayed and then expressed the following words, 'Kenbō Shrine is the place where those who have worked and died for the emperor are celebrated. I always knew that members of one of our tribes who worked and died for Japan during the Musha Incident were also celebrated here. But, I had not imagined it would be this magnificent of a shrine. I suppose our tribe must be very satisfied that they are celebrated in such a magnificent place.'"[80]

Somewhat surprisingly (to this historian), this statement elicited no further comment from Matsuda. Rendered in polite but not honorific forms, the statement demonstrated considerable linguistic and cultural fluency on the part of its speaker. Perhaps this form of competence and this register of imperial subjectivity were now in the realm of the expected for Matsuda.

Later, however, Matsuda represented indigenous speech entirely differently on a visit Taroko Gorge in eastern Taiwan. In the words of the popular song "Taroko bushi" (Taroko melody), Taroko was the home of friendly Taroko maidens:

> Taiwan's Taroko, what is its specialty?
> Gold sand, gourds, Taroko paper, paulownia sandals of plums and
>   silk floss,
> a Taroko maiden's "hello"[81]

The image is similar to what Hayasaka conjured with his conversation with the "beautiful Korean women" on the train to Heijō: politeness and deference to the terms of Japanese rule through the proper use of Japanese language. Well known for its scenic beauty (Taroko would become one of Taiwan's three national parks the following year), Taroko increasingly attracted imperial travelers in the 1930s. Yet Matsuda objected when indigenous people stepped outside of their defined role as part of the scenery. Arriving at Taroko, two "savages" *(banjin)* offered to take a photo with him for ten *sen* each. Matsuda found this both exciting and troubling. "On the one hand, I felt very happy to find that savages also understand the value of money. They don't have tattoos, and they are wearing *yukata* and red *obi*—they are just like Japanese *(naichijin)*!" Similar to other imperial travelers, Matsuda thought the logic of capitalism to be foreign to colonized subjects and particularly to indigenous people, who were thought to not understand how money worked. The men's request for money might, Matsuda suggested, mean that they were now Japanese. But he quickly found a way to reinscribe difference as ethno-racial rather than linguistic: "But the threateningness of their eyes and their black faces are parts that just can't be disputed."[82]

Like Matsuda, imperial travelers often paired expectations about the content of speech with expectations about the nature of difference within a multiethnic nation. For Matsuda, faced with indigenous people speaking in a Japanese register, language could (suddenly) no longer overcome race. Other imperial travelers similarly reified ethno-racial difference by conceiving of language as a bridge between distinct peoples rather than as the manifestation of a national spirit. For these travelers, speech served as a conduit yet did not reveal the internal essence of the speaker. Travelers imagined that, with or without Japanese-language speech, Koreans, Taiwanese, Chinese, and especially indigenous people could not be known.

Whereas indigenous minds were once expected to be incoherent ("they speak!"), by the 1930s, imperial travelers expected fluency. Yet this fluency did not signify, as it had previously, the incorporation or inclusion of indigenous people within the Japanese nation. Language training did not make them Japanese. Instead, language training moved the definition of what Japanese was. By the 1930s, colonial officials in Taiwan treated Japanese-language speech by indigenous people as a performance of a bridge between two immutably different peoples. As Savage Manager *(ribanka)* Suzuki Tadashi explained in 1932, the purpose of national language education was to create a shared language that made clear the "shared consciousness" of Japanese and indigenous people, but which also fostered "close friendship" between the two peoples.[83] The first half of the sentence implied the possibility of a Japanese nation and national spirit that fully incorporated indigenous people. Yet the second half of the sentence undermined the first, representing the two peoples as essentially different.

The utility of language went both ways. In a report on its publication of training materials for "savage language" *(bango)*, the Taihoku Prefectural Department of Savage Management noted the recent rise in the use of native languages by savage managers. While the increase in communication was a positive trend, the department insisted that savage managers persist in setting the expectation that national language would be used at all times.[84] Language education was not for the purpose of increasing communication per se. Rather, national language education made possible the performance that Japanese travelers and colonial officials expected of indigenous people in order to prove what—it was presumed—could not be proved by sight alone: their submission to the power and norms of Japanese rule.

The "troubled, ill-defined" boundary between full and differential inclusion, between unselfconscious access and precarious performance, was precisely the expectation that indigenous people had to prove their fitness for inclusion.[85] But, as we see from the shifting expectations that both imperial travelers and the colonial governments applied to the Japanese-language speech of colonized subjects, this was an impossible task. If under the geography of civilization, the measure was pronunciation, comprehension, and the performance of obedience, under the geography of cultural pluralism, imperial travelers introduced explicitly racialized expectations that marked colonized subjects as unable to speak Japanese "like a Japanese person" even as they carried on conversations with colonized subjects in perfect Japanese. The expectation of difference became the imposition of difference.

## SILENCE, VIOLENCE, AND THE OPAQUE MIND

Under the geography of cultural pluralism, colonial boosters, imperial travelers, and even colonial policy styled language as a bridge that brought people together into a community of shared consciousness. But it did so by first constituting them as worlds apart. Linguistic anthropologists argue that the idea that other minds are "opaque" is a form of language ideology prevalent in local, non-Western communities. Indeed, the "opacity of other minds" is often treated as a cultural clash between a Western language ideology in which speech is a transparent reflection of intention (speech as equivalent to intention) and particular or local language ideologies that assume the impossibility of knowing what is going on in somebody else's head, regardless of what they say.[86] What is abundantly clear from the treatment of colonial Japanese-language speech is that Japanese colonial boosters and imperial travelers styled their speech as transparent in opposition to the opacity of the colonized. To rephrase the dichotomy, self-styled modern cultures have ideas about the distinct difference of Others, the first and foremost of which is the inability of language to make clear their intentions.[87]

The inscrutability of indigenous people appeared in imperial travelers' accounts of Taiwan as a fear of silence and expectation of violence. In the early years of colonialism, travelers portrayed Japanese-language greetings as a signal of safety. Ishikawa, for example, noted that the indigenous men who greeted him did so while gripping their "savage swords." Yet after being greeted with a polite hello, he relaxed and marveled at the bright future of colonialism and assimilation. Twenty years later, however, speech could not erase the fear of violence. "While it's to be expected that savage women and children will be polite," Matsuda Kiichi wrote after an encounter with a mother and child, "when you meet a savage man in his prime, you wonder, will he just not greet me or will he also pierce my body [with his sword]?"[88] Silence engendered a panic in Itagaki Hōki's account too. Writing in 1931, he used the silence of indigenous people to signify danger. Stopped in the car on their way to the town of Keishū (C. Xizhou), Itagaki asked the driver why they were stopped.

> When I asked the [Taiwanese] malaria assistant *(mararia joshu)*, he avoided an explanation with frighteningly simple Japanese:
> "Connection. Connection."
> The sun was blazing down, and it was very hot, so we settled into the middle of the car. As soon as we did so, a person peered into the car. We looked up: it was a savage. And not just one, but three or four, each doing his own painstaking investigation. I felt chills on my neck, as if our necks were being evaluated for head-hunting, just as the books on head-hunting said.
> "Connection. Connection."
> What was the malaria assistant thinking?[89]

In the end, Itagaki discovered that the assistant had stopped the car in order to transfer Itagaki and his wife to a different one, hence his statement of "connection, connection" *(renraku renraku)*. But the other car had not arrived before a group of indigenous men arrived and examined the car's inhabitants, leading Itagaki to wonder, "How long will we be pilloried for the savages?"[90]

The fear that Matsuda and Itagaki expressed was, in part, a response to an unexpected, violent, and widely reported anti-Japanese uprising in the village of Musha (C. Wushe) on October 27, 1930. On this day, a group of Atayal tribe members killed 134 Japanese officials and residents. Prior to the incident, Musha had been known as a model, "tamed" village. As one Government General of Taiwan publication put it in 1925, Musha offered an experience of the "magnificent beauty" of the savage world, "bathed in the atmosphere of the savage highlands."[91] After the Musha Incident *(Musha jiken)*, however, Musha became a site of uncanny silence. The actual village was destroyed, and its remaining residents were moved to a neighboring village. Tourist literature portrayed the Japanese-language voices of the village's past inhabitants as ghostly sounds, whose comprehensibility was shattered by the unexpected violence. The 1935 *Taiwan tetsudō ryokō annai* described the village before the incident as occupying an important position in Taiwan's "savage management" system, economy, and transportation network—a place where Japanese, islanders, and indigenous people lived together and where indigenous children "happily puppeted national language and sang 'Kimi ga yo' [the imperial anthem]."[92]

But to use the Musha Incident to divide the history of colonial Taiwan into two periods, one in which imperial travelers believed assimilation possible and one in which they recognized its futility, suggests the truth of the inscrutability thesis—that the actual inscrutability of the indigenous was just waiting to be discovered by the Japanese. Instead, it is far more accurate to point out that there had been violence between indigenous communities and the colonial government throughout the colonial period (much of it instigated by the colonial government). Moreover, as the comments by early Japanese travelers such as Ishikawa indicate, the idea that indigenous people were violent people, and in particular of indigenous people as "head-hunters," had been a central component of colonial discourse since the initial colonization of Taiwan.[93] What we see in post-1930 accounts of linguistic encounters is not the recognition of an extant opacity made apparent by sudden violence. Rather, we see the construction of a narrative of inscrutability, with the Musha Incident as its central evidence.

Tourist guidebooks and imperial travelers treated the Musha Incident as evidence of the impossibility that indigenous people could ever be fully incorporated into the Japanese nation. As the 1935 guidebook explained, Musha had been a place of Japanese-language conversation and interaction. But in the end, speech was not enough to prove the loyalty of the indigenous community. The guidebook assured travelers that the colonial government had exacted swift and overwhelming retribution to reassert Japanese authority. Following the uprising, the colonial government killed over one hundred Atayal people and removed nearly three hundred "submissive" indigenous people to a neighboring village.[94] For Nakanishi Inosuke, the village became a place of silence. He cut off sound by placing a transparent barrier between himself and indigenous people in a conversation with his travel companion:

Musha! [....]
"I'd like to see it one time. Are there still savages from that time alive?"
"I think so. Over that mountain ... in place called Kawanakashima...."
When the car passed by Hori [C. Puli], the figures of savages were visible through the car window.[95]

After Musha, imperial travelers routinely incorporated the idea that language signified transformation. But it was only a partial one, which could not fully overcome ancestry. Chōnan Kuranosuke, a member of the All-Japan Geography and History Teachers' Association who traveled with the group to Taiwan in 1932, brought this lens to bear on his encounter with indigenous students in Kappanzan, a popular stop for travelers to Taiwan. The group witnessed a special Japanese-language class. "If you listen to their speaking, they speak in fluent

FIGURE 12. School for indigenous children at Kappanzan, c. early 1930s. The students' clothing and haircuts emphasized their Japanification, in contrast to other representations, which exoticized the customary dress and tattoo practices of Taiwan's indigenous peoples. Schools were a central component of the imperial tourist circuit for Taiwan and a key site where imperial travelers would engage indigenous peoples in Japanese-language conversations. Digital image courtesy of East Asia Image Collection, Lafayette College Libraries, Easton, PA. Image ip1532.

standard Japanese *(hyōjungo)* with the correct pronunciation and no bad habits, not even an accent," he wrote.[96] The students carried the travelers' bags like they were their uncles. "It was cute!" he exclaimed.[97] For Chōnan, the enthusiastic and proper speech of the children signified their willingness to be part of the imperial nation. Yet it was an inclusion that was incomplete, as he also insisted on seeing the children as representatives of a local ethnic group first and as Japanese second: "You wouldn't believe that they were the children and grandchildren of the fierce and bloodthirsty Atayal tribe that we heard so much about."[98]

## CONCLUSION

Like local color, imperial travelers used language to put colonized peoples and their lands *in place* within a multiethnic and complementary Japanese nation. Imperial travelers used reports of their conversations with colonized subjects to represent the empire as a linguistic landscape. The landscape's borders were drawn along the lines of class, place, gender, ethnicity, and race. Increasingly, as the linguistic nationalism of the early imperial period gave way to a feeble multilingualism, imperial travelers drew the boundaries along racial and ethnic lines that drew more from their expectations about how people from particular places should speak rather than how they did speak.

In these accounts, the Japanese language was supposedly the glue that would bind the empire's disparate populations into a single nation. But speaking the language was a marker of inclusion that colonized subjects could never achieve. Rather, in the face of colonial fluency, imperial travelers differentiated language into, in the words of Osa Shizue, "both a culture and a skill."[99] Imperial travelers used the concepts of "proper" speech, content policing, and ethno-linguistic opacity to create a new hierarchy of imperial culture that situated imperial travelers as the examiners of linguistic skill and appropriateness, and colonized subjects as the examined. Imperial travelers placed colonized subjects in the category of the perpetually "not-quite" as "perfect speech" increasingly became an accomplishment that could be obtained only through study in the sterile linguistic environment of classroom, while Japanese people from the metropole demonstrated their authenticity through the deployment of dialect and jargon. Even if perfect Japanese speech was attained, it marked colonized subjects as colonial.

Local color and local language offered a distinctly pluralistic rather than genuinely multicultural vision of empire. Both sought to place colonized land, peoples, and cultures within imperial society without upsetting the fundamental basis for imperial rule, that is, the disenfranchisement of one political society at the hands of another.[100] They did this by treating culture as fixed and territorial and people as scenery; by defining certain peoples and cultures by locality, and others (the more powerful) by their mobility; and by representing language as a performance of political submission and a bridge between fundamentally different communities. The result was a new map of empire, one whose borders were drawn not along the lines of inner and outer territory, but along the intertwined axes of region, class, and ethnicity. It was also one from which, no matter how fluid, imperial travelers did not allow their objects to escape. While the categories they used to draw the maps changed over time, the fact that the map was drawn unilaterally and used in service of a narrative of imperial nationalism did not.

# Conclusion

The shift from empire as a project of territorial acquisition to empire as a project of territorial maintenance altered the meaning of colonial difference at the same time that it altered the meaning of what it meant to be Japanese. Imperial travelers and colonial boosters struggled over the course of the Japanese Empire to place colonized lands within the Japanese nation without abandoning colonial hierarchies. For them, these acts of placing aimed to reorder the space of Japan, to turn Taiwan and Korea into subregions of a Japanese nation-state, and Manchuria into a region (and later state) that was outside of China and in a relationship of natural complementarity with Japan. After World War I, imperial travelers and colonial boosters redefined the space of the nation. Under the geography of cultural pluralism, colonial boosters argued that Japan was a composite of diverse regions, with each territorial unit representing a distinct cultural and ethnic homeland that, when taken together, made up a multinational Japanese state and multiethnic Japanese nation. Acts of placing went beyond representations of land. Indeed, imperial travelers used techniques of placing to fix and refix social hierarchies of language and ethnicity as well as economic hierarchies with an imperial division of labor.

In their endeavors to construct a social and spatial imaginary of the nation that could inhabit colonized lands and incorporate colonized subjects, imperial travelers and colonial boosters promoted a worldview rooted in the tensions between liberal capitalist idealism, anti-imperial nationalism, and global imperialism. They shared with their readers a social imagination of imperial Japan that was conceived of as a space of complementary diversity—of labor, resources, and cultures—yet was, at the same time, unified through the operation of history.

From inner and new territories to commensurable cultural regions, imperial travelers and colonial boosters used concepts of place to locate Korea, Manchuria, and Taiwan and their populations within a shifting imperial social, political, and economic hierarchy. It was not the worldview that critics such as Nakanishi Inosuke wanted imperial travelers to have, nor was it the end to the uneven territorial-administrative structure of empire that anticolonial activists such as Cai Peihuo sought. It was, instead, a worldview that sustained unequal relations between colonizer and colonized—the "newness" of colonized lands, in the words of Nitobe Inazō—through the production of Korea, Taiwan, and Manchuria/Manchukuo as unique places within the empire and within the world. Such rhetoric rationalized inequality as a feature of cultural predispositions and natural resources, and it transformed the space of the nation and empire into a self-evident hierarchy of natural complementarity.

Place was a mechanism through which imperial elites reproduced a social imaginary that served their interests even as the basic conditions of empire changed. The elite students who embarked on the first school trips to Korea and Manchuria in 1906 experienced empire primarily as a matter of territorial conquest, which demonstrated and bestowed national strength. Yet by 1915, the next generation of travelers began to grapple with empire as an ambiguously temporary stage in historical development, which raised innumerable questions about how the nation of the future would fuse the territories and their populations, and how best to facilitate the resolution of this issue in the present. Travelers in the 1930s encountered empire as yet a different set of concerns, this time as a problem of how to maintain the legitimacy of colonial rule while, at the same time, decentering the inner territory as the cultural and social pinnacle of the nation. Weaving together each generation's concerns was the common thread of articulating concerns about the future of imperial society in the language of place: Where were Korea, Manchuria, and Taiwan located within the space and time of the Japanese nation? The territory of the Japanese state? What about their peoples?

Each generation of imperial travelers and colonial boosters territorialized different configurations of a Japanese nation on colonized land and used these senses of place to internalize and naturalize their own identities as "good" citizens of an imperial nation. By using the tools of tourism to shape how travelers observed and experienced the landscape itself, placing became a powerful strategy for reproducing a sense of Korea, Taiwan, and Manchuria as acceptable exceptions to the professed norms of the nation and to the liberal international system. Indeed, as the shift from surprise over the continued presence of recognizable markers of colonial difference (e.g., white robes) in the 1910s and 1920s to the *expectation* of such regional difference in 1930s shows, imperial tourism and its associated discourses of placing were quite successful in that endeavor.

## PLACING, EMPIRE, AND HISTORY

For imperial travelers and colonial boosters, place worked to naturalize an unequal political system by presenting social problems as problem places. The takeaway is not that travel writing distorted and therefore deceived or manipulated Japanese travelers into becoming willing participants of empire. Such a conclusion suggests that there were nonpolitical concepts of place that existed elsewhere. If place is part of how people imagine themselves within a society—and how they imagine the boundaries and contours of that society—then place is also always already political. Rather than treating certain manifestations of place as distorted, we are better off thinking of concepts of place as situational.[1] Acts of placing are extraordinarily political yet nonetheless fictive frameworks for ordering space into meaningful units and these units into meaningful relationships.

Writing about the relationship of nations to the territories they inhabit without recreating empire's spatial politics presents a challenge to the historian of the modern world. Empire continues to operate as a project of territorial maintenance. In the case of Japan, for example, previously colonized lands, such as Hokkaidō, are represented as the "national exotic," which, just as it did for Japanese travelers in the 1930s, justifies the differences between the histories and cultures of the region's peoples and those of the colonizing nation but, at the same time, domesticates the act of conquest by representing it as an element of a dead past. The result, as Michele Mason argues, is the representation of colonized cultures as facets of Japanese history—and the detachment of the modern moment from the fact and consequences of dispossession by treating it as an event in Japanese history rather than a living struggle.[2]

The challenge that this book poses for such a deeply rooted, institutionalized practice is to show how, over the course of a global shift from a world of empires to a world of nation-states, the act of placing took on powerful political overtones. In its narrative, affective, and material registers, imperial tourism constituted a body of national subjects with personal memories of and emotional ties to colonized territories. An imperial traveler claimed a sense of self as a member of a national people—the *kokumin*—who were anchored in a particular national land—the *kokudo*. From this perspective, the territorialization of the nation was an ongoing process rather than an outcome that, once achieved, was settled.[3] It required reproduction across generations and across different political circumstances.[4] Indeed, as scholars of tourism, colonialism, and empire have shown, placing was not a strategy limited to the Japanese Empire. Rather, hegemonic powers around the globe used tourism to naturalize imperial socio-spatial imaginaries throughout the twentieth century as anticolonial groups or other powers challenged their control over colonized land.[5] Recognizing the existence of such an ongoing spatial politics suggests that progressive historians must shoulder a particular burden: to approach place as a question, a debate, and a tool rather than a spatial container for the unfolding of an internal historical narrative.

For historians of Japan and the Japanese Empire, the history of spatial politics presented here suggests at least two concrete interventions into the writing of the history of the Japanese Empire. One, analyzing the history of colonial discourses and representations in the aggregate—that is, in the trans-colonial manner that we have done here—is as important as analyzing these phenomena in isolation. There is no better example than Manchuria/Manchukuo, which has been long singled out in the history of the Japanese Empire as a discursive outlier due to the uniquely informal or semicolonial nature of Japan's imperial endeavor there. Examined in conversation with the spatial discourses of Taiwan and Korea, however, the uniqueness of Manchuria and Manchukuo begins to erode. The tendency to focus studies of Manchuria on the post-1932 period, that is, the era of Manchukuo, obscures the way in which Manchuria was the object of considerable ideological production as early as 1906 and the fact that the idea of Manchuria as a uniquely multinational space began to appear in South Manchuria Railway Company guidebooks from at least as early as 1929. In fact, the South Manchuria Railway Company was late to the project of territorializing subnational ethnic identities—what I have called the spatial politics of "fromness"—which, at least in the context of imperial tourism, the Government General of Taiwan inaugurated in 1927. What we learn from analyzing Manchuria through a trans-colonial and longitudinal methodology is that colonial boosters' representations of Manchuria and Manchukuo reflected a much broader, empire-wide, and global shift from a spatial politics based on a geography of civilization and monocultural nationalism to a spatial politics based on a geography (and ethics) of cultural pluralism. Moreover, the particular spatial ideology that the Manchukuoan state adopted to legitimate its territorial claims relied on the emplacement of Manchukuo within a broader spatial order of territorialized ethnic identities that existed beyond the borders of the state. In this sense, analyzing the spatial politics of Manchukuo in a trans-colonial frame illuminates not the uniqueness of Manchukuo but rather the interrelationship of the dominant spatial imaginaries of Japan and Manchukuo in the 1930s. The particular spatial politics of Manchukuo's universal, multinational state relied on the idea that the state's "five races"—in particular, the Chinese—had authentic, territorial homelands *elsewhere*. Thus the spatial politics of Manchukuo, which emphasized the migrant and/or miscegenated nature of each of its ethnic groups, represent a mirror image of the spatial politics of 1930s Japan, where colonial boosters argued that a universal, multinational Japanese state represented the interests of the many ethnic nations and peoples who had authentic territorial claims to regions *within* the borders of the state.

Two, the spatial components of Japanese discourses of imperial nationalism and multinationality—what I have called the geography of cultural pluralism—were constitutive elements of the history of Japanese imperialism and the history of modern Japan. Analyses of the relationship of colonialism to the formation of modern Japanese national identity have neglected an analysis of spatial politics in favor of an emphasis on questions of race and ethnicity. The spatial component of the social imaginary has largely been treated as an aside to a larger intellectual history of "the national polity," what was known as the *kokutai*. Yet, in his path-breaking study of discourses of Japanese national identity under empire, Oguma Eiji noted that the idea of Japan as a multinational state appeared first and most emphatically in geography textbooks around 1918—just before Japanese officials began to impose a new round of mobility restrictions on colonized subjects and the newly domesticated imperial tourism industry began to advertise intra-imperial tourism as the right and duty of all imperial citizens. That insight was not followed up on, however, leaving the question of why it was that the determination of a spatial imaginary was so important to the determination of the social imaginary unanswered. What emerges from the present study is the fact that the social imaginary of the nation was inseparable from the spatial identity and spatial order of the nation. The territoriality of national identity had been a concern of the Japanese government from the first days of the modern Japanese nation-state, and this concern increased markedly following the acquisition of Manchuria in 1906. Thus the appearance of the geographic representation of multinational statehood that Oguma noted in 1918 was not the first instance, but rather the latest iteration in the ongoing project of territorializing a Japanese national identity in the face of expanding state borders, an industrializing economic structure, and the rise of liberal internationalism as the moral and institutional core of global politics.

But the 1918 textbook changes did reveal a significant shift in the spatial politics of empire. If, in the earlier era, spatial politics had relied on a geography of civilization that territorialized a Japanese national identity on colonized land by marking colonized subjects as out of place on that land, by the 1920s, spatial politics had adopted a geography of cultural pluralism, which argued that colonized subjects had a legitimate place in the nation, but one that was defined in terms of the contribution of colonized lands and peoples to an imperial whole. The dominant social imaginary of the Japanese nation in the post–World War I era was thus an inherently spatial one, which posited the existence of discrete ethnic identities, rooted in particular regions, that the state would bring together in relations of complementarity. It was this spatial component of the social imaginary that structured the conceptualization and enactment of colonial difference as the politics of "fromness," which came to inform and legitimate the exploitation of migrant Korean and Chinese laborers, the denial of Taiwanese Chinese demands for self-rule, and the imagination of an essential, internal difference between Japanese and colonized subjects that the use of a national language could bridge but not ameliorate.

## RE-PLACING JAPAN

The end of the Japanese Empire came suddenly in September 1945. The local color imaginary of Japan as a culturally pluralistic empire survived in the concept of Japan as a homogenous cultural region that was the authentic homeland of the Japanese ethnic nation. Yet the political space of Japan changed dramatically. The occupation government—in name a collaboration of all the Allied powers, but in practice a project directed mainly by U.S. forces under the leadership of Supreme Commander of Allied Powers (SCAP) General Douglas MacArthur—severed Japanese control over Taiwan, Korea, and Manchuria. Korea was quickly placed under the jurisdiction of its own U.S Occupation, which, in many cases, governed out of the same civil buildings and military bases that had anchored Japanese colonial rule.[6] Taiwan came under the control of the Kuomintang Nationalist government, led by Chiang Kai-Shek. Here, too, Taiwanese Chinese people quickly found themselves embroiled in a different, yet no less imperial, standoff as the United States began to draw the line of containment around Taiwan, Korea, and Japan in the burgeoning Cold War. Using language strikingly similar to that of the Japanese Great East Asia Co-Prosperity Sphere, U.S. Secretary of State Dean Acheson called for the United States to establish a "great crescent" of allied countries in Asia to prevent the expansion of Communism.[7] Manchukuo, invaded initially by Soviet forces, quickly became a battlefield between the Chinese Communist and Nationalist forces and, in 1949, came under the control the new People's Republic of China.

By the time war broke out in Korea, in June 1950, the political geography had changed to such a degree that a minor publishing industry emerged in Japan to educate Japanese citizens about the new map of East Asia. Books with titles such as *Futatsu no Chūgoku: tsuketari Nanboku-Sen Firipin* (The two Chinas, including North and South Korea and the Philippines) promised to bring Japanese readers up-to-date on the political status and recent history of China, Korea and Taiwan.[8] The Democratic People's Republic of Korea contributed its own voice to the project, publishing a colorful illustrated tourist pamphlet in 1959 entitled, *Chōsen no meishō* (The famous sights of Korea).[9]

The former new territories were not the only territories that needed to be re-placed in the aftermath of empire. Japan itself also had to be situated within a new spatial order—no longer the cultural and economic center of a vast empire, the Japanese government and the U.S. Occupation agreed that the new era required a new understanding of Japan's place in East Asia. Contrary to the actions of many Japanese people, who sought through travel writing to explore the relationship between the ghostly remnants of the imperial spatial imaginary and the new post-imperial map, the U.S. Occupation government moved quickly to erase all of Japan's ties to its former empire and to define Japan as a uniquely "peaceful" nation-state within East Asia.

One element of this project was the denaturalization of former colonized subjects residing in the inner territory. The U.S. Joint Chiefs of Staff found it difficult to place Koreans and Taiwanese Chinese in the turbulent geopolitical milieu. As the initial post-surrender instructions to General MacArthur stated: "You shall treat Formosans-Chinese and Koreans as liberated people in so far as military security permits. They are not to be included in the term 'Japanese,' . . . but they have been Japanese subjects and may be treated, in case of necessity, as enemy nationals. They should be identified as to nationality, place of residence, and present location. They may be repatriated if they so desire under such regulations as you may establish."[10]

The Occupation government encouraged the three million Koreans and Taiwanese residing in Japan to "repatriate" to territories many had never known. By the end of 1945, 1.3 million Koreans had left for Korea. Only able to carry with them one thousand yen (about 20 packs of cigarettes at that time) and faced with an outbreak of cholera in Korea, over six hundred thousand Koreans opted to stay. Members of the Japanese Diet and Occupation government often treated the Koreans who remained as criminals, blaming them for the spread of the black market and for promoting illegal migration. The 1947 Constitution and subsequent Nationality Law placed Koreans and Taiwanese Chinese people firmly outside of Japanese society by defining Japanese nationals as holders of Japanese household registrations. Koreans and Taiwanese Chinese residing in Japan lost the right to vote. In the words of the Ministry of Justice in 1952, the effect of the law was dramatic: "All Koreans and Taiwanese, even those on the home islands, lost their Japanese nationality. . . . In order for a Korean or Taiwanese person to become Japanese, he will need to undergo the same naturalization process as any other foreigner. The fact that he used to be a Japanese subject or is a person who had lost his Japanese citizenship makes no difference."[11]

The Occupation and Japanese government's move to denaturalize former colonized subjects was paired with the troubled re-naturalization of Japanese settlers. Former settlers found themselves subject to scorn and derision as they traveled back to the metropole. Over five million repatriates poured into the country from Korea, Taiwan, and most especially Manchuria between September 1945 and December 1946. The metropolitan press referred to them as "overseas brethren" (*kaigai dōhō*). But reports also circulated that described how the repatriates were being treated as a "distinctive kind of people."[12] The word "repatriate" (*hikiagesha*) contained the distinction within it—repatriates were people who were *coming back* to the patria; they were people who had been "lifted and landed" back in Japan.[13] They were out of place. Kazuko Kuramoto, who wrote about her experience as a repatriate in her memoir, *Manchurian Legacy*, described her first encounter with the sense of difference contained in the word *hikiagesha*: "[My cousin] Taro always referred to us as 'repatriates,' as if we were of another race, not 'real' Japanese. I had

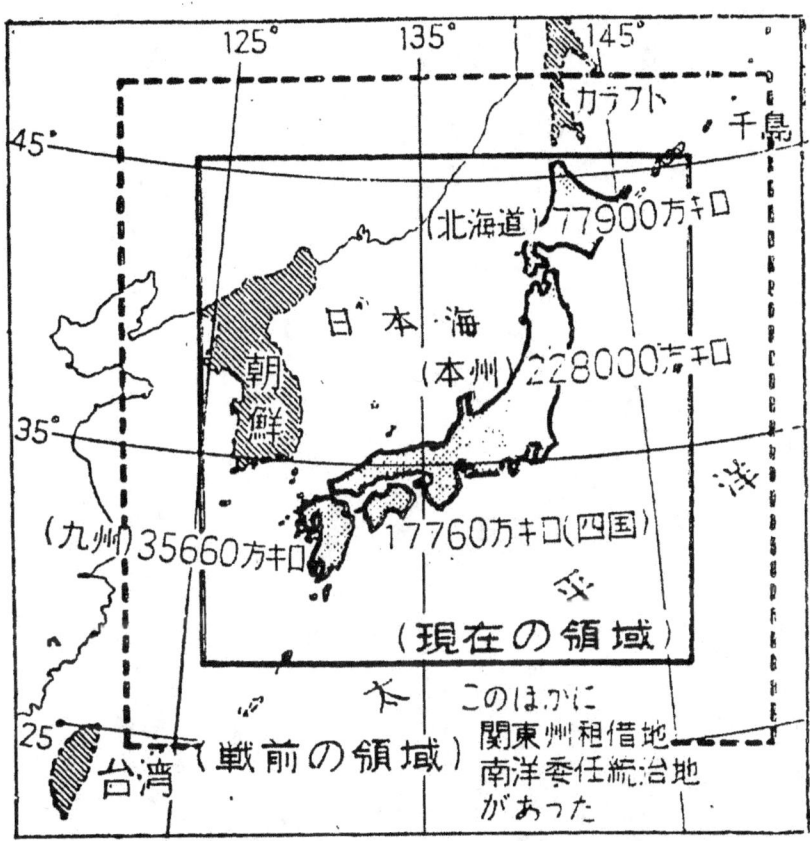

FIGURE 13. "Nihon han'i no shukushō to yon dai shima no mensekizu" (The reduction of the area of Japan and area map of the four main islands). The 1954 textbook map of Japan shaded the former colonial territories (Taiwan, Korea, and Karafuto) to mark the extent of the prewar territory of Japan.
SOURCE: Muramatsu Shigeki, *Chūgaku shakai: Nihon to sekai: Chiriteki naiyō o omo to suru mono* (Tokyo: Teikoku shoin, 1954). Courtesy of Teikoku-Shoin, Co., Ltd.

first heard this term, *hiki-age-sha*, at the Sasebo Port when we had arrived in Japan. The man who welcomed us had said, 'Welcome home my fellow repatriates.' He had not said, 'Welcome home, my fellow Japanese.'"[14]

Japanese geography textbooks also struggled with how to define the past and present of East Asian geography. One 1954 middle-school textbook positioned Ja-

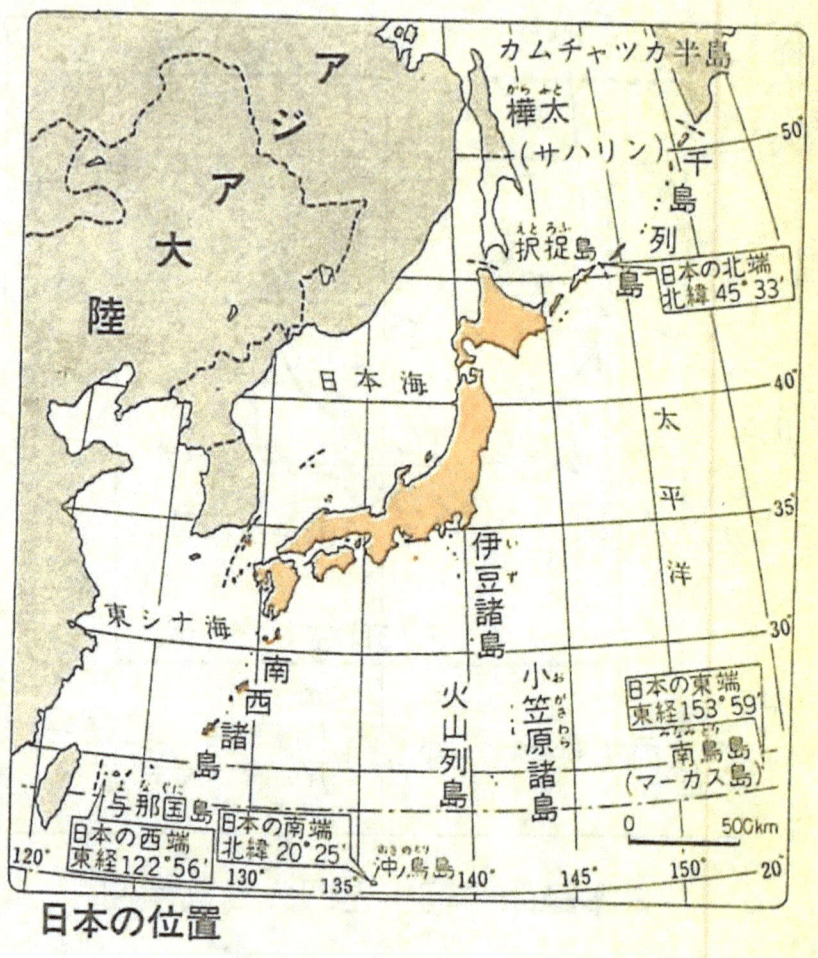

FIGURE 14. "Nihon no ichi" (The place of Japan). The 1974 textbook map of Japan shaded only the current territory of Japan, with the islands of Hokkaidō, Honshū, Shikoku, Kyūshū, and Okinawa marked in orange. There was no mention of the former empire.
SOURCE: Nō Toshio, Yazawa Taiji, Tanabe Ken'ichi, and Satō Hisashi, *Chūgaku shakaika chiri hatsu teiban* (Tokyo: Teikoku shoin, 1974). Courtesy of Teikoku-Shoin, Co., Ltd.

pan in East Asia in relation to its former territories—the map shaded in Korea and Taiwan and marked them as "prewar territories." Not until 1974 did this textbook series show Japan in East Asia as an "island nation" *(shimaguni).*[15] Place names, too, presented a particular challenge to textbook publishers. One 1955 textbook dealt with the issue by writing Korean and Chinese place names in *kanji* (characters) and then including the former Japanese pronunciation and the present-day pronunciation as *furigana* (superscript) above the characters. Seoul, for example, appeared as 京城 with *Keijō* written on one side in *hiragana* (the syllabary used for Japanese words) and Seoul written on the other side in *katakana* (the syllabary used for foreign words). In the entry on Manchuria (which all textbooks continued to treat as a distinct region within China), the textbook included a helpful mnemonic for those who still oriented themselves to the imperial map: the text represented Shenyang in characters, with the *katakana* and *hiragana* pronunciation on either side, followed by the statement in parenthesis "the former Hōten."[16] Only in 1964 did the publisher revise this practice, opting instead to represent now-foreign place names in *katakana* and including the Japanese characters only as superscript above the name.[17]

## THE SPATIAL POLITICS OF POST-IMPERIAL TOURISM

In the midst of this massive reordering of the spatial politics of East Asia, the Occupation government partnered with the Japan Tourist Bureau to reintroduce Japan as a tourist destination. For Occupation planners and the Japan Tourist Bureau, the biggest appeal was economic. Public opinion in the United States stood against the revival of Japanese industry. As a February 1950 memo from the Economic and Scientific Section to the Occupation's General Headquarters (GHQ) stated, "The tourist industry . . . is probably the only industry which Japan can actively advertise and promote without being subjected to attack by special pressure groups abroad."[18] For its part, the Japan Tourist Bureau supported GHQ's plan to revive Japan's foreign tourism industry. Commissions on ticket sales had made up over 80 percent of its prewar income. With the end of leisure travel under the Occupation, the bureau found itself in such dire financial circumstances that it considered selling romance novels and magazines to keep its doors open.[19]

Without the resources or desire to revamp the entire permit system that governed the entry and exit of foreign nationals in Occupied Japan, the promotion of tourism occupied a relatively minor place on the Occupation's hierarchy of needs in 1948. Yet as GHQ focused on stabilizing Japan's internal economy and resource pool, transportation companies scrambled to get a jump on the emerging market for tourism. On January 15, 1948, for example, Northwest Airlines submitted to GHQ a proposal to initiate tourist travel to Japan, precipitating a study by members of GHQ's Economic and Scientific Section (ESS) as to the feasibility of opening the country to tourist travel.[20] Whereas in October of 1947, the Civil Transportation Section (CTS) had declared that "fostering tourism is not feasible at this time,"[21] by June 1948, SCAP approved "the idea" of tourist travel and set representatives of ESS, CTS, and Public Health and Works (PHW) to work on figuring out the details. Stumbling blocks included, but were not limited to, logistical support for nonofficial travel, entry procedures, and the lack of available hotel beds in the Tokyo metropolitan area (the Western-style hotels were full of GIs). To minimize these potential problems and any potential drain on the limping Japanese economy, it was decided that "logistic support, including fuel oil and tires for motor vehicles, [would be] provided by the SCAP Revolving Fund." Furthermore, tour groups were limited to twenty-four people, as opposed to the initially proposed twenty-five, so that they would fit in one rail carriage. SCAP also began the arduous process of rearranging the allocation of hotel space in the Tokyo area in order to liberate the rooms that tourists would require.[22] On June 25, 1948, SCAP sent a memo to the Japanese government's Board of Trade and the Ministry of Commerce and Industry, signaling approval of the Japan Tourist Bureau's plan to conduct seven-day tours for up to twenty-four individuals.[23]

The opening of Japan to foreign visitors did not immediately result in a tourism boom. Yet, here and there, a few tourists arrived for the regular seven-day itinerary or a "special tour" whose details had been prearranged with Japan Tourist Bureau and SCAP. Joe Merider and Olive Boxley participated in one such special tour, which had been arranged for them by Pan-American Airlines and the Japan Tourist Bureau. The two-day tour took Merider and Boxley first on a motor tour of Tokyo, including the Imperial Palace, Diet Building, and the Nihonbashi shopping area. On the second day, Merider and Boxley visited the Hachiman Shrine and Stone Buddha at Kamakura before returning to Tokyo. The Japan Tourist Bureau conducted "overland" tours as well for passengers of steamships. A two-day overland tour for passengers of the S.S. President Wilson began with the Imperial Palace Grounds and Heian Shrine in Kyōto and ended the second day with a motor coach tour of Kamakura.[24] By the end of 1949, SCAP had approved standard two-, three-, seven-, thirteen-, fourteen-, twenty-three-, and thirty-one-day itineraries.[25] In January of 1950, the Japan Tourist Bureau's English-language publication, *Travel News*, reported that nine thousand foreign tourists had visited Japan in 1949.[26] Following the rise in tourist traffic and expecting further increases, Pan-American proposed the construction of a one-thousand-room hotel in Tokyo in March of 1950.[27]

Only three years removed from the end of World War II—and surrounded by civil and anti-imperial wars—"peaceful Japan" became the overarching message of the GHQ/Japan Tourist Bureau tourist narrative.[28] As the Tourism Division of the Ministry of Transportation (Un'yushō kankōkakari) wrote in 1948, "Because at heart, even looking historically, we are a people who love peace, the tourism industry can work to recover our reputation in the world. Though the nation (*kokumin*) known as the Japanese people for a very short time became conceited and committed a grave mistake, we still have not thrown it [peace] away."[29] Tourist pamphlets published by the Japan Tourist Bureau emphasized the "peaceful" character of Japan. The cherry blossoms on the cover of one pamphlet "symbolize

Peaceful Japan." Another pamphlet even suggested that "Peaceful Japan" was a particular place, not to be confused with other Japans out there: "Now the procedures to secure entry to peaceful Japan are very simple," it stated, and laid out how to arrange for a Japan Tourist Bureau package tour through a steamship or airline travel agent.[30]

The emphasis on the peacefulness of the country was not just for foreign consumption. The Ministry of Transportation combined peace with the promotion of Japan's history of grassroots democracy in its revisions to the Japanese-language *Nihon annai ki* (Guide to Japan), with the central goal of removing all references to militarism or warrior prowess and increasing the number of sights and emphasis on popular movements and peaceful, "cultural" history. The revised editions abounded with references to churches, none of which were included in the 1932 version, and the Ministry of Transportation removed many references to the imperial line. Statements such as, "the founding of the country by Jimmu Tennō" became "the myth of the founding of the country" with no reference to Jimmu Tennō, the mythical first emperor of Japan.[31] The new guidebooks also translated imperial calendar years into Western calendar years (i.e., "Meiji 43" became "1910").[32]

References to Japan's empire disappeared as well. While it makes sense that the Japan Tourist Bureau and Ministry of Transportation ceased publishing on travel to Korea, Manchuria, and Taiwan—given the impossibility of any Japanese travelers actually visiting these areas in the immediate postwar period—the removal of references to "the empire within" is not so easily written off. For example, the revised edition of the *Nihon annai ki* volume on the Kinki region, which appeared in 1949, altered the significance of Kyōto's Higashi Honganji Temple to reflect Japan's newly shrunken borders. While in 1932 Higashi Honganji constituted a significant player "in the religious world of our country, spreading the faith in first the inner territory, Korea, and Manchuria, then China and even as far as North America," in 1949 Higashi Honganji had been reduced to "constituting an important role in the religious world of our country and endeavoring to proselytize."[33]

## THE COUNTRY THAT IS BOTH CLOSE AND FAR AWAY

Despite GHQ's attempt to distinguish Japan from the rest of East Asia, Japanese commentators grappled publically with the past places of the Japanese Empire and their significance for the present moment. In the 1949 introduction to *Futatsu no Chūgoku: tsuketari Nanboku Sen, Firipin*, Mizuno Masanao argued that despite the restructuring of political relationships in the immediate postwar, Japan's future still lay with East Asia: "Although Japan is in the special state of being under occupation, Japan is an East Asian nation-state and cannot help but be significantly influenced by how the situation in East Asia changes."[34]

In the early years of the postwar period, the theme of imperial travel served as a site for plumbing the fraught question of how to define social relations between a newly constructed and confined Japanese nation (made up of metropolitan Japanese and repatriates) and the peoples of the former colonized territories. Was there a relationship? Writing for *Tabi* in 1951, novelist Kitabayashi Tōma struggled to articulate the responsibility that he felt toward his former Korean countrymen *(dōhō)* as they now suffered civil war. The impetus for his contribution, a recollection of a trip to a hot spring in Manchukuo, was the press coverage of the war in Korea: "When I hear the names, 'Keijō,' 'Suiden,' 'Taikyō,' 'North Korea's Heijō,' and 'Kaijō,' what I remember is the Korea of eighteen years ago." Kitabayashi indicated that he intended for the characters of these place names to be pronounced with their Japanese readings to draw a link between the liberated Korea of 1951 and the colonial Korea he visited on his way to Manchukuo in 1933.[35] Reminiscing about his previous travel to Korea, he wondered what had happened to the people he had met. The youth were probably divided into north and south, carrying guns and fighting. The women who wore white robes while doing the laundry on the banks of the Han River had perhaps fled their homes.[36] "When I think of these things, a feeling of pain comes over my chest," Kitabayashi wrote. He continued in this vein, expressing a feeling of responsibility toward Korean society, albeit one that borrowed more from the colonial discourse of Japanese colonialism as an act of rescuing Koreans from bad government than from any interrogation of the responsibility of ordinary Japanese citizens for the violence of imperialism: "You know, the Korea of that time was, in fact, peaceful. Even if we take into account the Manchurian Incident, which took place on the opposite side of the Yalu River, it had nothing to do with ordinary Koreans. Even us travelers, when I think of it now, were so carefree it's funny."[37]

To illustrate the contrast, Kitabayashi recounted a story of his visit to a hot spring known as Goryūhai in Manchuria. Upon his arrival, he found that the town's sole hotel was completely booked. The scene at the station was so deserted that he described it like landing "in an American Western."[38] The stationmaster suggested that Kitabayashi try to find a place in Hōten, which Kitabayashi compared to arriving in the Japanese hot spring town of Atami (near Tokyo) and being told to look for a place in Kyōto. He finally got into the hotel the next day, at which point he discovered that it was under near constant attack by bandits. The hot spring itself was nice. The whole experience, however, was strange and unsettling. On a tip from the hotel's Korean maid, Kitabayashi then returned to Korea in search of a more relaxing hot spring adventure. He eventually settled on Kaiundai hot spring before "repatriating" *(hikiageru)* to the inner territory. He marveled at how he could not remember much from the peaceful, Korean portion of his trip, except that at the hot spring, he recalled sharing a bath with "rich-looking Koreans and shrinking back from the garlic smell."[39]

In contrasting "peaceful Korea" to "dangerous Manchuria," Kitabayashi's tale of hot springs adventure differed little from accounts of the Korea-Manchuria border during the 1930s. In his ending, however, Kitabayashi attempted to carry the story forward, mixing racist tropes of Korean laziness from the colonial era with post-imperial nostalgia and a sense of displacement. He did not, or could not, articulate what that future would look like. "Whatever happened to those people?" he wondered. "My memories and my impressions are only of calm and lazy people and yet, as I wrote in the beginning, I am filled with something like deep emotion."[40]

Others tried to find a language to rearticulate memories that relied on a now-obsolete geography. Mizutani Chōzaburō, a member of the House of Representatives during the 1930s and early 1940s and a two-time minister of commerce and industry in the postwar period, recalled how the history of socialist struggle against militarism and economic inequality was woven through the history of his travels around Japan, the empire, and the world. Perhaps because he was writing as one of the more well-known names of the Occupation-era government, Mizutani aimed particularly to articulate how Japan's loss of international power and prestige affected the current generation of students, who would not enjoy the same experiences and opportunities that he had. He bridled at a statement by General MacArthur, who declared in 1945 that Japan had "fallen to a fourth-rate nation." "When I was a student," Mizutani reminisced, "it was a time when the 'Great Empire of Japan' had joined the world's Five Great Powers. (Today's 'Fourth-Rate Nation' Japan is one of these five great countries only in terms of population.) When I compare [my life then] to the lives of students, who are pressed by part-time work, now, my student years seem like a total dream world. From this blessed earthly paradise, I spread my wings wide and flew."[41]

Mizutani lamented the loss of Taiwan. Unlike Kitabayashi, Mizutani made clear that he held Japanese imperialism responsible for the perpetration of enormous social and political injustice. Yet, rather than consider the specific injustice of colonialism, Mizutani lamented the violence and inequality of imperial society as a whole. He located the problem in the time period, not the specific relationship: "The police suppression tactics of that era were so unreasonable that young people today can not imagine even a little bit what they were like." As a member of the Marxist Labor-Farmer Party, he had come "very close to being arrested" during the mass arrest of Communist Party members in 1928. It was under this cloud that he traveled to Taiwan in 1928, only to find that police suppression there was no better: "Because I was a member of the House of Representatives, the police restrained themselves with me. Instead, when I lectured at Taiwanese gatherings, they did harassing things like ordering my Taiwanese translator to stop translating."[42] His second trip to Taiwan, in 1941, also suffered from political unrest, in this case in the upset after the Minseitō political party expelled Representative

Saitō Takao from the Diet for questioning the legitimacy of the army's "holy war" in China in 1940. Mizutani and a few others were also expelled from the Social Masses Party for protesting the expulsion of Saitō. Traveling together to Taiwan, the expelled MPs "traveled like 'social outcasts.'"[43]

For Mizutani, the loss of empire was the loss of the potential for a powerful Japan to be a force for social progress in East Asia. Implicitly reflecting the right-wing socialist motives that had circulated through much of the argument for pan-Asianism and the Great East Asia Co-Prosperity Sphere, Mizutani critiqued the wealth and power of government officials, who stood between the emperor and the people. "When I went to Taiwan . . . the travel of the governor general was more ostentatious than the imperial processions of the Japanese emperor." Perhaps as a result, the war was lost, and "Taiwan drifted away from the hand of Japan to become the land of Chiang Kai-Shek's government-in-exile. Even my black eyes," he lamented, "have come to see the extremes of fate."[44] For Mizutani, the most unfortunate result of such failed government was that the empire was never given a proper chance to succeed: "In the postwar, when I had become a minister, Taiwan was no longer part of the territory of Japan. So, it came to pass that I never got an opportunity to travel to Taiwan squarely before the eyes of the people."[45]

For Japanese travel writers, past places eventually settled into a present map of ambiguous relations. The Japanese government normalized relations with the Republic of China (Taiwan) in 1952, Korea in 1965, and the People's Republic of China in 1972 (which abrogated the previous agreement with Taiwan). And once again, in 1964, Japanese citizens began to travel abroad for leisure. The government of South Korea, which had established its own National Tourism Corporation in 1962, eagerly sought foreign tourists for the boost they would bring the Korean economy.[46] Japanese tourists were among the largest group of foreign travelers to arrive in Korea, growing from fewer than two thousand in 1964 to over four hundred thousand in 1973.[47] More than 90 percent of these travelers were male, and a large number of them traveled for a combination of business and sex tourism.[48] At the same time, many Japanese also returned to see their old homes and visit with former classmates.[49]

The lingering ties of empire that continued to trouble the place of Japan in Asia came to have their own name: the country that is both close and far away (*chikakute tōi kuni*). The phrase appeared first in 1956, in the title of a travelogue by Kinoshita Junji, and then with increasingly frequency in the 1960s and 1970s. In this period, it almost always referred to Korea. Such language recalled the spatial politics of empire and its insistence on the complementary difference of Korea and Japan—a place that is so different yet so close, as Kobayashi Chiyoko wrote for *Tabi* magazine in 1935. Yet by the 1970s, travel writers used the trope of being both far and close to ask questions about the responsibility of Japan toward its former colonial territories. As Satō Sanae wrote in her 1972 *Dare mo kakanakatta Kankoku*

(The Korea that nobody wrote about), "Korean attitudes toward Japanese ... were not born in a single day and night." For that reason, Satō traveled to Korea to learn from ordinary Koreans *(shomin)* about the present state of Korea and to teach Japanese readers about "the faces of the neighbors who are both close and far away." For Satō, who went on to become a prolific author of books on war memory and the Japanese diaspora, international boundaries could not erase the colonial and imperial past. Rather, the memory of that encounter constituted the fundamental subtext of Korean-Japanese relations: "To answer the question of what we are supposed to do now with this country that neighbors Japan, this friendly nation, we must try once to go back to the starting point and think about [Korean-Japanese relations] again."[50]

With this statement, Satō signaled that place best remained a question, an opportunity to explore the many layers and scales of history, rather than a framework for fixing relations outside of history. For nationalists, place will continue to serve as a tool for rationalizing the politics of the moment. Yet for others more inclined to challenge rather than reproduce the status quo, attempts to fix relations between people by naturalizing particular spatial orders should continue to raise questions about the work that such placing does. As we embark on a new era of spatial politics—of battles over islands in the South China Sea, of independence movements in naturalized colonies, and of fights to right the increasingly reified inequalities of global economic interdependence—the history of placing in the Japanese Empire suggests that each attempt to produce a shared spatial imaginary must always be met with a simple yet powerful question: Whose map?

## APPENDIX

TABLE 3 Place names.

| Japanese | Characters | Chinese (pinyin) | Korean (McCune-Reischauer) | Korean (hangul) |
|---|---|---|---|---|
| Antō | 安東 | Andong | | |
| Arisan | 阿里山 | Alishan | | |
| Bujun | 撫順 | Fushun | | |
| Chōshun | 長春 | Changchun | | |
| Daidō | 大同 | | Taedong | 대동강 |
| Daikoku | 大黒山 | Dahei | | |
| Dairen | 大連 | Dalian | | |
| Eikō | 栄口 | Yingkou | | |
| Gensan | 元山 | | Wŏnsan | 원산 |
| Harbin | 哈爾濱 | Ha'erbin | | |
| Heijō | 平壤 | | P'yŏngyang | 평양 |
| Heitō | 屏東 | Pingtung | | |

177

178 APPENDIX: PLACE NAMES

| Japanese | Characters | Chinese (pinyin) | Korean (McCune-Reischauer) | Korean (hangul) |
|---|---|---|---|---|
| Hokkō | 北港 | Beigang | | |
| Hokutō | 北投 | Beitou | | |
| Hori | 埔里 | Puli | | |
| Hōten | 奉天 | Fengtian | | |
| Jinsen | 仁川 | | Inch'ŏn | 인천 |
| Kagi | 嘉義 | Chiayi | | |
| Kaijō | 開城 | | Kaesŏng | 개성 |
| Kappanzan | 角板山 | Jiaobanshan | | |
| Keishū (Korea) | 慶州 | | Kyŏngju | 경주 |
| Keishū (Taiwan) | 溪州 | Xizhou | | |
| Kinshū | 錦州 | Jinzhou | | |
| Kiryū | 基隆 | Jilong | | |
| Maruyama | 円山 | Yuanshan | | |
| Musha | 霧社 | Wushe | | |
| Nichigetsutan (Sun-Moon Lake) | 日月潭 | Riyuetan | | |
| Niitaka | 新高 | Yushan | | |
| Ryojun (Port Arthur) | 旅順 | Lushun | | |
| Pusan | 釜山 | | Busan | 부산 |
| Puyo | 扶余 | | Buyŏ | 부여 |
| Ryōyō | 遼陽 | Liaoyang | | |

APPENDIX: PLACE NAMES 179

| Japanese | Characters | Chinese (pinyin) | Korean (McCune-Reischauer) | Korean (hangul) |
|---|---|---|---|---|
| Shingishū | 新義州 | | Sinŭiju | 신의주 |
| Taichū | 台中 | Taichung | | |
| Taihoku | 台北 | Taipei | | |
| Tainan | 台南 | Tainan | | |
| Taroko | タロコ | Taroko | | |
| Tōkōshi | 湯崗子 | Tanggangzi | | |
| Tsugitaka | 次高山 | Xueshan | | |

# NOTES

## PREFACE AND ACKNOWLEDGMENTS

1. Mark R. Peattie, "Japanese Attitudes toward Colonialism, 1895–1937," in *The Japanese Colonial Empire, 1895–1937*, ed. Ramon H. Myers and Mark R. Peattie (Princeton, NJ: Princeton University Press, 1984), 6.
2. Ibid., 7.
3. Ann Laura Stoler and Frederick Cooper, "Between Metropole and Colony: Rethinking a Research Agenda," in *Tensions of Empire: Colonial Cultures in a Bourgeois World* (Berkeley: University of California Press, 1997), 23.
4. Antoinette Burton, "Introduction: On the Inadequacy and Indispensability of the Nation," in *After the Imperial Turn: Thinking with and through the Nation* (Durham, NC: Duke University Press, 2003), 5, 12; Ann Laura Stoler, "On Degrees of Imperial Sovereignty," *Public Culture* 18, no. 1 (2006): 125–46; and Jane Burbank and Frederick Cooper, *Empires in World History: Power and the Politics of Difference* (Princeton, NJ: Princeton University Press, 2010).
5. The term "space of exception" comes from Nasser Hussain, *The Jurisprudence of Emergency: Colonialism and the Rule of Law* (Ann Arbor: University of Michigan Press, 2003), 20, 31.

## INTRODUCTION

1. Quoted in Jun Uchida, *Brokers of Empire: Japanese Settler Colonialism in Korea, 1876–1945* (Cambridge: Harvard University Asia Center, 2011), 299.
2. Samuel P. S. Ho, *The Economic Development of Taiwan, 1860–1970* (New Haven, CT: Yale University Press, 1978), 29.
3. Stoler, "Degrees of Imperial Sovereignty," 128, 136–37.

4. Paul Kramer calls the externalization of empire a "spatial ideology of impressive durability." Paul Kramer, "Power and Connection: Imperial Histories of the United States and the World," *American Historical Review* 116, no. 5 (2011): 1357. On the issue of how of comparing the "good" nationalism of the United States with the "bad" imperialism of Japan has shaped the historiography of race and empire in both countries, see Takashi Fujitani, *Race for Empire: Koreans As Japanese and Japanese As Americans during World War II* (Berkeley: University of California Press, 2011), 7–17.

5. Giovanni Arrighi, *The Long Twentieth Century: Money, Power, and the Origins of Our Times* (London: Verso, 1994).

6. Prasenjit Duara, "Asia Redux: Conceptualizing a Region for Our Times," *Journal of Asian Studies* 69, no. 4 (2010): 964, 966.

7. Hussain, *The Jurisprudence of Emergency*, 20, 31.

8. Yamamuro Shin'ichi, *Manchuria under Japanese Domination*, trans. Joshua A. Fogel (Philadelphia: University of Pennsylvania Press, 2006).

9. Hiroko Matsuda, "Becoming Japanese in the Colony," *Cultural Studies* 26, no. 5 (2012): 692–93.

10. Barbara J. Brooks, "Japanese Colonialism, Gender, and Household Registration: Legal Reconstruction of Boundaries," in *Gender and Law in the Japanese Imperium*, ed. Susan L. Burns and Barbara J. Brooks, 219–39 (Honolulu: University of Hawai'i Press, 2014), 235.

11. Tessa Morris-Suzuki, *Reinventing Japan: Time, Space, and Nation* (Armonk, NY: M. E. Sharpe, 1998), 189.

12. H. Matsuda, "Becoming Japanese," 694. Okamoto Makiko, *Shokuminchi kanryō no seijishi, Chōsen Taiwan sōtokufu to teikoku Nihon* (Tokyo: Sangensha, 2008).

13. Fujitani, *Race for Empire*.

14. Brooks, "Japanese Colonialism," 233–34. The marriage of Korean women to Japanese men appears to have been infrequent, which Brooks speculates may account for the government's enthusiastic promotion of these unions.

15. On the social character of space, see Henri Lefebvre, *The Production of Space*, trans. Donald Nicholson-Smith (Oxford: Blackwell, 1991). On ways that geographers in the Marxist tradition have grappled with the relationship between social and spatial orders, see Edward W. Soja, "The Socio-Spatial Dialectic," *Annals of the Association of American Geographers* 70, no. 2 (1980): 207–25.

16. John Urry, *The Tourist Gaze: Leisure and Travel in Contemporary Societies* (London: Sage, 1990).

17. Peter Duus, "Imperialism without Colonies: The Vision of a Greater East Asia Co-Prosperity Sphere," *Diplomacy and Statecraft* 7, no. 1 (1996): 54–72; and Susan Pedersen, *The Guardians: The League of Nations and the Crisis of Empire* (New York: Oxford University Press, 2015).

18. Shelley Baranowski, Christopher Endy, Waleed Hazbun, Stephanie Malia Hom, Gordon Pirie, Trevor Simmons, and Eric G. E. Zuelow, "Discussion: Tourism and Empire," *Journal of Tourism History* 7, no. 1–2 (2015): 100–130.

19. Jason Ruiz, *Americans in the Treasure House: Travel to Porfirian Mexico and the Cultural Politics of Empire* (Austin: University of Texas Press, 2014); Christine M. Skwiot, *The Purposes of Paradise: U.S. Tourism and Empire in Cuba and Hawai'i* (Philadelphia: University of Pennsylvania Press, 2010); Vernadette Vicuña-Gonzalez, *Securing Paradise:*

*Tourism and Militarism in Hawai'i and the Philippines* (Durham, NC: Duke University Press, 2013).

20. Ellen Furlough, "*Une leçon de choses:* Tourism, Empire, and the Nation in Interwar France," *French Historical Studies* 25, no. 3 (2002): 441–73; and Inderpal Grewal, *Home and Harem: Nation, Gender, Empire and the Cultures of Travel* (Durham, NC: Duke University Press, 1996).

21. Ann Laura Stoler suggests the term *imperial formation* rather than *empire* as a way of refocusing on the processes of imperial "decimation, displacement, and reclamation" that continue beyond the fixed form of empire. I'm indebted to her analysis here for drawing my attention to how such an approach can productively illuminate the ways in which empire was never Empire but always a formation in process. See Stoler, "Imperial Debris: Reflections on Ruins and Ruination," *Cultural Anthropology* 23, no. 2 (2008): 191–219. In the Japanese Empire, *terra nullius* (in Japanese, *mushu no chi*) arguments were used in legal proceedings concerning the colonization of Ainu land in Hokkaidō and indigenous land in Taiwan. On *terra nullius / mushu no chi* and the legal colonization of Hokkaidō, see Katsuya Hirano, "Thanatopolitics and the Making of Japan's Hokkaidō: Settler Colonialism and Primitive Accumulation," *Critical Historical Studies* 2, no. 2 (2015): 197. On *mushu no chi* arguments in the case of Taiwan, see chapter 4. On *terra nullius* in the colonization of North America, Pacific islands, and Australia, see Stuart Banner, *Possessing the Pacific: Land, Settlers, and Indigenous Peoples from Australia to Alaska* (Cambridge: Harvard University Press, 2007).

22. On imperial tourism as "self-administered citizenship training" in the context of the 1940 celebrations of the 2,600th anniversary of the Japanese imperial household, see Kenneth J. Ruoff, *Imperial Japan at Its Zenith: The Wartime Celebration of the Empire's 2,600th Anniversary* (Ithaca: Cornell University Press, 2010), esp. chap. 5. On tourism to Port Arthur as a "memory industry," see Gao Yuan, "Kioku sangyō toshite no tsūrizumu: sengo ni okeru Nihonjin no 'Manshū' kankō," *Gendai shisō* 29, no. 3 (2001): 219; and Gao Yuan, "'Rakudo' o hashiru kankō basu," in *Kakudai suru modanitii: 1920–1930 nendai 2*, ed. Yoshimi Shun'ya (Tokyo: Iwanami shoten, 2002). See also Louise Young, *Japan's Total Empire: Manchukuo and the Culture of Wartime Imperialism* (Berkeley: University of California Press, 1998); Soyama Takeshi, *Shokuminchi Taiwan to kindai tsūrizumu* (Tokyo: Seikyūsha, 2003); Hyung Il Pai, *Heritage Management in Korea and Japan: The Politics of Antiquity and Identity* (Seattle: University of Washington Press, 2013); Paul D. Barclay, "Peddling Postcards and Selling Empire: Image-Making in Taiwan under Japanese Colonial Rule," *Japanese Studies* 30, no. 1 (2010): 81–110; Osa Shizue, "'Manshū' tsūrizumu to gakkō teikoku kūkan senjō: Joshi kōtō shihan gakkō no 'tairiku ryokō' kiroku o chūshin ni," in *Teikoku to gakkō*, ed. Komagome Takeshi and Hashimoto Nobuya, 337–77 (Kyōto: Shōwadō, 2007).

23. David Howell describes the "geography of civilization" as a way of conceiving of early modern Japan that defined the borders of the realm and the differences between subjects of the shogun from others as the separation of "the civilized from the barbarian." In Howell's argument, the Meiji state spatialized the status component of this geography—over time, equating Japanese ethnicity with civility and the space of civilization with the territory of the state. I also use the term to evoke the kind of core-periphery geography that Howell is describing. But as I use it, the modern geography of civilization was not a totalizing

geography of state-ethnicity-territory. Rather, it encapsulated a number of modes of territorial incorporation that relied on the core-periphery idea, but each represented distinct spatializations of the Japanese nation. See Howell, *Geographies of Identity in Nineteenth-Century Japan* (Berkeley: University of California Press, 2005), 3, 131–54.

24. In formulating this concept, I draw inspiration from recent studies of the spatial history of imperialism, such as those by Sylvia Sellers-García and Paul Kosmin, which demonstrate that spatial concepts such as "distance" and "territory" have served as powerful methods for naturalizing empire across a broad span of human history. Sylvia Sellers-García, *Distance and Documents at the Spanish Empire's Periphery* (Stanford: Stanford University Press, 2014); Paul Kosmin, *The Land of the Elephant Kings: Space, Territory, and Ideology in the Seleucid Empire* (Cambridge, MA: Harvard University Press, 2014).

25. Lauren Benton, "Spatial Histories of Empire," *Itinerario* 30, no. 3 (2006): 20 suggests, for example, that "micro-regions represented a grammar for spatial organization in European empire" that can be approached by historians within the framework of a non-completist, non-jigsaw puzzle, non-universalizing approach to imperial geographies.

26. The project bridges a gap between spatial histories of early modern Japan, which trace the history of the emergence of Japan's modern geobody, and cultural histories of the Japanese Empire, which have taken space as a key topic of analysis but which have not extended the analysis to the study of the spatial imaginary of modern Japan itself. On the spatial history of early modern Japan, see Kären E. Wigen, *A Malleable Map: Geographies of Restoration in Central Japan, 1600–1912* (Berkeley: University of California Press, 2010); Howell, *Geographies of Identity*; David Howell, "Territoriality and Collective Identity in Tokugawa Japan," *Daedalus* 127, no. 3 (1998): 105–32; Katō Takashi, "Governing Edo," in *Edo and Paris: Urban Life and the State in the Early Modern Era*, ed. James L. McClain, John M. Merriman, and Ugawa Kaoru, 41–67 (Ithaca: Cornell University Press, 1994). See also Marcia Yonemoto, *Mapping Early Modern Japan: Space, Place, and Culture in the Tokugawa Period, 1603–1868* (Berkeley: University of California Press, 2003). On the spatial aspects of the history of the Japanese Empire, see E. Taylor Atkins, *Primitive Selves: Koreana in the Japanese Colonial Gaze, 1910–1945* (Berkeley: University of California Press, 2010); Kimberley Brandt, *Kingdom of Beauty: Mingei and the Politics of Folk Art in Imperial Japan* (Durham, NC: Duke University Press, 2007); Noriko Aso, *Public Properties: Museums in Imperial Japan* (Durham, NC: Duke University Press, 2014); Prasenjit Duara, *Sovereignty and Authenticity: Manchukuo and the East Asian Modern* (Lanham, MD: Rowman and Littlefield, 2003); L. Young, *Japan's Total Empire*.

27. Stefan Tanaka, *Japan's Orient: Rendering Pasts into History* (Berkeley: University of California Press, 1993), 244–55.

28. The history of imperial tourism's spatial politics elucidates how the theories of multiethnic Japanese national identity and culture that circulated in the realm of intellectual debate and policy were made tangible to a popular audience. Komagome Takeshi, *Shokuminchi teikoku Nihon no bunka tōgō* (Tokyo: Iwanami shoten, 1996) and Komagome Takeshi, *Sekaishi no naka no Taiwan shokuminchi shihai: Tainan chōrōkyō chūgakkō kara no shiza* (Tokyo: Iwanami shoten, 2015); Haruyama Meitetsu, *Kindai Nihon to Taiwan: Musha jiken shokuminchi tōchi seisaku no kenkyū* (Tokyo: Fujiwara shobō, 2008); Oguma Eiji, *'Nihonjin' no kyōkai: Okinawa, Ainu, Taiwan, Chōsen, shokuminchi shihai kara fukki undō made* (Tokyo: Shin'yōsha, 1998); Morris-Suzuki, *Reinventing Japan: Time, Space, and Nation;*

and Oguma Eiji, *A Genealogy of "Japanese" Self-Images*, trans. David Askew (Melbourne, Australia: Trans Pacific Press, 2002), 133, 134–37. It is, in fact, in Oguma Eiji's famous study of concepts of Japanese ethnicity and national identity under empire that we get a glimpse of the centrality of place to the history of empire. Oguma specifically highlighted how changes to the spatial representation of Japan in the 1920s were part of the broader embrace of a multiethnic imaginary of the Japanese nation. The "most marked transition" in descriptions of the Japanese Empire was found in geography textbooks, he writes, which, after 1918, "clearly adopted the view that Japan was a multi-national empire."

29. Peter Jackson and Jan Penrose, "Introduction: Placing 'Race' and Nation," in *Constructions of Race, Place, and Nation* (London: University College London Press, 1994); Tracey Banivanua-Mar and Penelope Edmonds, "Making Space in Settler Colonies," in *Making Settler Colonial Space: Perspectives on Race, Place, and Identity* (New York: Palgrave MacMillan, 2010), 2. Though we arrived at the term separately, Banivanua-Mar and Edmonds also use *spatial politics* to describe how settler colonial societies used representations of space to facilitate the dispossession of indigenous populations and the possession of these lands by expanding nation-states. They also caution against conflating the spatial politics of settler colonialism with other kinds of colonialism. Here, I have opted to focus less on the specifics of settler colonialism within the Japanese Empire in favor of an approach that highlights how spatial politics operated in the heterogeneous colonial formations of Japanese imperialism. Indeed, one of the most significant elements of spatial politics was the way in which it sought to transform these heterogeneous formations into the singular space of the nation. On settler colonialism in the Japanese Empire compared to settler colonialism elsewhere, see J. Uchida, *Brokers of Empire*, 11–25. For a global perspective, see Caroline Elkins and Susan Pedersen, eds., *Settler Colonialism in the Twentieth Century: Projects, Practices, Legacies* (New York: Routledge, 2005).

30. There is a robust field of scholarship on the spatial history of empire, much of it focused on cartographic and other technologies for making the terrain legible to imperial states and on the construction of urban spaces under colonial modernity. It does not, however, address the liminality of nation and empire, and thus it tends to pathologize geographies of dominance as "imperial" rather than examining their shifting uses. For an overview of this scholarship, see Daniel Clayton, "Critical and Imperial Geographies," in *Handbook of Cultural Geography*, ed. Kay Anderson, Mona Domosh, Steve Pile, and Nigel Thrift, 354–68 (Thousand Oaks, CA: Sage, 2003). For a critique of the overemphasis on imperial geographies at the expense of colonized geographies, see Brenda S. A. Yeoh, "Historical Geographies of the Colonised World," in *Modern Historical Geographies*, ed. Catherine Nash and B. J. Graham, 146–66 (London: Longman, 2000); Étienne Balibar and Immanuel Wallerstein, *Race, Nation, Class: Ambiguous Identities* (London: Verso, 1991); Mae M. Ngai, *Impossible Subjects: Illegal Aliens and the Making of Modern America* (Princeton, NJ: Princeton University Press, 2004); Natalia Molina, *How Race Is Made in America: Immigration, Citizenship, and the Historical Power of Racial Scripts* (Berkeley: University of California Press, 2014). For a powerful argument on the racial character of capitalism, see Cedric J. Robinson, *Black Marxism: The Making of the Black Radical Tradition* (Chapel Hill: University of North Carolina Press, 2000).

31. Tim Cresswell, *Place: A Short Introduction* (Malden, MA: Blackwell, 2004), 15.

32. Jeff E. Malpas, *Place and Experience: A Philosophical Topography* (Cambridge: Cambridge University Press, 1999), 36, quoted in Cresswell, *Place: A Short Introduction*, 31.

33. Yi-Fu Tuan, "Space and Place: Humanistic Perspective" (1974), in *Human Geography: An Essential Anthology*, eds. John Agnew, David Livingstone, and Alistair Rodgers, 444–57 (Oxford: Blackwell, 1996); John Agnew, "Representing Space: Space, Scale and Culture in Social Science," in *Place/Culture/Representation*, ed. James Duncan and David Ley (London: Routledge, 1993), 263.

34. Rob Shields, *Places on the Margins: Alternative Geographies of Modernity* (London: Routledge, 1991).

35. Doreen Massey, "Power-Geometry and a Progressive Sense of Place," in *Mapping the Futures: Local Cultures, Global Change*, ed. John Bird, Barry Curtis, Tim Putnam, and Lisa Tickner (London: Routledge, 1993), 66.

36. David Harvey, *Justice, Nature, and the Geography of Difference* (Malden, MA: Blackwell Publishing, 1996), 261, 264.

37. John Agnew, "No Borders, No Nations: Making Greece in Macedonia," *Annals of the Association of American Geographers* 97, no. 2 (2007): 398–422. The nation-state was not the only model that anti-imperial activists promoted to address the problem of equality and political emancipation. See Frederick Cooper, *Africa in the World: Capitalism, Empire, Nation-State* (Cambridge, MA: Harvard University Press, 2014).

38. Benedict Anderson, *Imagined Communities: Reflections on the Origin and Spread of Nationalism* (London: Verso, 1983); Eric Hobsbawm, *Nations and Nationalism since 1780: Programme, Myth, Reality* (Cambridge: Cambridge University Press, 1992); Étienne Balibar, "The Nation Form," in *Race, Class, Nation: Ambiguous Identities*, ed. Étienne Balibar and Immanuel Wallerstein, 86–106 (London: Verso, 1991).

39. Edward W. Soja, *The Political Organization of Space* (Washington, DC: The Association of American Geographers, 1971).

40. Itty Abraham, *How India Became Territorial: Foreign Policy, Diaspora, Geopolitics* (Stanford, CA: Stanford University Press, 2014), 18. See also 107–40.

41. Alexander B. Murphy presents a compelling history of this shift in "The Sovereign State System As Political-Territorial Ideal: Historical and Contemporary Considerations," in *State Sovereignty As Social Construct*, ed. Thomas J. Biersteker and Cynthia Weber, 81–120 (Cambridge: Cambridge University Press, 1996).

42. Patrick Wolfe, *Settler Colonialism* (New York: Bloomsbury, 1999), 2.

43. Anthony D. Smith, *The Nation in History: Historiographical Debates about Ethnicity and Nationalism* (Hanover, NH: University Press of New England, 2000), 21.

44. Ibid., 4–26, esp. 10–15, quote on 21. Smith relies heavily on Homi K. Bhabha, ed., *Nation and Narration* (London: Routledge, 1990).

45. Agnew, "No Borders, No Nations," 416; Thongchai Winikachul, *Siam Mapped: A History of the Geo-Body of the Nation* (Honolulu: University of Hawai'i Press, 1994).

46. A. D. Smith, "States and Homelands: The Social and Geopolitical Implications of National Territory," *Millennium: Journal of International Studies* 10, no. 3 (1981): 187.

47. David H. Kaplan, "Territorial Identities and Geographic Scale," in *Nested Identities: Nationalism, Territory, and Scale*, ed. Guntram Henrik Herb and David H. Kaplan (Lanhan, MD: Rowman & Littlefield, 1999), 34–38.

48. Kaplan, "Territorial Identities and Geographic Scale." See also Anssi Paasi, *Territories, Boundaries, and Consciousness: The Changing Geographies of the Finnish-Russian Border* (Chichester, England: J. Wiley and Sons, 1996).

49. Yamazaki Naomasa, *Futsū kyōiku Nihon chiri kyōkasho* (Tokyo: Tokyo kaiseikan, 1919), 5.

50. Nitobe Inazō, "Shokuminchi seisaku kōgi oyobi ronbun" (c. 1915), in *Nitobe Inazō zenshū*, vol. 4, ed. Nitobe Inazō zenshū henshū iinkai (Tokyo: Kyōbunkan, 1969), 57. See also Asada Kyōji, *Nihon shokuminchi kenkyū shiron* (Tokyo: Miraisha, 1990), 37, n. 3.

51. Nitobe, "Shokuminchi," 61.

52. Nitobe, "Shokuminchi," 57.

53. Asada, *Nihon shokuminchi kenkyū shiron*, 32.

54. Nitobe, "Shokuminchi," 63.

55. This is not an argument against Said's imaginative geographies. Said argued quite clearly, especially in his later work on place and memory, that his concept of imaginative geographies includes their use as tools for dispossession. Rather, spatial politics seeks to keep the discursive always in conversation with the material by emphasizing the relationship between the spatial imaginary of the nation and the practices that sustained unequal forms of citizenship within the territory of the state. Edward W. Said, *Orientalism* (London: Verso, 1978), and Said, "Invention, Memory, and Place," *Critical Inquiry* 26, no. 2 (2000): 175–92. For uses of Said that pay particular attention to the material consequences of spatial discourse, see Gary Fields, "Enclosure Landscapes: Historical Reflections on Palestinian Geography," *Historical Geography* 39 (2011): 182–207; and Gary Fields, "This Is Our Land: Collective Violence, Property Law, and Imagining the Geography of Palestine," *Journal of Cultural Geography* 29, no. 3 (2012): 267–91.

56. On wartime tourism to occupied China, see Kenneth J. Ruoff, "Japanese Tourism to Mukden, Nanjing, and Qufu, 1938–1943," *Japan Review* 27 (2014): 171–200.

57. See, for example, Peter Duus, Ramon H. Myers, and Mark R. Peattie, *The Japanese Informal Empire in China, 1895–1937* (Princeton: Princeton University Press, 1989). More recently, Louise Young argues that Japanese imperialism contained both formal and informal elements. The point I make here is that the field of Japanese Empire studies treats Japanese Manchuria as a different historical phenomenon than that of "formal" Japanese colonialism in Taiwan and Korea. Young, *Japan's Total Empire*, 11.

58. The government held a 50 percent stake and the Imperial House held a 1 percent stake. Y. Tak Matsusaka, *The Making of Japanese Manchuria, 1904–1932* (Cambridge: Harvard University Asia Center, 2001), 71, 90.

59. Manshū senseki hozonkai (1914) at Japan Center for Asian Historical Records (A14080166600).

60. The phrase *semantic depth* comes from Nicholas J. Entrikin, *The Betweenness of Place: Towards a Geography of Modernity* (Baltimore: Johns Hopkins University Press, 1991). For the classic study of place names and imperial spatial imaginaries, see Paul Carter, *The Road to Botany Bay: Explorations in Landscape and History* (New York: Knopf, 1988). Engseng Ho's *Graves of Tarim: Genealogy and Mobility across the Indian Ocean* (Berkeley: University of California Press, 2006) and Rian Thum's recent *The Sacred Routes of Uyghur History* (Cambridge, MA: Harvard University Press, 2014) show how certain texts and place names can become anchors through which diasporic and otherwise mobile communities construct spatial identities.

61. Andre Schmid, *Korea between Empires, 1895–1919* (New York: Columbia University Press, 2002), 72–78, 74.

62. Richard Siddle, "The Making of Ainu Moshiri: Japan's Indigenous Nationalism and Its Cultural Fictions," in *Nationalisms in Japan*, ed. Naoko Shimazu, 110–30 (New York: Routledge, 2006).

1. SEEING LIKE THE NATION

1. Nakanishi Inosuke, *Shina Manshū Chōsen* (Tokyo: Jissensha, 1936), 3–4.

2. Andre Haag describes Nakanishi as a "one-man contact zone" for his role in facilitating connections between Japanese and Korean writers. See Haag's insightful chapter on Nakanishi's "anti-travelogues" in "Fear and Loathing in Imperial Japan: The Cultures of Korean Peril, 1919–1923," PhD diss., Stanford University, 2013, 200–69. For more on Nakanishi's writings on Korea, see Nakane Takayuki, *"Chōsen" hyōshō no bunka shi: Kindai Nihon to tasha o meguru chi no shokuminchika* (Tokyo: Shin'yōsha, 2004). Haag's characterization of Nakanishi as being particularly attuned to the way that "the system of colonialism warps the inner world of Japanese settlers" is in contrast to Kawamura Minato's reading of his work—Kawamura suggests that Nakanishi "lacked any self-reflection on how the Japanese self appeared to Koreans." Kawamura Minato, "Puroreteria bungaku no naka no minzoku mondai," *Kokubungaku kaishaku to kanshō* 75, no. 4 (2010): 63, quoted and translated in Haag, "Fear and Loathing in Imperial Japan," 265. From my readings of Nakanishi's later travelogues for Korea, Manchuria, and Taiwan, I am inclined to follow Haag's reading of Nakanishi as particularly insightful, if unruly, critic of colonialism's cultural politics. For more on Nakanishi's writings in the contact zone, see Karen Thornber, *Empire of Texts in Motion: Chinese, Korea, and Taiwanese Transculturations of Japanese Literature* (Cambridge, MA: Harvard University Asia Center, 2009).

3. Nakanishi, *Shina Manshū Chōsen*, 56.

4. James C. Scott, *Seeing Like a State: How Certain Schemes to Improve the Human Condition Have Failed* (New Haven, CT: Yale University Press, 1998).

5. Gotō Shinpei, "Taiwan kankō jun," *Tabi* 1925, no. 12: 2–3.

6. Mary Louise Pratt, *Imperial Eyes: Travel Writing and Transculturation*, 2nd ed. (New York: Routledge, 2008), 3.

7. Bernard S. Cohn terms this the "observational/travel modality" of producing colonial knowledge in which the itinerary provides a narrative for organizing knowledge. Cohn, *Colonialism and Its Forms of Knowledge: The British in India* (Princeton, NJ: Princeton University Press, 1996), 6–7.

8. Helen J. S. Lee, "Voices of the 'Colonists,' Voices of the 'Immigrants': 'Korea' in Japan's Early Colonial Travel Narratives and Guides, 1894–1914," *Japanese Language and Literature* 41, no. 1 (2007): 7.

9. A classic example of this argument is Marius B. Jansen, "Japanese Imperialism: Late Meiji Perspectives," in *The Japanese Colonial Empire, 1895–1945*, ed. Ramon H. Myers and Mark R. Peattie, 61–79 (Princeton: Princeton University Press, 1989). Other prominent examples include, Akira Iriye, "Japan's Drive to Great-Power Status," in *The Cambridge History of Japan*, vol. 5, *The Nineteenth Century*, ed. Marius B. Jansen, 721–82 (Cambridge:

Cambridge University Press, 1989); William Lockwood, *The Economic Development of Japan* (Princeton: Princeton University Press, 1954). The description of Japanese imperial expansion as a logical, necessary, and generally uncontested step in Japan's industrial development appears more recently in Burbank and Cooper, *Empires in World History*, 302–3. Other historians, especially those writing in Japanese, have developed a considerably more circumspect position on the preordained nature of Japanese imperial expansion. See, for example, Komori Yōichi and Narita Ryūichi, eds., *Nichi-Ro sensō sutadīzu* (Tokyo: Kinokuniya shoten, 2004).

10. Peter B. High, *The Imperial Screen: Japanese Film Culture in the Fifteen Years' War* (Madison: University of Wisconsin Press, 2003), 3–8; and T. Fujitani, *Splendid Monarchy: Power and Pageantry in the Making of Modern Japan* (Berkeley: University of California Press, 1996), 127–32.

11. "Man-Kan jun'yū sen," *Tokyo Asahi shinbun*, July 25, 1906, morning edition.

12. Shumpei Okamoto, "The Emperor and the Crowd: The Historical Significance of the Hibiya Riot," in *Conflict in Modern Japanese History: The Neglected Tradition*, ed. Tetsuo Najita and J. Victor Koschmann, 258–75 (Princeton: Princeton University Press, 1982); Andrew Gordon, *Labor and Imperial Democracy in Prewar Japan* (Berkeley: University of California Press, 1991), 26–33.

13. Narita Ryūichi, "'Kokumin' no hikōteki keisei: Nichi-Ro sensō to minshū undō," in *Nichi-Ro sensō sutadīzu*, ed. Komori Yōichi and Narita Ryūichi (Tokyo: Kinokuniya shoten, 2004), 122; Naoko Shimazu, "The Myth of the 'Patriotic Soldier': Japanese Attitudes toward Death in the Russo-Japanese War," *War & Society* 19, no. 2 (2001): 75.

14. The comment is from Ōmachi Keigetsu in *Taiyō* magazine. Quoted in Naoko Shimazu, *Japanese Society at War: Death, Memory, and the Russo-Japanese War* (Cambridge: Cambridge University Press, 2009), 41.

15. Yosano Akiko, "You Must Not Die," trans. Atsumi Ikuko and Graeme Wilson, in Atsumi Ikuko and Graeme Wilson, "The Poetry of Yosano Akiko," *Japan Quarterly* 21, no. 2 (1974), 184, quoted in Shimazu, *Japanese Society at War*, 31–32.

16. Narita, "'Kokumin' no hikōteki keisei," 128.

17. Sho Konishi, *Anarchist Modernity: Cooperatism and Japanese-Russian Relations in Modern Japan* (Cambridge, MA: Harvard University Asia Center, 2013), 169.

18. Kevin M. Doak, *A History of Nationalism in Modern Japan: Placing the People* (Leiden: Brill, 2007), 148–215, esp. 194. See also Yoon, Keun Cha, *Nihon kokuminron: Kindai Nihon no aidentiti* (Tokyo: Chikuma shobō, 1997). J. Uchida, *Brokers of Empire*, 24, translates *kokumin* as "citizen-subjects" to emphasize the slippery status of settlers as Japanese outside of the territorial jurisdiction of the Constitution, as well as the empire's practice of separating nationality from citizenship. But since, legally speaking, *kokumin*-ness was not a determination of citizenship, I have opted here to simply leave the word in its Japanese form. On the disconnect between *kokumin* as "national people" and "citizen," see Douglas R. Howland, *Translating the West: Language and Political Reason in Nineteenth-Century Japan* (Honolulu: University of Hawai'i Press, 2002), 185–88.

19. Ishida Takeshi, "Dōka seisaku to tsukurareta kannen toshite no 'Nihon,'" *Shisō*, no. 892 (1998): 48.

20. Doak, *A History of Nationalism*, 165–77.

21. Carol Gluck, *Japan's Modern Myths: Ideology in the Late Meiji Period* (Princeton: Princeton University Press, 1985); Kevin M. Doak, "What Is a Nation and Who Belongs? National Narratives and the Ethnic Imagination in Twentieth-Century Japan," *American Historical Review* 102, no. 2 (1997): 287.

22. Konishi, *Anarchist Modernity*, 157.

23. This paragraph is indebted to Sho Konishi's insightful analysis of the Nonwar movement and its critiques of modern international relations. Konishi, *Anarchist Modernity*, 148–54. See also Beate Jahn, "IR and the State of Nature: The Cultural Origins of a Ruling Ideology," *Review of International Studies* 25 (1999): 411–34.

24. S. Okamoto, "The Emperor and the Crowd," 274–75. For an analysis of the content of ethics textbooks, see Samuel Hideo Yamashita, "Confucianism and the Japanese State, 1904–1945," in *Confucian Traditions in East Asian Modernity: Moral Education and Economic Culture in Japan and the Four Mini-Dragons*, ed. Tu Wei-Ming, 132–54 (Cambridge: Harvard University Press, 1996).

25. Ariyama Teruo, *Kaigai kankō ryokō no tanjō* (Tokyo: Yoshikawa kōbunkan, 2002), 57–58.

26. Ibid., 54.

27. Ibid.

28. Ruoff, *Imperial Japan at Its Zenith*, 8.

29. On nationalism and the "understanding of globality as a shared historical condition" in the case of China, see Rebecca Karl, *Staging the World: Chinese Nationalism at the Turn of the Twentieth Century* (Durham: Duke University Press, 2002), quote from 195.

30. See Laura Nenzi, *Excursions in Identity: Travel at the Intersection of Place, Gender, and Status in Edo Japan* (Honolulu: University of Hawai'i Press, 2008); Imai Kingō, *Edo no tabi fūzoku: dōchūki o chūshin ni* (Tokyo: Ōzorasha, 1997); Uchida Aya, "Kinsei gōki ni okeru onsenchi e no tabi to taizai seikatsu ni kansuru kenkyū," PhD diss., Rikkyō daigaku, 2011.

31. Hoi-Eun Kim, *Doctors of Empire: Medical and Cultural Encounters between Imperial Germany and Meiji Japan* (Toronto: University of Toronto Press, 2014), 54–61; Ishizuka Minoru, *Kindai Nihon no kaigai ryūgakushi* (Tokyo: Chūō kōron, 1972); Ardath W. Burks, ed., *The Modernizers: Overseas Students, Foreign Employees, and Meiji Japan* (Boulder, CO: Westview Press, 1985)

32. Soshiroda Akira, "Inbound Tourism Policies in Japan from 1859 to 2003," *Annals of Tourism Research* 32, no. 4 (2005): 1100–20.

33. The word that I translate as "observation" here, *shisatsu*, has also been translated in this context as "investigation" and "inspection," as in "tours of inspection." I use "observation" in order to situate it within the wider context of the eighteenth- and nineteenth-century turn to the production of knowledge through visual rather than textual or metaphorical means, as well as to emphasize the eyewitness or first-hand nature of the knowledge travelers were meant to gain. The idea of travel as the observation of the real was also implicated in the construction of the individual self within the shifting frameworks of self-knowledge of the day, in this case, the idea of a national subject. Thus, as Jilly Traganou argues, "looking with 'one's own eyes' is not a spectator's natural capacity, but rather a constructed condition that has been valorized through the modern faith in the power of individuality." This individuality was constituted within, as Noriko Aso has argued, a "exhibitionary complex" that

staged (in Tim Mitchell's words) "the world as representation" in which the individual is conceived of as a spectator of a world that exists outside of his or her own encounter with it. As I am arguing here, this individuality was the conceptual precursor for the internalization of national identity based on how one saw and interacted with sites designated as "national land." Judith Adler, "The Origins of Sightseeing," *Annals of Tourism Research* 16 (1989): 7-29; Jilly Traganou, *The Tōkaidō Road: Traveling and Representation in Edo and Meiji Japan* (New York: RoutledgeCurzon, 2004), 2; Jonathan Crary, *Techniques of the Observer: On Vision and Modernity in the Nineteenth Century* (Cambridge, MA: MIT Press, 1990); Karatani Kōjin, *Kindai Nihon bungaku no kigen* (Tokyo: Kōdansha, 1988). Aso, *Public Properties*, 15-16; Timothy Mitchell, *Colonising Egypt* (Berkeley: University of California Press, 1991), 6; Timothy Mitchell, "The Stage of Modernity," in *Questions of Modernity* (Minneapolis: University of Minnesota Press, 2000), 20. For one example of a work that uses "inspection" rather than "observation," see Sonia Ryang, "Japanese Travellers' Accounts of Korea," *East Asian History* 13/14 (1997): 133-52.

34. *Ryōtō shūgaku ryokō ki* (Tokyo: Tokyo kōtō shihan gakkō shūgaku ryokō dan kiroku kakari, 1907), 2.

35. Ibid.

36. The quoted phrase is from Maki Fukuoka, *The Premise of Fidelity: Science, Visuality, and Representing the Real in Nineteenth-Century Japan* (Stanford, CA: Stanford University Press, 2012), 6. Fukuoka refers to the meaning of the word *shashin*, commonly translated as "photograph" and implicated in a telos of imaginative to real technologies of visual representation.

37. On the developmental learning movement and Japanese professional educators' embrace of Pestalozzian thought, see Mark E. Lincicome, *Principles, Praxis, and the Politics of Educational Reform in Meiji Japan* (Honolulu: University of Hawai'i Press, 1995). In geography education, see Wigen, *A Malleable Map*, 173.

38. Stefan Tanaka, "Childhood: Naturalization of Development into a Japanese Space," in *Cultures of* Scholarship, ed. Sarah C. Humphreys (Ann Arbor, MI: University of Michigan Press, 1997), 24.

39. Kären Wigen, "Teaching about Home: Geography at Work in the Prewar Nagano Classroom," *Journal of Asian Studies* 59, no. 3 (2000): 554, 556.

40. Ibid., 556. The term *metageography* comes from Martin Lewis and Kären Wigen, *The Myth of Continents: A Critique of Metageography* (Berkeley: University of California Press, 1997).

41. Wigen, *A Malleable Map*, 176.

42. Chiri rekishi kenkyūkai, *Nihon zenkoku jun'yū gakusei ensoku shūgaku ryokō annai* (Osaka: Tanaka sōeidō, 1902).

43. Quote is from S. Tanaka, "Childhood," 25. He is referring specifically to the function of childhood in the construction of the temporality of the nation here, but the context more broadly is the "convergence of nature and thought in the construction of the nation-state" (24).

44. "Jun'yū shokan," *Tokyo Asahi shinbun*, September 10, 1906, morning edition.

45. Peter J. Taylor, "Metageographical Moments: A Geohistorical Interpretation of Embedded Statism and Globalization," in *Rethinking Global Political Economy: Emerging Issues, Unfolding Odysseys*, eds. Mary Ann Tétreault, Robert A. Denmark, Kenneth P. Thomas, and Kurt Burch (New York: Routledge, 2003), 48-55.

46. "Rosettamaru jun'yū shokan (tsutsuki)," *Tokyo Asahi shinbun*, September 12, 1906, morning edition.
47. Duara, *Sovereignty and Authenticity*, 44–47.
48. Mitchell, *Colonising Egypt*, 6.
49. Dean MacCannell, *The Tourist: A New Theory of the Leisure Class* (New York: Schocken Books, 1976), 135–43.
50. Entrikin, *The Betweenness of Place*.
51. On memory as reenactment rather than recollection, see Marita Sturken, *Tangled Memories: The Vietnam War, the AIDS Epidemic, and the Politics of Remembering* (Berkeley: University of California Press, 1997), 24.
52. Tokutomi Sohō, "Seinen no fūki," *Dairokunichiyō kōdan* (1905), quoted in Oka Yoshitake, "Generational Conflict after the Russo-Japanese War," in *Conflict in Modern Japanese History: The Neglected Tradition*, eds. Tetsuo Najita and J. Victor Koschmann (Princeton: Princeton University Press, 1982), 201.
53. Hiroshima kōtō shihan gakkō, *Tairiku shūgaku ryokō ki* ([Hiroshima]: Hiroshima kōtō shihan gakkō, 1915), 55.
54. Ibid.
55. Ibid., 122.
56. Ibid., 140.
57. Ibid., 50.
58. Hamamoto Hiroshi, *Ryojun* (Tokyo: Rokkō shōkai shuppanbu, 1942), 12, for a description of the tour guides as performers with particular specialties, whose performances focused on eliciting emotional responses to the battlefields. David Wharton Lloyd, *Battlefield Tourism: Pilgrimage and the Commemoration of the Great War in Britain, Australia, and Canada, 1919–1939* (Oxford: Berg, 1998), 117, notes this practice also occurred at World War I battlefield memorials in Europe.
59. *Ryōtō shūgaku ryokō ki*, 217–18. The phrase "fast gathering darkness" is confusing in the context. It is possible that he elided the passage of an entire day's worth of time between this sentence and the previous one. It is also possible that the student made a mistake in his word choice. The student, who was part of the English Club, published his account in English.
60. Ibid.
61. Hiroshima kōtō shihan gakkō, *Tairiku shūgaku ryokō ki*, 99–100.
62. Moto Jun, "Dairen Ryojun," in *Kōyūkaishi (Keijō chū)* (March 1, 1935): 247. This particular student was probably Korean; one way to read his surname is Ho. In this case, however, his recollection differs little from that of his Japanese colleagues. On the experience of Korean students at these sites, see Woo Miyeong, "Trip to Empire on Display and Colonized Subjects," *Tong-Asia munhwa yŏn'gu* 48 (2010): 33–68.
63. "Manshū senseki hozonkai no jigyō ni kansuru kengi" (1914), Japan Center for Asian Historical Records. A14080166600.
64. Yosano traveled to Manchuria and Mongolia in the late 1920s, though her travel account repeats rather than challenges much of what would become the standard discourse of imperial travel in Manchuria. See Yosano Akiko, *Travels in Manchuria and Mongolia: A Feminist Poet from Japan Encounters Prewar China*, trans. Joshua A. Fogel (New York: Columbia University Press, 2001).

65. Monbushō, ed., *Jinjō shōgaku Nihon rekishi* (Tokyo: Monbushō, 1904), *Jinjō shōgaku Nihon rekishi* (Tokyo: Monbushō, 1909), and *Jinjō shōgaku kokushi* (1920), all reprinted in Kaigo Tokiomi and Naka Arata, eds., *Nihon kyōkasho taikei*, Kindai-hen rekishi, vol. 19 (Tokyo: Kōdansha, 1965), 443–44, 534–36, 626–28. On the use of the mythical history of Mimana to justify the annexation of Korea in 1910, see Oguma, *A Genealogy of "Japanese" Self-Images*, 84.

66. Schmid, *Korea between Empires*, 72–78.

67. George L. Mosse, *Fallen Soldiers: Reshaping the Memory of the World Wars* (New York: Oxford University Press, 1991), 7. Lloyd, *Battlefield Tourism*.

68. Kikuchi Kunisaku, *Chōhei kihi no kenkyū* (Tokyo: Rippū shobō, 1977), 110–11, quoted in Shimazu, "Myth of the 'Patriotic Soldier,'" 73.

69. Kikuchi, *Kunisaku kihi no kenkyū*, 111, 176–78, 197, 427.

70. Konishi, *Anarchist Modernity*, 184.

71. Ibid., 183–87. Though the *Heimin shinbun* printed a translation of Tolstoy's "Bethink Yourselves," a critique of the Russo-Japanese War, the newspaper's editors also challenged Tolstoy for portraying the cause of the war as lost religious faith. In an article published in the following issue, editor Kōtoku Shūsui argued that the cause of war was rather "the intensifying economic competition between major powers." For that reason, "if we wish to eliminate wars between nations, . . . we must overthrow the capitalist system and put a socialist system in its place." Kōtoku Shūsui, "A Critique of Tolstoy's Pacifism," *Heimin shinbun*, August 14, 1904, quoted in Robert Tierney, *Monster of the Twentieth Century: Kōtoku Shūsui and Japan's First Anti-Imperialist Movement* (Berkeley: University of California Press, 2015), 111. On the *Heimin shinbun* and the people's *(heimin)* movement, see Tierney, *Monster of the Twentieth Century*, 96–114.

72. Tayama Katai, "Ippei sotsu" (1908), translated as "One Soldier," in *Modern Japanese Literature, An Anthology*, trans. and ed. Donald Keene, 142–58 (New York: Grove Press, 1956).

73. Ishimitsu Makiyo, "Bōkyō no uta," in *Ishimitsu Makiyo no shuki* (Tokyo: Chūō kōronsha, 1978), 668, quoted in Shimazu, "Myth of the 'Patriotic Soldier,'" 81.

74. Shimazu, "Myth of the 'Patriotic Soldier.'"

75. Jordan Sand, "Imperial Tokyo As Contact Zone: The Metropolitan Tours of Taiwanese Aborigines," *The Asia-Pacific Journal* 12, issue 10, no. 4 (March 10, 2014).

76. Zheng Zhengcheng, *Ren shi ta zhe de tian kong: Ri zhi shi qi Taiwan yuan zhu min de guan guang xing lü* (Taipei shi: Bo yang wenhua shiye youxian gongsi, 2005), 37–77.

77. Senjū Hajime, "Nihon tōchika Nan'yō guntō ni okeru naichi kankōdan no seiritsu," *Rekishi hyōron*, no. 661 (2005): 52–68; Cho Sŏng-un, *Singminji kŭndae kwan'gwang kwa Ilbon sich'al* (Seoul: Kyŏngin munhwasa, 2011).

78. Zheng argues that the emphasis on military might and submission continued until the 1930s, when the itineraries shifted to inspiring political loyalty. These later itineraries devoted only a few hours to military sites and instead focused on temples, shrines, and agriculture. Zheng, *Ren shi ta zhe de tian kong*, 78–129.

79. "Dai 4-kai naichi kankō banjin kansō hōkoku" (1913), Japan Center for Asian Historical Records, C08020372800, frames 3–4; also cited in Sand, "Imperial Tokyo As Contact Zone." Following the annexation in 1910, members of the Korean aristocracy also undertook widely publicized tours of the metropole, where they met with the members of the Japanese

imperial family and government officials and toured local sights. In bringing members of the two aristocracies together, these tours "demonstrated Korean acceptance" of the new Japan-Korea relationship and, in particular, its "hierarchical construction." Mark Caprio, "Marketing Assimilation: The Press and the Formation of the Japanese-Korean Colonial Relationship," *Journal of Korean Studies* 16, no. 1 (2011): 2.

80. "Dai 4-kai naichi kankō banjin kansō hōkoku" (1913), Japan Center for Asian Historical Records, C08020372800, frames 3–4.

81. Cho, *Singminji kŭndae kwan'gwang kwa Ilbon sich'al*, 199.

82. Tōyō takushoku kabushiki kaisha, ed., *Chōsenjin naichi shisatsu Taishō 2-nen shūki* (Keijō: Tōyō takushoku, 1913), 14–19, 27. At the Ishimori co-op, the travelogue reported that the travelers were impressed with the savings and stability of the co-op, and argued that the stable development of Korean villages would have to be based on such organizations.

83. Howland, *Translating the West*, 38–40. *Bunmei kaika* did not equal "civilization and enlightenment" really until the advent of modernization theory in the 1950s; until then, it was simply translated as "civilization."

84. Ariyama, *Kaigai kankō ryokō*, 37–39.

85. Ibid., 38. For example, the Tokyo Prefectural Legislature voted unanimously to fund the travel of students and teachers at prefectural schools, a total of 2,022 yen. In Mie Prefecture, the government offered each elementary school teacher who traveled a 15-yen fellowship and each prefectural school principal a 25-yen fellowship.

86. This, for example, is Urry's description of tourism. Buzard points out though that even the Grand Tour, often used to contrast early modern "travel" with modern "tourism," was undertaken primarily by members of the middle class, who embarked on more or less standard itineraries that were designed to increase their knowledge of Europe and forge potential commercial connections. In this, it was not unlike imperial tourism in Japan. Urry, *The Tourist Gaze*; James Buzard, *The Beaten Track: European Tourism, Literature, and the Ways to Culture* (Oxford: Oxford University Press, 1993). For an overview of the debate, see Rudy Koshar, *German Travel Cultures* (Oxford: Berg, 2001), 4–5.

87. Gao Yuan, "Kankō no seijigaku: Senzen sengo ni okeru Nihonjin no 'Manshū' kankō" (PhD diss., University of Tokyo, 2004), 65–66.

88. Japan Tourist Bureau, ed., *Ryotei to hiyō gaisan Taishō 12-nen* (Tokyo: Japan Tourist Bureau, 1923), 259. The estimated cost included a Japan-Korea-Manchuria Leisure Ticket *(Nissenman shūyū ken)*, two round-trip fares from Dairen to Ryojun and Hōten to Bujun (not covered by the discount ticket), hotel, sleeper car and carriage expenses, and meals.

89. Shūkan Asahi, ed., *Nedanshi nenpyō: Meiji, Taishō, Shōwa* (Tokyo: Asahi shinbunsha, 1989 [1988]), 116. The tuition figures do not include lab and other fees *(jisshūryō)*.

90. "Taiwan e no tabi," *Umi* 1924, no. 8, 31–32. Japan Tourist Bureau, ed., *Ryotei to hiyō gaisan Taishō 12-nen*, 287–95. First-class travel was 326.42 yen; second class ran 232.96 yen (no third class yet offered).

91. Itō Takeo, *Life along the South Manchurian Railway: The Memoirs of Itō Takeo*, trans. Joshua A. Fogel (Armonk, NY: M. E. Sharpe, 1998), 30.

92. Abe Yasunari, "Tairiku ni kōfun suru shūgaku ryokō—Yamaguchi kōtō shōgyō gakkō ga yuku 'Man-Kan-Shi' 'Sen-Man-Shi,'" *Chūgoku* 21, no. 29 (March 2008): 226–28.

93. William Lockwood, *The Economic Development of Japan*, expanded ed. (Princeton: Princeton University Press, 1968), 272–73.

94. One description of a settler journey can be found in Kurose Yūji, *Tōyō takushoku kaisha: Nihon teikoku shugi to Ajia taiheiyō* (Tokyo: Nihon keizai hyōronsha, 2003), 39–44.

95. Man-Kan kankō dan, *Man Kan kankō dan shi* (Utsunomiya: Man-Kan kankō dan, 1911), 13, 27.

96. Ibid., 155.

97. Ibid., 35. The South Manchuria Railway also inaugurated the practice of sponsoring the travel of influential writers to Manchuria, beginning with Natsume Sōseki in 1909. Sōseki published his lightly critical account of the Railway Zone in the *Tokyo Asahi Newspaper* as "Man-Kan tokoro dokoro" (Here and there in Manchuria and Korea). It subsequently became one of the most famous travel accounts of Korea and Manchuria. Although Sōseki is considered the "father of modern Japanese literature," in the aftermath of empire, "Man-Kan tokoro dokoro" was written out of his oeuvre and the canon of modern Japanese literature as part of a larger project of casting the story of modern Japanese literature as one of Japan encountering the West, rather than of Japan colonizing Asia. James A. Fujii, "Writing Out Asia: Modernity, Canon, and Natsume Sōseki's *Kokoro*," positions 1, no. 1 (1993): 194–223. For an excellent English translation of Sōseki's account, see Natsume Sōseki, *Man-Kan tokoro dokoro*, reprinted in *Rediscovering Natsume Sōseki, with the First English Translation of Travels in Manchuria and Korea*, trans. Inger Sigrun Brodey and Sammy I. Tsunematsu (Kent, England: Global Oriental, 2000).

98. "Ryokōbu buhō," *Kōyūkai zasshi*, no. 243 (March 17, 1915): 50–51.

99. Kōbe kōtō shōkō gakkō, *Kaigai ryokō chōsa hōkoku (Taishō 7-nen kaki)*, (Kōbe: Kōbe kōtō shōkō gakkō, 1919), preface.

100. See Ugaramon's critique of *shisatsuka*, which Lee translates as "surveyors" in Ugaramon, *Chōsen e yuku hito ni* (Tokyo: Chōsen e yuku hito hensanjo, 1914), cited in H. Lee, "Voices of the 'Colonists,'" 27.

101. Hiroshima kōtō shihan gakkō, *Tairiku shūgaku ryokō ki*, 36. David R. Ambaras, "Social Knowledge, Cultural Capital, and the New Middle Class in Japan," *Journal of Japanese Studies* 24, no. 1 (1998): 22.

102. Daniel T. Rodgers, *Atlantic Crossings: Social Politics in a Progressive Age* (Cambridge, MA: Belknap Press, 1998).

103. "Man-Sen ryokōki," *Kōyūkai zasshi*, no. 219 (November 21, 1912): 100.

104. Ibid., 128.

105. Hiroshima kōtō shihan gakkō, *Tairiku shūgaku ryokō ki*, 56.

106. Ibid., 100.

107. Zheng, *Ren shi ta zhe de tian kong*, 286.

108. Kate McDonald, "Speaking Japanese: Language and the Expectation of Empire," in *The Affect of Difference: Representations of Race in the Japanese Empire*, ed. Christopher P. Hanscom and Dennis Washburn (Honolulu: University of Hawai'i Press, 2016), 167.

109. Ji Seon Bang, "A School Excursion of the Middle School Managed by Korean to Japan, Manchuria in 1920-30s," [in Korean]. *Sŏktang nonch'ong* 44 (2009): 167–216.

110. Hiroshima kōtō shihan gakkō, *Tairiku shūgaku ryokō ki*, 49.

111. Marilyn Ivy, *Discourses of the Vanishing: Modernity, Phantasm, Japan* (Chicago: University of Chicago Press, 1995); Ann Laura Stoler and Carole McGranahan, "Refiguring Imperial Terrains," *Ab Imperio* 2 (2006): 52.

112. Mariko Tamanoi, *Memory Maps: The State and Manchuria in Postwar Japan* (Honolulu: University of Hawai'i Press, 2009), 159–60; Kawamura Minato, " 'Senseki' to iu tēma pāku," in *Nichiro sensō sutadīzu*, ed. Komori Yōichi and Narita Ryūichi, 217–19 (Tokyo: Kinokuniya shoten, 2004).

113. Scott Laderman, *Tours of Vietnam: War, Travel Guides, and Memory* (Durham, NC: Duke University Press, 2009) gives an excellent example of how this works in the context of American tourism to post–Vietnam War Vietnam.

114. In this case, the response to the problem of territorial memory operates differently than what Lauren A. Rivera describes in the former Yugoslavia. Lauren A. Rivera, "Managing 'Spoiled' National Identity: War, Tourism, and Memory in Croatia," *American Sociological Review* 73, no. 4 (2008): 613–34.

## 2. THE NEW TERRITORIES

1. Liisa Malkki, "National Geographic: The Rooting of Peoples and the Territorialization of National Identity among Scholars and Refugees," *Cultural Anthropology* 7, no. 1 (1992): 24–44.

2. Johannes Fabian, *Time and the Other: How Anthropology Makes Its Object* (New York: Columbia University Press, 1983), 31. Paul Barclay argues that allochronic discourse provided the "governing metaphor" for photographic representations of indigenous people in Taiwan during the 1930s. While I agree in principle, my research suggests that allochrony dominated the 1910s and 1920s but was then superseded by a geocultural discourse of identity, which synchronized difference by ascribing culture to territory rather than people. See Barclay, "Peddling Postcards and Selling Empire," 86. Allochrony also structures Stefan Tanaka's interpretation of how Orientalist historians produced a modern history of Japan that distinguished Japan as a historical nation from China by locating China as Japan's past. Here I argue that while allochrony did and would continue to structure discourses of Chinese difference (China as *Shina*) allochrony did not and could not hold for Korea, Taiwan, and, somewhat ambiguously, Manchuria, as the state sought to consolidate and maintain its imperial territory as the space of the Japanese nation. Tanaka, *Japan's Orient*, 244–55.

3. J. Uchida, *Brokers of Empire*, 231–33; H. Matsuda, "Becoming Japanese in the Colony," 705; Okamoto Makiko, "Shokuminchi zaijūsha no seiji sanka o meguru sōkoku," *Shakai kagaku*, no. 89 (2010): 95–131.

4. See, e.g., Margueritte Shaffer, *See America First: Tourism and National Identity, 1880–1940* (Washington, DC: Smithsonian Institution Press, 2001); Kynan Gentry, *History, Heritage, and Colonialism: Historical Consciousness, Britishness, and Cultural Identity in New Zealand, 1870–1940* (Manchester, England: Manchester University Press, 2015); Skwiot, *The Purposes of Paradise*.

5. Yamaji Katsuhiko, *Kindai Nihon no shokuminchi hakurankai* (Tokyo: Fūkyōsha, 2008).

6. Wolfgang Schivelbusch calls this "railway space" and describes how the railway transformed landscape by embedding the traveler in a systematized, network space removed from any organic sense of duration or sequential topography. In the colonial context, however, place was temporal as well as spatial. Wolfgang Schivelbusch, *The Railway Journey: The*

*Industrialization of Time and Space in the 19th Century* (Berkeley: University of California Press, 1986), 52–55.

7. Taylor, "Metageographical Moments," 48–55. Banner, *Possessing the Pacific*.

8. Jürgen Osterhammel, *The Transformation of the World: A Global History of the Nineteenth Century*, trans. Patrick Camiller (Princeton, NJ: Princeton University Press, 2014), 394–96.

9. Christopher L. Hill, *National History and the World of Nations: Capital, State, and the Rhetoric of History in Japan, France, and the United States* (Durham, NC: Duke University Press, 2008).

10. "National-historical space" comes from Hill, *National History and the World of Nations*, 50.

11. Yamaji Katsuhiko, "Nanjō jiken to 'senjūmin' mondai: Shokuminchi Taiwan to tochiken no kisū," *Kansai gakuin daigaku shakai gakubu kiyō* 109 (March 2010): 23–50.

12. Edwin H. Gragert, *Landownership under Colonial Rule: Korea's Japanese Experience* (Honolulu: University of Hawai'i Press, 1994), 71–72.

13. Chulwoo Lee, "Modernity, Legality, and Power," in *Colonial Modernity in Korea*, eds. Gi-Wook Shin and Michael Robinson (Cambridge, MA: Harvard University Asia Center, 1999), 26; Daniel Botsman, *Power and Punishment in the Making of Modern Japan* (Princeton, NJ: Princeton University Press, 2005), 211–20.

14. Erik Esselstrom, *Crossing Empire's Edge: Foreign Ministry Police and Japanese Expansionism in Northeast Asia* (Honolulu: University of Hawai'i, 2009). The state of Manchukuo abrogated the extraterritorial rights of Japanese residents in 1937. This did little, however, to change the balance of power in the puppet state. Tamanoi, *Memory Maps*, 42–43; Yamamuro Shin'ichi, *Japanese Domination of Manchuria*, 178–79.

15. Carl Walter Young, *Japanese Jurisdiction in the South Manchuria Railway Areas* (Baltimore: Johns Hopkins University Press, 1931).

16. Emer O'Dwyer, *Significant Soil: Settler Colonialism and Japan's Urban Empire in Manchuria* (Cambridge, MA: Harvard University Asia Center, 2015), 72.

17. Itō Hirobumi to Prime Minister Prince Saionji at an interministerial conference in May 1906, quoted in Matsusaka, *The Making of Japanese Manchuria, 1904–1932*, 84. Itō Hirobumi drafted the 1889 Constitution, served as Japan's first prime minister, and, from 1905 until his assassination in 1909, served as the first resident general of Korea.

18. We see this most clearly in the 1922 Washington Conference and the Nine-Power Treaty's insistence on protecting the "territorial integrity" of China, which, since it did not come with the return of tariff autonomy to China, was also seen as an excuse for blocking Japanese expansion into Asia in the name of maintaining China as a territory of exploitation for the other Great Powers. Akira Iriye, *After Imperialism: The Search for a New Order in the Far East, 1921–1931* (Cambridge, MA: Harvard University Press, 1965); Susan Pedersen, "Back to the League of Nations," *American Historical Review* 112, no. 4 (2007): 1091–117.

19. Okita Kinjō, *Rimen no Kankoku* (Osaka: Kibunkan, 1905), 33; quoted in Peter Duus, *The Abacus and the Sword: The Japanese Penetration of Korea, 1895–1910* (Berkeley: University of California Press, 1995), 401–2. For more on Japanese travel writings on Korea before the annexation, see 397–423.

20. Duus, *The Abacus and the Sword*, 401; Todd A. Henry, "Sanitizing Empire: Japanese Articulations of Korean Otherness and the Construction of Early Colonial Seoul," *Journal of Asian Studies* 64, no. 3 (2005): 639–75.

21. Settlers particularly chafed against the Company Law, which required companies to receive the approval of the Government General before they could be formed. The Government General implemented the policy in the name of preventing "frivolous" Korean companies from wasting capital that could otherwise be used more productively, but a joint Korean-Japanese Chamber of Commerce argued that it was having the effect of preventing the industrial development of the peninsula as a whole. J. Uchida, *Brokers of Empire*, 231–33.

22. Todd A. Henry, "Assimilation's Racializing Sensibilities: Colonized Koreans As *Yobos* and the '*Yobo*-ization' of Expatriate Japanese," in *The Affect of Difference: Representations of Race in the Japanese Empire*, ed. Christopher P. Hanscom and Dennis Washburn (Honolulu: University of Hawai'i Press, 2016), 91–94.

23. On the external orientation of assimilation versus the internal orientation of the later policy of "imperialization" *(kōminka)*, see Leo T. S. Ching, *Becoming "Japanese": Colonial Taiwan and the Politics of Identity Formation* (Berkeley: University of California Press, 2001), 89–132.

24. "Shasetsu: Chōsen kyōshinkai," *Tokyo Asahi shinbun*, September 11, 1915, morning edition. To this end, local Japanese residents established the Chōsen kenkyūkai (Korea research association), which disseminated publications about Korea and Koreans through the empire, often with the imprimatur of the Government General. J. Uchida, *Brokers of Empire*, 193–202.

25. Kimura Matsuhiko, "Public Finance in Korea under Japanese Rule: Deficit in the Colonial Account and Colonial Taxation," *Explorations in Economic History* 26 (1989): 288–89.

26. See the *Fūzoku gahō* special issues on the invasion of Taiwan: issues 98, 101, 103, 105 (1895); 109 (1896); on the pacification of Chinese rebels *(dohi)*, issue 111 (1896); and on "savage customs" *(banjin fūzoku)*, 129 (1896). At least one of these representations borrowed explicitly from woodblock prints from the late Tokugawa period, which depicted Commodore Perry groveling before a triumphant samurai general. At the same time, they made slight changes to fit Taiwan and civilization within the context of European modernity rather than Japanese civilization. One anonymously published print from 1874, rendered a Japanese general as a samurai leader receiving the scraping bows of the indigenous leaders. Though in almost all respects a repurposing of the Perry image, in this case the samurai general sat upon a chair rather than a stool. The chair, which was a ubiquitous a symbol of the "civilization and enlightenment" discourse of the early Meiji period, situated indigenous people and the Japanese in a universalized hierarchy of civilizational development. Robert Eskildsen, "Of Civilization and Savages: The Mimetic Imperialism of Japan's 1874 Expedition to Taiwan," *American Historical Review* 107, no. 2 (2002): 410, 418.

27. Chih-ming Ka, *Japanese Colonialism in Taiwan: Land Tenure, Development, and Dependency, 1895–1945* (Boulder, CO: Westview Press, 1995), 58–62.

28. Go Kōmei, "Kindai Nihon no Taiwan ninshiki: 'Taiwan kyōkai kaihō' 'Tōyō jihō' o chūshin ni," in *Kindai Nihon no Ajia ninshiki*, ed. Furuya Tetsuo (Kyōto: Kyōto daigaku jinbun kagaku kenkyūjo, 1994), 225–26.

29. Ibid., 213. The image of Taiwan as a lawless place was further underscored by a violent rebellion of Taiwanese Chinese in the village of Ta-pa-ni in 1915. Brought about by the pressures of colonial economic policy, especially the Government General's land taxes,

sugar monopoly, and the practice of confiscating forest land, the colonial administration and metropolitan media nevertheless portrayed the uprising as the work of "bandits" *(dohi)* out to upset the law and order of the colony. In the aftermath, members of the Japanese parliament called (unsuccessfully) for the resignation of colonial authorities. Paul Katz, *When Valleys Turned Blood Red: The Ta-pa-ni Incident in Colonial Taiwan* (Honolulu: University of Hawai'i Press, 2005), 2–8, 210.

30. Go, "Kindai Nihon no Taiwan ninshiki," 228. On *wajin* in the context of nineteenth-century Japanese-Ainu relations, see Howell, *Geographies of Identity*.

31. The settlers who are quoted in J. Uchida, *Brokers of Empire*, do this, though the book does not address the distinction directly.

32. Gao Yuan, "Kankō no seijigaku," 290–96. The numbers jumped higher after 1918. By the mid-1920s, the improvements in the speed of steamship travel made Taiwan a more popular destination as well, though the numbers of travelers to Taiwan would never rival those of the continent.

33. Nihon kōtsū kōsha, ed. *Gojūnen shi* (Tokyo: Nihon kōtsū kōsha, 1962), 104 and chronology (paginated separately) pp. 1–2, 13–14; Minami Manshū tetsudō kabushiki kaisha, *Minami Manshū tetsudō kabushiki kaisha dai nijūnen shi*, vol. 1 (Dairen: Minami Manshū tetsudō kabushiki kaisha, 1929), 126–27.

34. Japan Tourist Bureau, ed., *Ryotei to hiyō gaisan* (Tokyo: Japan Tourist Bureau, 1920); Mantetsu Man-Sen annaijo, ed., *Sen-Man-Shina ryotei to hiyō gaisan* (Tokyo: Mantetsu Man-Sen annaijo, 1923).

35. Tsurumi Yūsuke, *Seiden Gotō Shinpei*, vol. 5 (Tokyo: Fujiwara shoten, 2005), 237, quoted in Oikawa Yoshinobu, "Kaidai," in *Tōa eibun ryokō annai*, reprinted in Modern Tourism Library Series (Tokyo: Edition Synapse, 2008 [Tokyo: Japanese Government Railways, 1913–1917]), 4–5. On the history of tourist guidebooks in the context of metropolitan Japan, see Nakagawa Zōichi, *Tabi no bunkashi: gaidobukku to jikokuhyō to ryokōshatachi* (Tokyo: Dentō to gendaisha, 1979). On the history of the Baedeker in the European context, see Rudy Koshar, "'What Ought to Be Seen': Tourists' Guidebooks and National Identities in Modern Germany and Europe," *Journal of Contemporary History* 33, no. 3 (1998): 23–40.

36. Japanese Government Railways, ed., *An Official Guide to Eastern Asia*, 5 vols. (Tokyo: Japanese Government Railways, 1913–1918).

37. Chōsen sōtokufu tetsudōkyoku, ed., *Chōsen tetsudō ryokō annai: tsuketari Kongōsan annai* (Keijō: Chōsen sōtokufu tetsudōkyoku, 1915), preface (n. p.).

38. Pierre L. van den Berghe and Charles F. Keyes, "Introduction: Tourism and Re-Created Ethnicity," *Annals of Tourism Research* 11 (1984): 345.

39. Tetsudōin, ed., *Chōsen Manshū Shina annai* (Tokyo: Teibi shuppansha, 1919), 2.

40. Kate McDonald, "Imperial Mobility: Circulation As History in East Asia under Empire," *Transfers* 4, no. 3 (2014): 68–87. Aaron S. Moore argues that the "technological imaginary" undergirded the pan-Asianist visions of Japanese engineers in the 1930s. Here I show that colonial boosters used the idea of circulation as civilization to justify Japanese colonialism and to define the space of the Japanese Empire as early as the 1910s. See Moore, *Constructing East Asia: Technology, Ideology, and Empire in Japan's Wartime Era, 1937–1945* (Stanford: Stanford University Press, 2013). See also Daqing Yang, *Technology of Empire: Telecommunications and Japanese Expansion in Asia, 1883–1945* (Cambridge, MA: Harvard

University Asia Center, 2010); Kate McDonald, "Asymmetrical Integration: Lessons from a Railway Empire," *Technology and Culture* 56, no. 1 (2015): 115–49.

41. Chōsen sōtokufu ed., *Chōsen tetsudō ryokō benran* (Keijō: Chōsen sōtokufu, 1923), 1.

42. Minami Manshū tetsudō kabushiki kaisha Keijō kanrikyoku, ed., *Chōsen tetsudō ryokō annai* (Keijō: Minami Manshū tetsudō kabushiki kaisha Keijō kanrikyoku, 1921), 9.

43. Kerry D. Smith, *A Time of Crisis: Japan, the Great Depression, and Rural Revitalization* (Cambridge: Harvard University Asia Center, 2001), 22–24.

44. Japan Tourist Bureau, ed., *Ryotei to hiyō gaisan Taishō 12-nen ban*, 287–92.

45. Taiwan sōtokufu, *Taiwan tetsudō ryokō annai* (Taihoku: Taiwan sōtokufu, 1921), 12.

46. Kaneko Fumio, *Kindai Nihon ni okeru tai Manshū tōshi no kenkyū* (Tokyo: Kondō shuppansha, 1991), 111.

47. Minami Manshū tetsudō kabushiki kaisha, *Minami Manshū tetsudō annai* (Dairen: Minami Manshū tetsudō kabushiki kaisha, 1909), 13.

48. Hiroshima kōtō shihan gakkō, *Tairiku shūgaku ryokō ki*, 47–48; Alice Mah, *Port Cities and Global Legacies: Urban Identity, Waterfront Work, and Radicalism* (New York: Palgrave Macmillan, 2014), 89–109.

49. Soyama, *Shokuminchi Taiwan to kindai tsūrizumu*, 190–91.

50. Taiwan sōtokufu, *Taiwan tetsudō ryokō annai* (Taihoku: Taiwan sōtokufu, 1916), 52.

51. Ibid., 39.

52. Taiwan sōtokufu, *Taiwan tetsudō ryokō annai* (Taihoku: Taiwan sōtokufu, 1927), 203.

53. Ibid., 135–36.

54. Minami Manshū tetsudō kabushiki kaisha, *Minami Manshū tetsudō ryokō annai* (Dairen: Minami Manshū tetsudō kabushiki kaisha,1919), n. pag between pp. 8–9.

55. "Man-Sen ryokōki," 111.

56. Anshan Iron and Steel Works, which was built in 1918, would become another major site.

57. Minami Manshū tetsudō kabushiki kaisha, *Minami Manshū tetsudō ryokō annai* (1919), 141–42.

58. Aoi Akihito, "Transplanting State Shintō: The Reconfiguration of Existing Built and Natural Environments," in *Constructing the Colonized Land: Entwined Perspectives of East Asia around World War II*, ed. Izumi Kuroishi (Burlington, VT: Ashgate, 2014), 100. In a discourse similar to that directed at commodity production—that Japanese imperialism was allowing the essence of Taiwan, Korea, and Manchuria to become part of the global market—Aoi argues that in the context of Japanese colonialism and the Shintō discourse on nature, the built environment was what made the natural environment possible. Although Shintō shrines were clearly the product of human hands, the inner shrine environment was the true "natural" (*shizen*) environment to which the "built" (*kōchiku*) environment was compared. Aoi Akihito, *Shokuminchi jinja to teikoku Nihon* (Tokyo: Yoshikawa kōbunkan, 2005), 10–12.

59. In this, the prince provided a nearly perfect vehicle for promoting the humanitarian nature of what Gotō Shinpei called Japan's "scientific colonialism" in Taiwan. The Government General targeted cholera, and later malaria, in large-scale efforts to eradicate these diseases on the island. While the impetus was largely self-serving—it was hard to exploit the camphor and sugar resources of the island if the labor force was constantly getting ill—the Government General used these campaigns to emphasize its desire to improve the welfare of the "entire island," in contrast to the previous Spanish, Dutch, and Qing colonial regimes,

which had only sought to extract resources from the island or improve the plains areas where colonial officials resided. Travelers also visited shrines in Korea. But in contrast to the trail of Prince Kitashirakawa, Korean shrines did not draw their meaning from the experience of the "actuality" of a national past, but rather in the planting of deities associated strongly with the Imperial House on Korean soil. In Korea, travelers stopped at Keijō Shrine and, after its construction in 1925, Chōsen Shrine, where they could pay their respects to the deities Amaterasu, the mythical mother of the Japanese imperial line, and the Meiji Emperor, who had overseen Japan's industrialization and imperial expansion before his death in 1912. Todd A. Henry, *Assimilating Seoul: Japanese Rule and the Politics of Public Space in Korea, 1910–1945* (Berkeley: University of California Press, 2014), 62–64.

60. Taiwan sōtokufu, *Taiwan tetsudō ryokō annai* (1921), 21.

61. Minami Manshū tetsudō kabushiki kaisha, *Minami Manshū tetsudō ryokō annai* (1919), 75–83.

62. Minami Manshū tetsudō kabushiki kaisha Keijō kanrikyoku, ed., *Chōsen tetsudō ryokō annai* (1921), 57–58.

63. Ibid., 66–67.

64. Ibid., 63.

65. Ibid., 62–63.

66. Aso, *Public Properties*, 95–126.

67. Todd A. Henry, "Respatializing Chosŏn's Royal Capital: The Politics of Japanese Urban Reforms in Early Colonial Seoul," in *Sitings: Critical Approaches to Korean Geography*, ed. Timothy Tangherlini and Sallie Yea (Honolulu: University of Hawai'i Press, 2007), 21. For a genealogy of the term "public" in Japanese usage, see Aso, *Public Properties*, 10–12. On the use of the relationship between the ruler and the people to connote a particularly "Asian" mode of governance in the 1930s, see Duara, *Sovereignty and Authenticity*.

68. Minami Manshū tetsudō kabushiki kaisha Keijō kanrikyoku, ed., *Chōsen tetsudō ryokō annai* (1921), 58.

69. On the distinction between racial and state theories of Korean origins, see Hyung Il Pai, *Constructing "Korean" Origins: A Critical Review of Archaeology, Historiography, and Racial Myth in Korean State-Formation Theories* (Cambridge, MA: Harvard University Asia Center, 2000), chaps. 3 and 4. On Sin Ch'ae-ho and his history of Tan'gun and the Korean nation (K. minjok; J. minzoku), see Schmid, *Korea Between Two Empires*, 171–98; and Henry Em, *The Great Enterprise: Sovereignty and Historiography in Modern Korea* (Durham, NC: Duke University Press, 2013), 79–84.

70. Minami Manshū tetsudō kabushiki kaisha Keijō kanrikyoku, ed., *Chōsen tetsudō ryokō annai* (1921), 101, 105.

71. Ibid., 105.

72. Ibid., 111.

73. Ibid., 111–12.

74. Ibid.

75. For some examples of this, see Michael Kim, "Re-Conceptualizing the Boundaries of Empire: The Imperial Politics of Chinese Labor Migration to Manchuria and Colonial Korea," *Sungkyun Journal of East Asian Studies* 16, no. 1 (2016): 1–24; Jun Uchida, "'A Scramble for Freight': The Politics of Collaboration along and across the Railway Tracks of Korea under Japanese Rule," *Comparative Studies in Society and History* 51, no. 1 (2009): 117–50;

Mark Driscoll, *Absolute Erotic, Absolute Grotesque: The Living, Dead, and Undead in Japan's Imperialism, 1895–1945* (Durham, NC: Duke University Press, 2010), 25–55.

76. Tim Cresswell, *In Place/Out of Place: Geography, Ideology, and Transgression* (Minneapolis: University of Minnesota Press, 1996), 8.

77. Arakawa Seijirō, *Sen-Man jitsugyō shisatsu danshi* (N.p., 1918), 85.

78. Asai Yumeji, "Keijō kenbun inshō roku," *Chōsen oyobi Manshū*, no. 99 (October 1915): 110.

79. Kawahigashi Hekigotō, "Chōsen no aki kakite," in *Shin Nihon kenbutsu*, ed. Kanao Shujirō (Tokyo: Kanao bun'endō, 1918), 141.

80. Nagasawa Sokichi, *Tōbu Taiwan jundanki* (Tokyo: Meibunsha, 1916), 24–25.

81. Hiroshima kōtō shihan gakkō, *Tairiku shūgaku ryokō ki*, 53.

82. Ibid., 114.

83. Hayasaka Yoshio, *Konran no Shina o tabishite* (Utsunomiya-shi: Hayasaka Yoshio, 1922), 30–33.

84. Yoshino Sakuzō, "Man-Kan o shisatsu shite," *Chūō kōron* (June 1916), reprinted in *Yoshino Sakuzō senshū*, vol. 9, ed. Matsuo Takayoshi, Mitani Taichirō, and Iida Taizō (Tokyo: Iwanami shoten, 1995), 6.

85. Basil Hall Chamberlain, *Things Japanese: Being Notes on Various Subjects Connected with Japan for the Use of Travellers and Others*, 5th ed. rev. (London: John Murray, 1905), 407.

86. On Barak, *On Time: Technology and Temporality in Egypt* (Berkeley: University of California Press, 2013), 37. See also Marian Aguiar, *Tracking Modernity: India's Railway and the Culture of Modernity* (Minneapolis: University of Minnesota Press, 2011).

87. See Michael Adas, *Machines As the Measure of Men: Science, Technology, and Ideologies of Western Dominance* (Ithaca: Cornell University Press, 1989), 199–270. The quote is from George Otto Trevelyan, *The Competition Wallah* (London: MacMillan and Co., 1895 [1864]), cited in Adas, *Machines As the Measure of Men*, 228.

88. Tayama Katai, *Man-Sen no kōraku* (Tokyo: Ōsakayagō shoten, 1924), 8.

89. Ibid., 334–35.

90. On the generically modern style of Japanese architecture in Dairen, see Nishizawa Yasuhiro, "Kenchiku no chōkyō to shokumin toshi kensetsu," in *"Teikoku" Nihon no gakuchi 8: Kūkan keisei Kūkan keisei to sekai ninshiki*, ed. Yamamuro Shin'ichi, 235–76 (Tokyo: Iwanami shoten, 2006). One of the most visible elements of the later shift to a geography of cultural pluralism would be the construction of official buildings meant to evoke a sense of authentic local architecture. On the Government General of Korea's construction of "Korean-style" exhibition buildings for the 1929 Chōsen Exhibition, see Hong Kal, "Modeling the West, Returning to Asia: Shifting Politics of Representation in Japanese Colonial Exposition in Korea," *Comparative Studies in Society and History* 47, no. 3 (2005): 507–31.

91. Maeda Ai, "Utopia of the Prisonhouse: A Reading of *In Darkest Tokyo*," in *Text and the City: Essays on Japanese Modernity*, ed. James A. Fujii, 21–64 (Durham, NC: Duke University Press, 2004); Jeffrey E. Hanes, *The City As Subject: Seki Hajime and the Reinvention of Modern Osaka* (Berkeley: University of California Press, 2002).

92. Yamamuro Shin'ichi, "Kūkan ninshiki no shikaku to kūkan no seisan," in *"Teikoku" Nihon no gakuchi 8: Kūkan keisei to sekai ninshiki*, ed. Yamamuro Shin'ichi (Tokyo: Iwanami shoten, 2006), 3.

93. Driscoll, *Absolute Erotic, Absolute Grotesque*; Henry, "Sanitizing Empire."

## 3. BOUNDARY NARRATIVES

1. This scene, as described by protagonist Yi Inhwa as he arrives in Pusan on the Kobe-Pusan steamer, is from Yŏm Sangsŏp's "Mansejŏn" (On the Eve of the Uprising), first published in 1924. Yŏm Sangsŏp, "On the Eve of the Uprising," in *On the Eve of the Uprising and Other Stories from Colonial Korea*, trans. Sunyoung Park with Jefferson J. A. Gattrall (Ithaca, NY: Cornell University Press, 2010), 46–48.

2. Rather than distinguish here between "ethnic" and "civic" nationalisms, as Kevin M. Doak has suggested, I am drawing on Tessa Morris-Suzuki's argument that national belonging operated in multiple realms in this era. I also draw on Naoki Sakai's notion of imperial nationhood, in which he points out how ethnic and civic nationalism were necessarily intertwined in the context of cultural pluralism and multiethnic nationalism. While there were, of course, actors who articulated one kind of nationalism over or against the other, it was the slippage between the two that defined the everyday experience of empire. Tessa Morris-Suzuki, "Migrants, Subjects, Citizens: Comparative Perspectives on Nationality in the Prewar Japanese Empire," *The Asia-Pacific Journal* 6, issue 8, number 0 (August 2008), 2; Naoki Sakai, "Subject and Substratum: On Japanese Imperial Nationalism," *Cultural Studies* 14, no. 3–4 (2000): 462–530; Doak, "What Is the Nation and Who Belongs?"

3. Morris-Suzuki, "Migrants, Subjects, Citizens," 3.

4. Erez Manela, *The Wilsonian Moment: Self-Determination and the International Origins of Anticolonial Nationalism* (New York: Oxford University Press, 2007), 201. A Korean nationalist group in China, the New Korea Youth Association, succeeded in sending a delegation to the conference, led by Kim Kyu-sik. Chong-Sik Lee, *The Politics of Korean Nationalism* (Berkeley: University of California Press, 1963), 103.

5. Hsu Chien-Jung, *The Construction of National Identity in Taiwan's Media, 1896–2012* (Leiden: Brill, 2014), 32.

6. Tim Cresswell, "Citizenship in Worlds of Mobility," in *Critical Mobilities*, ed. Ola Söderström, Shalini Randeria, Didier Ruedin, Gianni D'Amato, Francesco Panese, 105–124 (New York: Taylor & Francis, 2013). On the reliance of cultural pluralism on a set of "common terms" that are coded as the culture of public life but, in fact, represent the ethics and mores of the dominant cultural group, see David Theo Goldberg, "Multicultural Conditions," in *Multiculturalism: A Critical Reader* (Oxford: Blackwell, 1994), 6. Goldberg contrasts the cultural politics of "integration" with "incorporation," which involves "dual transformations that take place in the dominant values and in those of the insurgent group as the latter insists on more complete incorporations into the body politic and the former grudgingly gives way" (9).

7. Oguma, *A Genealogy of Japanese Self-Images*.

8. Ngai, *Impossible Subjects*, 227–34.

9. On the post–World War I "crisis of empire," see J. Adam Tooze, *The Deluge: the Great War, America, and the Remaking of Global Order, 1916–1931* (New York: Viking, 2014); and Pedersen, *The Guardians*. I refer to those movements that sought independence as "anti-imperial" and those that sought the complete incorporation of the colonies into the metropole as "anticolonial." In the Japanese Empire, the paradigmatic example of the former is the Korean independence movement, while the latter is represented by some aspects of the Taiwanese Chinese assimilation and self-rule movements in colonial Taiwan.

10. Gary Wilder, "Framing Greater France between the Wars," *Journal of Historical Sociology* 14 (2001): 201, quoted in Furlough, "*Une leçon de choses*," 442. For a discussion of the discourse of Greater France, see Gary Wilder, *The French Imperial Nation-State: Negritude and Colonial Humanism between the Two World Wars* (Chicago: University of Chicago Press, 2005), 29–36.

11. Francine Hirsch, *Empire of Nations: Ethnographic Knowledge and the Making of the Soviet Union* (Ithaca: Cornell University Press, 2005), 63–64.

12. Frederick Cooper notes, but does not elaborate on, this aspect of the debates over imperial citizenship in France. See Cooper, *Citizenship between Empire and Nation: Remaking France and French Africa* (Princeton, NJ: Princeton University Press, 2014).

13. Tooze, *The Deluge*.

14. Manela, *The Wilsonian Moment*, 6. Derek Heater, *National Self-Determination: Woodrow Wilson and His Legacy* (Houndsmill: Macmillan, 1994), 1–14. Derek Heater traces the origin of the idea of national self-determination to eighteenth-century Europe; Erez Manela points out that in the years preceding the Paris Peace Conference, the Bolshevik leaders V. I. Lenin and Leon Trotsky articulated the principle of nationality most forcefully. My point in drawing attention to the "pre" history of self-determination is to re-center Wilson's articulation of national self-determination firmly within the scope of imperialist responses to a multifaceted crisis of empire rather than portray Wilson as an idealist outlier who challenged the idea of empire.

15. Pedersen, *The Guardians*, 4, 23–24.

16. Bang, "A School Excursion of the Middle School Managed by Korean to Japan, Manchuria in 1920–30s."

17. The Government General of Taiwan responded, for example, with extreme force to a rebellion of Taiwanese Chinese residents of southern Taiwan in 1915, an incident known as the Ta-pa-ni Incident. Led by Yü Ch'ing-fang, a former police officer, and Chiang Ting, a former district head, the uprising involved both Taiwanese Chinese and indigenous rebels and lasted for over a month. Over one thousand villagers and Japanese people died in the fighting at the village of Ta-pa-ni. Nearly two thousand individuals were arrested in conjunction with the uprising and 915 were sentenced to death. Over one hundred actual executions took place, with many more individuals dying in prison. Katz, *When Valleys Turned Blood Red*, 1–2.

18. Edward I-Te Chen, "Formosan Political Movements under Japanese Colonial Rule, 1914–1937," *Journal of Asian Studies* 31, no. 3 (1972): 477–97; and Henry J. Lamley, "Assimilation Efforts in Colonial Taiwan: The Fate of the 1914 Movement," *Monumenta Serica* 29 (1970–1971): 496–520.

19. "Declaration of Independence," quoted in Henry Chung, *The Case of Korea: A Collection of Evidence on the Japanese Domination of Korea, and on the Development of the Korean Independence Movement* (New York: Fleming H. Revell, 1921), 200.

20. Japan Chronicle, ed., "Eight Japanese and 150 Koreans Killed," *The Independence Movement in Korea: A Record of Some of the Events of the Spring of 1919* (Kobe: Japan Chronicle, 1919), 30. The statistic was originally printed in the *Japan Chronicle* on April 16, 1919. For a detailed treatment of the March First Movement, see Frank Baldwin, "The March First Movement: Korean Challenge and Japanese Response" (PhD diss., Columbia University, 1969).

21. Chow Tse-tsung, *The May Fourth Movement: Intellectual Revolution in Modern China* (Stanford: Stanford University Press, 1960).
22. Jonathan D. Spence, *The Search for Modern China* (New York: W. W. Norton, 1991), 310. Spence notes that the term "May Fourth Movement" refers to both the immediate events of May 4, 1919, and to the broader anti-imperial nationalist movement that followed.
23. Hara Takashi, "Opinion on the Rule of Korea," quoted in Oguma, *"Nihonjin" no kyōkai,* 245.
24. Michael E. Robinson, *Cultural Nationalism in Colonial Korea, 1920–1925* (Seattle: University of Washington, 1988), 4.
25. Harry Lamley, "Taiwan under Japanese Rule, 1895–1945," in *Taiwan: A New History,* ed. Murray A. Rubinstein (Armonk, NY: M. E. Sharpe, 1999), 220–23.
26. *Dōmin* 7 (1924): 22–23, quoted in J. Uchida, *Brokers of Empire,* 185.
27. Hamada Tsunenosuke, *Waga shokuminchi* (Tokyo: Toyamabō, 1928), 451.
28. Anssi Paasi, "Boundaries As Social Processes: Territoriality in the World of Flows," in *Boundaries, Territory and Postmodernity,* ed. David Newman (London: Frank Cass, 1999), 75.
29. Miriam Silverberg, *Erotic Grotesque Nonsense: The Mass Culture of Japanese Modern Times* (Berkeley: University of California Press, 2006), 14, 20–28.
30. Nihon kotsū kōsha, *Gojūnen shi,* 104.
31. Chōsen sōtokufu, ed., *Chōsen tetsudō ryokō benran* (1923), 1.
32. Chōsen sōtokufu tetsudōkyoku, ed., *Chōsen tetsudō ryokō annai* (1915), 97.
33. "Shuchō: Man-Sen no renraku naru," *Chōsen* 1911, no. 12: 12; "Honshi no kōdai," *Chōsen oyobi Manshū* 1912, no. 1: 10.
34. Taiwan sōtokufu kōtsūkyoku tetsudōbu, ed., *Taiwan tetsudō shi,* vol. 3 (Taihoku [Taipei]: Taiwan sōtokufu tetsudōkyoku, 1910– 1911), 489–90, 506–8, 537, 543.
35. Tanaka Keiji, "Shoken," Zenkoku chūtō gakkō chiri rekishi ka kyōinkai, ed., *Zenkoku chūtō gakkō chiri rekishika kyōin dai 9-kai kyōgikai oyobi Taiwan nan-Shi ryokō hōkoku,* 327–30 (Tokyo: Zenkoku chūtō gakkō chiri rekishika kyōin kyōgikai, 1932), 327.
36. Silverberg, *Erotic Grotesque Nonsense,* 22.
37. Hayashi Takahisa, Preface to *Shiroi kimono to kuroi ishō,* ed. Miyazaki kenritsu Miyakonojō shōkō gakkō (Tojō: Miyazaki kenritsu Miyakonojō shōkō gakkō, 1931), n. pag.
38. Nihon kōtsū kōsha, *Gojūnen shi,* 77–78. The Traveling Club (Nihon ryokō kurabu) was established to interface between local travel clubs and transportation and hotel enterprises. It was founded by several famous members of the Tokyo Arukōkai (Let's walk society), including novelist Tayama Katai, poet Ōmachi Keigetsu, and the noted conservative scholar of law Uesugi Shinkichi. The first president of the Travel Culture Association was Nomura Ryūtarō, the former president of the South Manchuria Railway. The Bureau of Railways became the Ministry of Railways in 1924.
39. Arai Gyōji, "Tabi no shakaika, minshūka," *Tabi* 1924, no. 7: 2–3.
40. Tonomura Masaru, *Zainichi Chōsenjin shakai no rekishigakuteki kenkyū: keisei kōzō hen'yō* (Tokyo: Ryokuin shobō, 2004), 32–34.
41. Cai Peihuo, *Nihon honkokumin ni atau* (Tokyo: Taiwan mondai kenkyūjo, 1928).
42. Seiji Shirane, "Mediated Empire: Colonial Taiwan in Japan's Imperial Expansion in South China and Southeast Asia, 1895–1945," PhD diss., Princeton University, 2014, 93–95.

43. Nakano Shigeharu, "Mosukowa sashite," *Musan shinbun* (October 5, 1928); and Annika A. Culver, Introduction to "Heading to Moscow" (Chicago: University of Chicago, The Center for East Asia Studies, 2012), https://ceas.uchicago.edu/sites/ceas.uchicago.edu/files/uploads/Sibley/Heading%20for%20Moscow%20Introduction.pdf.

44. Japan Tourist Bureau, *Ryotei to hiyō gaisan Taishō 12-nen ban*, 256–58.

45. Japan Tourist Bureau, *Ryotei to hiyō gaisan Shōwa 6-nen ban* (Tokyo: Hakubunkan, 1931), 546.

46. Hiroshima kōtō shihan gakkō, *Tairiku shūgaku ryokō ki*, 140.

47. Hayasaka, *Konran no Shina o tabi shite*, 62.

48. Ibid., 12.

49. Yŏm, "On the Eve of the Uprising," 29.

50. Ibid., 37–42.

51. The phrase "differential mobility" comes from Ginnete Verstraete, *Tracking Europe: Mobility, Diaspora, and the Politics of Location* (Durham, NC: Duke University Press, 2009).

52. Like most of our colonial interlocutors, Yŏm Sangsŏp's life and sense of self are not reducible to a binary of Korean (resistance) versus Japanese (empire). Yŏm Sangsŏp, "Yŏm Sangsŏp," in *On the Eve of the Uprising and Other Stories from Colonial Korea*, translated by Sunyoung Park, with Jefferson J. A. Gattrall (Ithaca, NY: Cornell University Press, 2010), 1–3.

53. Go Dōshi, "Hitori Taiwanjin no kokuhaku," *Tōyō jihō* no. 258–59 (March 4, 1920), quoted in Go Kōmei, "Kindai Nihon no Taiwan ninshiki," 234.

54. Taiwan sōtokufu, *Taiwan tetsudō ryokō annai* (Taihoku: Taiwan sōtokufu, 1927), 278–79. "Taiwan kara Shina e! Nan'yō e!" *Umi* 1924, no. 4: 19–20.

55. Matsuda Kyōko, "Shokuminchi shihaika no Taiwan genjūmin o meguru 'bunrui' no shikō to tōchi jissen," *Rekishigaku kenkyū*, no. 846 (2008): 99. Matsuda cites a report from the Taihoku Prefectural Police. Matsushita Kentarō, ed., *Taihokushū ribanshi gekan* (Taihoku: Taihokushū kenmubu, 1923), 64.

56. Paul D. Barclay, "Cultural Brokerage and Interethnic Marriage in Colonial Taiwan: Japanese Subalterns and Their Aboriginal Wives, 1895–1930," *Journal of Asian Studies* 64, no. 2 (2005): 345.

57. This is a shortened version of the story of Yayutz Bleyh. Kirsten L. Ziomek, "The Possibility of Liminal Colonial Subjecthood," *Critical Asian Studies* 47, no. 1 (2015): 123–50.

58. Taiwan sōtokufu, *Tetsudō ryokō annai* (1916), 25.

59. Ōgi Zenzō, "Taiwan kengaku nikki," *Umi* 1924, no. 9: 27.

60. Japan Tourist Bureau, *Ryotei to hiyō gaisan Shōwa 6-nen ban*, 534.

61. Kō Sonbon, *Shokuminchi no tetsudō* (Tokyo: Nihon keizai hyōronsha, 2006), 174.

62. Ibid.

63. Akimori Tsunetarō, *Chōsen shokan* (Osaka: Akimori Tsunetarō, 1935), 6.

64. Even though this policy was most likely unofficial, I say "enforced" because there is evidence that the conductors attempted to prevent Taiwanese Chinese from entering second-class cabins. Kō Sonbon describes one June 1929 case in *Shokuminchi no tetsudō*, 174. See also Soyama Takeshi, "Nihon tōchiki Taiwan no tsūrizumu saikō," *Tamagawa*

*daigaku kankō gakubu kiyō* 3 (2015): 71. Soyama's account is based on interviews with Taiwanese Chinese who traveled during the colonial era.

65. "Sen-Man-Shina ryokōki oyobi ryokōbu buhō," *Kōyūkai zasshi*, no. 278 (15 September 1919): 119.

66. Matsuda Kiichi, *Taiwan Okinawa no tabi* (Osaka: Yanagihara shoten, 1937), 46.

67. See "Keijō dayori," in *Kōgakkō yō Kokugo dokuhon 7-kan*, 42–48 (Taihoku: Taiwan sōtokufu, 1931 [1924]), and "Kiryū kara Kōbe," in *Kōgakkō yō kokugo dokuhon 10-kan*, 7–20 (Taihoku: Taiwan sōtokufu, 1935 [1926]); and "Renrakusen ni notta," in *Futsū gakkō kokugo dokuhon 7-kan*, 78–84 (Keijō: Chōsen sōtokufu, 1924).

68. "Renrakusen ni notta," 78, 84.

69. Ibid., 82.

70. Tsukahara Zenki, "Kansō," in *Zenkoku chūtō gakkō chiri rekishika kyōin dai 9-kai kyōgikai oyobi Taiwan nan-Shi ryokō hōkoku*, ed. Zenkoku chūtō gakkō chiri rekishika kyōin kyōgikai (Tokyo: Zenkoku chūtō gakkō chiri rekishika kyōin kyōgikai, 1932), 345.

71. Urakami Shūe, "Taiwan Nan-Shi ryokō shokan," in *Zenkoku chūtō gakkō chiri rekishika kyōin dai 9-kai kyōgikai oyobi Taiwan nan-Shi ryokō hōkoku*, ed. Zenkoku chūtō gakkō chiri rekishika kyōin kyōgikai (Tokyo: Zenkoku chūtō gakkō chiri rekishika kyōin kyōgikai, 1932), 348–349.

72. Ibid., 349.

73. Yamaguchi Shunsaku, "Miyage banashi," in *Zenkoku chūtō gakkō chiri rekishika kyōin dai 9-kai kyōgikai oyobi Taiwan nan-Shi ryokō hōkoku*, ed. Zenkoku chūtō gakkō chiri rekishika kyōin kyōgikai (Tokyo: Zenkoku chūtō gakkō chiri rekishika kyōin kyōgikai, 1932), 354.

74. I am indebted to Kapil Raj, whose proposal to treat "circulation as a site" helped me to conceive of this approach of tourism's history. Kapil Raj, *Relocating Modern Science: Circulation and the Construction of Knowledge in South Asia and Europe, 1650–1900* (New York: Palgrave MacMillan, 2007).

75. Saskia Sassen, *Territory, Authority, Rights: From Medieval to Global Assemblages* (Princeton: Princeton University Press, 2008), 4.

## 4. LOCAL COLOR

1. E. Taylor Atkins, "The Dual Career of 'Arirang': The Korean Resistance Anthem That Became a Japanese Pop Hit," *Journal of Asian Studies* 66, no. 4 (2007): 666–67.

2. Kobayashi Chiyoko, "Hakui no Chōsen o iku," *Tabi* 1935, no. 7: 14.

3. Nagata Shunsui, "Tabako-tō Chōsenjin," *Tabi* 1935, no. 5: 25.

4. This suggests that under the geography of cultural pluralism, observation not only produced knowledge of the colonized but was also seen as a way of knowing the imperial nation. Cf. Cohn, *Colonialism and Its Forms of Knowledge*, 6–7.

5. This is the fundamental feature of what Pierre L. van den Berghe and Charles F. Keyes term "ethnic tourism," in which "the native is not simply 'there' to serve the needs of the tourist; he is himself 'on show,' a living spectacle to be scrutinized, photographed, tape recorded, and interacted with in some particular ways." See van den Berghe and Keyes, "Introduction: Tourism and Re-Created Ethnicity," 345.

6. Charles Taylor, "Modern Social Imaginaries," *Public Culture* 14, no. 1 (2002): 101. For Taylor, the key difference between these premodern social imaginaries and the modern social imaginary is the question of the basic unit of differentiation within relations of exchange and mutual benefit. If, in the medieval period, the social order imagined these relations by type—the clergy prayed for the laity, the laity work for the clergy; the peasants farmed for the samurai, the samurai fought for the peasants—in the modern period, "we start with individuals and their debt of mutual service; the divisions emerge as a way to most effectively discharge this debt" (96). Yet, as the history of local color shows, a notion of the hierarchical complementarity of ethnic groups played a key role in defining the hegemonic imaginary of social relations within the culturally pluralistic, imperial Japanese nation of the late 1920s and 1930s.

7. Silverberg, *Erotic Grotesque Nonsense*, 4.

8. Driscoll, *Absolute Grotesque, Absolute Erotic*, 161–201.

9. Though generally known as one of the most famous early Korean nationalist historians, in the mid-1920s, Sin Ch'ae-ho began publishing anarchist histories instead. See Henry Em, *The Great Enterprise*, 107–9.

10. Louise Young, *Beyond the Metropolis: Second Cities and Modern Life in Interwar Japan* (Berkeley: University of California Press, 2013), 141–87.

11. Duara, *Sovereignty and Authenticity*, 9–40.

12. Thomas G. Andrews, "'Made by Toile?' Tourism, Labor, and the Construction of the Colorado Landscape, 1858–1917," *Journal of American History* 82, no. 3 (2005): 837–63.

13. Matsukawa Jirō, *Shi go nichi no tabi* (Tokyo: Yūseidō shoten, 1925), 472.

14. "Jo," in Miyazaki kenritsu Miyakonojō shōkōgakkō, ed., *Shiroi kimono to kuroi ishō*, n. p.

15. Itō Ken, *Taiwan annai* (Tokyo: Shokumin jijō kenkyūsha, 1935), 2.

16. Fujitani, *Race for Empire*, 23–24. Fujitani notes that only 9.3 percent of the Korean population in Japan was eligible to vote in the 1928 election, compared with 20 percent of the Japanese population. See also Matsuda Toshihiko, *Senzenki no zainichi Chōsenjin to sanseikan* (Tokyo: Akashi shoten, 1995). On mobile Korean labor in Japan during the 1920s and 1930s, see Ken C. Kawashima, *The Proletarian Gable: Korean Workers in Interwar Japan* (Berkeley: University of California Press, 2009).

17. J. Uchida, *Brokers of Empire*, 273, 284.

18. See chapter 2.

19. H. Matsuda, "Becoming Japanese in the Colony," 690.

20. O'Dwyer, *Significant Soil*, 216–18.

21. Hamada, *Waga shokuminchi*, 477–78.

22. Kawamura Minato, *Sakubun no naka no dai Nihon teikoku* (Tokyo: Iwanami shoten, 2000), 72–77.

23. Officials were particularly concerned about ethnic tensions in the aftermath of the massacres of Koreans that had followed the 1923 Great Tokyo Earthquake.

24. Cai, *Nihon honkokumin ni atau*, 62–63.

25. Ibid., 30–32.

26. Katō Kiyofumi, "Seitō naikaku kakuritsuki ni okeru shokuminchi shihai taisei no mosaku: Takumushō setchi mondai no kōsatsu," *Higashi Ajia kindai shi* 1, no. 1 (1998): 41, 49.

27. On the history of the term *gaichi*, see Nakamura Akira, "Shokuminchi hō," in *Kindai Nihonhō hattatsu shi*, vol. 5, ed. Ukai Nobushige et al (Tokyo: Keisō shobō, 1958). Mizuno Naoki outlines the changes to the administrative divisions of the empire after 1929 as the central government moved to fully unify the administration of the metropole and the colonies. See Mizuno Naoki, "Senjiki no shokuminchi shihai to 'nai gai chi gyōsei ichigenka,'" *Jinbun gakuhō* 79 (1997): 77–102.

28. Mariko Tamanoi, "Knowledge, Power, and Racial Classifications: The 'Japanese' in Manchuria," *Journal of Asian Studies* 59, no. 2 (2000): 250, 255.

29. Elizabeth A. Povinelli, *The Cunning of Recognition: Indigenous Alterities and the Making of Australian Multiculturalism* (Durham, NC: Duke University Press, 2002), 32.

30. Taiwan sōtokufu, *Taiwan tetsudō ryokō annai* (1927).

31. See, for example, the Government General of Korea's new guidebook series, *Chōsen ryokō annai ki*, which debuted in 1929, the 1929 *Minami Manshū tetsudō ryokō annai*, and the Ministry of Railway's nine-volume *Nihon annai ki* series, which replaced the older *Tetsudō ryokō annai* series, beginning with a volume on Hokkaidō in 1929.

32. Mōri Motoyoshi, "Chihō shoku o omonzeyo," *Kokusai kankō* 3, no. 2 (April 1935): 18. Emphasis in original.

33. Keijō kankō kyōkai, *Keijō annai Shōwa 8-nen ban* (Keijō: Keijō kankō kyōkai, 1933), 1.

34. Kobayashi, "Hakui no Chōsen," 15

35. Hamada, *Waga shokuminchi*, 91–93.

36. "Tairiku o miyo! Sen-Man o miyo!" *Tabi* 1929, no. 9: 86.

37. Miyazaki kenritsu Miyakonojō shōkō gakkō, ed., *Shiroi kimono to kuroi ishō*, 150.

38. Tokyo furitsu dai-ichi shōgyō gakkō kōyūkai, ed., *Bokura no mitaru Man-Sen-nan Shi* (Tokyo furitsu dai-ichi shōgyō gakkō kōyūkai, 1932), 303–7.

39. Matsuda Kiichi, *Taiwan Okinawa no tabi*, 49.

40. Minami Manshū tetsudō kabushiki kaisha Keijō kanrikyoku, ed., *Chōsen tetsudō ryokō annai* (1921), 9. See chapter 2.

41. Hiroshima kōtō shihan gakkō, *Tairiku shūgaku ryokō ki*, 56.

42. Miyazaki kenritsu Miyakonojō shōkō gakkō, ed., *Shiroi kimono to kuroi ishō*, 124.

43. Ibid., 117.

44. Ibid., 129–31. This account was from 1926.

45. Ibid., 130.

46. Ibid., 141.

47. Takahashi Gentarō, *Shin Manshūkoku kenbutsu* (Tokyo: Ōsakayagō shoten, 1934), 108–10.

48. Ibid., 110–11.

49. Taiwan sōtokufu, *Taiwan tetsudō ryokō annai* (1927), 22.

50. Chōsen sōtokufu tetsudōkyoku, ed., *Chōsen ryokō annai ki* (Keijō: Chōsen sōtokufu tetsudōkyoku, 1929), 5.

51. Chōsen sōtokufu tetsudōkyoku, ed., *Chōsen ryokō annai ki* (Keijō: Chōsen sōtokufu tetsudōkyoku, 1934), 44.

52. Minami Manshū tetsudō kabushiki kaisha, *Minami Manshū tetsudō ryokō annai* (Dairen: Minami Manshū tetsudō kabushiki kaisha, 1929), 280.

53. L. Young, *Japan's Total Empire*, 29.
54. Arjun Appadurai, "Putting Hierarchy in Its Place," *Cultural Anthropology* 3, no. 1 (1988): 37.
55. Ōtsu Toshiya, *Manshūkoku ryokō annai* (Tokyo: Shinkōsha, 1935 [1932]), n.pag. (preface).
56. Minami Manshū tetsudō kabushiki kaisha, *Minami Manshū tetsudō ryokō annai* (Dairen: Minami Manshū tetsudō kabushiki kaisha, 1935), 31–32.
57. Minami Manshū tetsudō kabushiki kaisha, *Minami Manshū tetsudō ryokō annai* (1929), 280–281.
58. Ibid., 281.
59. Ibid.
60. Yuko Kikuchi, Introduction to *Refracted Modernity: Visual Culture and Identity in Colonial Taiwan*, ed. Yuko Kikuchi (Honolulu: University of Hawai'i Press, 2007), 13.
61. Matsuzawa Akira, *Tai-Nai ōrai ryokō* (Taihoku: Taihoku kappansha shuppanbu, 1929), 16.
62. Ibid., 24.
63. Morishige Shūzō, "Taiwan no konjaku," *Tabi* 1925, no. 1: 48.
64. Cai, *Nihon honkokumin ni atau*, 101–2.
65. Morishige, "Taiwan no konjaku," 50.
66. Go, "Kindai Nihon no Taiwan ninshiki," 236–37. On the self-rule movement's attempt to distance itself from the image of Taiwan's indigenous peoples, see Wakabayashi Masahiro, *Taiwan kōnichi undōshi kenkyū* (Tokyo: Kenbun shuppan, 1983). Aso, *Public Properties*, 103–7, also notes that the colonial government museum's emphasis on Taiwan's natural resources was part of a move to "de-Sinify" Taiwan, especially after the Manchuria Incident in 1931.
67. Go, "Kindai Nihon no Taiwan ninshiki," 234.
68. Jason Ruiz argues that travelers' emphasis on the figure of the "burden bearer" played a central role in facilitating the U.S. "economic conquest" of Porfirian Mexico, because such images served as evidence that "a large and docile pool of labor resided south of the border." Ruiz, *Americans in the Treasure House*, 49–50.
69. Arakawa, *Sen-Man jitsugyō shisatsu danshi*, 173.
70. Chōsen sōtokufu tetsudōkyoku, ed., *Chōsen ryokō annai ki* (1934), 12.
71. Ibid.
72. "'Utsukushii shima' Taiwan o nozoku," *Tabi* 1939, no. 5: n. pag.
73. The exact date of the policy change is unclear. In 1937, the Government General of Taiwan prohibited the use of the term "raw savages" in official discourse. Ching, *Becoming "Japanese,"* 211n3. In an earlier work, Ching states that the change in naming policy came in June 1935. Leo T. S. Ching, "Savage Construction and Civility Making: The Musha Incident and Aboriginal Representations in Colonial Taiwan," *positions* 8, no. 3 (2000): 804.
74. Denny Roy, *Taiwan: A Political History* (Ithaca, NY: Cornell University Press, 2003), 12.
75. On the uses of "Chineseness" in representations of Manchuria's walled cities, see Kari Shepherdson-Scott, "Race behind the Walls: Contact and Containment in Japanese Images of Urban Manchuria," in *The Affect of Difference: Representations of Race in the Japanese Empire*, ed. Christopher P. Hanscom and Dennis Washburn, 186–206 (Honolulu: University of Hawai'i Press, 2016).

76. See, for example, the title of the Miyakonojō Higher Commercial School's 1930 account of their trip to Korea and Manchuria: *Shiroi kimono kuroi ishō*, "White robes, black robes."
77. Takahashi, *Shin Manshūkoku kenbutsu*, 75–76.
78. Taguchi Mizuho, "Saikin no Manshū tokoro dokoro," *Tabi* 1936, no. 6: 102–3.
79. M. Kim, "Re-Conceptualizing the Boundaries of Empire," 17.
80. Takahashi, *Shin Manshūkoku kenbutsu*, 76.
81. "Life of the Poor Classes," *Manshū gurafu* 4, no. 5 (May 1936), 91. A special thanks to Kari Shepherdson-Scott for pointing me to this source.
82. Nakanishi, *Shina Manshū Chōsen*, 74.
83. Driscoll, *Absolute Erotic, Absolute Grotesque*, 40–41 and 315n2.
84. For example, the lack of middle management is evident in the following report by Hashiguchi Minato, director general of Yalu Lumber Company. Hashiguchi told the *Manchuria Daily News* (Manshū nichi nichi shinbun), that in 1909 that his company employed forty-five corporate staff members—twenty-three Japanese and twenty-two Chinese—and thirty thousand North Chinese migrants. He intended to expand that number to fifty thousand in the coming years. *Manshū nichi nichi shinbun*, January 10, 1909, quoted in Driscoll, *Absolute Erotic, Absolute Grotesque*, 39.
85. "Coolies Longshoring at the Dairen Wharves," *Manshū gurafu* (May 1936): 87.
86. Aoi Ikko, "Han Nihonka no Keijō," *Tabi* 1929, no. 6: 76.
87. Kyūshū teikoku daigaku, *Chōsen Manshū ryokō: Kyūshū teikoku daigaku gakusei shisatsu dan* (Hakozaki-chō [Fukuoka-ken]: Kyūshū teikoku daigaku haizoku shōkō shitsu, 1933), 66.
88. Kyōto-shi kyōiku-bu shakai-ka, "Kyōto-shi ni okeru hiyatoi rōdōsha ni kansuru chōsa," (Kyōto-shi, 1931), 19, quoted in Kawashima, *The Proletarian Gamble*, 61.
89. Sakai Toshio, Osaka City Bureau of Labor, quoted in Kawashima, *The Proletarian Gamble*, 47.
90. Akimori, *Chōsen shokan*, 6.
91. While Maruyama Hiroshi points out that the heyday of national park designation in Japan and around the world was the high point of ethnic nationalism, it was also during this period that empires and settler colonial nation-states found ways to transform the scenery of colonized lands into paradigmatic examples of national identity. During the 1920s and 1930s, states established over 150 national parks, nearly half of which were located in colonized territories or in U.S. Commonwealth or British Dominion territories. In the United States, national parks were established in Hawai'i in 1916 and in Alaska in 1918, long before these territories became states. Likewise, the French established national parks in Cambodia and Singapore, and the British colonial governments established national parks in India and Sri Lanka, while the settler colonial dominion governments established dozens of parks in the Union of South Africa and Australia. Maruyama Hiroshi, *Kindai Nihon kōenshi no kenkyū* (Kyōto: Shibunkaku shuppan, 1994), 298–99. See also International Commission on National Parks, *1973 United Nations List of National Parks and Equivalent Reserves* (Morges: IUCN, 1973), https://portals.iucn.org/library/node/6229.
92. Morioka Jirō, "Taiwan kokuritsu kōen no shitei wo iwasu," *Kokuritsu kōen* 10, no. 1 (1938): 2.
93. Tamura Tsuyoshi, "Nihonjin no fūkeikan to kokuritsu kōen," *Kokuritsu kōen* 7, no. 6 (1935): 2–3.

94. Kanda Kōji, *Kankō kūkan no seisan to chiriteki shizōryoku* (Kyōto: Nakanishiya shuppan, 2012), 73–109.

95. Ohama Jōkō, "Taiwan kokuritsu kōen no shimei," *Kokuritsu kōen* 8, no. 8 (1936): 5.

96. Ishikawa Sadatomo, "Nihon ni okeru kokuritsu kōen no enkaku," *Kokuritsu kōen* 10, no. 1 (1938): 7, quoted in Nishida Masanori, "Nihon tōchi jidai ni okeru Taiwan no kokuritsu kōen," *Chiiki sōzōgaku kenkyū* 22, no. 2 (2012): 120.

97. Saitō Itsuki, "Niitaka to Arisan," *Tabi* 1932, no. 10: 42.

98. Takahashi, "Banchi ni okeru kokuritsu kōen to riban to no ninshiki," *Riban no tomo* 1938, no. 3: 2–4.

99. Aso, *Public Properties*, 105.

100. Inagaki Ryūichi, "Taiwan ni okeru kokuritsu kōen mondai," *Kokuritsu kōen* 8, no. 1 (1936): 7.

101. Yokō Kōsuke. "Banzan no shinbi o Takasagozoku ni kiku," *Kokuritsu kōen* 10, no. 1 (1938): 65.

102. Ohama, "Taiwan kokuritsu kōen no shimei," 5.

103. Yamaji, "Nanjō jiken to 'senjūmin' mondai: Shokuminchi Taiwan to tochiken no kisū," 37–45.

104. Quoted in Nishida, "Nihon tōchi jidai ni okeru Taiwan no kokuritsu kōen," 128.

105. Tamura Tsuyoshi, *Arisan fūkei chōsa sho* (Taihoku: Taiwan sōtokufu eirinjo, 1930), 60, quoted in Nishida, "Nihon tōchi jidai ni okeru Taiwan no kokuritsu kōen," 131.

106. Yamaji, "Nanjō jiken to 'senjūmin' mondai," 45. See also Kondō Masami, "Taiwan sōtokufu no riban taisei to Musha jiken," in *Iwanami kōza kindai Nihon to shokuminchi 2*, ed. Ōe Shinobu, 35–58 (Tokyo: Iwanami shoten, 1993); and Uesugi Mitsuhiko, "'Takasagozoku' no ijū ni tsuite (1)," *Takachiho ronsō* 24, no. 3 (1990): 39–101.

107. Tamura Tsuyoshi, *Kokuritsu kōen kōwa* (Tokyo: Meiji shoin, 1948), 180–83, cited in Nishida, "Nihon tōchi jidai ni okeru Taiwan no kokuritsu kōen," 128–29.

108. MacCannell, *The Tourist*, 55–57.

109. Povinelli, *The Cunning of Recognition*, 32.

110. Duara, *Sovereignty and Authenticity*, 9.

111. As in the Japanese case, these "local colors" were curated to fit the needs of the colonizing power. Thus, in the case of California, the cultivators of California's "regional identity" emphasized its Spanish imperial past—signified primarily through architectural codes that required red-tile roofs—rather than its indigenous or Mexican pasts. See Phoebe S. Kropp, *California Vieja: Culture and Memory in a Modern American Place* (Berkeley: University of California Press, 2006).

## 5. SPEAKING JAPANESE

1. Ueda Kazutoshi, "Kokugo to kokka to," (1894) in *Meiji bungaku zenshū*, vol. 44 (Tokyo: Chikuma shobō, 1968), 110, quoted in Miyako Inoue, *Vicarious Language: Gender and Linguistic Modernity in Japan* (Berkeley: University of California Press, 2006), 87.

2. Michael Silverstein, "Metapragmatic Discourses and Metapragmatic Function," in *Reflexive Language: Reported Speech and Metapragmatics*, ed. John A. Lucy, 33–58 (Cambridge: Cambridge University Press, 1993).

3. Hiraku Shimoda, "Tongues-Tied: The Making of a 'National Language' and the Discovery of Dialects in Meiji Japan," *American Historical Review* 115, no. 3 (2010): 714–31.

4. Shimoda, "Tongues-Tied," 729.

5. Ueda Kazutoshi, "Shōgaku no kyōka ni kokugo ni ikka o moukuru no gi," *Dai Nippon kyōikukai zasshi*, special ed. 2 (1884): 138, quoted in Shimoda, "Tongues-Tied," 722.

6. The seminal work in the ideology of landscape is Denis Cosgrove, *Social Formation and Symbolic Landscape* (Madison: University of Wisconsin Press, 1984); and Denis Cosgrove and Stephen Daniels, eds., *The Iconography of Landscape: Essays on Symbolic Representation, Design, and Use of Past Environments* (Cambridge: Cambridge University Press, 1988). On linguistic landscapes, see Adam Jaworski, "Mobile Language in Mobile Places," *International Journal of Bilingualism* 18, no. 5 (2014): 524–33.

7. Arakawa, *Sen-Man jitsugyō shisatsu danshi*, 42.

8. Ibid., 25.

9. Hiroshima kōtō shihan gakkō, ed., *Tairiku shūgaku ryokō ki*, 55.

10. Ibid., 127.

11. Ted Mack has recently been working on the question of how to classify Japanese language communities in Brazil, which were composed of people who settled there with the encouragement of the government but whose relationship with Brazil was never codified into the formal arrangement that we now think of as "colonialism." Japanese settler communities in Brazil published Japanese-language newspapers, imported Japanese-language books from the metropole, and even produced Japanese-language literature. Though excluded from the territories covered by Kawamura Minato's definition of "colonial literature," the Japanese-language community of Brazil raises an intriguing set of questions about the relationship between language, politics, and literature. See Edward Mack, "Ōtaku Wasaburō's Dictionaries and the Japanese 'Colonization' of Brazil," *Dictionaries: Journal of the Dictionary Society of North America*, no. 31 (2010): 46–68. On colonial literature, see Kawamura Minato, "Shokuminchi bungaku to wa nani ka," in *Nan'yō Karafuto no Nihon bungaku* (Tokyo: Chikuma shobō, 1994).

12. Hiroshima kōtō shihan gakkō, ed., *Tairiku shūgaku ryokō ki*, 48.

13. "Man-Sen ryokōki," 112.

14. Ibid., 114.

15. Ibid., 115.

16. Ishikawa Toraji, "Taiwan ryokō," in *Shin Nihon kenbutsu*, ed. Kanao Shujirō (Tokyo: Kanao Bun'endō, 1918), 70. Matsuda Yoshirō, *Taiwan genjūmin to Nihongo kyōiku: Nihon tōchi jidai Taiwan genjūmin kyōikushi kenkyū* (Kyōto: Kyōto shobō, 2004), 48.

17. E. Patricia Tsurumi, *Japanese Colonial Education in Taiwan, 1895–1945* (Cambridge, MA: Harvard University Press, 1978), 2.

18. Eika Tai, "*Kokogo* and Colonial Education in Taiwan," *positions* 7, no. 2 (1999): 524.

19. Ibid., 524. Tai is quoting Yamaguchi Kiichirō, *Taiwan kyōiku zasshi* 27 (1904), cited in Komagome Takeshi, "I-minzoku shihai no 'kyōgi'," in *Tōgō to shihai no ronri*, ed. Asada Kyōji Kindai (Tokyo: Iwanami shoten, 1993), 140.

20. Tsurumi, *Japanese Colonial Education in Taiwan*, 15–16.

21. Ibid., 18. See also Yoshino Hidekimi, *Taiwan kyōiku shi* (Taihoku: Yoshino Hidekimi, 1927).

22. Matsuda Y., *Taiwan genjūmin to Nihongo kyōiku*, 48.

23. Kitamura Kae, *Nihon shokuminchika no Taiwan genjūmin kyōiku shi* (Sapporo: Hokkaidō daigaku shuppankai, 2008), 86, 112.
24. Taiwan kyōikukai, ed., *Taiwan kyōiku enkaku shi* (Taihoku: Taiwan kyōikukai, 1939), 501; Matsuda, *Taiwan genjūmin to Nihongo kyōiku*, 54.
25. Kitamura, *Nihon shokuminchika no Taiwan genjūmin kyōiku shi*, 202–3; Matsuda Y., *Taiwan genjūmin to Nihongo kyōiku*, 56.
26. Taiwan sōtokufu keimukyoku, *Banjin kyōiku gaikyō* (Taihoku: Taiwan sōtokufu keimukyoku, 1934). 1.
27. Taiwan sōtokufu keimukyoku, *Takasagozoku no kyōiku* (Taihoku: Taiwan sōtokufu keimukyoku, 1936), frontispiece graph of "Shuzoku betsu jidō tsūgaku buai nami kokugo fukyū oyobi buai."
28. Tsurumi, *Japanese Colonial Education in Taiwan*, 133.
29. E. Patricia Tsurumi, "Colonial Education in Korea and Taiwan," in *The Japanese Colonial Empire, 1895–1945*, ed. Ramon H. Myers and Mark R. Peattie (Princeton, NJ: Princeton University Press, 1984), 299.
30. Hamada, *Waga shokuminchi*, 594.
31. Ibid., 315.
32. Shimoda, "Tongues-Tied," 718.
33. Nanette Twine, *Language and the Modern State: The Reform of Written Japanese* (London: Routledge, 1991), 105–6.
34. Twine, *Language and the Modern State*, 171.
35. Florian Coulmas, "Language Policy in Modern Japanese Education," in *Language Policies in Education: Critical Issues*, ed. James W. Tollefson (Mahwah, NJ: Lawrence Erlbaum Associates, 2002), 213.
36. Twine, *Language and the Modern State*, 163.
37. Quoted in Yeongsuk Lee, *The Ideology of Kokugo: Nationalizing Language in Modern Japan*, trans. Maki Hirano Hubbard (Honolulu: University of Hawaii Press, 2010), 51. This is Hubbard's translation.
38. Quoted in Yeounsuk Lee, *The Ideology of Kokugo*, 51. This is Hubbard's translation.
39. Yeounsuk Lee, *The Ideology of Kokugo*, 64.
40. Hiroshima kōtō shihan gakkō, ed., *Tairiku shūgaku ryokō ki*, 107.
41. Ibid.
42. Miyazaki kenritsu Miyakonojō shōkō gakkō, *Shiroi kimono to kuroi ishō*, 143.
43. Ibid., 124.
44. The term *Sengo* is a derogatory term for the Korean language, similar to the use of *Senjin* rather than *Chōsenjin* when referring to Korean people. While the term *Chōsengo*—*go* being the character that denotes language—would have been the official term for Korean at the time, it is possible that the emphasis on national language in Korea led the guidebook editors to diminish the status of Korean through derogatory terminology.
45. Chōsen sōtokufu, ed., *Chōsen ryokō annai ki* (1934), 109.
46. Mantetsu Sen-Man annaijo, ed., *Chōsen Manshū ryokō annai: tsuketari Shina ryokō annai* (Tokyo: Mantetsu Sen-Man annaijo, 1926), 78.
47. Kokusai kankō kyoku Manshū shibu, *Manshū kanban ōrai* (Hōten: Kokusai kankō kyoku Manshū shibu, 1941), 5.

48. Minami Manshū tetsudō kabushiki kaisha, *Minami Manshū tetsudō ryokō annai* (1935), inside cover.
49. Ivy, *Discourses of the Vanishing*; Harry D. Harootunian, "Figuring the Folk: History, Poetics, and Representation," in *Mirror of Modernity: Invented Traditions in Modern Japan*, ed. Stephen Vlastos, 144–59 (Berkeley: University of California Press, 1997).
50. Matsuda Kyōko, *Teikoku no shisen: Hakurankai to ibunka hyōzō* (Tokyo: Yoshikawa kōbunkan, 2003), 110.
51. Tamanoi, "Knowledge, Power, and Racial Classifications," 258.
52. Tetsudōshō, ed., *Nihon annai ki Kyūshū hen* (Tokyo: Hakubunkan, 1935), 27. The volume on the Chūbu region (the central mountainous region of the main island of Honshū) describes the dialect as broken up into east and west but puts no temporal reference on the two dialects. "In Kyūshū, a dialect different from that of Honshū or Shikoku is used. In Honshū, 'ji' and 'zhi,' and 'zu' and 'du' have come to be confused. Yet in the greater part of Kyūshū, these are pronounced distinctly, taking the figure *(sugata)* of ancient language."
53. Hayasaka, *Konran no Shina o tabishite*, 24.
54. Nagasawa, *Tōbu Taiwan jūdanki*, 26–27.
55. Hayasaka, *Konran no Shina o tabishite*, 24.
56. Nagasawa, *Tōbu Taiwan jūdanki*, 26–27.
57. Motoyama Yukihiko, "Meiji kokka no kyōiku shisō: Taishō no kyōiku to no kanren o chūshin ni," in *Taishō no kyōiku*, ed. Ikeda Susumu and Motoyama Yukihiko, 39–162 (Tokyo: Daiichi hōki shuppan, 1978).
58. Kitamura, *Nihon shokuminchika no Taiwan genjūmin kyōiku shi*, 202.
59. Kawanishi Hidemichi, "Tōhoku wa Nihon no Sukottorando ka," in *Rōkaru hisutorī kara gurōbaru hisutorī e: tabunka no rekishigaku to chiikishi*, ed. Kawanishi Hidemichi, Namikawa Kenji, and M. William Steele, 207–23 (Tokyo: Iwata shoin, 2005); Oguma Eiji, "The Hidden Face of Disaster: 3.11, the Historical Structure and Future of Japan's Northeast," *The Asia-Pacific Journal* vol. 9, issue 31, no. 6 (August 1, 2011).
60. Andre Gunder Frank, "The Development of Underdevelopment," *The Monthly Review* 18, no. 4 (1966): 17–31.
61. Hayasaka, *Konran no Shina o tabishite*, 24; Nagasawa, *Tōbu Taiwan jūdanki*, 26–27.
62. Hiroshima kōtō shihan gakkō, ed., *Tairiku shūgaku ryokō ki*, 128.
63. Steve A. Caton, "The Importance of Reflexive Language in G. H. Mead's Theory of Self and Communication," in *Reflexive Language: Reported Speech and Metapragmatics*, ed. John A. Lucy (Cambridge: Cambridge University Press, 1993), 327.
64. Hayasaka, *Konran no Shina o tabishite*, 51–52.
65. Ibid., 31.
66. Robinson, *Cultural Nationalism in Colonial Korea*.
67. Tsurumi, *Japanese Colonial Education in Taiwan*, 99.
68. "Separate but equal" is from Michael J. Seth, *Education Fever: Society, Politics, and the Pursuit of Schooling in South Korea* (Honolulu: University of Hawaii, 2002), 20, 22. Private academies continued to operate in both Taiwan and Korea. In Korea, they were required to teach in Japanese. Missionaries also operated schools in colonial Korea.
69. Yeounsuk Lee, *The Ideology of Kokugo*, 174–75.

70. Byron K. Marshall and other historians of Japanese education emphasize "centralization, nationalism, and elitism" as defining features of the prewar Japanese education system. This critique replicates the immediate postwar analysis of the Japanese education system promoted by U.S. military personnel working for the U.S. Occupation, who, in their eagerness to correct "what went wrong" with Japan, found in the education system a useful scapegoat. Yet, as scholarship on modern education in the United States, Britain, and France has shown, elitism, nationalism, and the tension between centralization and local autonomy are a feature of modern public education as such, not a pathology unique to Japan. Indeed, it is Marshall himself who points to the relatively meritocratic rather than elite nature of prewar Japanese education when he shows that Japanese higher schools enrolled a considerably higher proportion of the student population than did the British or French higher schools. Marshall, *Learning to Be Modern: Japanese Political Discourse on Education* (Boulder, CO: Westview Press, 1994), 2, 40–47.

71. The difficulty of getting in to higher schools in Korea and Taiwan had the paradoxical effect of pushing more Taiwanese Chinese and Korean students to study at higher schools in the inner territory, where the competition was less steep and the ethnic discrimination less stark. See Thornber, *Empire of Texts in Motion*, 34–41.

72. Ming-Cheng M. Lo, *Doctors within Borders: Profession, Ethnicity, and Modernity in Colonial Taiwan* (Berkeley: University of California Press, 2002), 60.

73. Tsurumi, "Colonial Education in Korea and Taiwan," 304.

74. Lo, *Doctors within Borders*, 60.

75. Tsurumi, *Japanese Colonial Education in Taiwan*, 97, 103.

76. Tai, "*Kokogo* and Colonial Education in Taiwan," 516.

77. Tsurumi, *Japanese Colonial Education in Taiwan*, 97.

78. Fujitani defines the shift as a shift "from treating these [racialized, colonized] populations as simply objects of rule, without significant interiority, to attempting to constitute them as self-reflexive and knowledgeable subjects who would participate at least to some extent in their own regulation." I should say that I am in agreement with Fujitani's conclusion, if not with the vulgar/polite terminology. Fujitani, *Race for Empire*, 25.

79. It is closer to what Todd Henry describes as "affective racism" in the context of colonial Korea: "the insidious practices of differential incorporation that relied on ethnic proximity and the lure of cultural assimilation as the basis for temporarily, if not permanently, marking the inherently porous boundaries between model Japanese subjects and colonized Korean others." Henry, "Assimilation's Racializing Sensibilities," 14.

80. Matsuda Kiichi, *Taiwan Okinawa no tabi*, 29.

81. Quoted in Nakanishi Inosuke, *Taiwan kenbunki* (Tokyo: Jissensha, 1937), 583.

82. Matsuda Kiichi, *Taiwan Okinawa no tabi*, 117.

83. Suzuki Tadashi, "Bandō kyōiku no ni dai ganmoku," *Riban no tomo* 1, no. 1 (January 1932): 7.

84. Taihokushū ribanka, "Taihokushū ribanka hakkō no gakujutsu kōshūyō bango shiryō ni tsuite," *Riban no tomo* 1, no. 4 (April 1932): 10.

85. Stoler, "On Degrees of Imperial Sovereignty," 128, 136–37.

86. For the cultural clash model of transparent/opaque language ideology, see Joel Robbins and Alan Rumsey, "Cultural and Linguistic Anthropology and the Opacity of Other Minds," *Anthropological Quarterly* 82, no. 2 (2008): 407–20.

87. Michelle Z. Rosaldo famously argued that speech act theory is itself a local language ideology in her seminal article, "The Things We Do with Words: Ilongot Speech Acts and Speech Act Theory in Philosophy," *Language in Society* 11, no. 2 (1982): 203–37. On speech act theory, she writes, "our theoretical attempts to understand how language works are like the far less explicated linguistic thoughts of people elsewhere in the world, in that both inevitably tend to reflect locally prevalent views about the given natures of those human persons by whom language is used" (203).

88. Matsuda Kiichi, *Taiwan Okinawa no tabi*, 120.

89. Itagaki Hōki, *Taiwan kenbutsu Man-Sen manpo* (Tokyo: Itagaki Rikiko, 1931), 154.

90. Ibid., 155.

91. Taiwan sōtokufu, *Saikin no Taiwan* (Taihoku: Taiwan sōtokufu, 1925), 30.

92. Japan tsūrisuto byūrō Taiwan shibu, ed., *Taiwan tetsudō ryokō annai* (1935), 142.

93. See chapter 2.

94. Japan tsūrisuto byūrō Taiwan shibu, ed., *Taiwan tetsudō ryokō annai* (1935), 143.

95. Nakanishi, *Taiwan kenbunki*, 272.

96. Zenkoku chūtō gakkō chiri rekishika kyōin kyōkigai, ed., *Zenkoku chūtō gakkō chiri rekishika kyōin dai 9-kai kyōgikai oyobi Taiwan nan-Shi ryokō hōkoku* (Tokyo: Zenkoku chūtō chiri rekishika kyōin kyōgikai, 1932), 266.

97. Ibid.

98. Ibid.

99. Osa Shizue, *Kindai Nihon to kokugo nashonarizumu* (Tokyo: Yoshikawa kōbunkan, 1998), 5–6.

100. Jane Burbank and Frederick Cooper argue for this broad definition of empire across world history. See Burbank and Cooper, *Empires in World History*.

## CONCLUSION

1. The concept of situational knowledge, as opposed to knowledge as "a view from nowhere," has a rich literature in science and technology studies. I draw my understanding from Donna Haraway's "situated knowledge." See Haraway, "Situated Knowledges: The Science Question in Feminism and the Privilege of Partial Perspective," *Feminist Studies* 14, no. 3 (1988): 575–99.

2. Michele Mason, *Dominant Narratives of Colonial Hokkaidō and Imperial Japan: Envisioning the Periphery and the Modern Nation-State* (New York: Palgrave Macmillan, 2012), 148–60.

3. Sebastian Conrad, *Globalisation and the Nation in Imperial Germany*, trans. Sorcha O'Hagan (Berkeley: University of California Press, 2010).

4. Here, I register my disagreement with narratives of modern history that pinpoint specific moments as "crises of territoriality," rather than a human geographic approach to territory in which territoriality is understood as a process of creating territories. Such a process is always in some sense in crisis, either in the geopolitical sense of contested territories or from the phenomenological perspective of trying to make the state's territoriality dominate over the multiple "geographic arrangements and understandings" that constitute the lived reality of human social relations. On definitions of territoriality, see Alexander B. Murphy, "Entente Territorial: Sack and Raffestin on Territory," *Environment and Plan-*

*ning D: Space and Society* 30, no. 1 (2012): 163. To put it differently, it is a rare privilege in this modern world to be able to be able to constrain "crisis" to a particular time period. As Walter Benjamin wrote, "The tradition of the oppressed teaches us that the 'state of emergency' in which we live is not the exception but the rule." Walter Benjamin, "Theses on the Philosophy of History," in *Illuminations*, ed. Hannah Arendt, trans. Harry Zohn (New York: Schocken Books, 1969), 257, quoted in T. Fujitani, Geoffrey M. White, and Lisa Yoneyama, introduction to *Perilous Memories: The Asia-Pacific War(s)*, ed. T. Fujitani, Geoffrey M. White, and Lisa Yoneyama (Durham, NC: Duke University Press, 2001), 21. On the idea of the 1980s and 1990s as a "crisis of territoriality," see Charles S. Maier, "Consigning the Twentieth Century to History: Alternative Narratives for the Modern Era," *American Historical Review* 105, no. 3 (2000): 808.

5. Rebecca L. Stein, *Itineraries of Conflict: Israelis, Palestinians, and the Political Lives of Tourism* (Durham, NC: Duke University Press, 2008).

6. Lori Watt, "Embracing Defeat in Seoul: Rethinking Decolonization in Korea, 1945," *Journal of Asian Studies* 74, no. 1 (2015): 153–74.

7. Bruce Cumings, *Parallax Visions: Making Sense of American-East Asian Relations* (Durham, NC: Duke University Press, 1999), 212.

8. Mizuno Masanao, *Futatsu no Chūgoku: tsuketari Nanboku-Sen, Firipin* (Tokyo: Kokudosha, 1949). The book was published as part of the series "Kokumin daigaku" (Citizens' university). Other titles included *Eikoku kenpō* (The English Constitution) and *Chihō zaisei* (Regional tax systems). Based on his other publications, it seems as if the author worked as a researcher in the South Manchuria Railway Company's East Asia Economic Research Bureau. See also Obara Kuniyoshi, *Chishima Karafuto Chōsen Chūgoku Ryūkyū Nan'yō chiri gakushi shinkenshi* (Tokyo: Tamagawa daigaku shuppanbu, 1952).

9. There were dozens of first-hand accounts of North Korea published by Japanese and Korean travelers in the early postwar period. The earliest was published by the Nagano Branch of the League of Korean Residents in Japan, which translated one Korean journalist's account of his 1948 trip north of the 38th parallel. See Jo Kōsei, *Kita Chōsen kikō: Nihongo ban* (Nagano: Zainichi Chōsenjin renmei Nagano honbu shuppanbu, 1948).

10. Joint Chiefs of Staff, "Basic Directive for Post-Surrender Military Government in Japan Proper (November 3, 1945)."

11. Tanaka Hiroshi, *Zainichi gaikokujin* (Tokyo: Iwanami shoten, 1991), 66–67, cited in Lori Watt, *When Empire Comes Home: Repatriation and Reintegration in Postwar Japan* (Cambridge, MA: Harvard University Asia Center, 2009), 96.

12. Watt, *When Empire Comes Home*, 57.

13. Ibid., 56.

14. Kazuko Kuramoto, *Manchurian Legacy: Memoirs of a Japanese Colonist* (East Lansing: Michigan State University Press, 2004), 118, quoted in Watt, *When Empire Comes Home*, 56.

15. Muramatsu Shigeki, *Chūgaku shakai: Nihon to sekai: Chiriteki naiyō o omo to suru mono* (Tokyo: Teikoku shoin, 1954), 7; Nō Toshio, Yazawa Taiji, Tanabe Ken'ichi, and Satō Hisashi, *Chūgaku shakaika chiri hatsu teiban* (Tokyo: Teikoku shoin, 1974), 17.

16. Satō Hiroshi et al, *Chūgaku shakai Nihon no kokudo to sekai: Chiri teki naiyō o omo to shita mono* (Tokyo: Shimizu shoin, 1955), 176.

17. Ibid., 166; Asaka Yukio, *Chūgaku shakai Nihon no kokudo to sekai, shin hen* (Tokyo: Shimizu shoin, 1964), 192.

18. "Brief—Program for Tourist Trade," February 9, 1950, National Archives and Records Administration, Records of the General Headquarters Supreme Commander for the Allied Powers (GHQ SCAP), RG 331, Box 8334, Folder: Program for Promotion of Tourist Trade. National Diet Library, Tokyo, Japan. (Hereafter cited as GHQ SCAP.)

19. Letter to CIS, June 1948, GHQ SCAP, Box 8649, Folder title: "Japan Travel Bureau (1); Translation of *Shinbun no shinbun* article, 20 May 1949, GHQ SCAP, Box 8613, Folder title: "Japan Travel Bureau (Kotsu kosha) (27)."

20. ESS, Chief of Staff, "Northwest Airlines' Proposal for Initiation of Limited Tourist Travel into Japan," March 25, 1948, GHQ SCAP, Box 9412, Folder title "Japanese Hotels—Tourist Travel, Trade, etc., #1 (1949–1950)." The memo references a letter to ESS from Northwest Airlines on January 15, 1948 containing a proposal for tourist travel. I have yet to find the original letter, proposal, or subsequent staff study.

21. Memo, CTS to AG-OS, October 27, 1947, GHQ SCAP, Box 8721, Folder title "Tourist Industry, 1947–1951."

22. "Memo of Conference in Re: Tourist Travel," Memo No. 98-0, June 10, 1948, GHQ SCAP Box 8721, Folder title "Tourist Industry, 1947–1951."

23. GHQ/SCAP Memo to Board of Trade and Ministry of Commerce and Industry, Signed by M.H. Halff, Ex. Officer, ESS, June 25, 1948, GHQ SCAP Box 8721, Folder title "Tourist Industry, 1947–1951."

24. "Two-Day Tokyo-Kamakura Tour Itinerary," September 22, 1949, and "2-day Overland Tour Itinerary for President Wilson Passenger Party," September 21, 1949, GHQ SCAP, Box 230, Folder Title: Japan Tourist, July 1949–September 1949 (2).

25. "Special Overland Tour 29 Dec, 4-day," GHQ SCAP, Box 230, Folder title: "Japan Tourist, November 1949–January 1950."

26. "9,000 Tourists Visit Japan During Past Year," *Travel News* 5, no. 2 (January 15, 1950), GHQ SCAP, Box 8334, Folder Title: "Program for Promotion of Tourist Trade."

27. "Pan American World Airways and its wholly-owned subsidiary Intercontinental Hotels Corporation: Proposal for 1,000-room Hotel in Tokyo," 14 March 1950, GHQ SCAP, Box 5979, Folder title: "Pan American World Airways (51)." SCAP authorized regular passenger service to and from Tokyo for Pan-American, Northwest, and five other foreign carriers on June 26, 1950. Takayama Kichirō, ed., *Nihon kōkū jūnen no ayumi, 1951–1961* (Tokyo: Nihon kōkū kabushiki kaisha, 1964), 132.

28. "Welcome to Japan," GHQ SCAP, Box 8334, Folder Title: "Program for Promotion of Tourist Trade." See also "Peaceful Japan: Land of Color, Charm and Courtesy" in same folder.

29. Un'yushō kankōka, ed., *Kankō jigyō no shiori kaichōban* (Tokyo: Un'yushō, 1948), 12.

30. "Tours in Japan: Shore Arrangement by Japan Travel Bureau," GHQ SCAP, Box 8334, Folder Title: "Program for Promotion of Tourist Trade."

31. Tetsudōshō, ed., *Nihon annai ki Kinki hen jō* (Tokyo: Hakubunkan, 1932), 39, and Un'yushō, ed., *Nihon annai ki Kinki hen jō kaichōban* (Tokyo: Un'yushō, 1949), 15.

32. Un'yushō, ed., *Nihon annai ki Kinki hen jō kaichōban* (1949), 1.

33. Tetsudōshō, ed., *Nihon annai ki Kinki hen jō* (1932), 114, and Un'yushō, ed., *Nihon annai ki Kinki hen jō kaichōban* (1949), 91.

34. Mizuno M., *Futatsu no Chūgoku*, preface (n. pag.). This book was the fiftieth in the series, "Citizens' university library" (Kokumin daigaku bunko) and the only one to offer place-knowledge. Other volumes offered introductions to the constitutions of the United

States and Great Britain and to political problems such as spreading democracy to rural areas. They were published by the Association for Political Education (Seiji kyōiku kyōkai), which had also published an early work on international relations by Kamikawa Hirokatsu in 1927.

35. Kitabayashi Tōma, "Chōsen ryokō to onsen," *Tabi* 1951, no. 3: 84.
36. Ibid.
37. Ibid.
38. Ibid.
39. Ibid., 87.
40. Ibid.
41. Mizutani Chōzaburō, "Waga tabi, waga tōsō," *Tabi* 1952, no. 1: 16.
42. Ibid., 17.
43. Ibid.
44. Ibid.
45. Ibid.
46. Young-sook Lee, "The Korean War and Tourism: Legacy of the War on the Development of the Tourism Industry in South Korea," *International Journal of Tourism Research* 8 (2006): 161.
47. Okpyo Moon, "Japanese Tourists in Korea: Colonial and Post-Colonial Encounters," in *Japanese Tourism and Travel Culture*, ed. Sylvie Guichard-Anguis and Okpyo Moon (New York: Routledge, 2009), 152.
48. Ibid., 152–53.
49. Ibid., 155.
50. Satō Sanae, *Dare mo kakanakatta Kankoku: chikakute tōi rinjin tachi no sugao* (Tokyo: Sankei shinbunsha, 1974), 13, 15.

SELECTED BIBLIOGRAPHY

*Newspapers*
*Tokyo Asahi shinbun*
*Musan shinbun*

*Archives*
Japan Center for Asian Historical Records, Tokyo, Japan. www.jacar.go.jp.
National Archives and Records Administration. Records of the General Headquarters Supreme Commander for the Allied Powers (GHQ SCAP). RG 331. National Diet Library, Tokyo, Japan.

*Published Books and Articles*
Abe Yasunari. "Tairiku ni kōfun suru shūgaku ryokō: Yamaguchi kōtō shōgyō gakkō ga yuku 'Man-Kan-Shi' 'Sen-Man-Shi.'" *Chūgoku 21*, no. 29 (March 2008): 219–36.
Abraham, Itty. *How India Became Territorial: Foreign Policy, Diaspora, Geopolitics*. Stanford: Stanford University Press, 2014.
Adas, Michael. *Machines As the Measure of Men: Science, Technology, and Ideologies of Western Dominance*. Ithaca: Cornell University Press, 1989.
Adler, Judith. "The Origins of Sightseeing." *Annals of Tourism Research* 16 (1989): 7–29.
Agnew, John. "Representing Space: Space, Scale and Culture in Social Science." In *Place/Culture/Representation*, edited by James Duncan and David Ley, 251–71. London: Routledge, 1993.
———. "No Borders, No Nations: Making Greece in Macedonia." *Annals of the Association of American Geographers* 97, no. 2 (2007): 398–422.
Aguiar, Marian. *Tracking Modernity: India's Railway and the Culture of Modernity*. Minneapolis: University of Minnesota Press, 2011.

Akimori Tsunetarō. *Chōsen shokan*. Osaka: Akimori Tsunetarō, 1935.
Ambaras, David R. "Social Knowledge, Cultural Capital, and the New Middle Class in Japan." *Journal of Japanese Studies* 24, no. 1 (1998): 1–33.
Anderson, Benedict. *Imagined Communities: Reflections on the Origin and Spread of Nationalism*. London: Verso, 1983.
Andrews, Thomas G. "'Made by Toile?' Tourism, Labor, and the Construction of the Colorado Landscape, 1858–1917." *Journal of American History* 82, no. 3 (2005): 837–63.
Aoi Akihito. *Shokuminchi jinja to teikoku Nihon*. Tokyo: Yoshikawa kōbunkan, 2005.
———. "Transplanting State Shintō: The Reconfiguration of Existing Built and Natural Environments." In *Constructing the Colonized Land: Entwined Perspectives of East Asia around World War II*, edited by Izumi Kuroishi, 97–122. Burlington, VT: Ashgate, 2014.
Aoi Ikko. "Han Nihonka no Keijō." *Tabi* 1929, no. 6: 76–79.
Appadurai, Arjun. "Putting Hierarchy in Its Place." *Cultural Anthropology* 3, no. 1 (1988): 36–49.
Arai Gyōji. "Tabi no shakaika, minshūka." *Tabi* 1924, no. 7: 2–3.
Arakawa Seijirō. *Sen-Man jitsugyō shisatsu danshi*. N.p., 1918.
Ariyama Teruo. *Kaigai kankō ryokō no tanjō*. Tokyo: Yoshikawa kōbunkan, 2002.
Armitage, David. *Foundations of Modern International Thought*. Cambridge: Cambridge University Press, 2013.
Arrighi, Giovanni. *The Long Twentieth Century: Money, Power, and the Origins of Our Times*. London: Verso, 1994.
Asada Kyōji. *Nihon shokuminchi kenkyū shiron*. Tokyo: Miraisha, 1990.
Asai Yumeji. "Keijō kenbun inshō roku." *Chōsen oyobi Manshū*, no. 99 (October 1915): 110–11.
Asaka Yukio. *Chūgaku shakai Nihon no kokudo to sekai, shin hen*. Tokyo: Shimizu shoin, 1964.
Aso, Noriko. *Public Properties: Museums in Imperial Japan*. Durham, NC: Duke University Press, 2014.
Atkins, E. Taylor. "The Dual Career of 'Arirang': The Korean Resistance Anthem That Became a Japanese Pop Hit." *Journal of Asian Studies* 66, no. 4 (2007): 645–87.
———. *Primitive Selves: Koreana in the Japanese Colonial Gaze, 1910–1945*. Berkeley: University of California Press, 2010.
Atsumi Ikuko and Graeme Wilson. "The Poetry of Yosano Akiko." *Japan Quarterly* 21, no. 2 (1974): 181–87.
Baldwin, Frank. "The March First Movement: Korean Challenge and Japanese Response." PhD diss., Columbia University, 1969.
Balibar, Étienne. "The Nation Form." In *Race, Class, Nation: Ambiguous Identities*, edited by Étienne Balibar and Immanuel Wallerstein, 86–106. London: Verso, 1991.
Balibar, Étienne, and Immanuel Wallerstein. *Race, Nation, Class: Ambiguous Identities*. London: Verso, 1991.
Ballantyne, Tony, and Antoinette Burton. *Empires and the Reach of the Global, 1870–1945*. Cambridge, MA: Belknap Press, 2014.
Bang, Ji Seon. "A School Excursion of the Middle School Managed by Korean to Japan, Manchuria in 1920-30s" [in Korean]. *Sŏktang nonch'ong* 44 (2009): 167–216.

Banivanua-Mar, Tracey, and Penelope Edmonds. "Making Space in Settler Colonies." In *Making Settler Colonial Space: Perspectives on Race, Place, and Identity*, edited by Tracey Banivanua-Mar and Penelope Edmonds, 1–24. New York: Palgrave MacMillan, 2010.
Banner, Stuart. *Possessing the Pacific: Land, Settlers, and Indigenous People from Australia to Alaska*. Cambridge, MA: Harvard University Press, 2007.
Barak, On. *On Time: Technology and Temporality in Egypt*. Berkeley: University of California Press, 2013.
Baranowski, Shelley, Christopher Endy, Waleed Hazbun, Stephanie Malia Hom, Gordon Pirie, Trevor Simmons, and Eric G. E. Zuelow. "Discussion: Tourism and Empire." *Journal of Tourism History* 7, no. 1–2 (2015): 100–130.
Barclay, Paul D. "Cultural Brokerage and Interethnic Marriage in Colonial Taiwan: Japanese Subalterns and Their Aboriginal Wives, 1895–1930." *Journal of Asian Studies* 64, no. 2 (2005): 323–60.
———. "Peddling Postcards and Selling Empire: Image-Making in Taiwan under Japanese Colonial Rule." *Japanese Studies* 30, no. 1 (2010): 81–110.
Benjamin, Walter. "Theses on the Philosophy of History." In *Illuminations*, edited by Hannah Arendt, translated by Harry Zohn. New York: Schocken Books, 1969.
Benton, Lauren. "Spatial Histories of Empire." *Itinerario* 30, no. 3 (2006): 19–24.
Bhabha, Homi K., ed. *Nation and Narration*. London: Routledge, 1990.
Botsman, Daniel. *Power and Punishment in the Making of Modern Japan*. Princeton, NJ: Princeton University Press, 2005.
Bowen-Struyk, Heather, and Norma Field, eds. *For Dignity, Justice, and Revolution: Anthology of Japanese Proletarian Literature*. Chicago: University of Chicago Press, 2016.
Brandt, Kimberley. *Kingdom of Beauty: Mingei and the Politics of Folk Art in Imperial Japan*. Durham, NC: Duke University Press, 2007.
Brooks, Barbara J. "Japanese Colonialism, Gender, and Household Registration: Legal Reconstruction of Boundaries." In *Gender and Law in the Japanese Imperium*, edited by Susan L. Burns and Barbara J. Brooks, 219–39. Honolulu: University of Hawai'i Press, 2014.
Burbank, Jane, and Frederick Cooper. *Empires in World History: Power and the Politics of Difference*. Princeton, NJ: Princeton University Press, 2010.
Burks, Ardath W., ed. *The Modernizers: Overseas Students, Foreign Employees, and Meiji Japan*. Boulder, CO: Westview Press, 1985.
Burton, Antoinette. "Introduction: On the Inadequacy and Indispensability of the Nation." In *After the Imperial Turn: Thinking with and through the Nation*, 1–23. Durham, NC: Duke University Press, 2003.
Buzard, James. *The Beaten Track: European Tourism, Literature, and the Ways to Culture*. Oxford: Oxford University Press, 1993.
Cai Peihuo. *Nihon honkokumin ni atau*. Tokyo: Taiwan mondai kenkyūjo, 1928.
Caprio, Mark. "Marketing Assimilation: The Press and the Formation of the Japanese-Korean Colonial Relationship." *Journal of Korean Studies* 16, no. 1 (2011): 1–25.
Carter, Paul. *The Road to Botany Bay: Explorations in Landscape and History*. New York: Knopf, 1988.
Caton, Steve A. "The Importance of Reflexive Language in G. H. Mead's Theory of Self and Communication." In *Reflexive Language: Reported Speech and Metapragmatics*, edited by John A. Lucy, 315–37. Cambridge: Cambridge University Press, 1993.

Chamberlain, Basil Hall. *Things Japanese: Being Notes on Various Subjects Connected with Japan for the Use of Travellers and Others.* 5th ed. rev. London: John Murray, 1905.
Chen, Edward I-Te. "Formosan Political Movements under Japanese Colonial Rule, 1914–1937." *Journal of Asian Studies* 31, no. 3 (1972): 477–97.
Ching, Leo T. S. "Savage Construction and Civility Making: The Musha Incident and Aboriginal Representations in Colonial Taiwan." *positions* 8, no. 3 (2000): 795–818.
———. *Becoming "Japanese": Colonial Taiwan and the Politics of Identity Formation.* Berkeley: University of California Press, 2001.
Chiri rekishi kenkyūkai. *Nihon zenkoku jun'yū gakusei ensoku shūgaku ryokō annai.* Osaka: Tanaka sōeidō, 1902.
Cho Sŏng-un. *Singminji kŭndae kwan'gwang kwa Ilbon sich'al.* Seoul: Kyŏngin munhwasa, 2011.
Chōsen sōtokufu, ed. *Chōsen tetsudō ryokō benran.* Keijō: Chōsen sōtokufu, 1923.
Chōsen sōtokufu tetsudōkyoku, ed. *Chōsen tetsudō ryokō annai: tsuketari Kongōsan annai.* Keijō: Chōsen sōtokufu tetsudōkyoku, 1915.
———. *Chōsen ryokō annai ki.* Keijō: Chōsen sōtokufu tetsudōkyoku, 1929.
———. *Chōsen ryokō annai ki.* Keijō: Chōsen sōtokufu tetsudōkyoku, 1934.
Chow Tse-tsung. *The May Fourth Movement: Intellectual Revolution in Modern China.* Stanford: Stanford University Press, 1960.
Christy, Alan S. "The Making of Imperial Subjects in Okinawa." *positions* 1, no. 3 (1993): 607–39.
Chung, Henry. *The Case of Korea: A Collection of Evidence on the Japanese Domination of Korea, and on the Development of the Korean Independence Movement.* New York: Fleming H. Revell Company, 1921.
Clayton, Daniel. "Critical and Imperial Geographies." In *Handbook of Cultural Geography,* edited by Kay Anderson, Mona Domosh, Steve Pile, and Nigel Thrift, 354–68. Thousand Oaks, CA: Sage Publications, 2003.
Cohn, Bernard S. *Colonialism and Its Forms of Knowledge: The British in India.* Princeton, NJ: Princeton University Press, 1996.
Conrad, Sebastian. *Globalisation and the Nation in Imperial Germany.* Translated by Sorcha O'Hagan. Berkeley: University of California Press, 2010.
———. "Enlightenment in Global History: A Historiographical Critique." *American Historical Review* 117, no. 4 (2012): 999–1027.
"Coolies Longshoring at the Dairen Wharves." *Manshū gurafu* (May 1936): 87.
Cooper, Frederick. *Africa in the World: Capitalism, Empire, Nation-State.* Cambridge, MA: Harvard University Press, 2014.
———. *Citizenship between Empire and Nation: Remaking France and French Africa.* Princeton, NJ: Princeton University Press, 2014.
Cosgrove, Denis. *Social Formation and Symbolic Landscape.* Madison: University of Wisconsin Press, 1984.
Cosgrove, Denis, and Stephen Daniels, ed. *The Iconography of Landscape: Essays on Symbolic Representation, Design, and Use of Past Environments.* Cambridge: Cambridge University Press, 1988.

Coulmas, Florian. "Language Policy in Modern Japanese Education." In *Language Policies in Education: Critical Issues*, edited by James W. Tollefson. Mahwah, NJ: Lawrence Erlbaum Associates, 2002.

Crary, Jonathan. *Techniques of the Observer: On Vision and Modernity in the Nineteenth Century*. Cambridge, MA: MIT Press, 1990.

Cresswell, Tim. *In Place/Out of Place: Geography, Ideology, and Transgression*. Minneapolis: University of Minnesota Press, 1996.

———. *Place: A Short Introduction*. Malden, MA: Blackwell, 2004.

———. "Citizenship in Worlds of Mobility." In *Critical Mobilities*, edited by Ola Söderström, Shalini Randeria, Didier Ruedin, Gianni D'Amato, and Francesco Panese, 105–24. New York: Taylor & Francis, 2013.

Cronon, William. *Changes in the Land: Indians, Colonists, and the Ecology of New England*. New York: Hill and Wang, 2003.

Culver, Annika A. "Introduction to 'Heading to Moscow.'" Chicago: The Center for East Asian Studies, 2012. https://ceas.uchicago.edu/sites/ceas.uchicago.edu/files/uploads/Sibley/Heading%20for%20Moscow%20Introduction.pdf.

Cumings, Bruce. *Parallax Visions: Making Sense of American-East Asian Relations*. Durham, NC: Duke University Press, 1999.

Dickinson, Frederick R. *World War I and the Triumph of a New Japan, 1919–1930*. Cambridge: Cambridge University Press, 2013.

Doak, Kevin M. "What Is a Nation and Who Belongs? National Narratives and the Ethnic Imagination in Twentieth-Century Japan." *American Historical Review* 102, no. 2 (1997): 283–309.

———. *A History of Nationalism in Modern Japan: Placing the People*. Leiden: Brill, 2007.

Dodge, Tony. *Inventing Iraq: The Failure of Nation-Building and a History Denied*. New York: Columbia University Press, 2003.

Driscoll, Mark. *Absolute Erotic, Absolute Grotesque: The Living, Dead, and Undead in Japan's Imperialism, 1895–1945*. Durham, NC: Duke University Press, 2010.

Duara, Prasenjit. *Sovereignty and Authenticity: Manchukuo and the East Asian Modern*. Lanham, MD: Rowman and Littlefield, 2003.

———. "Asia Redux: Conceptualizing a Region for Our Times." *Journal of Asian Studies* 69, no. 4 (2010): 963–83.

Dudden, Alexis. *Japan's Colonization of Korea: Discourse and Power*. Berkeley: University of California Press, 2005.

Duus, Peter. *The Abacus and the Sword: The Japanese Penetration of Korea, 1895–1910*. Berkeley: University of California Press, 1995.

———. "Imperialism without Colonies: The Vision of a Greater East Asia Co-Prosperity Sphere." *Diplomacy and Statecraft* 7, no. 1 (1996): 54–72.

Duus, Peter, Ramon H. Myers, and Mark R. Peattie. *The Japanese Informal Empire in China, 1895–1937*. Princeton, NJ: Princeton University Press, 1989.

Elkins, Caroline, and Susan Pedersen, eds. *Settler Colonialism in the Twentieth Century: Projects, Practices, Legacies*. New York: Routledge, 2005.

Em, Henry. *The Great Enterprise: Sovereignty and Historiography in Modern Korea*. Durham, NC: Duke University Press, 2013.

Entrikin, Nicholas J. *The Betweenness of Place: Towards a Geography of Modernity*. Baltimore: Johns Hopkins University Press, 1991.

Eskildsen, Robert. "Of Civilization and Savages: The Mimetic Imperialism of Japan's 1874 Expedition to Taiwan." *American Historical Review* 107, no. 2 (2002): 388–418.

Esselstrom, Erik. *Crossing Empire's Edge: Foreign Ministry Police and Japanese Expansionism in Northeast Asia*. Honolulu: University of Hawai'i Press, 2009.

Fabian, Johannes. *Time and the Other: How Anthropology Makes Its Object*. New York: Columbia University Press, 1983.

Fields, Gary. "Enclosure Landscapes: Historical Reflections on Palestinian Geography." *Historical Geography* 39 (2011): 182–207.

———. "This Is Our Land: Collective Violence, Property Law, and Imagining the Geography of Palestine." *Journal of Cultural Geography* 29, no. 3 (2012): 267–91.

Frank, Andre Gunder. "The Development of Underdevelopment." *The Monthly Review* 18, no. 4 (1966): 17–31.

Fujii, James A. "Writing Out Asia: Modernity, Canon, and Natsume Sōseki's *Kokoro*." *positions* 1, no. 1 (1993): 194–223.

Fujitani, Takashi. *Splendid Monarchy: Power and Pageantry in Modern Japan*. Berkeley: University of California Press, 1996.

———. *Race for Empire: Koreans As Japanese and Japanese As Americans during World War II*. Berkeley: University of California Press, 2011.

Fujitani, Takashi, Geoffrey M. White, and Lisa Yoneyama. Introduction to *Perilous Memories: The Asia-Pacific War(s)*. Durham, NC: Duke University Press, 2001.

Fukuoka, Maki. *The Premise of Fidelity: Science, Visuality, and Representing the Real in Nineteenth-Century Japan*. Stanford: Stanford University Press, 2012.

Furlough, Ellen. "Une leçon de choses: Tourism, Empire, and the Nation in Interwar France." *French Historical Studies* 25, no. 3 (2002): 441–73.

Gao Yuan. "Kioku sangyō toshite no tsūrizumu: sengo ni okeru Nihonjin no 'Manshū' kankō." *Gendai shisō* 29, no. 3 (2001): 219–29.

———. "'Rakudo' o hashiru kankō basu." In *Kakudai suru modanitii: 1920–1930 nendai 2*, edited by Yoshimi Shun'ya, 216–53. Tokyo: Iwanami shoten, 2002.

———. "Kankō no seijigaku: Senzen sengo ni okeru Nihonjin no 'Manshū' kankō." PhD diss., University of Tokyo, 2004.

Gentry, Kynan. *History, Heritage, and Colonialism: Historical Consciousness, Britishness, and Cultural Identity in New Zealand, 1870–1940*. Manchester, England: Manchester University Press, 2015.

Gluck, Carol. *Japan's Modern Myths: Ideology in the Late Meiji Period*. Princeton, NJ: Princeton University Press, 1985.

Go Kōmei. "Kindai Nihon no Taiwan ninshiki: 'Taiwan kyōkai kaihō' 'Tōyō jihō' o chūshin ni." In *Kindai Nihon no Ajia ninshiki*, edited by Furuya Tetsuo, 211–41. Kyōto: Kyōto daigaku jinbun kagaku kenkyūjo, 1994.

Goldberg, David Theo. "Multicultural Conditions." In *Multiculturalism: A Critical Reader*, 1–41. Oxford: Blackwell, 1994.

Gordon, Andrew. *Labor and Imperial Democracy in Prewar Japan*. Berkeley: University of California Press, 1991.

Gotō Shinpei. "Taiwan kankō jun." *Tabi* 1925, no. 12: 2–3.

Gragert, Edwin H. *Landownership under Colonial Rule: Korea's Japanese Experience*. Honolulu: University of Hawai'i Press, 1994.
Grewal, Inderpal. *Home and Harem: Nation, Gender, Empire and the Cultures of Travel*. Durham, NC: Duke University Press, 1996.
Haag, Andre. "Fear and Loathing in Imperial Japan: The Cultures of Korean Peril, 1919–1923." PhD diss., Stanford University, 2013.
Hamada Tsunenosuke. *Waga shokuminchi*. Tokyo: Toyamabō, 1928.
Hamamoto Hiroshi. *Ryojun*. Tokyo: Rokkō shōkai shuppanbu, 1942.
Han, Sun-Jung. *An Imperial Path to Modernity: Yoshino Sakuzō and a New Liberal Order in East Asia, 1905–1937*. Cambridge, MA: Harvard University Asia Center, 2012.
Hane, Mikiso. *Modern Japan: A Historical Survey*. Boulder, CO: Westview Press, 1986.
Hanes, Jeffrey E. *The City As Subject: Seki Hajime and the Reinvention of Modern Osaka*. Berkeley: University of California Press, 2002.
Haraway, Donna. "Situated Knowledges: The Science Question in Feminism and the Privilege of Partial Perspective." *Feminist Studies* 14, no. 3 (1988): 575–99.
Harootunian, Harry D. "Figuring the Folk: History, Poetics, and Representation." In *Mirror of Modernity: Invented Traditions in Modern Japan*, edited by Stephen Vlastos, 144–59. Berkeley: University of California Press, 1997.
Haruyama Meitetsu. *Kindai Nihon to Taiwan: Musha jiken shokuminchi tōchi seisaku no kenkyū*. Tokyo: Fujiwara shobō, 2008.
Harvey, David. *Justice, Nature, and the Geography of Difference*. Malden, MA: Blackwell, 1996.
Hayasaka Yoshino. *Konran no Shina o tabishite*. Utsunomiya-shi: Hayasaka Yoshio, 1922.
Hayashi Takahisa. Preface to *Shiroi kimono to kuroi ishō*, edited by Miyazaki kenritsu Miyakonojō shōkō gakkō. Tojō: Miyazaki kenritsu Miyakonojō shōkō gakkō, 1931.
Heater, Derek. *National Self-Determination: Woodrow Wilson and His Legacy*. New York: St. Martin's Press, 1994.
Henry, Todd A. "Sanitizing Empire: Japanese Articulations of Korean Otherness and the Construction of Early Colonial Seoul." *Journal of Asian Studies* 64, no. 3 (2005): 639–75.
———. "Respatializing Chosŏn's Royal Capital: The Politics of Japanese Urban Reforms in Early Colonial Seoul." In *Sitings: Critical Approaches to Korean Geography*, edited by Timothy Tangherlini and Sallie Yea, 15–38. Honolulu: University of Hawai'i Press, 2007.
———. *Assimilating Seoul: Japanese Rule and the Politics of Space in Colonial Korea, 1910–1945*. Berkeley: University of California Press, 2014.
———. "Assimilation's Racializing Sensibilities: Colonized Koreans As *Yobos* and the '*Yobo*-ization' of Expatriate Japanese." In *The Affect of Difference: Representations of Race in the Japanese Empire*, edited by Christopher P. Hanscom and Dennis Washburn, 81–107. Honolulu: University of Hawai'i Press, 2016.
High, Peter B. *The Imperial Screen: Japanese Film Culture in the Fifteen Years' War*. Madison, WI: University of Wisconsin Press, 2003.
Hill, Christopher L. *National History and the World of Nations: Capital, State, and the Rhetoric of History in Japan, France, and the United States*. Durham, NC: Duke University Press, 2008.
Hirano, Katsuya. "Thanatopolitics and the Making of Japan's Hokkaidō: Settler Colonialism and Primitive Accumulation." *Critical Historical Studies* 2, no. 2 (2015): 191–218.

Hiroshima kōtō shihan gakkō. *Tairiku shūgaku ryokō ki.* [Hiroshima]: Hiroshima kōtō shihan gakkō, 1915.

Hirsch, Francine. *Empire of Nations: Ethnographic Knowledge and the Making of the Soviet Union.* Ithaca, NY: Cornell University Press, 2005.

Ho, Engseng. *Graves of Tarim: Genealogy and Mobility across the Indian Ocean.* Berkeley: University of California Press, 2006.

Ho, Samuel P. S. *The Economic Development of Taiwan, 1860–1970.* New Haven, CT: Yale University Press, 1978.

Hobsbawm, Eric. *Nations and Nationalism since 1780: Programme, Myth, Reality.* Cambridge: Cambridge University Press, 1992.

"Honshi no kōdai." *Chōsen oyobi Manshū* 1912, no. 1: 10.

Howell, David. "Territoriality and Collective Identity in Tokugawa Japan." *Daedalus* 127, no. 3 (1998): 105–32.

———. *Geographies of Identity in Nineteenth-Century Japan.* Berkeley: University of California Press, 2005.

Howland, Douglas R. *The Borders of Chinese Civilization: Geography and History at Empire's End.* Durham, NC: Duke University Press, 1996.

———. *Translating the West: Language and Political Reason in Nineteenth-Century Japan.* Honolulu: University of Hawai'i Press, 2002.

Hsu Chien-Jung. *The Construction of National Identity in Taiwan's Media, 1896–2012.* Leiden: Brill, 2014.

Hussain, Nasser. *The Jurisprudence of Emergency: Colonialism and the Rule of Law.* Ann Arbor: University of Michigan Press, 2003.

Imai Kingō. *Edo no tabi fūzoku: dōchūki o chūshin ni.* Tokyo: Ōzorasha, 1997.

Inagaki Ryūichi. "Taiwan ni okeru kokuritsu kōen mondai." *Kokuritsu kōen* 8, no. 1 (1936): 6–9.

Inoue, Kota. "A Little Story of Settler Colonialism: Imperialist Consciousness and Children's Literature in the 1920s." In *Reading Colonial Literature in Japan: Text, Context, Critique,* edited by Michele M. Mason and Helen J. S. Lee, 188–208. Stanford: Stanford University Press, 2012.

Inoue, Miyako. *Vicarious Language: Gender and Linguistic Modernity in Japan.* Berkeley: University of California Press, 2006.

International Commission on National Parks. *1973 United Nations List of National Parks and Equivalent Reserves.* Morges: IUCN, 1973.

Iriye, Akira. *After Imperialism: The Search for a New Order in the Far East, 1921–1931.* Cambridge, MA: Harvard University Press, 1965.

———. "Japan's Drive to Great-Power Status." In *The Cambridge History of Japan,* vol. 5, *The Nineteenth Century,* edited Marius B. Jansen, 721–82. Cambridge: Cambridge University Press, 1989.

Ishida Takeshi. "Dōka seisaku to tsukurareta kannen toshite no 'Nihon.'" *Shisō,* no. 892 (1998): 47–75.

Ishikawa Sadatomo. "Nihon ni okeru kokuritsu kōen no enkaku." *Kokuritsu kōen* 10, no. 1 (1938): 7.

Ishikawa Toraji. "Taiwan ryokō." In *Shin Nihon kenbutsu,* edited by Kanao Shujirō. Tokyo: Kanao Bun'endō, 1918.

Ishimitsu Makiyo. "Bōkyō no uta." In *Ishimitsu Makiyo no shuki*. Tokyo: Chūō kōronsha, 1978.
Ishizuka Minoru. *Kindai Nihon no kaigai ryūgakushi*. Tokyo: Chūō kōron, 1972.
Itagaki Hōki. *Taiwan kenbutsu Man-Sen manpo*. Tokyo: Itagaki Rikiko, 1931.
Itō Ken. *Taiwan annai*. Tokyo: Shokumin jijō kenkyūsha, 1935.
Itō Takeo. *Life along the South Manchurian Railway: The Memoirs of Itō Takeo*. Translated by Joshua A. Fogel. Armonk, NY: M. E. Sharpe, 1998.
Ivy, Marilyn. *Discourses of the Vanishing: Modernity, Phantasm, Japan*. Chicago: University of Chicago Press, 1995.
Jackson, Peter, and Jan Penrose. "Introduction: Placing 'Race' and Nation." In *Constructions of Race, Place, and Nation*. London: University College London Press, 1994.
Jahn, Beate. "IR and the State of Nature: The Cultural Origins of a Ruling Ideology." *Review of International Studies* 25 (1999): 411–34.
Jansen, Marius B. "Japanese Imperialism: Late Meiji Perspectives." In *The Japanese Colonial Empire, 1895–1945*, edited by Ramon H. Myers and Mark R. Peattie, 61–79. Princeton, NJ: Princeton University Press, 1989.
Japan Chronicle, ed. "Eight Japanese and 150 Koreans Killed." *The Independence Movement in Korea: A Record of Some of the Events of the Spring of 1919*. Kobe: Japan Chronicle, 1919.
Japan Tourist Bureau, ed. *Ryotei to hiyō gaisan*. Tokyo: Japan Tourist Bureau, 1920.
———, ed. *Ryotei to hiyō gaisan Taishō 12-nen*. Tokyo: Japan Tourist Bureau, 1923.
———, ed. *Ryotei to hiyō gaisan Shōwa 6-nen ban*. Tokyo: Hakubunkan, 1931.
Japan tsūrisuto byūrō Taiwan shibu, ed. *Taiwan tetsudō ryokō annai*. Taihoku: Japan tsūrisuto byūrō Taiwan shibu, 1935.
Japanese Government Railways, ed. *An Official Guide to Eastern Asia*. 5 vols. Tokyo: Japanese Government Railways, 1913–1918.
Jaworski, Adam. "Mobile Language in Mobile Places." *International Journal of Bilingualism* 18, no. 5 (2014): 524–533.
Jo Kōsei. *Kita Chōsen kikō: Nihongo ban*. Nagano: Zainichi Chōsenjin renmei Nagano honbu shuppanbu, 1948.
Ka, Chih-ming. *Japanese Colonialism in Taiwan: Land Tenure, Development, and Dependency, 1895–1945*. Boulder, CO: Westview Press, 1995.
Kal, Hong. "Modeling the West, Returning to Asia: Shifting Politics of Representation in Japanese Colonial Exposition in Korea." *Comparative Studies in Society and History* 47, no. 3 (2005): 507–31.
Kanda Kōji. *Kankō kūkan no seisan to chiriteki shizōryoku*. Kyōto: Nakanishiya shuppan, 2012.
Kaneko Fumio. *Kindai Nihon ni okeru tai Manshū tōshi no kenkyū*. Tokyo: Kondō shuppansha, 1991.
Kaplan, David H. "Territorial Identities and Geographic Scale." In *Nested Identities: Nationalism, Territory, and Scale*, edited by Guntram Henrik Herb and David H. Kaplan, 31–49. Lanhan, MD: Rowman & Littlefield, 1999.
Karatani Kōjin. *Kindai Nihon bungaku no kigen*. Tokyo: Kōdansha, 1988.
Karl, Rebecca. *Staging the World: Chinese Nationalism at the Turn of the Twentieth Century*. Durham, NC: Duke University Press, 2002.

Katō Kiyofumi. "Seitō naikaku kakuritsuki ni okeru shokuminchi shihai taisei no mosaku: Takumushō setchi mondai no kōsatsu." *Higashi Ajia kindai shi* 1, no. 1 (1998): 39–58.
Katō Takashi. "Governing Edo." In *Edo and Paris: Urban Life and the State in the Early Modern Era*, edited by James L. McClain, John M. Merriman, and Ugawa Kaoru, 41–67. Ithaca, NY: Cornell University Press, 1994.
Katz, Paul. *When Valleys Turned Blood Red: The Ta-pa-ni Incident in Colonial Taiwan.* Honolulu: University of Hawai'i Press, 2005.
Kawahigashi Hekigotō. "Chōsen no aki kakite." In *Shin Nihon kenbutsu*, edited by Kanao Shujirō. Tokyo: Kanao bun'endō, 1918.
Kawamura Minato. "Shokuminchi bungaku to wa nani ka." In *Nan'yō Karafuto no Nihon bungaku*. Tokyo: Chikuma shobō, 1994.
———. *Sakubun no naka no dai Nihon teikoku*. Tokyo: Iwanami shoten, 2000.
———. "'Senseki' to iu tēma pāku." In *Nichiro sensō sutadīzu*, edited by Komori Yōichi and Narita Ryūichi, 217–19. Tokyo: Kinokuniya shoten, 2004.
———. "Puroretaria bungaku no naka no minzoku mondai." *Kokubungaku kaishaku to kanshō* 75, no. 4 (2010): 58–65.
Kawanishi Hidemichi. "Tōhoku wa Nihon no Sukottorando ka." In *Rōkaru hisutorī kara gurōbaru hisutorī e: tabunka no rekishigaku to chiikishi*, edited by Kawanishi Hidemichi, Namikawa Kenji, and M. William Steele, 207–23. Tokyo: Iwata shoin, 2005.
Kawashima, Ken C. *The Proletarian Gamble: Korean Workers in Interwar Japan.* Berkeley: University of California Press, 2009.
Kearney, Reginald. "The Pro-Japanese Utterances of W. E. B. Du Bois." *Contributions in Black Studies* 13/14 (1995/1996): 201–17.
———. *African American Views of the Japanese: Solidarity or Sedition?* Albany: SUNY Press, 1998.
"Keijō dayori." In *Kōgakkō yō kokugo dokuhon 7-kan*. Taihoku: Taiwan sōtokufu, 1931 [1924].
Keijō kankō kyōkai. *Keijō annai Shōwa 8-nen ban*. Keijō: Keijō kankō kyōkai, 1933.
Kikuchi Kunisaku. *Chōhei kihi no kenkyū*. Tokyo: Rippū shobō, 1977.
Kikuchi, Yuko. Introduction to *Refracted Modernity: Visual Culture and Identity in Colonial Taiwan*, edited by Yuko Kikuchi, 1–20. Honolulu: University of Hawai'i Press, 2007.
Kim, Hoi-Eun. *Doctors of Empire: Medical and Cultural Encounters between Imperial Germany and Meiji Japan.* Toronto: University of Toronto Press, 2014.
Kim, Michael. "Re-Conceptualizing the Boundaries of Empire: The Imperial Politics of Chinese Labor Migration to Manchuria and Colonial Korea." *Sungkyun Journal of East Asian Studies* 16, no. 1 (2016): 1–24.
Kimura Matsuhiko. "Public Finance in Korea under Japanese Rule: Deficit in the Colonial Account and Colonial Taxation." *Explorations in Economic History* 26 (1989): 285–310.
"Kiryū kara Kōbe." In *Kōgakkō yō kokugo dokuhon 10-kan*. Taihoku: Taiwan sōtokufu, 1935 [1926].
Kitabayashi Tōma. "Chōsen ryokō to onsen." *Tabi* 1951, no. 3: 84–87.
Kitamura Kae. *Nihon shokuminchika no Taiwan genjūmin kyōiku shi*. Sapporo: Hokkaidō daigaku shuppankai, 2008.
Kō Sonbon. *Shokuminchi no tetsudō*. Tokyo: Nihon keizai hyōronsha, 2006.
Kobashi Miyoko. "Chōsen mita mama no ki." *Chōsen*, no. 34 (1910): 37–39.
Kobayashi Chiyoko. "Hakui no Chōsen o iku." *Tabi* 1935, no. 7: 14–36.

Kōbe kōtō shōkō gakkō. *Kaigai ryokō chōsa hōkoku (Taishō 7-nen kaki).* Kōbe: Kōbe kōtō shōkō gakkō, 1919.
Kokusai kankō kyoku Manshū shibu. *Manshū kanban ōrai.* Hōten: Kokusai kankō kyoku Manshū shibu, 1941.
Komagome Takeshi. "I-minzoku shihai no 'kyōgi'." In *Tōgō to shihai no ronri*, edited by Asada Kyōji, 137–55. Tokyo: Iwanami shoten, 1993.
———. *Shokuminchi teikoku Nihon no bunka tōgō.* Tokyo: Iwanami shoten, 1996.
———. *Sekaishi no naka no Taiwan shokuminchi shihai: Tainan chōrōkyō chūgakkō kara no shiza.* Tokyo: Iwanami shoten, 2015.
Komori Yōichi and Narita Ryūichi, eds. *Nichi-Ro sensō sutadīzu.* Tokyo: Kinokuniya shoten, 2004.
Kondō Masami. "Taiwan sōtokufu no riban taisei to Musha jiken." In *Iwanami kōza kindai Nihon to shokuminchi 2*, edited by Ōe Shinobu, 35–58. Tokyo: Iwanami shoten, 1993.
Konishi, Sho. *Anarchist Modernity: Cooperatism and Japanese-Russian Relations in Modern Japan.* Cambridge, MA: Harvard University Asia Center, 2013.
Kōno Shinji. *Taiwan tōgyō kan.* Kōbe: Nikkan shinpōsha, 1915.
Koshar, Rudy. "'What Ought to Be Seen': Tourists' Guidebooks and National Identities in Modern Germany and Europe." *Journal of Contemporary History* 33, no. 3 (1998): 23–40.
———. *German Travel Cultures.* Oxford: Berg, 2001.
Kosmin, Paul. *The Land of the Elephant Kings: Space, Territory, and Ideology in the Seleucid Empire.* Cambridge, MA: Harvard University Press, 2014.
Kramer, Paul. "Power and Connection: Imperial Histories of the United States and the World." *American Historical Review* 116, no. 5 (2011): 1348–91.
Kropp, Phoebe S. *California Vieja: Culture and Memory in a Modern American Place.* Berkeley: University of California Press, 2006.
Kuramoto, Kazuko. *Manchurian Legacy: Memoirs of a Japanese Colonist.* East Lansing: Michigan State University Press, 2004.
Kurose Yūji. *Tōyō takushoku kaisha: Nihon teikoku shugi to Ajia taiheiyō.* Tokyo: Nihon keizai hyōronsha, 2003.
Kyōto-shi kyōiku-bu shakai-ka. "Kyōto-shi ni okeru hiyatoi rōdōsha ni kansuru chōsa." Kyōto-shi, 1931.
Kyūshū teikoku daigaku. *Chōsen Manshū ryokō: Kyūshū teikoku daigaku gakusei shisatsu dan.* Hakozaki-chō [Fukuoka-ken]: Kyūshū teikoku daigaku haizoku shōkō shitsu, 1933.
Laderman, Scott. *Tours of Vietnam: War, Travel Guides, and Memory.* Durham, NC: Duke University Press, 2009.
Lamley, Henry J. "Assimilation Efforts in Colonial Taiwan: The Fate of the 1914 Movement." *Monumenta Serica* 29 (1970–1971): 496–520.
———. "Taiwan under Japanese Rule, 1895–1945." In *Taiwan: A New History*, edited by Murray A. Rubinstein, 201–60. Armonk, NY: M. E. Sharpe, 1999.
Lee, Chulwoo. "Modernity, Legality, and Power." In *Colonial Modernity in Korea*, edited by Gi-Wook Shin and Michael Robinson, 21–51. Cambridge, MA: Harvard University Asia Center, 1999.
Lee, Chong-Sik. *The Politics of Korean Nationalism.* Berkeley: University of California Press, 1963.

Lee, Helen J. S. "Voices of the 'Colonists,' Voices of the 'Immigrants': 'Korea' in Japan's Early Colonial Travel Narratives and Guides, 1894–1914." *Japanese Language and Literature* 41, no. 1 (2007): 1–36.

Lee, Yeounsuk. *The Ideology of Kokugo: Nationalizing Language in Modern Japan.* Translated by Maki Hirano Hubbard. Honolulu: University of Hawai'i Press, 2010.

Lee, Young-sook. "The Korean War and Trism: Legacy of the War on the Development of the Tourism Industry in South Korea." *International Journal of Tourism Research* 8 (2006): 157–70.

Lefebvre, Henri. *The Production of Space.* Translated by Donald Nicholson-Smith. Oxford: Blackwell, 1991.

Lewallen, Ann-Elise. "Performing Identity, Saving Land: Ainu Indigenous Ecotourism As a Stage for Reclaiming Rights in Japan." In *Kokusai shinpojiumu: Kankō kara miru higashi Ajia no esunishiti to kokka.* [Yokohama]: Kanazawa daigaku jinbun shakai kenkyūjo, 2011.

Lewis, Michael. *Rioters and Citizens: Mass Protest in Imperial Japan.* Berkeley: University of California Press, 1990.

Lewis, Martin, and Kären Wigen. *The Myth of Continents: A Critique of Metageography.* Berkeley: University of California Press, 1997.

"Life of the Poor Classes." *Manshū gurafu* 4, no. 5 (May 1936): 91.

Lincicome, Mark E. *Principles, Praxis, and the Politics of Educational Reform in Meiji Japan.* Honolulu: University of Hawai'i Press, 1995.

Lloyd, David Wharton. *Battlefield Tourism: Pilgrimage and the Commemoration of the Great War in Britain, Australia, and Canada, 1919–1939.* Oxford: Berg, 1998.

Lo, Ming-Cheng M. *Doctors within Borders: Profession, Ethnicity, and Modernity in Colonial Taiwan.* Berkeley: University of California Press, 2002.

Locke, John. *Two Treatises of Government,* edited by Peter Laslett. Rev. ed. Cambridge: Cambridge University Press, 1963.

Lockwood, William. *The Economic Development of Japan.* Princeton, NJ: Princeton University Press, 1954.

——. *The Economic Development of Japan.* Expanded ed. Princeton, NJ: Princeton University Press, 1968.

MacCannell, Dean. *The Tourist: A New Theory of the Leisure Class.* New York: Schocken Books, 1976.

Mack, Edward. "Ōtaku Wasaburō's Dictionaries and the Japanese 'Colonization' of Brazil." *Dictionaries: Journal of the Dictionary Society of North America* 31 (2010): 46–68.

Maeda Ai. "Utopia of the Prisonhouse: A Reading of *In Darkest Tokyo*." In *Text and the City: Essays on Japanese Modernity.* Edited by James A. Fujii. Translated by Seiji M. Lippit and James A. Fujii, 21–64. Durham, NC: Duke University Press, 2004.

Mah, Alice. *Port Cities and Global Legacies: Urban Identity, Waterfront Work, and Radicalism.* New York: Palgrave Macmillan, 2014.

Maier, Charles S. "Consigning the Twentieth Century to History: Alternative Narratives for the Modern Era." *American Historical Review* 105, no. 3 (2000): 807–31.

Malkki, Liisa. "National Geographic: The Rooting of Peoples and the Territorialization of National Identity among Scholars and Refugees." *Cultural Anthropology* 7, no. 1 (1992): 24–44.

Manela, Erez. *The Wilsonian Moment: Self-Determination and the International Origins of Anticolonial Nationalism*. Oxford: Oxford University Press, 2007.
Man-Kan kankō dan. *Man Kan kankō dan shi*. Utsunomiya: Man-Kan kankō dan, 1911.
"Man-Sen ryokōki." *Kōyūkai zasshi*, no. 219 (November 21, 1912): 100–130.
Mantetsu Man-Sen annaijo, ed. *Sen-Man-Shina ryotei to hiyō gaisan*. Tokyo: Mantetsu Man-Sen annaijo, 1923.
———. *Chōsen Manshū ryokō annai: tsuketari Shina ryokō annai*. Tokyo: Mantetsu Sen-Man annaijo, 1926.
Marshall, Byron K. *Learning to Be Modern: Japanese Political Discourse on Education*. Boulder, CO: Westview Press, 1994.
Maruyama Hiroshi. *Kindai Nihon kōenshi no kenkyū*. Kyōto: Shibunkaku shuppan, 1994.
Mason, Michele. *Dominant Narratives of Colonial Hokkaidō and Imperial Japan: Envisioning the Periphery and the Modern Nation-State*. New York: Palgrave Macmillan, 2012.
Massey, Doreen. "Power-Geometry and a Progressive Sense of Place." In *Mapping the Futures: Local Cultures, Global Change*, edited by John Bird, Barry Curtis, Tim Putnam, and Lisa Tickner, 59–69. London: Routledge, 1993.
Matsuda, Hiroko. "Becoming Japanese in the Colony." *Cultural Studies* 26, no. 5 (2012): 688–709.
Matsuda Kiichi. *Taiwan Okinawa no tabi*. Osaka: Yanagihara shoten, 1937.
Matsuda Kyōko. *Teikoku no shisen. Hakurankai to ihunka hyōzō*. Tokyo: Yoshikawa kōbunkan, 2003.
———. "Shokuminchi shihaika no Taiwan genjūmin o meguru 'bunrui' no shikō to tōchi jissen." *Rekishigaku kenkyū*, no. 846 (2008): 99–107.
Matsuda Toshihiko. *Senzenki no zainichi Chōsenjin to sanseikan*. Tokyo: Akashi shoten, 1995.
Matsuda Yoshirō. *Taiwan genjūmin to Nihongo kyōiku: Nihon tōchi jidai Taiwan genjūmin kyōikushi kenkyū*. Kyōto: Kyōto shobō, 2004.
Matsukawa Jirō. *Shi go nichi no tabi*. Tokyo: Yūseidō shoten, 1925.
Matsuoka Yōsuke. "Ugoku Man-Mō." In *Ugoku Man-Mō*. Tokyo: Senshinsha, 1931.
Matsusaka, Y. Tak. *The Making of Japanese Manchuria, 1904–1932*. Cambridge, MA: Harvard University Asia Center, 2001.
Matsushita Kentarō, ed. *Taihokushū ribanshi gekan*. Taihoku: Taihokushū kenmubu, 1923.
Matsuzawa Akira. *Tai-Nai ōrai ryokō*. Taihoku: Taihoku kappansha shuppanbu, 1929.
Mattelart, Armand. *The Invention of Communication*, translated by Susan Emanuel. Minneapolis: University of Minnesota Press, 1996.
McDonald, Kate. "Imperial Mobility: Circulation As History in East Asia under Empire." *Transfers* 4, no. 3 (2014): 68–87.
———. "Asymmetrical Integration: Lessons from a Railway Empire." *Technology and Culture* 56, no. 1 (2015): 115–49.
———. "Speaking Japanese: Language and the Expectation of Empire." In *The Affect of Difference: Representations of Race in the Japanese Empire*, edited by Christopher P. Hanscom and Dennis Washburn, 159–79. Honolulu: University of Hawai'i Press, 2016.
Mehta, Uday Singh. *Liberalism and Empire: A Study in Nineteenth-Century British Liberal Thought*. Chicago: University of Chicago Press, 1999.

Mimura, Janis. *Planning for Empire: Reform Bureaucrats and the Japanese Wartime State.* Ithaca, NY: Cornell University Press, 2011.
Minami Manshū tetsudō kabushiki kaisha. *Minami Manshū tetsudō annai.* Dairen: Minami Manshū tetsudō kabushiki kaisha, 1909.
———. *Minami Manshū tetsudō ryokō annai.* Dairen: Minami Manshū tetsudō kabushiki kaisha, 1919.
———. *Minami Manshū tetsudō ryokō annai.* Dairen: Minami Manshū tetsudō kabushiki kaisha, 1929.
———. *Minami Manshū tetsudō kabushiki kaisha dai nijūnen shi.* Vol. 1. Dairen: Minami Manshū tetsudō kabushiki kaisha, 1929.
———. *Minami Manshū tetsudō ryokō annai.* Dairen: Minami Manshū tetsudō kabushiki kaisha, 1935.
Minami Manshū tetsudō kabushiki kaisha Keijō kanrikyoku, ed. *Chōsen tetsudō ryokō annai.* Keijō: Minami Manshū tetsudō kabushiki kaisha Keijō kanrikyoku, 1921.
———. *Chōsen no fūkō.* [Keijō]: Minami Manshū tetsudō kabushiki kaisha Keijō kanrikyoku, 1922.
Mitchell, Timothy. *Colonising Egypt.* Berkeley: University of California Press, 1991.
———. "The Stage of Modernity." In *Questions of Modernity.* Minneapolis: University of Minnesota Press, 2000.
Miyazaki kenritsu Miyakonojō shōkō gakkō, ed. *Shiroi kimono to kuroi ishō.* Tojō: Miyazaki kenritsu Miyakonojō shōkō gakkō, 1931.
Mizuno Masanao. *Futatsu no Chūgoku: tsuketari Nanboku-Sen, Firipin.* Tokyo: Kokudosha, 1949.
Mizuno Naoki. "Senjiki no shokuminchi shihai to 'nai gai chi gyōsei ichigenka'." *Jinbun gakuhō* 79 (1997): 77–102.
Mizutani Chōzaburō. "Waga tabi, waga tōsō." *Tabi* 1952, no. 1: 16–19.
Molina, Natalia. *How Race Is Made in America: Immigration, Citizenship, and the Historical Power of Racial Scripts.* Berkeley: University of California Press, 2014.
Monbushō, ed. *Jinjō shōgaku Nihon rekishi.* 1904. Reprinted in *Nihon kyōkasho taikei,* edited by Kaigo Tokiomi and Naka Arata, Kindai-hen rekishi, vol. 19. Tokyo: Kōdansha, 1965.
———. *Jinjō shōgaku Nihon rekishi.* 1909. Reprinted in *Nihon kyōkasho taikei,* edited by Kaigo Tokiomi and Naka Arata, Kindai-hen rekishi, vol. 19. Tokyo: Kōdansha, 1965.
———. *Jinjō shōgaku kokushi.* 1920. Reprinted in *Nihon kyōkasho taikei,* edited by Kaigo Tokiomi and Naka Arata, Kindai-hen rekishi, vol. 19. Tokyo: Kōdansha, 1965.
Moon, Okpyo. "Japanese Tourists in Korea: Colonial and Post-Colonial Encounters." In *Japanese Tourism and Travel Culture,* edited by Sylvie Guichard-Anguis and Okpyo Moon, 147–71. New York: Routledge, 2009.
Moore, Aaron S. *Constructing East Asia: Technology, Ideology, and Empire in Japan's Wartime Era, 1937–1945.* Stanford: Stanford University Press, 2013.
Morioka Jirō. "Taiwan kokuritsu kōen no shitei o iwasu." *Kokuritsu kōen* 10, no. 1 (1938): 2.
Morishige Shūzō. "Taiwan no konjaku." *Tabi* 1925, no. 1: 48–50.
Mōri Motoyoshi. "Chihō shoku o omonzeyo." *Kokusai kankō* 3, no. 2 (April 1935): 18–19.
Morris-Suzuki, Tessa. *Reinventing Japan: Time, Space, and Nation.* Armonk, NY: M. E. Sharpe, 1998.

———. "Migrants, Subjects, Citizens: Comparative Perspectives on Nationality in the Prewar Japanese Empire." *Asia-Pacific Journal* 6, issue 8, no. 0 (August 2008).
Mosse, George L. *Fallen Soldiers: Reshaping the Memory of the World Wars*. Oxford: Oxford University Press, 1991.
Moto Jun. "Dairen Ryojun." In *Kōyūkaishi (Keijō chū)* 1 March 1935: 245–54.
Motoyama Yukihiko. "Meiji kokka no kyōiku shisō: Taishō no kyōiku to no kanren o chūshin ni." In *Taishō no kyōiku*, edited by Ikeda Susumu and Motoyama Yukihiko, 39–162. Tokyo: Daiichi hōki shuppan, 1978.
Muramatsu Shigeki. *Chūgaku shakai: Nihon to sekai: Chiriteki naiyō o omo to suru mono*. Tokyo: Teikoku shoin, 1954.
Murphy, Alexander B. "The Sovereign State System As Political-Territorial Ideal: Historical and Contemporary Considerations." In *State Sovereignty As Social Construct*, edited by Thomas J. Biersteker and Cynthia Weber, 81–120. Cambridge: Cambridge University Press, 1996.
———. "Entente Territorial: Sack and Raffestin on Territory." *Environment and Planning D: Space and Society* 30, no. 1 (2012): 159–72.
Nagasawa Sokichi. *Tōbu Taiwan jundanki*. Tokyo: Meibunsha, 1916.
Nagata Shunsui. "Tabako-tō Chōsenjin." *Tabi* 1935, no. 5: 25.
Nakagawa Zōichi. *Tabi no bunkashi: gaidobukku to jikokuhyō to ryokōshatachi*. Tokyo: Dentō to gendaisha, 1979.
Nakamura Akira. "Shokuminchi hō." In *Kindai Nihonhō hattatsu shi*, vol. 5, edited by Ukai Nobushige. Tokyo: Keisō shobō, 1958.
Nakane Takayuki. *"Chōsen" hyōshō no bunka shi: Kindai Nihon to tasha o meguru chi no shokuminchika*. Tokyo: Shin'yōsha, 2004.
Nakanishi Inosuke. *Shina Manshū Chōsen*. Tokyo: Jissensha, 1936.
———. *Taiwan kenbunki*. Tokyo: Jissensha, 1937.
Nakano Ryoko. "Uncovering *Shokumin*: Yanaihara Tadao's Concept of Global Civil Society." *Social Science Journal Japan* 9, no. 2 (2006): 187–202.
Narita Ryūichi. "'Kokumin' no hikōteki keisei: Nichi-Ro sensō to minshū undo." In *Nichi-Ro sensō sutadīzu*, edited by Komori Yōichi and Narita Ryūichi, 114–28. Tokyo: Kinokuniya shoten, 2004.
Natsume Sōseki. *Man-Kan tokoro dokoro*. 1909. Reprinted in *Rediscovering Natsume Sōseki, with the First English Translation of Travels in Manchuria and Korea*. Translated by Inger Sigrun Brodey and Sammy I. Tsunematsu. Kent, England: Global Oriental, 2000.
Nenzi, Laura. *Excursions in Identity: Travel at the Intersection of Place, Gender, and Status in Edo Japan*. Honolulu: University of Hawai'i Press, 2008.
Ngai, Mae M. *Impossible Subjects: Illegal Aliens and the Making of Modern America*. Princeton, NJ: Princeton University Press, 2004.
Nihon kōtsū kōsha. *Gojūnen shi*. Tokyo: Nihon kōtsū kōsha, 1962.
Nishida Masanori. "Nihon tōchi jidai ni okeru Taiwan no kokuritsu kōen." *Chiiki sōzōgaku kenkyū* 22, no. 2 (2012): 97–136.
Nishizawa Yasuhiro. "Kenchiku no chōkyō to shokumin toshi kensetsu." In *"Teikoku" Nihon no gakuchi 8: Kūkan keisei to sekai ninshiki*, edited by Yamamuro Shin'ichi, 235–76. Tokyo: Iwanami shoten, 2006.

Nitobe Inazō. "Shokuminchi seisaku kōgi oyobi ronbun" (c. 1915). In *Nitobe Inazō zenshū*, edited by Nitobe Inazō zenshū henshū iinkai. Vol. 4. Tokyo: Kyōbunkan, 1969.

Nō Toshio, Yazawa Taiji, Tanabe Ken'ichi, and Satō Hisashi. *Chūgaku shakaika chiri hatsu teiban*. Tokyo: Teikoku shoin, 1974.

Obara Kuniyoshi. *Chishima Karafuto Chōsen Chūgoku Ryūkyū Nan'yō chiri gakushi shinkenshi*. Tokyo: Tamagawa daigaku shuppanbu, 1952.

O'Dwyer, Emer. *Significant Soil: Settler Colonialism and Japan's Urban Empire in Manchuria*. Cambridge, MA: Harvard University Asia Center, 2015.

Ōgi Zenzō. "Taiwan kengaku nikki." *Umi* 1924, no. 9: 26–28.

Oguma Eiji. *Tan'itsu minzoku shinwa no kigen: "Nihonjin" no jigazō no keifu*. Tokyo: Shin'yōsha, 1995.

———. *"Nihonjin" no kyōkai: Okinawa, Ainu, Taiwan, Chōsen, shokuminchi shihai kara fukki undō made*. Tokyo: Shin'yōsha, 1998.

———. *A Genealogy of "Japanese" Self-Images*. Translated by David Askew. Melbourne, Australia: Trans Pacific Press, 2002.

———. "The Hidden Face of Disaster: 3.11, the Historical Structure and Future of Japan's Northeast." *Asia-Pacific Journal* 9, issue 31, no. 6 (August 1, 2011).

Ohama Jōkō. "Taiwan kokuritsu kōen no shimei." *Kokuritsu kōen* 8, no. 8 (1936): 4–5.

Oikawa Yoshinobu. "Kaidai." In *Tōa eibun ryokō annai*. Tokyo: Edition Synapse, 2008 [Tokyo: Japanese Government Railways, 1913–1917].

Oka Yoshitake. "Generational Conflict after the Russo-Japanese War." In *Conflict in Modern Japanese History: The Neglected Tradition*, edited by Tetsuo Najita and J. Victor Koschmann, 197–225. Princeton, NJ: Princeton University Press, 1982.

Okamoto Makiko. *Shokuminchi kanryō no seijishi Chōsen Taiwan sōtokufu to teikoku Nihon*. Tokyo: Sangensha, 2008.

———. "Shokuminchi zaijūsha no seiji sanka o meguru sōkoku." *Shakai kagaku*, no. 89 (2010): 95–131.

Okamoto, Shumpei. "The Emperor and the Crowd: The Historical Significance of the Hibiya Riot." In *Conflict in Modern Japanese History: The Neglected Tradition*, edited by Tetsuo Najita and J. Victor Koschmann, 258–75. Princeton, NJ: Princeton University Press, 1982.

Okita Kinjō. *Rimen no Kankoku*. Osaka: Kibunkan, 1905.

Osa Shizue. *Kindai Nihon to kokugo nashonarizumu*. Tokyo: Yoshikawa kōbunkan, 1998.

———. "'Manshū' tsūrizumu to gakkō teikoku kūkan senjō: Joshi kōtō shihan gakkō no 'tairiku ryokō' kiroku o chūshin ni." In *Teikoku to gakkō*, edited by Komagome Takeshi and Hashimoto Nobuya, 337–77. Kyōto: Shōwadō, 2007.

Osterhammel, Jürgen. *The Transformation of the World: A Global History of the Nineteenth Century*. Translated by Patrick Camiller. Princeton, NJ: Princeton University Press, 2014.

Ōtsu Toshiya. *Manshūkoku ryokō annai*. Tokyo: Shinkōsha, 1935 [1932].

Paasi, Anssi. *Territories, Boundaries, and Consciousness: The Changing Geographies of the Finnish-Russian Border*. Chichester, England: J. Wiley and Sons, 1996.

———. "Boundaries As Social Processes: Territoriality in the World of Flows." In *Boundaries, Territory and Postmodernity*, edited by David Newman, 69–88. London: Frank Cass, 1999.

Pai, Hyung Il. *Constructing "Korean" Origins: A Critical Review of Archaeology, Historiography, and Racial Myth in Korean State-Formation Theories*. Cambridge, MA: Harvard University Asia Center, 2000.

———. *Heritage Management in Korea and Japan: The Politics of Antiquity and Identity*. Seattle: University of Washington Press, 2013.

Peattie, Mark R. "Japanese Attitudes toward Colonialism, 1895–1937." In *The Japanese Colonial Empire, 1895–1937*, edited by Ramon H. Myers and Mark R. Peattie, 80–127. Princeton, NJ: Princeton University Press, 1984.

Pedersen, Susan. "Back to the League of Nations." *American Historical Review* 112, no. 4 (2007): 1091–117.

———. *The Guardians: The League of Nations and the Crisis of Empire*. New York: Oxford University Press, 2015.

Perry, Samuel. *Recasting Red Culture in Proletarian Japan: Childhood, Korea, and the Historical Avant-Garde*. Honolulu: University of Hawai'i Press, 2014.

Povinelli, Elizabeth A. *The Cunning of Recognition: Indigenous Alterities and the Making of Australian Multiculturalism*. Durham, NC: Duke University Press, 2002.

Pratt, Mary Louise. *Imperial Eyes: Travel Writing and Transculturation*. 2nd ed. New York: Routledge, 2008.

Rafael, Vicente. *White Love and Other Events in Filipino History*. Durham, NC: Duke University Press, 2000.

Raj, Kapil. *Relocating Modern Science: Circulation and the Construction of Knowledge in South Asia and Europe, 1650–1900*. New York: Palgrave MacMillan, 2007.

"Renrakusen ni notta." In *Futsū gakkō kokugo dokuhon 7-kan*, Keijō: Chōsen sōtokufu, 1924.

Rivera, Lauren A. "Managing 'Spoiled' National Identity: War, Tourism, and Memory in Croatia." *American Sociological Review* 73, no. 4 (2008): 613–34.

Robbins, Joel, and Alan Rumsey. "Cultural and Linguistic Anthropology and the Opacity of Other Minds." *Anthropological Quarterly* 82, no. 2 (2008): 407–20.

Robinson, Cedric J. *Black Marxism: The Making of the Black Radical Tradition*. Chapel Hill: University of North Carolina Press, 2000.

Robinson, Michael E. *Cultural Nationalism in Colonial Korea, 1920–1925*. Seattle: University of Washington, 1988.

Rodgers, Daniel T. *Atlantic Crossings: Social Politics in a Progressive Age*. Cambridge, MA: Belknap Press, 1998.

Rosaldo, Michelle Z. "The Things We Do with Words: Ilongot Speech Acts and Speech Act Theory in Philosophy." *Language in Society* 11, no. 2 (1982): 203–237.

Roy, Denny. *Taiwan: A Political History*. Ithaca, NY: Cornell University Press, 2003.

Ruiz, Jason. *Americans in the Treasure House: Travel to Porfirian Mexico and the Cultural Politics of Empire*. Austin: University of Texas Press, 2014.

Ruoff, Kenneth J. *Imperial Japan at Its Zenith: The Wartime Celebration of the Empire's 2,600th Anniversary*. Ithaca, NY: Cornell University Press, 2010.

———. "Japanese Tourism to Mukden, Nanjing, and Qufu, 1938–1943." *Japan Review* 27 (2014): 171–200.

Ryang, Sonia. "Japanese Travellers' Accounts of Korea." *East Asian History* 13/14 (1997): 133–52.

"Ryokōbu buhō." *Kōyūkai zasshi*, no. 243 (March 17, 1915): 50–52.

*Ryōtō shūgaku ryokō ki*. Tokyo: Tokyo kōtō shihan gakkō shūgaku ryokō dan kiroku kakari, 1907.

Saaler, Sven. "Pan-Asianism in Modern Japanese History: Overcoming the Nation, Creating a Region, Forging an Empire." In *Pan-Asianism in Modern Japanese History: Colonialism, Regionalism, and Borders*, edited by Sven Saaler and J. Victor Koschmann, 1–18. London: Routledge, 2007.

Said, Edward W. *Orientalism*. London: Verso, 1978.

———. "Invention, Memory, and Place." *Critical Inquiry* 26, no. 2 (2000): 175–92.

Saitō Itsuki. "Niitaka to Arisan." *Tabi* 1932, no. 10: 40–45.

Sakai, Naoki. "Subject and Substratum: On Japanese Imperial Nationalism." *Cultural Studies* 14, no. 3–4 (2000): 462–530.

Sand, Jordan. "Imperial Tokyo As Contact Zone: The Metropolitan Tours of Taiwanese Aborigines." *Asia-Pacific Journal* 12, issue 10, no. 4 (March 10, 2014).

Sassen, Saskia. *Territory, Authority, Rights: From Medieval to Global Assemblages*. Princeton, NJ: Princeton University Press, 2008.

Satō Hiroshi et al. *Chūgaku shakai Nihon no kokudo to sekai: Chiri teki naiyō o omo ni shita mono*. Tokyo: Shimizu shoin, 1955.

Satō Sanae. *Dare mo kakanakatta Kankoku: chikakute tōi rinjin tachi no sugao*. Tokyo: Sankei shinbunsha, 1974.

Sawada Hisao. *Nihon chimei daijiten*. Vol. 2. Tokyo: Nihon shobō, 1937.

Schivelbusch, Wolfgang. *The Railway Journey: The Industrialization of Time and Space in the 19th Century*. Berkeley: University of California Press, 1986.

Schmid, Andre. *Korea between Empires, 1895–1919*. New York: Columbia University Press, 2002.

Scott, James C. *Seeing Like a State: How Certain Schemes to Improve the Human Condition Have Failed*. New Haven, CT: Yale University Press, 1998.

Sellers-García, Sylvia. *Distance and Documents at the Spanish Empire's Periphery*. Stanford: Stanford University Press, 2014.

Senjū Hajime. "Nihon tōchika Nan'yō guntō ni okeru naichi kankōdan no seiritsu." *Rekishi hyōron*, no. 661 (2005): 52–68.

"Sen-Man-Shina ryokōki oyobi ryokōbu buhō." *Kōyūkai zasshi*, no. 278 (September 15, 1919): 61–63.

Seth, Michael J. *Education Fever: Society, Politics, and the Pursuit of Schooling in South Korea*. Honolulu: University of Hawai'i Press, 2002.

Shaffer, Margueritte. *See America First: Tourism and National Identity, 1880–1940*. Washington, DC: Smithsonian Institution Press, 2001.

Shepherdson-Scott, Kari. "Race behind the Walls: Contact and Containment in Japanese Images of Urban Manchuria." In *The Affect of Difference: Representations of Race in the Japanese Empire*, edited by Christopher P. Hanscom and Dennis Washburn, 186–206. Honolulu: University of Hawai'i Press, 2016.

Shields, Rob. *Places on the Margins: Alternative Geographies of Modernity*. London: Routledge, 1991.

Shimazu, Naoko. "The Myth of the 'Patriotic Soldier': Japanese Attitudes toward Death in the Russo-Japanese War." *War & Society* 19, no. 2 (2001): 69–89.

———. *Japanese Society at War: Death, Memory, and the Russo-Japanese War*. Cambridge: Cambridge University Press, 2009.

Shimoda, Hiraku. "Tongues-Tied: The Making of a 'National Language' and the Discovery of Dialects in Meiji Japan." *American Historical Review* 115, no. 3 (2010): 714–31.

Shirane, Seiji. "Mediated Empire: Colonial Taiwan in Japan's Imperial Expansion in South China and Southeast Asia, 1895–1945." PhD diss., Princeton University, 2014.
"Shuchō: Man-Sen no renraku naru." *Chōsen* 1911, no. 12.
Shūkan Asahi, ed. *Nedanshi nenpyō: Meiji, Taishō, Shōwa*. Tokyo: Asahi shinbunsha, 1989.
Siddle, Richard. "The Making of Ainu Moshiri: Japan's Indigenous Nationalism and Its Cultural Fictions." In *Nationalisms in Japan*, edited by Naoko Shimazu, 110–30. New York: Routledge, 2006.
Silverberg, Miriam. *Erotic Grotesque Nonsense: The Mass Culture of Japanese Modern Times*. Berkeley: University of California Press, 2006.
Silverstein, Michael. "Metapragmatic Discourses and Metapragmatic Function." In *Reflexive Language: Reported Speech and Metapragmatics*, edited by John A. Lucy, 33–58. Cambridge: Cambridge University Press, 1993.
Skwiot, Christine M. *The Purposes of Paradise: U.S. Tourism and Empire in Cuba and Hawai'i*. Philadelphia: University of Pennsylvania Press, 2010.
Smith, Anthony D. *The Nation in History: Historiographical Debates about Ethnicity and Nationalism*. Hanover, NH: University Press of New England, 2000.
Smith, A. D. "States and Homelands: The Social and Geopolitical Implications of National Territory." *Millennium: Journal of International Studies* 10, no. 3 (1981): 187–202.
Smith, Kerry D. *A Time of Crisis: Japan, the Great Depression, and Rural Revitalization*. Cambridge, MA: Harvard University Asia Center, 1994.
Soja, Edward W. *The Political Organization of Space*. Washington, DC: The Association of American Geographers, 1971.
———. "The Socio-Spatial Dialectic." *Annals of the Association of American Geographers* 70, no. 2 (1980): 207–25.
Soshiroda Akira. "Inbound Tourism Policies in Japan from 1859 to 2003." *Annals of Tourism Research* 32, no. 4 (2005): 1100–20.
Soyama Takeshi. *Shokuminchi Taiwan to kindai tsūrizumu*. Tokyo: Seikyūsha, 2003.
———. "Nihon tōchiki Taiwan no tsūrizumu saikō." *Tamagawa daigaku kankō gakubu kiyō* 3 (2015): 65–77.
Spence, Jonathan D. *The Search for Modern China*. New York: W. W. Norton, 1991.
Stein, Rebecca L. *Itineraries of Conflict: Israelis, Palestinians, and the Political Lives of Tourism*. Durham, NC: Duke University Press, 2008.
Stoler, Ann Laura. "On Degrees of Imperial Sovereignty." *Public Culture* 18, no. 1 (2006): 125–46.
———. "Imperial Debris: Reflections on Ruins and Ruination." *Cultural Anthropology* 23, no. 2 (2008): 191–219.
Stoler, Ann Laura, and Frederick Cooper. "Between Metropole and Colony: Rethinking a Research Agenda." In *Tensions of Empire: Colonial Cultures in a Bourgeois World*, 1–56. Berkeley: University of California Press, 1997.
Stoler, Ann Laura, and Carole McGranahan. "Refiguring Imperial Terrains." *Ab Imperio* 2 (2006): 17–58.
Sturken, Marita. *Tangled Memories: The Vietnam War, the AIDS Epidemic, and the Politics of Remembering*. Berkeley: University of California Press, 1997.
Suzuki Sakutarō. *Taiwan no banzoku kenkyū*. Taihoku: Taiwan shiseki kankōkai, 1932.
Suzuki Tadashi. "Bandō kyōiku no ni dai ganmoku." *Riban no tomo* 1, no. 1 (January 1932): 7.

Taguchi Mizuho. "Saikin no Manshū tokoro dokoro." *Tabi* 1936, no. 6: 102–3.
Tai, Eika. *"Kokugo* and Colonial Education in Taiwan." *positions* 7, no. 2 (1999): 503–40.
Taihokushū ribanka. "Taihokushū ribanka hakkō no gakujutsu kōshūyō bango shiryō ni tsuite." *Riban no tomo* 1, no. 4 (April 1932): 9–10.
Tainan jinja shamusho, ed. *Tainan jinjashi.* Taihoku: Tainan jinja shamusho, 1928.
"Tairiku o miyo! Sen-Man o miyo!" *Tabi* 1929, no. 9: 86–87.
"Taiwan e no tabi." *Umi* 1924, no. 8: 31–32.
"Taiwan kara Shina e! Nan'yō e!" *Umi*, no. 4 (1924): 19–20.
Taiwan kyōikukai, ed. *Taiwan kyōiku enkaku shi.* Taihoku: Taiwan kyōikukai, 1939.
Taiwan sōtokufu. *Taiwan tetsudō ryokō annai.* Taihoku: Taiwan sōtokufu, 1916.
———. *Taiwan tetsudō ryokō annai.* Taihoku: Taiwan sōtokufu, 1921.
———. *Saikin no Taiwan.* Taihoku: Taiwan sōtokufu, 1925.
———. *Taiwan tetsudō ryokō annai.* Taihoku: Taiwan sōtokufu, 1927.
Taiwan sōtokufu keimukyoku. *Banjin kyōiku gaikyō.* Taihoku: Taiwan sōtokufu keimukyoku, 1934.
———. *Takasagozoku no kyōiku.* Taihoku: Taiwan sōtokufu keimukyoku, 1936.
Taiwan sōtokufu kōtsūkyoku tetsudōbu, ed. *Taiwan tetsudō shi.* Vol. 3. Taihoku [Taipei]: Taiwan sōtokufu tetsudōkyoku, 1910–1911.
Takahashi. "Banchi ni okeru kokuritsu kōen to riban to no ninshiki." *Riban no tomo*, no. 3 (1938): 2–4.
Takahashi Gentarō. *Shin Manshūkoku kenbutsu.* Tokyo: Ōsakayagō shoten, 1934.
Takayama Kichirō, ed. *Nihon kōkū jūnen no ayumi, 1951–1961.* Tokyo: Nihon kōkū kabushiki kaisha, 1964.
Takeuchi Yoshimi, ed. *Ajiashugi.* Tokyo: Chikuma shobō, 1963.
Tamanoi, Mariko. "Knowledge, Power, and Racial Classifications: The 'Japanese' in Manchuria." *Journal of Asian Studies* 59, no. 2 (2000): 248–76.
———. *Memory Maps: The State and Manchuria in Postwar Japan.* Honolulu: University of Hawai'i Press, 2009.
Tamura Tsuyoshi. *Arisan fūkei chōsa sho.* Taihoku: Taiwan sōtokufu eirinjo, 1930.
———. "Nihonjin no fūkeikan to kokuritsu kōen." *Kokuritsu kōen* 7, no. 6 (1935): 2–3.
———. *Kokuritsu kōen kōwa.* Tokyo: Meiji shoin, 1948.
Tanaka Hiroshi. *Zainichi gaikokujin.* Tokyo: Iwanami shoten, 1991.
Tanaka Keiji. "Shoken." In *Zenkoku chūtō gakkō chiri rekishika kyōin dai 9-kai kyōgikai oyobi Taiwan nan-Shi ryokō hōkoku*, edited by Zenkoku chūtō gakkō chiri rekishika kyōin kyōgikai. Tokyo: Zenkoku chūtō gakkō chiri rekishi ka kyōinkai, 1932.
Tanaka, Stefan. *Japan's Orient: Rendering Pasts into History.* Berkeley: University of California Press, 1993.
———. "Childhood: Naturalization of Development into a Japanese Space." In *Cultures of Scholarship*, edited by Sarah C. Humphreys, 21–56. Ann Arbor: University of Michigan Press, 1997.
Tayama Katai. *Man-Sen no kōraku.* Tokyo: Ōsakayagō shoten, 1924.
———. "Ippei sotsu." In *Modern Japanese Literature, An Anthology*, translated and edited Donald Keene, 142–58. New York: Grove Press, 1956.
Taylor, Charles. "Modern Social Imaginaries." *Public Culture* 14, no. 1 (2002): 91–124.

Taylor, Peter J. "Metageographical Moments: A Geohistorical Interpretation of Embedded Statism and Globalization." In *Rethinking Global Political Economy: Emerging Issues, Unfolding Odysseys*, edited by Mary Ann Tétreault, Robert A. Denmark, Kenneth P. Thomas, and Kurt Burch, 46–64. New York: Routledge, 2003.

Tetsudōin, ed. *Chōsen Manshū Shina annai*. Tokyo: Teibi shuppansha, 1919.

Tetsudōshō. *Nihon annai ki Kinki hen jō*. Tokyo: Hakubunkan, 1932.

———. *Nihon annai ki Kyūshū hen*. Tokyo: Hakubunkan, 1935.

Thornber, Karen. *Empire of Texts in Motion: Chinese, Korea, and Taiwanese Transculturations of Japanese Literature*. Cambridge, MA: Harvard University Asia Center, 2009.

Thum, Rian. *The Sacred Routes of Uyghur History*. Cambridge, MA: Harvard University Press, 2014.

Tierney, Robert. *Tropics of Savagery: The Culture of Japanese Empire in Comparative Frame*. Berkeley: University of California Press, 2010.

———. *Monster of the Twentieth Century: Kōtoku Shūsui and Japan's First Anti-Imperialist Movement*. Berkeley: University of California Press, 2015.

Tokyo furitsu dai-ichi shōgyō gakkō kōyūkai, ed. *Bokura no mitaru Man-Sen-nan-Shi*. Tokyo: Tokyo furitsu dai-ichi shōgyō gakkō kōyūkai, 1932.

Tonomura Masaru. *Zainichi Chōsenjin shakai no rekishigakuteki kenkyū: keisei kōzō hen'yō*. Tokyo: Ryokuin shobō, 2004.

Tooze, J. Adam. *The Deluge: The Great War, America, and the Remaking of Global Order, 1916–1931*. New York: Viking, 2014.

Tōyō takushoku kabushiki kaisha, ed. *Chōsenjin naichi shisatsu Taishō 2-nen shūki*. Keijō: Tōyō takushoku, 1913.

Traganou, Jilly. *The Tōkaidō Road: Traveling and Representation in Edo and Meiji Japan*. New York: RoutledgeCurzon, 2004.

Tsukahara Zenki. "Kansō." In *Zenkoku chūtō gakkō chiri rekishika kyōin dai 9-kai kyōgikai oyobi Taiwan nan-Shi ryokō hōhoku*, edited by Zenkoku chūtō gakkō chiri rekishika kyōin kyōgikai. Tokyo: Zenkoku chūtō gakkō chiri rekishika kyōin kyōgikai, 1932.

Tsurumi, E. Patricia. *Japanese Colonial Education in Taiwan, 1895–1945*. Cambridge, MA: Harvard University Press, 1978.

———. "Colonial Education in Korea and Taiwan." In *The Japanese Colonial Empire, 1895–1945*, edited by Ramon H. Myers and Mark R. Peattie, 275–311. Princeton, NJ: Princeton University Press, 1984.

Tsurumi Yūsuke. *Seiden Gotō Shinpei*. Vol. 5. Tokyo: Fujiwara shoten, 2005.

Tuan, Yi-Fu. "Space and Place: Humanistic Perspective." In *Human Geography: An Essential Anthology*, edited by John Agnew, David Livingstone, and Alistair Rodgers, 444–57. Oxford: Blackwell, 1996.

Twine, Nanette. *Language and the Modern State: The Reform of Written Japanese*. London: Routledge, 1991.

Tze, Loo. *Heritage Politics: Shuri Castle and Okinawa's Incorporation into Modern Japan, 1879–2000*. Lanham, MD: Lexington Books, 2014.

Uchida Aya. "Kinsei gōki ni okeru onsenchi e no tabi to taizai seikatsu ni kansuru kenkyū." PhD diss., Rikkyō daigaku, 2011.

Uchida, Jun. "'A Scramble for Freight': The Politics of Collaboration along and across the Railway Tracks of Korea under Japanese Rule." *Comparative Studies in Society and History* 51, no. 1 (2009): 117–50.

———. *Brokers of Empire: Japanese Settler Colonialism in Korea, 1876–1945*. Cambridge, MA: Harvard University Asia Center, 2011.

Ueda Kazutoshi. "Shōgaku no kyōka ni kokugo ni ikka o moukuru no gi." *Dai Nippon kyōikukai zasshi*, special ed. 2 (1884).

———. "Kokugo to kokka to." In *Meiji bungaku zenshū*. Vol. 44. Tokyo: Chikuma shobō, 1968.

Uesugi Mitsuhiko. "'Takasagozoku' no ijū ni tsuite (1)." *Takachiho ronsō* 24, no. 3 (1990): 39–101.

Ugaramon. *Chōsen e yuku hito ni*. Tokyo: Chōsen e yuku hito hensanjo, 1914.

Un'yushō, ed. *Nihon annai ki Kinki hen jō kaichōban*. Tokyo: Un'yushō, 1949.

Un'yushō kankōka, ed. *Kankō jigyō no shiori kaichōban*. Tokyo: Un'yushō, 1948.

Urakami Shūe. "Taiwan nan-Shi ryokō shokan." In *Zenkoku chūtō gakkō chiri rekishika kyōin dai 9-kai kyōgikai oyobi Taiwan nan-Shi ryokō hōkoku*, edited by Zenkoku chūtō gakkō chiri rekishika kyōgikai. Tokyo: Zenkoku chūtō gakkō chiri rekishi ka kyōinkai, 1932.

Urry, John. *The Tourist Gaze: Leisure and Travel in Contemporary Societies*. London: Sage, 1990.

"'Utsukushii shima' Taiwan o nozoku." *Tabi* 1939, no. 5.

van den Berghe, Pierre L., and Charles F. Keyes. "Introduction: Tourism and Re-Created Ethnicity." *Annals of Tourism Research* 11 (1984): 343–52.

Verstraete, Ginnete. *Tracking Europe: Mobility, Diaspora, and the Politics of Location*. Durham, NC: Duke University Press, 2009.

Vicuña-Gonzalez, Vernadette. *Securing Paradise: Tourism and Militarism in Hawai'i and the Philippines*. Durham, NC: Duke University Press, 2013.

Wakabayashi Masahiro. *Taiwan kō-Nichi undōshi kenkyū*. Tokyo: Kenbun shuppan, 1983.

Watt, Lori. *When Empire Comes Home: Repatriation and Reintegration in Postwar Japan*. Cambridge, MA: Harvard University Asia Center, 2009.

———. "Embracing Defeat in Seoul: Rethinking Decolonization in Korea, 1945." *Journal of Asian Studies* 74, no. 1 (2015): 153–74.

Wigen, Kären E. "Teaching about Home: Geography at Work in the Prewar Nagano Classroom." *Journal of Asian Studies* 59, no. 3 (2000): 550–74.

———. *A Malleable Map: Geographies of Restoration in Central Japan, 1600–1912*. Berkeley: University of California Press, 2010.

Wilder, Gary. *The French Imperial Nation-State: Negritude and Colonial Humanism between the Two World Wars*. Chicago: University of Chicago Press, 2005.

Winikachul, Thongchai. *Siam Mapped: A History of the Geo-Body of the Nation*. Honolulu: University of Hawai'i Press, 1994.

Wolfe, Patrick. *Settler Colonialism*. New York: Bloomsbury, 1999.

Woo Miyeong. "Trip to Empire on Display and Colonized Subjects." *Tong-Asia munhwa yŏn'gu* 48 (2010): 33–68.

Yamaguchi Shunsaku. "Miyage banashi." In *Zenkoku chūtō gakkō chiri rekishika kyōin dai 9-kai kyōgikai oyobi Taiwan nan-Shi ryokō hōkoku*, edited by Zenkoku chūtō gakkō chiri rekishika kyōin kyōgikai. Tokyo: Zenkoku chūtō gakkō chiri rekishika kyōin kyōgikai, 1932.

Yamaji Katsuhiko. *Kindai Nihon no shokuminchi hakurankai.* Tokyo: Fūkyōsha, 2008.

———. "Nanjō jiken to 'senjūmin' mondai: Shokuminchi Taiwan to tochiken no kisū." *Kansai gakuin daigaku shakai gakubu kiyō* 109 (March 2010): 23–50.

Yamamuro Shin'ichi. *Manchuria under Japanese Domination.* Translated by Joshua A. Fogel. Philadelphia: University of Pennsylvania Press, 2006.

———. "Kūkan ninshiki no shikaku to kūkan no seisan." In *"Teikoku" Nihon no gakuchi 8: Kūkan keisei to sekai ninshiki,* edited by Yamamuro Shin'ichi, 1–18. Tokyo: Iwanami shoten, 2006.

Yamashita, Samuel Hideo. "Confucianism and the Japanese State, 1904–1945." In *Confucian Traditions in East Asian Modernity: Moral Education and Economic Culture in Japan and the Four Mini-Dragons,* edited by Tu Wei-Ming, 132–54. Cambridge, MA: Harvard University Press, 1996.

Yamazaki Naomasa. *Futsū kyōiku Nihon chiri kyōkasho.* Tokyo: Tokyo kaiseikan, 1919.

Yang, Daqing. *Technology of Empire: Telecommunications and Japanese Expansion in Asia, 1883–1945.* Cambridge, MA: Harvard University Asia Center, 2010.

Yeoh, Brenda S. A. "Historical Geographies of the Colonised World." In *Modern Historical Geographies,* edited by Catherine Nash and B. J. Graham, 146–66. London: Longman, 2000.

Yokō Kōsuke. "Banzan no shinbi o Takasagozoku ni kiku." *Kokuritsu kōen* 10, no. 1 (1938): 65–70.

Yŏm Sangsŏp. "On the Eve of the Uprising." In *On the Eve of the Uprising and Other Stories from Colonial Korea,* translated by Sunyoung Park, with Jefferson J. A. Gattrall, 5–111. Ithaca, NY: Cornell University Press, 2010.

———. "Yŏm Sangsŏp." In *On the Eve of the Uprising and Other Stories from Colonial Korea.* Translated by Sunyoung Park, with Jefferson J. A. Gattrall, 1–3. Ithaca, NY: Cornell University Press, 2010.

Yonemoto, Marcia. *Mapping Early Modern Japan: Space, Place, and Culture in the Tokugawa Period, 1603–1868.* Berkeley: University of California Press, 2003.

Yoon, Keun Cha. *Nihon kokuminron: Kindai Nihon no aidentiti.* Tokyo: Chikuma shobō, 1997.

Yosano Akiko. *Travels in Manchuria and Mongolia: A Feminist Poet from Japan Encounters Prewar China.* Translated by Joshua A. Fogel. New York: Columbia University Press, 2001.

Yoshino Hidekimi. *Taiwan kyōiku shi.* Taihoku: Yoshino Hidekimi, 1927.

Yoshino Sakuzō. "Man-Kan o shisatsu shite." *Chūō kōron* (June 1916). Reprinted in *Yoshino Sakuzō senshū,* edited by Matsuo Takayoshi, Mitani Taichirō, and Iida Taizō. Vol. 9. Tokyo: Iwanami shoten, 1995.

Young, Carl Walter. *Japanese Jurisdiction in the South Manchuria Railway Areas.* Baltimore: Johns Hopkins University Press, 1931.

Young, Louise. *Japan's Total Empire: Manchukuo and the Culture of Wartime Imperialism.* Berkeley: University of California Press, 1998.

———. *Beyond the Metropolis: Second Cities and Modern Life in Interwar Japan.* Berkeley: University of California Press, 2013.

Zenkoku chūtō gakkō chiri rekishika kyōin kyōgigai, ed. *Zenkoku chūtō gakkō chiri rekishika kyōin dai 9-kai kyōgikai oyobi Taiwan nan-Shi ryokō hōkoku.* Tokyo: Zenkoku chūtō gakkō chiri rekishika kyōin kyōgikai, 1932.

Zheng Zhengcheng. *Ren shi ta zhe de tian kong: Ri zhi shi qi Taiwan yuan zhu min de guan guang xing lü.* Taipei shi: Bo yang wenhua shiye youxian gongsi, 2005.

Ziomek, Kirsten L. "The Possibility of Liminal Colonial Subjecthood." *Critical Asian Studies* 47, no. 1 (2015): 123–50.

# INDEX

Acheson, Dean, 165
affective attachments: and difference, 114; to *kokudo* (national land), 15–16, 28, 35, 38, 58, 133; to territory, 10, 31, 35–40
agriculture, 2; as marker of Japanese superiority, 43. *See also under* Korea *and* Taiwan
anarchism, 105
annexation (*heigō*), 14, 40, 55, 69. *See also* words: *heigō*
Arai Gyōji, 92
Arakawa Seijirō, 74, 121, 137
Aso, Noriko, 190n33
assimilation (*dōka*): and anticolonial movement in Taiwan, 88, 110–11, 120; challenge of cultural pluralism to, 85–87; and changes to the land, 79; and *naichi enchō*, 88, 109. *See also* colonialism: policy of assimilation; language; people(s)
Australia, 133

Banivanua-Mar, Tracy, 185n29
*banjin kankō* (savage tours). *See under* words
Barclay, Paul D., 97, 196n2
Benjamin, Walter, 218n4
Benton, Lauren, 184n25
boundaries and borders: internal, 2, 7, 16–17, 83, 93–95, 97; international, 10; narratives about, 90–92
Brazil, 213n11
British Empire, 76, 86, 87

Brooks, Barbara, 4
Bunroku campaign, 72–73
Burbank, Jane, 189n9, 217n100
Buzard, James, 194n86

cadastral surveys, 26, 53
Cai Peihuo, 85, 110–12, 120, 161
capitalism: as cause of war, 193n71; and education, 146; and identity, 8; knowledge of, as marker of Japanese superiority, 74–75, 154; tension between imperialism and, 160
cartography. *See* maps
censorship, 47, 93, 124. *See also* mobility: political restrictions on
Chamberlain, Basil Hall, 76
Chiang Kai-Shek, 165, 174
*chige-kun* (Korean burden bearers). *See under* words
*chihō* (region). *See under* words
Chōsen (Korea). *See under* words
circulating mission. *See* colonialism: discourse of circulating mission
circulation, networks and sites of, 51, 58, 62–66, 68, 74–75, 105; as marker of Japanese superiority, 74–75, 86, 105. *See also* transportation
citizenship, 2, 6, 13, 17, 89, 100; colonized people as *Nihonjin*, 100; denaturalization of former colonized people, 166; and ethnicity, 4, 29, 57, 86; and place, 30, 57, 86; and space, 4.

245

citizenship (*continued*)
    *See also* law; rights; words: citizen; words: Nihonjin
coal, 66, 147
Cohn, Bernard S., 188n7
colonial boosters. *See under* local color; people(s); travel, imperial
colonialism: discourse of circulating mission, 62, 78, 84, 93, 99, 101–2; discourse of Japanese-Korean shared ancestry, 55; discourse of savagery, 56, 61; policy of assimilation (*dōka*), 61, 86; profitability, 54, 55–56, 86; settler, 185n29. *See also* imperialism; territorialization, modes of; words: policy of ethnic harmony (*yūwa*)
colonized lands: as cultural regions, 85, 103–34, 161; and "dis-placement" of colonial peoples, 50–77; malleability, 62; as peripheries, 1, 7, 16, 34, 47, 52, 56, 62, 86, 90, 183n23; as "national land," 58, 62–73 111; as "new territories," 13, 107, 135, 149, 161; as sites of extraction of labor and commodities, 63–66, 105, 107, 130, 161 (*see also* agriculture). *See also* colony(ies); Hokkaidō; Korea; Manchuria; Okinawa; Taiwan
colony(ies): definitions, 11, 112. *See also* colonized lands
commodities. *See* colonized lands: as sites of extraction
communism, 93
conscription. *See under* military service
consumption: and construction of *kokumin* (national subjects), 105–6; of the exotic, 105–6, 129–32
"coolies." *See under* labor. *See also* words: *kakō*
Cooper, Frederick, xiv, 189n9, 217n100
core-periphery distinction, 7. *See also* boundaries
corruption, 94, 124–25
Cresswell, Tim, 8–9
culture, 17, 106; change and stasis, 17; complementarity, 107–12, 114, 125, 132, 160–61; as consumable commodity, 105–6, 113, 129–32; cultural regions, 7, 17, 103–34; diversity, 14, 16, 17 (*see also* empire: multinational); and "local color," 17, 103–34; and nation, 106
Culver, Annika, 93
customs inspections, 83, 93–95

Dairen (Dalian), 34, 63–64
Diet, election of settlers to, 10
dissent: by colonized people, 7, 14, 47, 87–88, 93, 95, 110, 141, 156–58, 161; within inner territory, 6, 11, 25–26, 27, 28–29, 30–31, 40–41, 46, 54–56; literary, 25, 29, 41, 83, 93, 95; March First Movement, 88, 95; May Fourth Movement, 88; Movement for a Taiwan Parliament, 88, 109, 110, 120; Musha Incident (*see under* Taiwan); in post–World War Two Japan, 173; repression of, 66, 87–88, 156–58, 198n26, 199n29, 204n17; by settlers, 2, 7, 51, 54–56, 108, 198n21; Ta-pa-ni Incident (*see under* Taiwan); use of "local color" in, 106; violent, 87, 156–58. *See also* colonialism: anticolonial liberalism; imperialism: anti-imperial nationalism
Doak, Kevin M., 203n2
*dochaku no jūmin* (people who live on the land, i.e., indigenous Taiwan people). *See under* words
Doi Ichirō, 114
*dojin* (natives). *See under* words

Edmonds, Penelope, 185n29
education: and capitalism, 146; colonial policy studies, 13, 30, 46; in colonized lands, 136, 139–40, 110; colonized people as students in inner territory, 96, 216n71; and comprehension, 147–48; and construction of *kokumin*, 33, 92, 110, 146–47; ethnic segregation, 140, 150–52; geography, 11, 165, 167–69, 184n28; goals, 33, 146, 154; inequalities in, 47, 87, 96, 140, 146, 150–52; Japanese-language, 136, 139–40, 141–42; and labor, 151; as marker of Japanese superiority, 42; and race, 150; and social class, 146; textbooks, 11, 39–40, 98–99, 136, 141, 164, 167–69, 184n28; theories, 33; and tourism, 32–33, 43; in U.S.-occupied Japan, 216n70. *See also* Ministry of Education
empire: and capitalism, 3; definitions of, 2, 162, 183n21, 217n4; and distance, 184n24; multinational/multiethnic, 85–86, 105–7, 133–34, 144, 160; relationship with nation and state (*see under* nation-state); and territory, 184n24. *See also* imperialism
enlightenment. *See* words: *kaika*; words: *keihatsu*
Entrikin, Nicholas, 35
"equal under the emperor's gaze," 88, 110
exhibitions/expositions, 36, 42, 45, 51, 55
exoticism, 105–6, 119–20, 125; "national exotic," 162
experience. *See* travel, imperial: "authentic knowledge" from; sensory experience
extraction, sites of. *See under* colonized lands
extraterritoriality. *See under* law

## INDEX

freedom: of movement (see mobility); political, 9
Freedom and Popular Rights Movement, 30
French Empire, 87
from-ness, 7, 17, 117–27, 164
Fujitani, Takashi, 216n78
Furlough, Ellen, 6

gaichi (outer territories). See under words
Gao Yuan, 183n22, 194n87, 199n32
gender: and rights of offspring, 4–5
genjūminzoku (indigenous peoples). See under words
geography(ies), 8–9; capital cities, significance of, 68, 71–73; of civilization, 6–7, 15–16, 32, 52, 54, 58, 95, 97, 103, 113, 117, 144, 149, 164, 183n23 (see also imperialism: civilizing mission; savagery, discourse of); of cultural pluralism, 6–7, 14, 16, 17, 18, 80, 85–102, 103, 117, 144, 149, 164; education in, 10–11, 165, 167–69, 184n28; feminist, 9; imaginative, 187n55; and nationalism, 33–35; of solidarity, 42; post-imperial, 165
Gluck, Carol, 30
Gotō Shinpei, 54, 58, 200n59
Government-General system, 1–2, 53, 89, 108–9, 110, 111–12, 198n21
Grand Tour, 41, 46, 194n86
Grewal, Inderpal, 6
guidebooks, 16, 25, 57–62, 90–91, 108, 112–13, 117–19, 121, 124–25, 144, 145, 149, 156; *Chōsen ryokō annai ki* (Notes for Travel in Korea), 121, 209n31; *Chōsen tetsudō ryokō annai* (Guide to railway travel in Korea), 57; *Minami Manshū tetsudō annai* (Guide to railway travel in southern Manchuria), 57, 63; *Minami Manshū tetsudō ryokō annai* (Guide to railway travel in southern Manchuria), 117, 145, 209n31; *Nihon annai ki* (Guide to Japan), 171, 209n31; *Taiwan tetsudō ryokō annai* (Guide to railway travel in Taiwan), 63, 96, 112, 117, 156; North Korean, 165. See also people(s): erasure/inclusion of colonized peoples

Haag, Andre, 188n2
Hamada Tsunenosuke, 89, 109–10, 114
Hara Takashi, 88–89
Haraway, Donna, 217n1
harmony. See words: *yūwa*
Harvey, David, 9
Hayasaka Yoshio, 75, 94, 146–49
Hayashi Takahisa, 91–92

head-hunters, representations of indigenous people as, 56, 156–57
Heater, Derek, 204n14
*heigō* (annexation). See under words
Heijō (P'yŏngyang), 36; as ancient capital, 68–73
Heijō Higher Common School, 137–38, 148
Henry, Todd, 216n79
Hideyoshi Toyotomi, 36, 39
*hikiagesha* (repatriation). See under World War Two and under words.
Hiraku Shimoda, 137
Hiroshima Higher Normal School, 36, 46–47, 64, 75, 94, 115, 148
Hirsch, Francine, 86
History, end of. See colonized lands: as "national land"
Hokkaidō, 1, 2, 4, 11, 14 18, 19, 30, 128, 183n21
*hontōjin* (islanders, i.e., Taiwanese Chinese). See under words
Hōten (Fengtian), 119, 122; as ancient and modern capital, 68–69, 75, 114
household registration system (*koseki seido*), 4–5
Howell, David, 183n23

identity: bases of (race, place, culture, etc.), 8–14, 17, 42; and capitalism, 8; and "from-ness" (see from-ness); national, 6, 164, 184n28, 190n33; and nationalism, 8; illegitimacy (of children), 5
Imjin War (Ming era), 72–73. See also Hideyoshi Toyotomi; Katō Kiyomasa; Konishi Yukinaga; Bunroku campaign
imperialism: anti-imperial nationalism, 77, 85–86, 90, 93, 105, 160 (see also dissent); civilizing mission, 51, 55, 86; global, 51, 68, 76, 160, 162; and imperial formations, 2, 7, 162, 183n21; Japanese, distinguished from others, xii–xiv, 68, 87; morality of, 86–87; as "necessary," 188n9; post-imperial, 134
imperial tourism. See tourism, imperial
imperial travel. See travel, imperial
indigeneity, as authentic, 117–21, 128–29, 144; definitions, 118; and place, 118. See also territory: authentic claims to
individualism, 30, 35–36, 46, 208n6
industry/industrialization: as beneficiary of tourism, 45–46; in colonized lands, 103; inner territory, 90; Korea, 3–4; Manchuria, 36; as marker of Japanese superiority, 43; and production of difference, 114; as sponsors of tourism, 44

inner territory *(naichi)*: changing meaning of, 3–4; and geography of civilization, 52, 78; and geography of cultural pluralism, 103, 113–16, 161. See also words: *naichi*
Inō Kanori, 145
Inoue Tetsujirō, 142
investment. See capitalism, knowledge of
Isawa Shūji, 142, 150
Ishikawa Toraji, 138–39, 155–56
Itagaki Hōki, 156
Italian Empire, 87
itineraries, 16, 58–63, 90–91, 93–94
Itō Hirobumi, 54
Itō Ken, 108, 109
Jackson, Peter, 8

Japan (as distinct from "colonies"). See inner territory
Japanese-ness, source of, 57, 86, 96
Japanification *(naichika)*, 62–64, 103, 115
Japanization, 55
Japan Tourist Bureau, 14, 50, 57–58, 84, 90, 92, 97, 103, 106, 114, 120, 169, 171. See also guidebooks; itineraries

*kaika* (the European Enlightenment). See under words
*kakō* (Chinese laborers; euphemism for "coolie"). See under words
*kanjin* (people of Chinese culture). See under words
Kappanzan (Jiaobanshan), 61, 97, 157–58
Katō Kiyomasa, 36
Kawamura Minato, 188n2, 213n11
Kazuko Kuramoto, 166–67
*keihatsu* (educational enlightenment, edification). See under words
Keijō (Seoul), 70–72, 125; as capital of the peninsula, 71
Keijō Girls' Higher Common School, 146
Keijō Public Middle School, 38
Keijō Tourism Association, 113
Kimi ga yo (Japanese imperial anthem), 138, 157
Kinki (region of Japan), 171
Kiryū (Jilong), 63
Kitabayashi Tōma, 172–73
Kitamura Kae, 146
Kitashirakawa, Prince, 66–67
Kō Sonbon, 97–98
Kobayashi Chiyoko, 103–5, 114, 125, 174
Kojong, king of Korea, 19, 70, 88

*kokkyō* (international border). See under words
*kokudo* (national land). See under affective attachments; travel, imperial; words
*kokugo* (national language). See under language; words
*kokumin* (people/subjects of the nation). See under words. See also under education; social class; travel, imperial
*kokutai* (national polity). See under words
*kōminka* (imperialization). See under words
Konishi Yukinaga, 36, 72–73
Korea: agriculture, 53, 109; annexation *(see* annexation; words: *heigō*); colonized subjects' tourism to inner territory, 42–43; as cultural region(s), 117, 118, 121; feudalism, 69; industrialization, 3–4, 62; instability and foreign domination, 68–69, 117, 118, 142, 148; Japanification, 62–63, 115, 125, 126–27; legal status, 28, 53; official narratives of Japanese relations with, 39–40; savagery, discourse of, 61; tourism to, 36, 39–40, 161, 175; tourism to North Korea (DPRK), 218n9; *yūwa* (ethnic harmony) policy, 89, 110; "white robes" as metonym for, 103, 114, 116, 122, 125, 126–27, 161, 172. See also colonialism: discourse of shared ancestry. See also under people(s)
*koseki seido* (household registration system), 4–5
Kosmin, Paul, 184n24
Kōtoku Shūsui, 193n71
Kramer, Paul, 182n4
*kyōdo* (national homeland). See under words
*kūrī* ("coolies"). See under labor. See also words: *kakō*

labor: "coolies" *(kūrī)*, 114, 117, 121–27; done by colonized peoples, 74, 75, 105; and education, 151; as essential attribute of colonized peoples, 105, 114, 117–27, 161; imperial division of, 107, 125, 160; and local color, 107; movements, 17, 25; and national parks, 129; wage inequality, 124–25, 127. See also colonized lands: as sites of extraction; laziness; people: Korean workers in inner territory
land ownership, 53–54
language: ambivalence about, 138–39, 141, 147, 154; and assimilation, 135, 137, 143, 150, 158, 159; and comprehension, 147–48; definitions of, 137, 146; colloquial vs. literary, 140, 141; as determiner of ethnicity, 145, 151, 154; dialect, 136, 142, 143, 146; fluency as carrier of status, 4, 96, 136, 146, 154; (il)literacy, 145;

indigenous, 154–55; and "inscrutability" of the Other, 155–58. Japanese, in Brazil, 213n11; Korean, derogatory term *(Sengo)* for, 214n44; linguistic nationalism, 135–37, 145; as local color, 144–49; as "national spirit," 140, 142; personal names, 96; as personality, 139; and place, 145–46; place names, 18–19, 113, 168–69 *(see also* Taiwan: names of); politeness, 139, 148–49; privileging of Japanese, 2, 17, 30, 55, 86, 93, 96, 135–59, 164; and race, 154, 158; speech act theory, 217n87; standardization of Japanese into "national language" *(kokugo)*, 136, 141–43; superiority of Japanese to Chinese, 142. See also under education
Law 63 and Law 30. See Government-General system
law: Constitution of 1889, 14, 30, 53, 88; Constitution of 1947, 166; differences/inequalities within empire, 4, 13, 53–54, 61, 85, 87–88, 89, 93–95; extraterritoriality, 54; legal status of colonized lands, 1, 53, 61; as marker of Japanese superiority, 117. See also citizenship; Government-General system; mobility; rights
laziness, as essential trait of colonized peoples, 114, 116, 125, 127
League of Nations, 5, 10, 87
Lee, Helen J.S., 27
Lenin, V.I., 204n14
local color, 103–34; and authenticity, 117–20, 144; in California, 212n111; colonial boosters' interest in, 107, 113–14, 120, 121; erasure of history by, 106, 130, 133; government's interest in, 106–7, 120; in inner territory, 106, 113; and labor, 107; and landscape, 107; language as, 143–49; and modernity, 113; uses of, 106, 117, 161, 213n111. See also culture: as consumable commodity; people: as scenery

MacArthur, Douglas, 165, 166
MacCannell, Dean, 35
Mack, Ted, 213n11
Manchuria: 203-Meter Hill, 37–40, 47; as cultural region, 118, 122; ethnic harmony *(yūwa)*, 116; (il)literacy in, 145; industrialization, 36, 63, 65–66; legal status, 14–15, 28, 34–35, 36, 53, 54; Manchukuo, 15, 112, 119; as multiethnic place, 116, 118–19, 122, 163; preservation of battlefields, 15, 38, 66; railway, 15, 28, 36, 74 *(see also* South Manchuria Railway Company); as separate from China, 51, 63, 106, 119, 160, 163; significance of Japanese language in, 138; tourism to, 27–41, 116, 161, 172, 192n64; as typical/atypical "colony," 163. See also race: in Manchukuo
Manela, Erez, 204n14
maps: 10, 11, 52–53, 63, 185n30
March First Movement. See under dissent
marriage and citizenship, 4–5, 29, 182n14; and ethnic harmony *(yūwa)*, 89
Marshall, Byron, K., 216n70
Mason, Michelle, 162
Massey, Doreen, 9, 42
Matsuda, Hiroko, 4
Matsuō Bashō, 92
May Fourth Movement. See under dissent
media: and dissent, 28–29; as tourism sponsors, 43, 45. See also censorship
Meiji emperor, 31, 46
meritocracy, 151
metageography, 33, 34; "jigsaw puzzle," 51; "mosaic," 51
metropole. See inner territory
Mexico, 210n68
military service: by colonized subjects, 4, 30; conscription, 28–29, 40; and disease, 41; romanticization of, 40; voluntary, 4
military, intimidation of colonized-subject tourists by, 42
Ministry of Colonial Affairs, 2, 111–12
Ministry of Education, 31, 136, 141, 146
*minzoku* (ethnic nation). See under words
Mitchell, Timothy, 35, 190n33
Miyakonojō Higher Commercial School, 91, 108, 114–15, 116, 143
Mizuno Masanao, 171
Mizuno Naoki, 209n27
Mizutani Chōzaburō, 173–74
mobility: freedom of, 2, 16–17; inequalities in, 84–86, 93–99, 105, 113; political restrictions on, 84, 93
modernity: and local color, 113, 116; as marker of Japanese superiority, 74–76, 84, 86, 107; transition to, 67, 66–73, 74–77, 86, 116. See also time
money. See capitalism, knowledge of
Moore, Aaron S., 199n40
Mori Arinori, 141
Mōri Motoyoshi, 113
Morris-Suzuki, Tessa, 84, 203n2
Motoyama Yukihiko, 146
Movement for a Taiwan Parliament. See under dissent
movement. See mobility

Nagasawa Sokichi, 75
*naichi* (inner territory). See inner territory. See also under words
*naichi enchō* (extending the metropole). See under words
*naichi kankō* (tours of the inner territory). See under words
*naichijin* (inner-territory people). See under words
*naichika* (Japanification). See Japanification. See also under words
Nakanishi Inosuke, 25–26, 106, 161
Nakano Shigeharu, 93
nation: definitions, 10–11, 106. See also under place; territory
nationalism, 105: anti-imperialist (*see under* imperialism); Chinese, 190n29; ethnic, 111; and identity, 8; mass, 27–31; and tourism, 6–7, 33–35, 46; U.S., 182n4
national parks, 128–32
nation-state: ideologies of, 30–32, 39–40, 50, 51–52, 55, 106; relationship among nation, state, and empire, 2–5, 8–14, 15–16; significance of territory to, 2–4, 6, 8–14
Natsume Sōseki, 195n97
nature, 76, 115, 128–30, 200n58; state of, 30
Ngai, Mae, 85
*Nihonjin* (legal Japanese citizen). See under citizenship *and under* words
*Nihon shinmin* (Japanese subjects). See under words
Nitobe Inazō, 13, 18, 30, 161
Nomura Ryūtarō, 205n38

observation: biases of, 26–27, 34–36, 40, 112–17; definitions of, 105, 115; and individualism, 190n33. See also tourism: observational travel
Odauchi Michitoshi, 11
O'Dwyer, Emer, 109
Oguma Eiji, 164, 184n28
Okada Kōyō, 132
Okinawa, 2, 4, 11, 14, 18, 30
Okita Kinjō, 55
Ōmachi Keigetsu, 205n38
*omoni* (Korean: wives). See under words
Orientalism, 196n2
Osa Shizue, 159, 183n22
Ōyama Takeshi, 140

Pai, Hyung Il, 183n22, 201n69
parties, political: advocacy of settler concerns, 109; post–World War Two, 173–74; and selection of prime minister, 88

Pedersen, Susan, 87
Penrose, Jan, 8
people(s): assimilation (*dōka*), 61, 86, 87, 89, 91, 95; colonial boosters, 50-51; colonized Chinese subjects in Taiwan, 56, 61, 85, 87–88, 89, 99–100, 109, 119–20, 139, 147; colonized students, 110, 216n71; colonized subjects in Korea, 61, 73, 75, 77, 83–84, 89, 93, 95, 125–27, 137–38, 140, 141, 146, 147–48; colonized subjects in Manchuria, 73, 75, 118–19, 138; colonized travelers (*see under* travel, imperial); erasure/inclusion of colonized peoples and cultures, 58–62, 73–77, 105, 112–13, 116, 125–27; imperial travelers (*see under* travel, imperial); indigenous people in Taiwan, 53, 56, 61, 73–74, 75, 97, 118, 119–20, 128–32, 138, 139–40, 146, 154, 156–58; inner-territory Japanese, 56–57; Japanese settlers in Brazil, 213n11; Japanese settlers in Manchuria, 54–55, 109, 166; Japanese settlers in Korea, 55–56, 166; Japanese settlers in Taiwan, 56, 109, 166; Korean workers in inner territory, 110, 127; as scenery, 73–77, 129–30; superiority/inferiority among, 42–43, 53–54, 74–75; words for (*see under* words). See also subheadings under dissent *and under* tourism, imperial; travel, imperial
Perry, Matthew, Commodore, 198n26
Pestalozzi, Johann Heinrich, 33
photography, 28, 45, 59–60, 61, 64, 65, 122, 132, 154, 191n36, 196n2, 207n5
place: and citizenship, 30, 61, 84–85, 166; and colonial difference, 8, 42, 104; and colonized peoples, 61; definitions of, 8–9, 13; names, 18–19, 113; and nation-state, 9–10. See also Japanese-ness
Povinelli, Elizabeth A., 133
production, sites of, 58, 62–66
public health, 200n59

race: and colonial difference, 8, 104; as focus of historical study of colonialism, 8, 164; in Manchukuo, 112, 118–19, 145, 163; and space, 8. See also education: and race; identity: bases of; language: and race
racism, vulgar and polite, 152
Renan, Ernest, 10
Rhee, Syngman, 84
rice, 2, 53, 122, 147
rights: and ethnicity, 4; and gender, 4–5; property, 110–11, 117, 130–32; and space, 4.

INDEX    251

*See also* citizenship; law; military service; mobility; suffrage
Roosevelt, Theodore, 30
Rosaldo, Michelle Z., 217n87
Ruiz, Jason, 5, 210n68
Ruoff, Kenneth J., 183n22, 187n56, 190n28
rural areas in inner territory. *See* Tōhoku
Russia, 34
Russo-Japanese War (1904–05): capitalism blamed for, 193n71; and nationalism, 28; and territorial acquisition, 15, 28. *See also* war memorials

Said, Edward, 13, 187n55
Saigyō Hōshi, 92
Saitō Makoto, 150–52
Saitō Takao, 174
Sakai, Naoki, 203n2
samurai, 29, 39
Sassen, Saskia, 100
Satō Sanae, 174–75
savagery, discourse of. *See under* colonialism. *See also* geography: of civilization
Savage Territory (Taiwan's special administrative zone), 97, 129, 155–58; as public land, 53, 130. *See also* boundaries and borders; national parks
Schivelbusch, Wolfgang, 196n6
Scott, James C., 26
*seiban* (raw savages). *See under* words
Sellers-García, Sylvia, 184n24
*Sengo/Senjin* (derogatory terms for Korean language/people). *See under* words
sensory experiences, 33, 62, 107, 114–15, 116. *See also* travel, imperial: "authentic knowledge"
settlers. *See under* dissent *and see subheadings under* people
Shimazu Naoko, 29
*shin ryōdo* (new territory of the state; colony). *See under* words
*Shina* (China). *See under* words
*shinmin* (emperor's subjects). *See under* words
Shintō, 66, 73, 171, 200n58, 200n59
Shiratori Naokichi, 142
*shisatsu* (observation). *See under* travel, imperial *and under* words
Sho Konishi, 30
*shokuminchi* (colony). *See under* words.
Silverberg, Miriam, 91
Silverstein, Michael, 137
Sin Ch'ae-ho, 106

Sino-Japanese War (1894–95): and nationalism, 28, 72, 73
Skwiot, Christine, 5
smell, 62, 115, 116, 172. *See also* sensory experience
Smith, Anthony D., 10
social class: and conscription, 40; and definition of *kokumin*, 29–30, 43; and education, 146; and imperialism, 25–26; as proxy for ethnicity, 97–98; of students, 45–46. *See also under* tourism, imperial; travel, imperial
social imaginary, 43; and difference in the modern era, 42; and the geography of civilization, 50, 74; and the geography of cultural pluralism, 85, 105, 132; and labor, 107, 121, 127; of modern Japan, re-routed through Manchuria, Korea, and Taiwan, 48; and place names, 18–19; *See also* geography(ies); spatial imaginary
Society for the Preservation of Manchuria's Battlefield Ruins, 15, 38
Soja, Edward W., 9
South Manchuria Railway Company: and cost of travel, 44; Korea-Manchuria Information Bureau, 58, 84; labor policies, 122–25; legal status, 15, 28, 38; management (*keiei*) of Manchuria by, 68, 118; representation of Manchuria by, 51, 57–58, 62, 66, 73, 78, 112, 118, 122, 163 (*see also* guidebooks; itineraries); and shipping, 62–66; as sponsor of tourism, 45, 51, 77, 195n97
sovereignty: and nation-state, 9–11; and tourism, 6–7. *See also* Manchuria: legal status
Soyama Takeshi, 183n22, 206n64
soybeans, 65
spatial imaginary: as component of nationalist ideology, 48–49, 79, 175; and geography of civilization, 16, 52, 77; and geography of cultural pluralism, 16, 121, 151; and modern Japan, 8; as object of memory, 17, 165, 167–69; and social imaginary, 2, 8, 42, 48, 160, 164. *See also* geography(ies); social imaginary
spatial politics, 1, 2, 185n29; and imaginative geography, 13–14; as maintenance of empire after World War One, 5; as means of "displacing" colonized peoples, 50–62, 73–77; as means of "placing" colonized peoples, 117–27; and nationalism, 10, 48; ongoing nature of, 19, 162, 169–75, 183n21, 217n4; and tourism, 5–8; and the writing of history, 162–63. *See also* from-ness; geography(ies); local color; place: names

## 252  INDEX

Stoler, Ann Laura, 2, 183n21
subjects. *See under* words
sublime, the, 114
suffrage, 17, 30, 85, 108–9, 112, 166
sugar, 66–67, 110, 122
*suljip* (Korean: sake shop). *See under* words

*Tabi* (Travel) magazine, 92, 103, 122, 124, 172, 174
Taihoku, 66; as modern capital, 68, 73–74
Taihoku Medical School, 151
Tainan, as ancient capital, 68, 73–74
Taiwan: agriculture, 64, 110; colonized subjects' tourism in inner territory, 42; legal status, 53, 183n21; as cultural region(s), 118–20, 121–22; discourse of savagery, 56, 61, 97; industrialization, 63–65, 130; invasion, 56, 198n26; Japanification, 63, 66–67, 135; Musha Incident, 47, 153, 156–58; names of, 56, 122; anticolonial activism in, 88, 109, 110, 120; Savage Territory (*see* Savage Territory); Ta-pa-ni Incident, 198n29, 204n17; travel/tourism to, 14, 25, 26, 42, 57, 63, 66–67, 73, 97, 118–20, 128, 132, 138–40, 153–54, 172; *yūwa* (ethnic harmony) policy, 89. *See also* subheadings *under* colonialism; dissent; people(s); *see also* words: *hontōjin* (islanders)
*Taiwanjin* (people of Taiwan). *See under* words
Takahashi Gentarō, 117
*Takasago-zoku* (tribal peoples of Taiwan). *See under* words
Tanaka Giichi, 2
Tanaka Keiji, 91
Tanaka, Stefan, 196n2
taxation, 30, 108
Tayama Katai, 41, 206n38
Taylor, Charles, 208n6
teachers. *See under* travel, imperial
Teachers' College (Taiwan), 151
*teikoku kokumin* (imperial national people). *See under* words
teleology (incorporation of colonized lands into Japanese nation as "end of History"). *See* colonized lands: as "national land"
*terra nullius* (unclaimed territory), 6, 31, 51, 55, 183n21
territorialization, modes of (economic, historical, nationalist, ethnographic), 52, 61–73, 78, 105
territory: asymmetry with space of nation, 10–13, 17–18, 52, 133; authentic claims to, 112, 117–21; Japanese empire as contiguous territory, xiv; and language, 144–46; legal distinction between colonized and Japanese territory, 1, 53–57, 111–12; and local color, 106–7; and nation, 6, 8, 9–10, 49; and place, 9, 13; territory of the state, xv, 3, 17, 52, 165, 174. *See also* law; place; rights; *terra nullius*; words: *gaichi*; words: *naichi*
textbooks. *See under* education
time, as means of "dis-placing" colonized peoples, 50, 54, 125, 196n2. *See also* modernity
Tōhoku: as cultural region, 146, 147; as inner-territory periphery, 62–63, 147
Tokutomi Sohō, 35–36, 46
Tokyo, cultural and linguistic privileging of, 106, 136
Tokyo Number One Higher School, 44–46, 65, 98, 138
Tokyo Prefectural Number One Commercial School, 114
Tolstoy, Leo, 41
tourism, ethnic, 61, 207n5
tourism, imperial: and citizenship, 84–85; as ideology, 84, 100–101; as mass travel, 84, 90, 92; and *ryokō bunka* (travel culture), 92. *See also* Japan Tourist Bureau; travel, imperial
tourism, post-imperial, 49, 169–71; internal Japanese politics of, 171; sex tourism, 174; to Vietnam by Americans, 196n113
Traganou, Jilly, 190n33
transportation, 5, 44, 63, 90–91; classes of, 97–98. *See also* Manchuria: railway; circulation
travel, imperial: "authentic knowledge" from, 18, 35, 114, 152–54, 217n1; and boundary narratives, Chap. 3 esp. 90–92; colonial boosters' interests in, 26, 28, 35–36, 39, 42, 51, 56, 58, 91–92, 103, 161; by colonized people, to inner territory *(naichi kankō; naichi shisatsu dan)*, 16, 32, 41–43, 87–88, 193n79; and construction of *kokudo* ("national land"), 28, 32–33, 38; and construction of *kokumin* ("national people/subjects"), 26–27, 31, 38, 43, 86, 92, 162; cost, 44, 84, 98; definitions, 5–6; dissemination of experiences/observations, 8, 16, 33, 43–45; domestic, 32; and economics, 6–7, 42, 62–66; educational, 32, 43; government's interests in, 5–6, 15–16, 31, 32, 43, 57, 78, 91, 103, 161; guides, 192n58; and "harmony" *(yūwa)*, 133; to historical/nationalist sites, 37–40, 47; and history, 6–7; by inner-territory residents, to colonized lands, 16, 25–49, 74, 85, 94; and military power, 42; and

nationalism, 6–7, 27–31, 33–35; as nostalgia, 49; settlers' interests in, 5–6; *shisatsu ryokō* ("observational travel"), 8, 16, 25–27, 31–41, 90, 190n33 (*see also* observation); and social class, 16–17, 27, 40, 43–44, 46, 84, 90; and sovereignty, 6–7; sponsors of, 43, 44, 45, 77, 84, 195n97; by students, 37–41, 43, 45–46, 83, 94, 114–16, 125–26, 161; by teachers and future teachers, 32–33, 43, 91, 99–100, 157–58; by writers, 195n97, 205n38. *See also* affective attachments; guidebooks; itineraries; tourism, imperial; travelogues
travel, imperial: encounters between imperial travelers and colonized people, 136–41, 144–45 148–49, 152–54, 156–58; fear of violence, 156–58
travelogues, 45, 94, 108, 124, 125, 138–39, 140, 144
travel writing, post-imperial, 165, 171–75
treaties, unequal, 54
Trevelyan, G.O., 76
Trotsky, Leon, 204n14
Tsukahara Zenki, 99
Tsurumi, E. Patricia, 139, 152
Twenty-One Demands, 55, 88

Ueda Kazutoshi, 135–37
Uesugi Shinkichi, 205n38
United Nations, 10
United States, as empire, 51, 85, 87, 210n68
Urakami Shūe, 100
urban planning, 26, 70
Urry, John, 194n86
USSR, as empire, 86

van den Berghe, Pierre L., 207n5
Vicuña-Gonzalez, Vernadette, 5

*wajin* (people of Japanese culture). *See under* words
war memorials, 29, 32, 36–41
Wigen, Kären E., 184n26, 191n37, 191n40
Wilder, Gary, 86
Wilson, Woodrow, 86–87, 204n14
Winikachul, Thongchai, 10
Wolfe, Patrick, 10
words, definitions and choices of; *chige-kun* (Korean burden bearers), 121; *banjin kankō* (savage tours), 97; *chihō* (region), 112; Chōsen (Korea), 19, 69; citizens, 17; *dochaku no jūmin* (people who live on the land, i.e., indigenous Taiwan people), 118; *dojin* (natives), 56; *gaichi* (outer territories), 3, 112;

*genjūminzoku* (indigenous peoples), 105; *heigō* (annexation), 14, 40, 55, 69; *hikiagesha* (repatriation), 166–67; *hontōjin* (islanders, i.e., Taiwanese Chinese), 56, 120; *kaika* (the European Enlightenment), 43, 92; *kakō* (Chinese laborers; euphemism for "coolie"), 122–24; *kanjin* (people of Chinese culture), 57; *keihatsu* (educational enlightenment, edification), 43, 92; *kokkyō* (international border), 91; *kokudo* (national land), 15–16, 27, 91; *kokugo* (national language), 136; *kokumin* (people/subjects of the nation), 13, 26, 29–30, 34–35, 37, 43, 86, 89, 105, 112, 189n18 (*see also under* education); *kokutai* (national polity), 164; *kōminka* (imperialization), 198n23; *kyōdo* (homeland), 10; *minzoku* (ethnic nation), 118; *naichi* (inner territory), 3, 42; *naichi enchō* (extending the metropole), 88, 109; *naichi kankō* (tours of the inner territory), 42–43; *naichijin* (inner-territory people), 56–57, 151; *naichika* (Japanification), 62–64, 103,115; *Nihon shinmin* (Japanese subjects), 57; *Nihonjin* (legal Japanese citizen), 29, 57, 100 (*see also under* citizenship); *omoni* (Korean: wives), 113; *seiban* (raw savages), 122, 210n73; *Sengo/Senjin* (derogatory terms for Korean language/people), 214n44; *shin ryōdo* (new territory of the state; colony), 13, 35; Shina (China), 196n2; *shinmin* (emperor's subjects), 30; *shisatsu* (observation), 190n33 (*see also under* travel, imperial); *shokuminchi* (colony), 87; subjects, 17; *suljip* (Korean: sake shop), 113; Taiwan, names of, 56, 122; *Taiwanjin* (people of Taiwan), 56; *Takasago-zoku* (tribal peoples of Taiwan), 210n73; *teikoku kokumin* (imperial national people), 57; *wajin* (people of Japanese culture), 57; *yobo* (derogatory term for Koreans), 55, 83; *yūwa* (policy of ethnic harmony), 89–90 (*see also under* citizenship; Korea; Manchuria; marriage; Taiwan; travel, imperial)
World War One, aftermath, 16, 86–87
World War Two, aftermath, 17–18; anti-imperialism, 173; comparison to breakup of Yugoslavia, 196n114; denaturalization and repatriation of Koreans and Taiwanese people, 166; dissent, 173; Japanese foreign relations, 173; Korea, 165; "peaceful" Japan, 165, 170–71; repatriation *(hikiagesha)* of settlers, 166–67, 172; Taiwan, 165; U.S. Occupation of Japan, 165, 169, 216n70

Yamaguchi Shunsaku, 100
Yamazaki Naomasa, 11
Yanagita Kunio, 145, 147
Yanaihara Tadao, 46
*yobo* (derogatory term for Koreans). *See under* words
Yŏm Sangsŏp, 95

Yosano Akiko, 29, 39
Yoshino Sakuzō, 75–76
Young, Louise, 187n57
*yūwa* (policy of ethnic harmony). *See under* citizenship; Korea; Manchuria; marriage; Taiwan; travel, imperial; words

www.ingramcontent.com/pod-product-compliance
Lightning Source LLC
Chambersburg PA
CBHW070757230426
43665CB00017B/2395